Guide to Information Sources in Mathematics and Statistics

**Recent Titles in
Reference Sources in Science and Technology**

American Military History: A Guide to Reference and Information Sources
Daniel K. Blewett

Education: A Guide to Reference and Information Sources
Nancy Patricia O'Brien

Northern Africa: A Guide to Reference and Information Sources
Paula Youngman Skreslet

Zoological Sciences: A Guide to Reference and Information Sources
Diane Schmidt

Guide to Information Sources in Mathematics and Statistics

Martha A. Tucker and Nancy D. Anderson

Reference Sources in Science and Technology
Judith A. Matthews, Series Editor

A Member of the Greenwood Publishing Group
Westport, Connecticut • London

Library of Congress Cataloging-in-Publication Data is available at www.loc.gov.

British Library Cataloguing in Publication Data is available.

Copyright © 2004 by Libraries Unlimited

All rights reserved. No portion of this book may be reproduced, by any process or technique, without the express written consent of the publisher.

ISBN: 1–56308–701–4

First published in 2004

Libraries Unlimited, 88 Post Road West, Westport, CT 06881
A Member of the Greenwood Publishing Group, Inc.
www.lu.com

Printed in the United States of America

The paper used in this book complies with the Permanent Paper Standard issued by the National Information Standards Organization (Z39.48–1984).

10 9 8 7 6 5 4 3 2 1

We dedicate this book to our colleagues of the Physics-Astronomy-Mathematics Division of SLA for their encouragement and support.

CONTENTS

Preface ix
Introduction: Mathematics Libraries—Time for Transition 1
Chapter 1: **Bibliographic Resources** 19
               Guides to the Literature 19
               Bibliographies 21
               Portals 28
               Library Catalogs 30
               New Books Information 31
               Document Delivery Vendors 32
Chapter 2: **Finding Tools** 35
               Databases and Indexes 35
               Search Engines 51
Chapter 3: **Selected Journals in Mathematics and Statistics** 53
               Journals 53
               Journal Resources 76
Chapter 4: **Dictionaries and Encyclopedias** 79
               Dictionaries 79
               Encyclopedias 97
Chapter 5: **Tables, Handbooks, Manuals, Guides** 107
               Tables 107
               Handbooks, Manuals, Guides 112
               Writing Guides 141
Chapter 6: **Directories and Department Guides** 145
Chapter 7: **Biographical and Historical Materials** 153
               Reference Resources 153
               Biographies 164
               Histories 173
Chapter 8: **Mathematics Books for Science Collections** 191
               General 192
               Mathematical Recreations 209
               Applications of Mathematics to Other Disciplines 213
               Mathematical and Statistical Computing 224

Chapter 9: Collected and Selected Works, Digital Collections 229
Collected and Selected Works
(arranged by individual) 229
Digital Collections 263
Digital Library Projects 269

Chapter 10: Monographic Series 273

Chapter 11: Major Societies and Publishers 281
Societies 281
Publishers 284

**Chapter 12: Additional Resources for Mathematics
Librarianship 287**
Readings of Interest 287
Surveys of Journal Prices in Mathematics 292
Newsletters/Listservs/Journals to Scan 292
Sources for Mathematical Multimedia 295
Miscellany 297

Author/Title Index 299

PREFACE

This book was conceived as a reference for librarians, mathematicians, and statisticians involved in college- and research-level mathematics and statistics in the twenty-first century. Now in a time of transition in scholarly communications in mathematics, practices that have changed little for a hundred years are giving way to new modes of accessing information. Where journals, books, indexes, and catalogs were once the physical representation of a good mathematics library, shelves have given way to computers, and users are often accessing information from remote places.

Professional mathematicians and statisticians working today demonstrate a variety of expertise in their use of the literature. Practitioners who have worked in the field for years may primarily use paper-based methods to do their research and increase current awareness; some may incorporate a blend of old and new approaches. Other researchers who have never even used a paper index and seldom physically come to a library still depend on knowledgeable librarians. Librarians serving this diverse population must be familiar with all resources and must also continuously teach their users when old techniques no longer work. This guide is our effort to highlight resources, both digital and paper, that we find useful.

The introductory chapter is a historical survey of the past 15 years tracking this huge transition in scholarly communications in mathematics. Mathematics is unique among the sciences in its dependence on both monographs and journals, old and new. Mathematicians care deeply about their literature, its quality, longevity, accessibility, and affordability now and in the distant future. Mathematicians are active in discussing and demonstrating new ways to communicate. A bibliography on scholarly communications in mathematics is included at the end of the introductory chapter.

The major portion of our book is the bibliography of resources we recommend to support the disciplines of mathematics and statistics. We have grouped these resources by type of material as indicated in the table of contents. Publication dates range from the 1800s onwards. Hundreds of electronic resources—some online, both dynamic and static, some in fixed media—are listed among the paper resources. Amazingly, a majority of listed electronic resources are free. This is a testament to mathematicians' desire to make their literature easily accessible to their community.

Readers will notice various notations in the left margin of some of the bibliographic citations. We felt strongly that certain kinds of resources should be marked for easy retrieval. As statistics is often subsumed within the broader discipline of mathematics, we marked resources in statistics with an **S**; mathematics resources are left unmarked. We especially wanted to highlight resources available electronically and so marked them with an **E**. Note that frequently the same title is also listed in its paper version as well. The entire scheme of notation is listed below:

- * undergraduate level resource
- **B** bibliographic resource
- **E** electronic resource
- **S** statistics resource
- **T** translated resource

Titles of electronic resources on the Web are italicized and marked with an **E**. Like print titles, electronic resources in a fixed format such as a CD-ROM have titles in bold, but are also marked with an **E**. For example, here are the bibliographic listings of a print, CD-ROM, and Web version of the same work:

Hazewinkel, M., ed. **Encyclopaedia of Mathematics.** Dordrecht, Holland; Norwell, MA: Kluwer Acad. Publ., 1987–1994. 10 vols. $806.00 pa.(set); $2,200.00 (set). ISBN 0-7923-4709-9 pa.(set); 1-556-08010-7 (set).

E Hazewinkel, M., ed. **Encyclopaedia of Mathematics on CD-ROM**. Norwell, MA: Kluwer Acad. Publ., 1997. Contains vols. 1–10, Supplement vol. 1. $235.00, single-user edition; $1,775.00, networked edition. ISBN 0-7923-4807-9.

E Hazewinkel, M., ed. *Encyclopaedia of Mathematics.* Kluwer Acad. Publ., 2001– . Contains vols. 1–10, Supplement vol. 1–3, and updates. Information available at: http://reference.kluweronline.com/?xmlid= 1402006098. $1,650.00–$3,300.00 + $330.00/yr.

The last chapter of this book is a listing of additional resources of particular interest to mathematics librarians. Many are authored by our librarian colleagues in mathematics as well as astronomy and physics; some are written by mathematicians with a deep interest in their libraries. These kinds of resources are an invaluable way to learn from our communities of users and colleagues.

This, of course, is not the kind of book one would read from cover to cover. Instead, we hope that readers will find it a handy reference for those just beginning to work with the mathematical literature and those who may only need to consult it on occasion for a particular need. Also, it is only a snapshot in time. Whereas paper resources are static, electronic resources can be quite fluid. URLs and names can change at any time. Those responsible today for online resources may allow them to lapse. This is very much a time of transition where the desire for open sources may be in conflict with the needs and costs of responsible stewardship. Librarians' and mathematicians' traditional concern for the literature should help solve the problems of preserving the past and present for the future.

Introduction: Mathematics Libraries— Time for Transition

From Indexes to Databases

The explosion of electronic resources in mathematics in the last 15 years has changed the research habits and lives of both mathematicians and mathematics librarians. The field of mathematics, along with physics and astronomy, appears to have recognized early on the benefits of making its research literature easily available and accessible to its community. The digital information revolution in mathematics has been led by energetic and innovative individual mathematicians and by its professional societies. The mathematics community currently has a wealth of material, both past and current, available electronically. Much of it is available for free or, for the most part, fairly reasonable prices. In the next 10 years, it is anticipated that most of mathematical literature—past, present, and future—will be available in digital format.

Life as a mathematics librarian before the dawn of the online age was challenging. Mathematics is a science that everyone has experience with at some level, but at the academic level is probably a mystery to most. Librarians without an advanced mathematical background worked hard to help patrons when doing subject searching. A fair knowledge of mathematics was needed to penetrate the AMS subject classification system or use Library of Congress subject headings. Even mathematicians working outside their own specialty acknowledged this. Subject searching was frequently done jointly with the patron who had the subject expertise while the librarian contributed the knowledge of information tools.

The dawn of the electronic age in mathematics began when the two main mathematical indexes became available as dial-up online databases in the1980s. The U.S.-based **Mathematical Reviews** offered its data first as **MathFile,** and the German **Zentralblatt für Mathematik** offered its as **MATH**. **MathFile** soon expanded its coverage to include statistics and computer science indexes and became known as **MathSci®.** The Institute for Scientific Information also offered online its **CMCI CompuMath Citation Index**, an offshoot of its science and social science citation databases. Its unique citation index feature offered a different approach to subject searching.

Available only through dial-up services such as Dialog, BRS, or STN, these tools were costly to access in both training time and online time, and there was a charge for each citation displayed or downloaded. Generally, only trained searchers, typically librarians, who were familiar with both the database and the search command language, accessed these databases. The charges were usually passed on to the researcher or his budget. Mathematicians were not frequent users of these services because of the expense and probably because they were not in immediate control of the search. **CMCI** got more use because researchers valued its unique citation searching capability. Because online searching allowed keyword searching of the full record, math librarians recognized early on how valuable these electronic tools could be if they were easier to use and cheaper to access. The pressure of the online clock was not conducive to exploratory searching and the cost of the citations was shocking to most patrons.

In 1989, the American Mathematical Society published **MathSci Disc**, a CD-ROM version of **Mathematical Reviews** and **Current Mathematical Publications**. Later, **CompactMath**, a CD-ROM version of **Zentralblatt für Mathematik**, was also released. Now, unlimited end-user electronic searching became available to all who could afford the CD-ROM, a PC, and related equipment. Primarily purchased by institutions for a single PC in a library setting, **MathSci Disc** became invaluable to librarians and academic researchers in mathematics and, to a lesser extent, those in statistics. Librarians had many reservations at the beginning. After all, how could we justify buying data we had already paid for once? Would the library administration purchase computer equipment for mathematics—not exactly the biggest science on campus? Most mathematicians were not computer users yet—would they use it? What would happen if it were cancelled—could the data be kept that had been paid for?

In time, mathematicians recognized what a powerful tool **MathSci Disc** was and, as they became more comfortable with computers in their own work, they began to use it more than the paper versions. Librarians helped by training end users in efficient searching methods. Gradually the search interface improved and bibliographic coverage was expanded back to 1940. Updated discs were published every six months. Unless someone was waiting in line, researchers could explore at their leisure the indexes of much of the past mathematical literature. The only drawbacks were that one had to come to the library to use it and only one person could use it at a time. Statisticians acknowledged that it was a good product, but its coverage of statistics was not comprehensive enough for them.

The American Mathematical Society eventually formulated a new pricing system for this additional version of **Mathematical Reviews**. A few years after **MathSci Disc** started, the AMS began its Data Access Fee pricing. The DAF pays for the expenses of compiling and maintaining **MR** data. Additional version fees paid for each version's development and customer support. AMS member institutions paid less than nonmember institutions. Personal subscriptions were available if the parent institution subscribed. Later, discounts were extended to institutions in less-developed countries and to library consortia. Most libraries in mathematically active institutions in the United States and Canada eventually were able to afford this new indexing tool by the mid-1990s. Some institutions bought **MathSci**® tapes and loaded them locally on their campuses.

From Paper to PDF

As the electronic tools for accessing mathematical literature were becoming more widespread, several trends such as the continuous rise in journal prices, the development of the Internet, and the widespread use of TeX, a mathematical typesetting program, combined to produce the first formal electronic-only primary literature in mathematics. Escalating journal prices had forced libraries around the world to start canceling subscriptions to journals. Stung by this loss to their laboratory, mathematicians, ahead of researchers in most other fields, began to see the developing Internet as the perfect medium to publish professional mathematics at practically no cost. Why not? they reasoned. Academic researchers authored, typeset, edited, and refereed papers already without extra pay. All that was needed was to make them publicly available. Posting papers on the Internet gave readers access without the expense of paper publishing and distribution.

E-mail became available to many in the late 1980s. The increasingly common use of TeX typesetting software allowed researchers to present their mathematical expressions exactly as intended. Data sharing via the Internet began with the use of UNIX programs such as FTP or Gopher. Researchers who were avid computer users began to store their papers online in order to share with their colleagues. Although not a user-friendly process, FTP allowed users to transfer papers from one computer to another and then process the papers through TeX in order to view and print them.

Ulam Quarterly, published out of the Ulam Center at Palm Beach Atlantic College and University of Florida, began online-only publication in 1992. Free to anyone, it contained carefully researched and referred mathematics produced by mathematicians without the services of a commercial publisher. The AMS began publishing its **Bulletin** in an electronic version that was (and still is) free to anyone. More AMS and SIAM print journals were offered electronically too and were free with a print subscription. The revolution in mathematics communication had begun! Other online-only e-journals in mathematics appeared. Both the **Electronic Journal of Differential Equations** and the **Electronic Transactions on Numerical Analysis** started in 1993, as did the **Journal of Statistics Education**. The **New York Journal of Mathematics** and the **Electronic Journal of Combinatorics** were launched in 1994; **Documenta Mathematica** in 1995. All of these online-only e-journals, except the **Ulam Quarterly**, are still publishing currently.

Mosaic, the first graphical browser for the Web, came into common use in libraries around 1994. Netscape arrived soon after. These graphical browsers were the "killer apps" for scholarly electronic communication. Now, rather than using FTP and Gopher to retrieve files, users could use a graphical search interface, click on hypertext links, and view the papers in various file formats. Whereas DVI and PS were popular file formats mathematicians were familiar with, in time Adobe Acrobat's PDF, which preserves the integrity of the printed page, came into common use.

MathSciNet made its appearance in January 1996 and became an instant hit with both researchers and librarians. Electronic-only journals and electronic versions of print journals multiplied. Academic and Springer were among the first commercial publishers to offer mathematics journals online. By 2001, most major commercial publishers and many small publishers had online versions of their journals. JSTOR mounted digital copies of backfiles of major core journals in mathematics and statistics online. *Zentralblatt MATH* and the *Current Index in Statistics* are also on the Web. Academic library users now can access these resources from the library, their offices, or remotely given the proper authentication. Librarians train users how to use these resources and provide expertise for difficult searches or technical difficulties. Paper indexes, if still published and purchased, are used mainly for browsing purposes now.

Partners in the Process

Late in the 1980s, the AMS invited librarians to serve on its new ad hoc AMS Library Committee. The AMS and math librarians already had a close relationship especially via the vendor/client relationship within the Physics-Astronomy-Mathematics Division of SLA, but this was their first formal involvement. As libraries are prime customers for the AMS publications program, it was natural to team up with each other. The AMS Library Committee was formed with four librarians and four mathematicians and charged with conducting surveys on the state of math libraries in the United States and Canada. Many other matters concerning scholarly communications in mathematics were discussed at committee meetings too. The committee began sponsoring sessions at the AMS/MAA Joint Meetings in order to inform mathematicians about the serious library problems affecting their research. The first library survey was conducted in the fall of 1990 (Anderson and Rovnyak 1991); a second library survey was conducted in 1996 (Anderson, Dilcher, and Rovnyak 1997).

By 1994, math librarians were struggling with the new technologies and new questions. Some working knowledge of DOS, Windows, Mac and/or Unix, e-mail, FTP, Internet browsers, the World Wide Web, TeX, and Postscript were now needed. Questions of what one did with the electronic-only titles arose. Were these electronic papers considered mainstream mathematics? Should libraries download, print, bind, and shelve? Will the mathematics indexes index them? Should libraries provide access via their catalogs to something virtual that was not "owned"? Would they be available in the future? How can we afford to provide computers and printers in the library in order to access this new format? Who should archive these titles in perpetuity and how?

In December 1994, **The Future of Mathematical Communication** conference was held at the Mathematical Sciences Research Institute in Berkeley. During that year, provocative papers by Frank Quinn (1995) and Andrew Odlyzko (1995) had circulated on the Internet. These men offered original perspectives from mathematicians' points of view. Quinn and Odlyzko were both invited to speak at FMC as was Paul Ginsparg, founder of the new Los Alamos electronic preprints archive in physics. The December gathering, very international in organization and attendance, was an exciting three days of interaction between mathematicians, publishers—both society and commercial—academic administrators, economists, librarians, physicists, and computer scientists from the United States and abroad (FMC 1994; Jackson 1995). A similar conference, **Conference on Electronic Communication in Mathematics**, occurred in Minneapolis in 1997 (CECM 1997). Another **Future of Mathematical Communications** conference took place in December 1999 with many of the same participants (FMC 1999). Topics at these conferences ranged from copyright, preprints, the demise of libraries, the viability of electronic archives, the economics of publishing, and the promise of MathML for publishing mathematics on the Web. Work on these questions continues, but certain trends became apparent.

Preprints Lead the Way

Formerly, math preprint series were distributed in paper by various institutes or departments and mailed to a limited number of interested researchers. Libraries may have subscribed to preprint series of interest to their faculty, but librarians were never quite sure what to do with this gray literature—shelve and routinely discard after a few years, review for formally published versions, or catalog and keep this rapidly growing type of literature permanently? Most preprints eventually were published in journals or proceedings and could be discarded, but verifying hundreds of preprints in the days before online databases was time consuming. Some preprints of importance are never published formally, and inevitably, if one was discarded, someone wanted it!

Since the mid-1990s, math preprints have become available online from a preprint archive or perhaps from an author's or department's home page. The world of preprints and of scholarly communications as a whole was revolutionized by the appearance of open access, centrally archived preprint collections such as the high-energy physics preprint archive originally known as the *xxx.lanl.gov* archive. Ginsparg, a physicist at Los Alamos National Laboratory, founded this archive in the early 1990s with support from the National Science Foundation. He and the archive, now renamed the *arXiv*, have since moved to Cornell University.

Early online math preprints were originally organized into specific subject archives without centralized indexing. This system worked fine for those who were active in that particular subject, but not for others. Several groups of mathematicians in the United States and in Europe saw the need for centralized access to preprints and began to promote mathematicians' use of either *xxx.lanl.gov/math* (now known as *arXiv*), a centralized archive, or *MPRESS*, a centralized index especially for European math preprints. Submissions increased and at present there are over 35,500 preprints from 1992 on in the mathematics *arXiv*. *MPRESS* covers European archives, math preprints in *arXiv,* as well as some subject-specific archives (Jackson 2002). It indexes over 66,000 preprints.

Several journals, including the highly regarded **Annals of Mathematics**, are currently published online as overlays of articles in the *arXiv*. The term for these *arXiv* documents has moved from preprint to "e-print" since some are now formally refereed and published. There is a growing impetus from the Open Archive movement led by Steven Harnad, cognitive sciences professor at University of Southampton, to post all academic papers on institutional e-print servers for free access. This would not preclude formal publication by societies or commercial publishers, but is merely advocated as a regular first step in the process of academic publication. Free OAI-compliant archiving software is available from the E-Prints organization (http://www.eprints.org/software.php) or from MIT's DSpace (http://www.dspace.org/). Libraries are beginning to offer this service, but making changes in the scholarly system is a slow process (Suber 2003).

Some mathematicians urge caution so as not to destroy what is valuable about the current environment. Like most mathematicians and librarians, John Ewing, AMS executive director and publisher, is very protective of the past literature. He writes, "The institution of journals exists because scholarly publishing is not meant only for today's scholars but for future scholars as well—for our children and our children's children. Scholarly communication is more than sending papers to one's colleagues. Validation? Archiving? Financial incentives? These are all about sustaining scholarship for the future, not about exchanging papers in the present. Who will watch over collections when enthusiastic volunteers move on? Who will pay the costs of ever-changing servers and software to keep papers accessible? Who will provide the huge sums for archiving—not only saving the bits but updating the format of millions of papers? Surely we should not rely on government agencies, which have an increasingly short-term view in all their activities" (Ewing 2002).

Mathematics Libraries Today

The academic mathematics library collection today may be a branch library located close to its client departments, or it may now be part of a consolidated library collection. Whereas university library administrators are increasingly looking to close small branch libraries in order to cut costs, most large mathematics departments are very protective of their mathematics library. The library is their laboratory, their meeting place, their archives, and their current awareness tool. The discipline of mathematics, unlike other sciences, depends a great deal on the older literature and on monographs. Like other sciences, journals are extremely important too. Browsing the shelves and new journal issues is a favorite and productive research tool. Browsing is increasingly difficult today because now it is nearly impossible to find a comprehensive physical collection of mathematics. Most academic libraries must store a large portion of their collection off-site. Budget cuts mean fewer purchases. The spiraling costs of journals have cut into funds for books and journals. Libraries are canceling paper copies of their journals subscriptions in favor of licensed electronic access only. Paper copies of the core mathematics and statistics journals digitally archived in the JSTOR collection are being moved out to make room for non-digitized materials (Seeds 2002).

Librarians have devised many ways to try to compensate for these problems as best they can. Shifting journals from paper subscription to licensed online access does save space and, in theory, processing expenses. It must be noted, though, that the licensing process has added greatly to libraries' workloads. Users are able to access these journals and databases anytime from anywhere. JSTOR backfiles and full-text searching makes older core journals available at a touch of a button. Interlibrary loan and document delivery provide users with books and journal articles not held locally more quickly and easily than before. Users themselves can request books located in other libraries while working in the online catalog. Consortia arrangements with other institutions stretch materials budgets by sharing electronic access to journals, by supporting patron-initiated interlibrary loans, and by cooperative collection development.

Despite 24-hour access to online journals, the ability to request materials, and better document delivery, many mathematicians and statisticians greatly miss the ease of browsing that accessible paper materials provide. Libraries can post weekly lists of links to new journal issues' tables of content whether subscribed to or not. Users can set up customized alerting of new journals in databases such as *Current Contents* or *Ingenta,* but journal coverage is not complete in either. The databases in the field, *MathSciNet, Zentralblatt MATH,* and *Current Index to Statistics* seem ideally suited to providing customizable current alerts, yet none do so yet. This is a missed opportunity for these databases to serve their disciplines.

Mathematics Libraries in the Future

Although the exact details of the future are not yet settled, it is obvious that the trend toward putting more and more mathematics into digital form is accelerating. There are a number of digital archives of older materials already in existence for mathematics and statistics:

- *Cornell University Library Historical Mathematics Monographs* is a collection of 576 selected monograph volumes with expired copyrights chosen from the mathematics field. Available at: http://library5.library.cornell.edu/math.html. Free.

- *DIEPER, Digitised European Periodicals* is a European effort to offer a central access point to journals that have been retrospectively digitized in Europe or anywhere else in the world. Available at: http://dieper.aib.uni-linz.ac.at/cgi-bin/project2/selbrowse.pl?Select=Periodicals. Free.

- *Gallica* is a Bibliothèque Nationale de France project with 244 digitized mathematics titles currently including many important nineteenth-century monographs, serial back sets, and collected works of mathematicians. Available at: http://gallica.bnf.fr/. Free.

- *GDZ (Göttinger Digitalisierungs-Zentrum), Mathematica* is a German retrospective digitization of eighteenth- and nineteenth-century journals, multivolume sets, and monographs. Available at: http://gdz.sub.uni-goettingen.de/en/index.html. Free.

- *JSTOR* is a broad collection of journal backfiles that includes 16 mathematics journals and 20 statistics journals. It also includes a number of general science journals that have mathematical and statistical articles. Available at: http://www.jstor.org/browse. Subscription.

- *NUMDAM, NUMérisation de Documents Anciens Mathématiques* is a French project to digitize French journals and seminars. Complete back runs of six journals are now available. Available at: http://www.numdam.org/en/. Free.

- *University of Michigan Historical Mathematics Collection* is a collection of nineteenth- and twentieth-century monographs in mathematics. Available at: http://www.hti.umich.edu/u/umhistmath/. Free.

Access to these archives is free with the exception of the materials in *JSTOR*. There doesn't yet seem to be any systematic cataloging done of these resources, but some libraries have submitted records to OCLC. *MathSciNet*, *Zentralblatt MATH* and *Jahrbuch Project* have added links from their existing records to materials in these archives. *MathSciNet* and *Zentralblatt MATH* are also retrospectively adding records to digitally archived articles that predate those databases (Jackson, 2003). Add these titles to all the current journals and monographs in digital form, and mathematicians have the beginnings of what could become a comprehensive archive in their discipline.

Indeed, in 2002, planning for a comprehensive archive of mathematics began with funding from a National Science Foundation grant for what is known as the Digital Mathematics Library. Led by mathematician Keith Dennis and librarians Sarah Thomas and Jean Poland, all of Cornell University, the DML planning group "strives to make the entirety of past mathematics scholarship available online, at reasonable cost, in the form of an authoritative and enduring digital collection, developed and curated by a network of institutions" (*Digital Mathematics Library* 2002). It is estimated that this will cost about $100 million to scan 50 million pages with partial optical character recognition, indexing, and other processing (Ewing 2002a). The DML plan hopes to develop a systematic, coordinated collaboration among funding agencies, institutions, libraries, scientific societies, technological innovators, and publishers to establish an archive of significant importance to mathematicians in all parts of the world.

In 2004 the National Science Foundation funded planning for the preservation and dissemination of newer digital mathematics and statistics journals. Cornell University Library and SUB Göttingen will partner with mathematics publishers on this effort to restore libraries' archival tradition. "We will develop an archive of serial mathematics literature that will be available to libraries worldwide and at the same time serve as a model for similar efforts in other disciplines within the library and publishing communities" (*Ensuring Access,* 2004).

Future of Mathematics Librarianship

What is the future of mathematics librarianship given the approach of having seemingly all mathematics in digital format? Libraries have very much been a valued part of the culture in mathematics. As every mathematics librarian knows, current daily activities include accessing and obtaining resources, organizing them for use, bibliographic citation chasing, management of physical collections, budgeting, license negotiation, serials management, and discovery of new products and resources. Training users in information literacy in this field is one of our most important roles. "To do research productively now, a library user must cope with more information, interpret different online frameworks, navigate a Web that adheres to few overarching organizational schemes, and understand how to access several portals or gateways. Because of the increasing complexity of the information environment and the growing requirement for specialized skills, scholars in mathematics need libraries and librarians today more than ever before" (Rutter 2002).

Mathematics librarians will continue to be a valued partner in mathematics research. Our role in the next decade most likely will be to participate in the process of digitizing mathematics past, present, and future, making sure it is archived and well indexed for future use in addition to doing all our usual activities. If we do it well, we could be putting ourselves out of a job, but given the complexities of scholarly communications, that is doubtful.

References

Anderson, Nancy D., and James L. Rovnyak. 1991. Mathematics Research Libraries: A 1990 Snapshot. *Notices of the American Mathematical Society* 38, no. 10 (December): 1258–1262.

Anderson, N. D., K. Dilcher, and J. Rovnyak. 1997. Mathematics Research Libraries at the End of the Twentieth Century. *Notices of the American Mathematical Society* 44, no. 11 (December): 1469–1472. Available at: http://www.ams.org/notices/199711/comm-rovnyak.pdf. Free.

Conference on Electronic Communication in Mathematics. 1997. Announcement available at: http://math.albany.edu:8800/hm/emj/1997/msg00071.html. The links are now dead, but the announcement gives a list of speakers. Free.

Digital Mathematics Library. 2002. Maintained by Kizer Walker, Cornell University Library. Available at: http://www.library.cornell.edu/dmlib/. Free.

Ensuring Access to Mathematics Over Time, 2004. Available at: http://www.library.cornell.edu/dlit/EATMOT/web/. Free.

Ewing, John. 2002. Predicting the Future of Scholarly Publishing. Version 2.5, 12/09/02. Based on a talk given at the Conference on Electronic Information and Communication, Tsinghua University, China, August 29–31, 2002. Available at: http://www.ams.org/ewing/Predicting25.pdf. Free. Also published in *Mathematical Intelligencer* 25, no. 2 (Spring 2003): 3–6.

———. 2002a. Twenty Centuries of Mathematics: Digitizing and Disseminating the Past Mathematical Literature. *Notices of the American*

Mathematical Society 49, no. 7 (August): 771–777. Available at: http://www.ams.org/notices/200207/fea-ewing.pdf. Free.

The Future of Mathematical Communications. 1994. Available at: http://www.msri.org/activities/events/9495/fmc/. Many of the links are now dead, but the site gives a list of speakers with links to some of the related materials. Free.

———. 1999. Available at: http://www.msri.org/activities/events/9900/fmc99/fmc_ABS.html. Abstracts of talks and streaming video available. Free.

Jackson, Allyn. 1995. MSRI Workshop. *Notices of the American Mathematical Society* 42, no. 5 (April): 445–449. Available at: http://www.ams.org/notices/199504/msri.pdf. Free.

———. 2002. From Preprints to E-prints: The Rise of Electronic Preprint Servers in Mathematics. *Notices of the American Mathematical Society* 47, no. 1 (January): 23–31. Available at: http://www.ams.org/notices/200201/fea-preprints.pdf. Free.

———. 2003. The Digital Mathematics Library. *Notices of the American Mathematical Society* 50, no. 8 (September): 918–923. Available at: http://www.ams.org/notices/200308/comm-jackson.pdf. Free.

Odlyzko, Andrew. 1995. Tragic Loss or Good Riddance? The Impending Demise of Traditional Scholarly Journals. Condensed version. *Notices of the American Mathematical Society* 42, no. 1 (January): 49–53. Available at: http://www.ams.org/notices/199501/forum.pdf. Free.

Quinn, Frank. 1995. Roadkill on the Electronic Highway: The Threat to the Mathematical Literature. *Notices of the American Mathematical Society* 42, no.1 (January): 53–56. Available at: http://www.ams.org/notices/199501/forum.pdf. Free.

Seeds, Robert S. 2002. Impact of a Digital Archive (JSTOR) on Print Collection Use. *Collection Building* 21, no. 3: 120–122. Available at: http://www.emeraldinsight.com/cb.htm. Subscription.

Suber, Peter. 2003. Removing Barriers to Research: An Introduction to Open Access for Librarians. *College & Research Library News* 64, no. 2 (February 2003): 92–94, 113.

Additional Readings on Scholarly Communications in Mathematics

E Alspach, Dale. "History of the Banach Space Archive and Implications for Electronic Archives of Publications." Text of January 8, 1999, talk. Available at: http://www.math.okstate.edu/~alspach/banach/banacharchist.ps. Free.

E Apt, Krzysztof. "Towards Free Access to Scientific Literature." *Nieuw Archief voor Wiskunde* 5:2, no. 3 (September 2001): 251–255. Available at: http://www.math.leidenuniv.nl/~naw/serie5/deel02/sep2001/pdf/apt.pdf. Free.

E Babbitt, Donald. "Mathematical Journals: Past, Present and Future—A Personal View." *Notices of the American Mathematical Society* 44, no. 1 (January 1997): 29–32. Available at: http://www.ams.org/notices/199701/comm-babbitt.pdf. Free.

E Barr, Michael. "Where Does the Money Go?" *Newsletter on Serials Pricing Issues*, no. 229 (July 13, 1999): 5p. Available at: http://www.lib.unc.edu/prices/1999/PRIC229.HTML. Free.

E Beschler, Edwin F. "Pricing of Scientific Publications: A Commercial Publisher's Point of View." *Notices of the American Mathematical Society* 45, no. 10 (November 1998): 1333–1343. Available at: http://www.ams.org/notices/199810/beschler.pdf. Free.

E Birman, Joan S. "Scientific Publishing: A Research Mathematician's Viewpoint." *Notices of the American Mathematical Society* 47, no. 7 (August 2000): 770–774. Available at: http://www.ams.org/notices/200007/forum-birman.pdf. Free.

E Branin, Jospeh J. and Mary Case. "Reforming Scholarly Publishing in the Sciences: A Librarian Perspective." *Notices of the American Mathematical Society* 45, no. 4 (April 1998): 475–486. Available at: http://www.ams.org/notices/199804/branin.pdf. Free.

E Burdzy, Krzysztof. "Mathematical Articles and Bottled Water." *Notices of the American Mathematical Society* 49, no. 5 (May 2002): 541. Available at: http://www.ams.org/notices/200205/commentary.pdf. Free.

S E Carroll, Raymond J. "Review Times in Statistical Journals: Tilting at Windmills?" *Biometrics* 57, no. 1 (2001): 1–6. Also available at: http://stat.tamu.edu/~biometrics/carroll.pdf. Free.

E Casselman, Bill. "Publishing on the Internet." *Notices of the American Mathematical Society* 47, no. 6 (June/July 2000): 629. Available at: http://www.ams.org/notices/200006/commentary.pdf. Free.

E [Cornell] University Faculty Forum. Open Access Scholarly Publishing: Opportunities and Obstacles, December 11, 2002: 22p. Transcript. Available at: http://web.cornell.edu/UniversityFaculty/forums/Scholarly%20Publishing/Forumtranscript.html. Free.

E Crawford, Walt. "Scholarly Journals and Grand Solutions." *Cites & Insights: Crawford at Large* 2, no. 9 (July 2002): 1–3. Available at: http://cites.boisestate.edu/civ2i9.pdf. Free.

E Ewing, John. DML: Moving Forward. Unpublished paper. 2003. Available at: www.ams.org/ewing/dml-moving-forward.pdf. Free.

E ——. "In Defense of Caution." *Learned Publishing* 15, no. 3 (July 2002): 231–233. Available at: http://ernesto.ingentaselect.com/vl=22384543/cl=41/nw=1/rpsv/~885/v15n3/s12/p231. Free.

E ——. "Mathematics: A Century Ago—A Century from Now." *Notices of the American Mathematical Society* 443, no. 6 (June 1996): 663–672. Available at: http://www.ams.org/notices/199606/ewing.pdf. Free.

Franks, John. "The Impact of Electronic Publication on Scholarly Journals." *Notices of the American Mathematical Society* 40, no. 9 (November 1993): 1200–1202.

E "From the AMS Secretary: Report of the Executive Director, State of the AMS, 2003" and "Report of the Treasurer (2002)." *Notices of the American Mathematical Society* 50, no. 7 (August 2003): 830–839. Available at: http://www.ams.org/notices/200307/from.pdf. Free. These annual reports include interesting details on the state and health of the publishing program of this scientific society.

E Gilbert, John D. "The Business of Scientific Communication." *Nieuw Archief voor Wiskunde* 5:3, no. 1 (March 2002): 49–51. Available at: http://www.math.leidenuniv.nl/~naw/serie5/deel03/mrt2002/pdf/gilbert.pdf. Free.

E International Mathematical Union. Committee on Electronic Information Communication. *Best Current Practices: Recommendations on Electronic Information Communication (2002)*. IMU, 2002. 5p. Available at: http://www.mat.univie.ac.at/~michor/ceic-best.pdf. Free.

E Jackson, Allyn. "The Slow Revolution of the Free Electronic Journal." *Notices of the American Mathematical Society* 47, no. 9 (October 2000): 1053–1059. Available at: http://www.ams.org/notices/200009/fea-eljnl.pdf. Free.

Kahin, Brian and Hal R. Varian, eds. *Internet Publishing and Beyond: The Economics of Digital Information and Intellectual Property*. Cambridge, MA: MIT Press, 2000.

E Kirby, Rob. "A Scenario for Publishing Mathematics in the Future." *Issues in Science and Technology Librarianship,* no. 20 (Fall 1998): 3p. Available at: http://www.istl.org/98-fall/article2.html. Free.

E ——. "Kirby Letter to Elsevier Officers." *Newsletter on Serials Pricing Issues,* no. 199 (January 21, 1998): 4p. Available at: http://www.lib.unc.edu/prices/1998/PRIC199.HTML#199.1. Free.

E Knuth, Donald. Knuth letter to Editorial Board, *Journal of Algorithms*. October 27, 2003: 14p. Available at: www-cs-faculty.stanford.edu/~knuth/joalet.pdf. Free. This letter to his fellow board members nicely surveys the recent history of scholarly publishing in computer science and mathematics.

E Kolman, Michiel. "Free Publishing." *Nieuw Archief voor Wiskunde* 5:2, no. 4 (December 2001): 349–350. Available at: http://www.math.leidenuniv.nl/~naw/serie5/deel02/dec2001/pdf/kolman.pdf. Free.

E Krantz, Stephen. "Mathematics Journals Should Be Electronic and Free." *Notices of the American Mathematical Society* 44, no. 8 (September 1997): 892. Available at: http://www.ams.org/notices/199708/page2.pdf. Free.

E Kuperberg, Greg. "Scholarly Mathematical Communication at a Crossroads." *Nieuw Archief voor Wiskunde* 5:3, no. 3 (September 2002): 262–264. Available at: http://www.math.leidenuniv.nl/~naw/serie5/deel03/sep2002/pdf/kuperberg.pdf. Free.

E Kuperberg, Greg, David Morrison, and Richard Palais. "Another Opinion: Mathematics Journals Should Be Electronic and Free(ly Accessible)." *Notices of the American Mathematical Society* 45, no. 7 (August 1998): 845. Available at: http://www.ams.org/notices/199807/commentary.pdf. Free.

E Levy, Silvio. "Remarks on Math Journals and Libraries." *Newsletter on Serials Pricing Issues,* no. 202 (March 12, 1998): 3p. Available at: http://www.lib.unc.edu/prices/1998/PRIC202.HTML#202.1. Free.

E Miner, Robert and Paul Topping. *Math on the Web: A Status Report, September 2003: Focus: Interactive Math*. Available at: http://www.mathtype.com/en/reference/webmath/status/status_Sep_03.htm. Free. Semi-annual reports on activities in the Math on the Web world.

E Odlyzko, Andrew. "Silicon Dreams and Silicon Bricks: The Continuing Evolution of Libraries." *Library Trends* 46, no. 1 (Summer 1997): 152–167. Also available at: http://www.dtc.umn.edu/~odlyzko/doc/silicon.dreams.txt. Free.

E ———. "The Economics of Electronic Journals." In Ekman, Richard and Richard E. Quandt, *Technology and Scholarly Communication*, Pittsburgh: University of California Press, published in association with the Andrew K. Mellon Foundation, 1999, 380–393. Also available at: http://www.dtc.umn.edu/~odlyzko/doc/economics.journals.txt.

E ———. "Competition and Cooperation: Libraries and Publishers in the Transition to Electronic Scholarly Journals." In Berry, R. Stephen and Anne Simon Moffat, editors, *The Transition from Paper: Where Are We Going and How Will We Get There?* Cambridge, MA: American Academy of Arts & Sciences, 1999: 19p. Available at: http://www.amacad.org/publications/trans13.htm. Free.

E ———. "The Rapid Evolution of Scholarly Communication." *Learned Publishing* 15, no. 1 (Janury 2002): 7–19. Available at: http://ernesto.ingentaselect.com/vl=22716232/cl=54/nw=1/rpsv/~885/v15n1/s2/p7. Free.

E Okerson, Ann. "Whose Article Is It Anyway? Copyright and Intellectual Property Issues for Researchers in the 90s." *Notices of the American Mathematical Society* 43, no. 1 (January 1996): 8–12. Available at: http://www.ams.org/notices/199601/okerson.pdf. Free.

E Pitman, Jim. A Strategy for Open Access to Society Publications. Proposal, January 28, 2004: 3p. Available at: http://stat-www.berkeley.edu/users/pitman/strategy.html. Free.

E ———. The Mathematics Survey Draft proposal, December 9, 2002. Available at: http://stat-www.berkeley.edu/users/pitman/mathsurvey/. Free.

E Quinn, Frank. "A Digital Archive for Mathematics." Preprint, 1996: 9p. Available at: http://www.math.vt.edu/people/quinn/epub/archive.html. Free.

E ———. "Postcommercial Scholarly Publication." Preprint, 1996. 2p. Available at: http://www.math.vt.edu/people/quinn/epub/postcommercial.html. Free.

E ———. "A Role for Libraries in Electronic Publication." *EJournal* 4, no. 2 (1994); reprinted in *Serials Review* 21, no. 1 (Spring 1995): 27–30. Available at: http://www.hanover.edu/philos/ejournal/archive/ej-4-2.txt; article starts on line 68. Free.

E Rehmann, Ulf. "Documenta Mathematica, A Community-Driven Scientific Journal" *HEP Libraries Webzine*, no. 8 (October 2003): 6p. Available at: http://library.cern.ch/HEPLW/8/papers/3/. Free.

E ———. "The Price Spiral of Mathematics Journals and What to Do About It." *European Mathematical Newsletter*, no. 38 (December 2000): 2p. Available at: http://www.mathematik.uni-bielefeld.de/~rehmann/EP/price_spiral_newsletter.pdf. Free.

E Rubenstein, Dan. "A Professor, his Periodicals, their Publication and Acquisition." *University of Alberta Folio* 37, no. 4 (October 15, 1999): 3p. Available at: http://www.ualberta.ca/~publicas/folio/37/04/focus.html. Free.

Schaffner, Ann C. "The Future of Scientific Journals: Lessons from the Past." *Information Technology and Libraries* 13 (Dec 1994): 239–47.

E Steinberger, Mark. "Electronic Mathematics Journals." *Notices of the American Mathematical Society* 43, no. 1 (January 1996): 13–17. Available at: http://www.ams.org/notices/199601/steinberger.pdf. Free.

E ———. "The Demands on Electronic Journals in the Mathematical Sciences." *Journal of Electronic Publishing* 4, no. 2 (December 1998): 8p. Available at: http://www.press.umich.edu/jep/04-02/steinberger.html. Free.

E Suber, Peter. "Open Access to the Scientific Journal Literature." *Journal of Biology* 1, no. 1 (June 2002): 3p. Available at: http://jbiol.com/content/pdf/1475-4924-1-3.pdf. Free.

E van der Geer, Gerard. "We *Can* Make a Change." *Notices of the American Mathematical Society* 51, no. 5 (May 2004): 493. Available at: http://www.ams.org/notices/200405/commentary.pdf. Free.

Wegner, Bernd, ed. "Electronic Publishing and Electronic Publications in Mathematics." In *European Congress of Mathematics, Budapest, July 22–26, 1996,* Vol. II, [Round Table A]: 397–430. Boston: Birkhäuser, 1998.

E Youngen, Ralph. "Toward a Mathematical Markup Language." *Notices of the American Mathematical Society* 43, no. 9 (October 1997): 1107–1109. Available at: http://www.ams.org/notices/199709/comm-youngen.pdf. Free.

1
Bibliographic Resources

Guides to the Literature

Anderson, Nancy D. and Lois M. Pausch, eds. **A Guide to Library Service in Mathematics: The Non-Trivial Mathematics Librarian.** Greenwich, CT: JAI Press, 1993. xi + 402p. $82.50. ISBN 1-55938-745-9.

Several chapters serve as guides to the literature: books and reference materials for the mathematics library, currently published journals of interest to mathematicians, and further readings. Author and subject index.

Dick, Elie M. **Current Information Sources in Mathematics: An Annotated Guide to Books and Periodicals, 1960–72.** Littleton, CO: Libraries Unlimited, 1973. x + 281p. Out of print. ISBN 0-87287-047-2.

Serves as a supplement to Parke's **Guide to the Literature of Mathematics and Physics** (see below). Covers 1,600 English-language mathematics monographs published from 1960 to 1972 in the form of a classified annotated bibliography. Sections on reference books, periodicals, publishers, and professional organizations.

S Dudewicz, Edward J. and Joo Ok Koo. **Complete Categorized Guide to Statistical Selection and Ranking Procedures.** Columbus, OH: American Sciences Press, 1982. v + 627p. (Series in Mathematical and Management Sciences; 6). $195.00 pa. ISBN 0-935950-03-6 pa.

This classified bibliography includes reports, theses, and published items. Index is by author and chronological indexes are by subjects and author. Reprints of reviews are included when available.

Fang, Joong. **Guide to the Literature of Mathematics Today.** Hauppauge, NY: Paideia, 1972. 267p. Out of print. ISBN 0-912490-10-1.

Classified arrangement based on author's particular philosophical approach to mathematics. Discussion and lists of major terms used in mathematics. Specific entries are very brief.

Fauvel, John. **Mathematics Through History: A Resource Guide.**
See complete entry in **Chapter 7, Biographical and Historical Materials.**

Fowler, Kristine K., ed. **Using the Mathematical Literature.** New York: Marcel Dekker, 2004. (Books in Library and Information Science Series; 66). vii + 389p. $165.00 ISBN: 0-8247-5035-7.

This expert guide to mathematical literature first surveys mathematics culture, and then discusses tools and strategies for searching and finding mathematics research and information. The second section of the book presents 12 bibliographies by specialists on: the history of mathematics, number theory, combinatorics, abstract algebra, algebraic and differential geometry, real and complex analysis, ordinary and partial differential equations, topology, probability theory and stochastic processes, numerical analysis, mathematical biology, and mathematics education.

E Hurt, Charlie Deuel. **Information Sources in Science and Technology.** 3rd edition. Englewood, CO: Libraries Unlimited, 1998. xvi + 346p. (Library and Information Science Text Series). $45.00 pa. ISBN 1-56308-531-3 pa. Also available electronically from *netLibrary*, http://www.netlibrary.com. ISBN 0-585-00152-9 E-book. Subscription.

Mathematics is 1 of 16 disciplines covered in this useful and updated book. Brief reviews given for guides to the literature, abstracts, indexes, bibliographies, encyclopedias, dictionaries, handbooks and tables, and directories.

S Koren, John. **History of Statistics, Their Development and Progress in Many Countries.**
See complete entry in **Chapter 7, Biographical and Historical Materials.**

Loria, Gino. **Guida allo Studio della Storia delle Matematiche: Generalit'a Didattica, Bibliografia. Appendice: Questioni Storiche Concernenti le Scienze Esatte.** 2nd edition, revised and augmented.

See complete entry in **Chapter 7, Biographical and Historical Materials.**

Müller, Felix. **Führer durch die Mathematische Literatur.** Abhandlungen zür Nendeln, The Netherlands: Kraus Reprint, 1979. x + 252p. (Geschichte der mathematischen Wissenschaften mit Einschluss ihrer Anwendungen; 27). Price not available. ISBN 3-262-01421-4.

Reprint of 1909 original, a guide to the mathematical literature with attention to historically important works.

Parke, Nathan Grier. **Guide to the Literature of Mathematics and Physics Including Related Works on Engineering Science.** 2nd revised edition. New York: Dover, 1958. xviii + 436p. Out of print.

Introduced by discussions of research and library use, the main body is a bibliography of 5,000 titles in classified arrangement with occasional notes. There is an emphasis on applied mathematics. A more current work is Dick's **Current Information Sources in Mathematics** (see above).

Pemberton, John E. **How to Find Out in Mathematics.** 2nd revised edition. Oxford: Pergamon Press, 1969. xiv + 193p. Out of print. ISBN 0-08-006823-5.

Somewhat dated, but still interesting guide to mathematics literature.

S Sachs, Lothar. **Guide to Statistical Methods and to the Pertinent Literature.** Berlin; New York: Springer-Verlag, 1986. xii + 212p. $49.95 pa. ISBN 0-387-16835-4 pa.

An English/German bilingual bibliography of 1,449 items with keyword and subject heading indexes of 5,500 terms. Intended for students and researchers using intermediate and multivariate methods.

Bibliographies

Anderson, Nancy D. **French Mathematical Seminars: A Union List.** 2nd edition. Providence, RI: American Mathematical Society, 1989. xv + 178p. $34.00 pa. ISBN 0-8218-0129-5 pa.

Union list for North American and a few French universities' holdings providing accurate bibliographic entries, cross references, sponsoring and issuing body, dates, normal form of entry, name and address of publisher, and other useful information.

S Anderson, T. W., et al. **Bibliography of Multivariate Statistical Analysis.** Huntington, NY: Krieger, 1977. Reprint of 1972 edition. x + 642p. $51.98. ISBN 0-88275-477-7.

An exhaustive compilation of literature on multivariate analysis to 1966 for articles and to 1970 for monographs. Provides author and subject access to some 6,250 papers and books. Useful background information.

Boncompagni, B., ed. **Bullettino di Bibliografia e di Storia della Scienze Matematiche e Fisiche.** v.1–20. 1868–1887. New York: Johnson Reprint Corp., 1964. Out of print. ISBN 03-84-06306-3.

Useful for referencing the older literature with contributions in Italian, French, or Latin. Index in v.20.

Brezinski, Claude. **A Bibliography on Continued Fractions, Padé Approximation, Sequence Transformation and Related Subjets.** 1a Ed. Ciencias; 3. Zaragoza: Universidad de Zaragoza, 1991. 348p. Price not available. ISBN 84-7733-238-X.

Contains more than 6,000 references on topics in title of book. Also includes references on related subjects such as moment problems and orthogonal polynomials.

Campbell, Paul J. and Louise S. Grinstein. **Mathematics Education in Secondary Schools and Two-Year Colleges: A Sourcebook.** New York: Garland, 1988. xvii + 439p. Out of print. ISBN 0-8240-8522-1.

An annotated bibliography of books and articles with brief essays by specialists at the beginning of each of 20 sections.

E Dauben, Joseph W. **History of Mathematics from Antiquity to the Present: A Selective Annotated Bibliography.**

See complete entry in **Chapter 7, Biographical and Historical Materials.**

Dell'Amico, Mauro, Francesco Maffioli, and Silvano Martello, eds. **Annotated Bibliographies in Combinatorial Optimization.** Chichester, England; New York: Wiley, 1997. xiii + 495p. $155.00. ISBN 0-471-965574-X.

Initial chapter reviews the most influential texts of the last decade. In addition to the annotated bibliographies, the authors provide a concise, comprehensive, and up-to-date survey of each topic. The 24 chapters, all by leading experts, cover both method and application oriented subjects. Many sections on available software.

De Morgan, Augustus. **Arithmetical Books from the Invention of Printing to the Present Time: Being Brief Notices of a Large Number of Works Drawn Up from Actual Inspection.** London: Taylor and Walton, 1847. xxviii + 124p. Out of print.

Chronological listing from 1491 to 1800 with an additional listing of 1,580 names of reported authors and editors.

Dilcher, Karl, Ladislav Skula, and Ilja Sh. Slavutskii, eds. **Bernoulli Numbers: Bibliography (1713–1990).** Kingston, ON: Queen's University, 1991. iv + 175p. (Queen's Papers in Pure & Applied Mathematics; 87). Out of print.

An enlarged edition of the 1988 original, listing 1,956 publications by 839 authors. Extensively indexed.

Forsythe, George Elmer. **Bibliography of Russian Mathematics Books.** New York: Chelsea, 1956. 106p. Out of print.

Listing of over 600 books in pure and applied mathematics published since 1930. Classified subject index and transliteration table.

Gaffney, Matthew P. and Lynn Arthur Steen. **Annotated Bibliography of Expository Writing in the Mathematical Sciences.** Washington, DC: Mathematical Association of America, 1976. xi + 282p. Out of print. ISBN 0-88385-422-8.

Classified, occasionally annotated listing of articles (some books) useful for university-level teaching. Seven major subject headings are divided by degree of difficulty plus related entries. Author index has complete citations.

S Harter, H. Leon. **Chronological Annotated Bibliography of Order Statistics.** Columbus, OH: American Sciences Press, 1983–1993. (American Series in Mathematical and Management Sciences; 7–8, 19–24). Vol. I. **Pre-1950.** iv + 515p. $195.00 pa. ISBN 0-9235950-04-4. Vol. II. **1950–1959.** vi + 993p. $195.00 pa. ISBN 0-935950-05-2. Vol. III. **1960–1961.** vi + 214p. $195.00 pa. ISBN 0-935950-21-4. Vol. IV. **1962–1963.** viii + 173. $195.00 pa. ISBN 0-935950-22-2. Vol. V. **1964–1965.** vi + 180p. Out of print. ISBN 0-935950-23-0. Vol. VI. **1966–1967.** vi + 232p. $195.00 pa. ISBN 0-935950-24-9. Vol. VII. **1968–1969.** vi + 292p. Out of print

ISBN 0-935950-25-7. Vol. VIII. **Indices, With a Supplement on 1970–1992.** vi + 267p. $195.00 pa. ISBN 0-935950-26-5.

An eight-volume set on books, articles, dissertations, theses, technical reports, and notes on order statistics, excluding rank statistics, for the periods indicated. Each succeeding volume, in addition to covering its time period, includes publications identified as relevant since the publishing of the previous volumes. Some simple citation indexing plus author and subject indexes. Volume 8 includes a section by N. Balakrishnan on developments in order statistics from 1970 to 1992.

Honda, Shojo, comp. **Pre-Meiji Works in the Library of Congress.** Washington, DC: Library of Congress, 1982. vii + 64p. Out of print. ISBN 0-8444-0392-X.

Bibliography of printed books and manuscripts from the Asian Division of the Library of Congress covering pre-Meiji Japanese mathematics from the seventeenth century to 1867. Entries arranged alphabetically. Titles Romanized using Hepburn system.

Høyrup, Else. **Women and Mathematics, Science and Engineering: A Partially Annotated Bibliography with Emphasis on Mathematics and with References on Related Topics.** Roskilde, Denmark: Roskilde University Library, 1978. vi + 62p. (Skriftserie fra Roskilde Universitetsbibliotek; 4). Not in trade.

Partially annotated bibliography of mainly American and Danish papers and books primarily from the sixties and seventies. Some of the topics include sex roles in textbooks, women mathematicians, and sex differences in spatial visualization, creativity, cognition, and problem solving.

Karpinski, Louis Charles. **Bibliography of Mathematical Works Printed in America through 1850.** Ann Arbor: University of Michigan Press; London: Oxford University Press, 1940. 4p. + vii–xxvi + 697p. Out of print.

Chronologically arranged coverage of over 1,000 mathematical books printed in America. Indexed by author and anonymous titles, topical, and publisher/printer indexes.

Karpinski, Louis Charles. **Bibliography of Mathematical Works Printed in America through 1850, Supplement** and **Second Supplement.** Reprint edition. New York: Arno, 1980. xxvi + 697p. + p.233–236 and p.173–176. Out of print.

Same as above, with the addition of two supplements that originally appeared in **Scripta Mathematica**, v.8 and v.12. Works consulted appears on p.613–618.

S Kendall, Maurice G. and Alison G. Doig. **Bibliography of Statistical Literature.** Vol. 1. **1950–1958.** xii + 297p. Vol. 2. **1940–1949.** 190p. Vol. 3. **Pre-1940.** vi + 356p. Salem, NH: Ayer, 1981. $75.00 (set). ISBN 0-405-13881-4 (set).

Comprehensive listing of major articles written on statistics since sixteenth century up to 1958. For more current bibliographic information, consult the statistics listings in **Chapter 2, Finding Tools.**

S Lancaster, Henry Oliver. **Bibliography of Statistical Bibliographies.** Edinburgh: Oliver and Boyd, 1968. ix + 103p. $18.00. ISBN 0-934454-12-4.

University-level materials in statistics, mathematical statistics, and probability. Arranged in two classes: "Persons," for contributors to statistical theory, and "Subject," containing methodology and applications. Author index includes authors, editors, compilers, and biographees.

Macfarlane, Alexander. **Bibliography of Quaternions and Allied Systems of Mathematics.** Dublin: Printed at the University Press by Ponsonby and Gibbs, 1904. 86p. Out of print.

Authors listed alphabetically with works arranged chronologically.

May, Kenneth O. **Bibliography and Research Manual of the History of Mathematics.**

See complete entry in **Chapter 7, Biographical and Historical Materials.**

Müller, Gert H. and Wolfgang Lenski, eds. **Omega—Bibliography of Mathematical Logic.** New York: Springer-Verlag, 1987. 6 vols. Vol. 1. **Classical Logic.** xxxix + 483p. Out of print. ISBN 0-387-17321-8. Vol. 2. **Non-Classical Logics.** xxxvii + 468p. Out of print. ISBN 0-387-15521-X. Vol. 3. **Model Theory.** xiv + 615p. Out of print. ISBN 0-387-15522-8. Vol. 4. **Recursion Theory.** xlv + 696p. Out of print. ISBN 0-387-15523-6. Vol. 5. **Set Theory.** li + 790p. Out of print. ISBN 0-387-15525-2. Vol. 6. **Proof Theory. Constructive Mathematics.** xli + 404p. Out of print. ISBN 0-387-15524-4.

Classified, comprehensive bibliography of works in mathematical logic published between 1879 and 1985 following MSC classification 03 categories with some modifications. Each volume includes an introduction, a subject index, an author index, and a source index.

Navia, Luis E. **Pythagoras: An Annotated Bibliography.**
See complete entry in **Chapter 7, Biographical and Historical Materials.**

O'Heigeartaigh, M., J. K. Lenstra, and A. H. G. Rinnooy Kan, eds. **Combinatorial Optimization: Annotated Bibliographies.** New York: Wiley, 1985. vii + 204p. Out of print. ISBN 0-471-90490-2.
Collection of annotated bibliographies covering several major areas within field of optimization.

Patil, Ganapati Parashuram and Sharadchandrea W. Joshi. **Dictionary and Bibliography of Discrete Distributions.** New York: Hafner, 1968. xii + 268p. Out of print.
Bibliography section contains over 2,900 entries arranged by author with a classified subject index. Dictionary section is classified and indexed.

Powell, Russell H., ed. **Handbooks and Tables in Science and Technology.** 2nd edition. Phoenix, AZ: Oryx, 1994. viii + 359p. $95.00. ISBN 0-89774-534-5.
Covers nearly 3,700 handbooks and tables in science and technology with thorough indexing. Each entry provides full bibliographic data. The more complex sources are described in annotations of 20–200 words. Very useful tool for evaluating sci-tech collections.

Rider, Robin E. **Bibliography of Early Modern Algebra, 1500–1800.**
See complete entry in **Chapter 7, Biographical and Historical Materials.**

Schaaf, William L. **Bibliography of Recreational Mathematics.** 4th edition. Reston, VA: National Council of Teachers of Mathematics, 1970–78. 4 vols. Out of print. Vol. 1. 148p. ISBN 0-87353-021-7. Vol. 2. 191p. ISBN 0-87353-022-5. Vol. 3. 187p. ISBN 0-87353-023-3. Volume 4. 178p. ISBN 0-87353-128-0.
Classified arrangement covers books and articles. Volumes overlap chronologically. Glossary in Volume 3 with supplement in Volume 4.

Smith, David Eugene. **Rara Arithmetica: A Catalogue of the Arithmetics Written Before the Year MDCI. . . .**

See complete entry in **Chapter 7, Biographical and Historical Materials.**

Sommerville, D. M. Y. **Bibliography of Non-Euclidean Geometry.** 2nd edition. New York: Chelsea, 1970. xii + 410p. $30.00. ISBN 0-8284-0175-6.

Some 4,500 entries arranged chronologically covering fourth century B.C. to 1911. One hundred twenty-five post-1911 items added in the reprint.

Steen, Lynn Arthur, ed. **Library Recommendations for Undergraduate Mathematics.** Washington, DC: Mathematical Association of America, 1992. xi + 194p. (MAA Reports; 4). $9.60 pa. ISBN 0-88385-076-1 pa.

Revision of MAA's long out-of-date **Basic Library List for Four-Year Colleges** (1976). Companion volume to **Two-Year College Mathematics Library Recommendations** (see below). Three thousand titles arranged in 25 chapters and coded with asterisks into 4 levels of priority (200 essential, 400 highly recommended, 800 recommended, and 1,600 listed). One of the purposes of this book is "to ensure that college libraries have important reference works and classic sources in the mathematical sciences." Both in-print and out-of-print titles have been selected. Also includes a section on periodicals and journals and an author index.

Steen, Lynn Arthur, ed. **Two-Year College Mathematics Library Recommendations.** Washington, DC: Mathematical Association of America, 1992. xi + 76p. (MAA Reports; 5). $6.00 pa. ISBN 0-88385-077-X pa.

The long-awaited revision of MAA's **Basic Library List for Two-Year Colleges** (1980). Organization and coverage is similar to its companion volume, **Library Recommendations for Undergraduate Mathematics** (see above). This list contains 1,200 titles specially selected from the 3,000 titles of the larger work.

Terquem, M., ed. **Bulletin de Bibliographie, d'Histoire et de Biographie Mathématiques.**

See complete entry in **Chapter 7, Biographical and Historical Materials.**

Tomber, Marvin, et al. **Tomber's Bibliography and Index in Nonassociative Algebras.** 3 vols. in 1. Nonantum, MA: Hadronic Press, 1984. 535p. Out of print. ISBN: 0-911767-17-7.

Contains early works on associative algebra compiled from a variety of sources, with **Mathematical Reviews** being the primary one.

Tsao, C. K., comp. **Bibliography of Mathematics Published in Communist China, 1949–1960.** Providence, RI: American Mathematical Society, 1961. 83p. Out of print.

As the title indicates, this is a bibliography of mathematics published in the Peoples' Republic of China, 1949–1960. There is a second part available from AMS that is a report on Chinese mathematical dictionaries by S. H. Gould (1969. ISBN 0-8218-0016-7. $9.00).

S Wold, Herman, ed. for the International Statistical Institute. **Bibliography on Time Series and Stochastic Processes: An International Team Project.** Cambridge, MA: MIT Press, 1965. xv + 516p. Out of print.

Covers research on time series and stochastic processes up to 1965.

Zhang Shu-yu, ed. **Bibliography on Chaos.** Singapore; River Edge, NJ: World Scientific, 1991. vi + 514p. (Directions in Chaos; 5). $91.00. ISBN 981-02-0580-5.

A list of books and articles related to chaotic dynamics that had appeared by the end of 1990.

Portals

The Web equivalent of bibliographies and guides to the literature are searchable and comprehensive subject-specific sites sometimes known as portals. Portals generally list only resources on the Web, not resources published in paper. In mathematics, there are many such sites compiled by knowledgeable mathematicians or librarians. Most listed electronic resources are available free.

E *EEVL: The Internet Guide to Engineering, Mathematics and Computing: [Mathematics].* EEVL, 2003. Available at: http://www.eevl.ac.uk/mathematics/index.htm.

Several British university libraries partnered to create the EEVL portal with access to quality resources in engineering, mathematics, and computer science. Entries are searchable in numerous ways and nicely annotated.

E *Math Archives*. Mathematics Archives, 1996–2001. Available at: http://archives.math.utk.edu/. Free.

Math Archives covers a wide array of math topics, math education, software, and miscellanies and may be searched by broad topic or by keyword. Each entry is marked with a useful icon indicating the minimum level of mathematical knowledge (five levels, from K6 through Graduate/Professional) needed to understand a significant portion of each site. Icons are also used to mark the presence of images, animation, Java programming, interactivity, or a collection of links to other sites. Some entries have added keywords.

E *The Math Forum Internet Mathematics Library*. The Math Forum@Drexel, 1994–2003. Available at: http://mathforum.org/library/. Free.

Nicely organized, this popular online forum and library is recommended as a first stop for math librarians and mathematicians. It has over 8,500 links to selected online resources in mathematics and mathematics education. They are arranged by topics, resource types, and education level and can be searched by any of these variables. Each record is annotated. The library is part of the larger *Math Forum@Drexel* site, which also offers a variety of links such as "Ask Dr. Math" and its archive, problems of the week, and "Teacher2Teacher." Originally funded by the National Science Foundation, *Math Forum* is now administered by Drexel University.

E *Math on the Web*. American Mathematical Society, 2003. Available at: http://www.ams.org/mathweb/. Free.

Clearly organized, the AMS site allows for quick retrieval. It has useful listings for handy reference items, online publications, mathematical publishers, electronic math journals, an annual list of new journals, and a set of links to over 500 math journal home pages.

E *Mathematical Atlas*. David Rusin; 2004. Available at: http://www.math-atlas.org/. Free.

This collection of articles is structured according to the Mathematics Subject Classification (MSC). Each section is an informative introduction to that specific area of mathematics with lists and links to other resources, both paper and electronic.

E *Mathematics WWW Virtual Library*. No copyright given. Available at: http://www.math.fsu.edu/Science/math.html. Free.

Part of the Virtual Library collection of sites, this site is organized by broad categories but is not searchable by keyword. Its Specialized Fields page lists topics alphabetically. Maintained by Florida State University's Department of Mathematics, it has a useful list of addresses and math department Web servers from around the world.

E *MathGuide*. SUB Göttingen, 1997–2001. Available at: http://www.mathguide.de/. Free.

Developed at SUB (Lower Saxony State and University Library) Göttingen, *MathGuide* selects and catalogs over 1,100 Internet resources in mathematics at the college and research levels. Each entry is described using Dublin Core metadata and evaluated for its content, clarity, indexing, links, and mathematical level with one to three stars. *MathGuide* can be searched by subject, MSC classification, source type, or keyword.

E *Resources in Mathematics*. Physics-Astronomy-Mathematics Division of SLA, 2004. Available at: http://www.sla.org/division/dpam/subjects/math.html. Free.

This is is a collection of links selected by mathematics librarians of the PAM Division of SLA. There are six sections: People, Professional Societies, Institutions, Reference, Preprints, and Pathfinders.

S E *StatLib*. Carnegie Mellon University, Department of Statistics, no copyright given. Available at: http://lib.stat.cmu.edu/. Free.

StatLib's collection of software, data sets, electronic journals, archives, and directories makes it the primary statistics portal for professional statisticians and academics. Its "Other Places" link lists statistics departments and societies worldwide.

Library Catalogs

Collection development and bibliographic verification are some of a librarian's main activities. With the advent of the Web, librarians and users can easily use library catalogs as bibliographic and collection development tools.

E California Digital Library. *Melvyl—The Catalog of the University of California Libraries.* The Regents of University of California, 2004. Available at: http://melvyl.cdlib.org. Free.

Melvyl contains over 9 million unique titles representing over 13.8 million holdings. It is a rich and useful resource for verification at the college and research levels. *Melvyl* includes holdings from nine University of California campuses, the California State Library, the California Academy of Sciences, the Center for Research Libraries, and the Graduate Theological Union in Berkeley.

E *LIBWEB; Library Servers via WWW.* Thomas Dowling, 1995–2003. Available at: http://sunsite.berkeley.edu/Libweb/. Free.

Need to check a specific library's catalog? LIBWEB links to over 6,100 library catalogs of all kinds from around the world.

E *OCLC Worldcat.* OCLC, 2003. Available at: http://www.oclc.org/firstsearch/databases/details/dbinformation_WorldCat.html. Subscription; price varies.

OCLC Worldcat is probably the most widely used union catalog in the United States and Canada. It contains over 48 million records contributed by its member libraries, including university libraries from the United States, Canada, and beyond; the Library of Congress; the British Library; the Canada Institute for Scientific and Technical Information (CISTI); and the Center for Research Libraries. Because it is so large, it is naturally the place to go first when trying to verify book and journal titles. It lists holding libraries for each record, thus facilitating interlibrary loan or document delivery service. Call numbers are now included in the catalog record. More than one record may exist for a title.

E *OhioLINK Central Catalog.* OhioLINK, no copyright given. Available at: http://olc1.ohiolink.edu/search/. Free.

OhioLink is one of the first large library catalogs to include book tables of contents in their catalog records. The TOC information comes from book vendor Blackwell North America and has appeared selectively since 1994. TOC information can be helpful when trying to decide whether to acquire a book or just get a chapter via document delivery.

New Books Information

Selection and acquisition decisions are frequently made in advance of publication when working from a book vendor's approval slips or a user's recommendation. One should be able to get prepublication verification, content, and price information from these sites.

E *AcqWeb's Directory of Publishers and Vendors.* AcqWeb, 1994–2001. Available at: http://acqweb.library.vanderbilt.edu/acqweb/pubr.html#alph. Free.

Publishers' catalogs sometimes offer more information on a book's or journal's contents, pricing, or availability than general catalogs or databases can convey. *AcqWeb*'s list of links is an easy way to find publisher sites. There is also a useful listing of out-of-print dealers at: http://acqweb.library.vanderbilt.edu/acqweb/verif_rare.html.

E *Amazon.com.* Amazon.com, Inc., 1996–2004. Available at: http://www.amazon.com. Free.

While primarily a book-selling site, one can use *Amazon.com* as a free books-in-print database—certainly users do! Records may include links to sample pages, customer reviews, tables of content, and related works. Some publishers allow users to see the full-text. Mathematics and statistics titles may have reviews, but they are not necessarily authoritative.

E *Books In Print*®. R.R. Bowker, LLC, 2004. Information Available at: http://www.booksinprint.com/bip/. Subscription; price varies.

The *Books In Print*® databases are available in many different forms from vendors as well as directly from the publisher. At this writing, there are about 2.7 million records of in-print, out-of-print, and forthcoming titles listed with bibliographic, price, and availability information.

Document Delivery Vendors

Libraries today have realized that even the largest libraries cannot continue to acquire everything. It has become cheaper and more efficient to offer patrons access to whatever they need rather than to try to anticipate all of their needs. Interlibrary loan and document delivery services help to fill in the gaps in library collections. These services at the university level may be available to users free or for a small fee. Although a central office usually manages transactions with other libraries, document delivery can be offered directly through subject librarians who know their field well. The document vendors listed below are among those found useful for mathematics and statistics documents. Some journal publishers and aggregators also offer pay-per-view services.

E *CISTI (Canada Institute for Scientific and Technical Information)*. NRC-CNRC, no copyright given. Available at: http://cat.cisti-icist.nrc-cnrc.gc.ca/search. Free registration; document delivery for a fee.

CISTI is one of the world's major sources for document delivery in all areas of science, technology, engineering, and medicine. *CISTI* has been responsible for nothing short of a revolution in the way science libraries provide information not held locally. The collection is vast and the document delivery process is efficient and timely. Document fees are affordable and the documents are clean and readable. *CISTI* delivers their documents by Ariel® (Research Libraries Group (RLG) document transmission system), PDF, fax, or courier. Fax images can be fuzzy and are not recommended whenever mathematics is involved. *CISTI* charges a document fee plus copyright. Turnaround time is usually 24–48 hours. If they do not have an item, *CISTI*'s LINK service, for a slight extra fee, expands their search to their partners, such as the British Library, some Far East partners, and the Institut de l'Information Scientifique et Technique (INIST) of France.

Users of *MathSciNet* can send orders directly to *CISTI* via the convenient DOCUMENT DELIVERY button offered on every *MathSciNet* record. The **MR** record is automatically transferred to *CISTI*. Registered users have only to input order numbers, maximum price, and any special instructions. It is recommended that one specify *CISTI*'s LINK service rather than their DIRECT service, so that orders automatically go beyond *CISTI* if needed. Copyright charges are available before ordering, but this information is not always accurate.

E *Ingenta*. Ingenta, 2001. Covers 1988– . Available at: http://www.ingenta.com/. Free searching; document delivery for a fee.

Ingenta is a large database of over 14 million journal article records taken from over 27,000 journals in all subjects that have appeared since fall 1988. Document delivery is available for a fee via e-mail, Ariel®, fax, or convenient and immediate PDF download.

E *Linda Hall Library Document Services*. Linda Hall Library, 2003. Available at: http://www.lindahall.org/services/document_delivery/index.shtml. Free registration; document delivery for a fee.

Linda Hall Library Document Services are reasonably priced, delivered on time, and have two advantages over *CISTI* services. Libraries can order articles from Linda Hall under the "fair use" clause and not pay for copyright until the library's "fair use" has been exceeded. Also, Linda Hall offers document delivery via PDF e-mail attachments in addition to delivery by Ariel®, fax, courier, or mail. PDF files can easily be delivered to the user's desktop.

2
Finding Tools

Databases and Indexes

The field of mathematics is blessed by the presence of a long tradition of high-quality indexing and abstracting. A structured classification system known as the Mathematics Subject Classification (MSC) has for many years been the chief subject access into the literature. The two major indexes use this system and most articles published in mathematics are given one or two MSC codes at the time of publication by their author(s). This system works well for mathematicians, but not so well for librarians or researchers outside the field. Fortunately, technology can help by providing online database searching by author, title, subject, and keywords. The two primary indexes in the field, **Mathematical Reviews** and **Zentralblatt für Mathematik und Ihre Grenzgebiete,** have migrated from paper indexes to dial-up searching through a vendor to CD-ROM to the Web over the last 25 years. The products get better and better in terms of searching functionality and output, and current prices are reasonable. Both *MathSciNet*, the Web version of **Mathematical Reviews**, and *Zentralblatt MATH*, the Web version of **Zentralblatt für Mathematik und ihre Grenzgebiete**, are compiled by scientific societies whose primary goals are to disseminate mathematics as broadly as possible rather than maximize their profits. The main U.S.-based statistics index, **Current Index to Statistics**, does not have as long a publishing history, nor does it have a structured classification system or review process. It has been slower to modernize, but substantial progress has been made in the last few years.

Where there are paper and electronic versions, the electronic version is discussed in more detail, as this is the dominant trend. Ancillary resources to the major indexes will be listed at the end of the main entry for the title as related resources. When a subscription is required, a range of prices for libraries may be given. Prices of electronic products vary a great deal depending on a variety of factors, such as an institution's size and membership in a society or in consortia. Contact the publisher directly for up-to-date information. Free resources are so indicated. In some cases, a product may exist only in paper or only on the Web. A paper-only product will get less and less use over time, but if it still has a unique value for particular dates or purposes, it will be listed here.

E *arXiv.org* (also known as xxx.lanl.gov or e-Print archive). Cornell University, no copyright given. Covers 1991– . Available at: http://arxiv.org or http://front.math.ucdavis.edu/ (math only). Free.

The original Los Alamos National Laboratory (LANL) physics preprints archive expanded to include nonlinear sciences, computer science, mathematics, and quantitative biology. Although the *arXiv* has had enormous success in physics, mathematicians have been slower to embrace the concept of a centralized preprint archive and its technology. Recently, however, there has been more movement toward using this site as a central depository for mathematics preprints and refereed e-journal articles. Unlike *MPRESS*, a European-based index to preprints in various repositories (see below), *arXiv* depends on authors (or their departments) to format and submit their papers to the centralized archive. There are over 35,500 math papers to date.

E *citebase Search.* [Open Archives], no date given. Available at: http://citebase.eprints.org/cgi-bin/search. Free.

This prototype site is part of the Open Archives services. It gives citation data according to various criteria for papers in open archives such as *arXiv*. Links to full text are there when available.

S E *Current Index to Statistics—Extended Database.* CIS, 2000. Updated annually. Release 11, 2003 covers pre-1975 to 2002 and some of 2003. Available at: http://www.statindex.org/CIS/query. $125.00–$720.00/yr. Access to **American Statistician** records and to pre-1995 records is free.

S E Current Index to Statistics—Extended Database CD-ROM. [Hayward, CA]: American Statistical Association and Institute of Mathematical Statistics, 2003. Release 11. Updated annually. $250.00–$1,440.00/yr. ISSN: 1094-7469.

S Current Index to Statistics. Alexandria, VA: American Statistical Association and Institute of Mathematical Statistics, 1975–1999. Vols. 1–25. Ceased.

Hungry for Web access to this small but important source, librarians and statisticians welcomed *CIS-ED* on the Web in 1999. *CIS-ED* is much more comprehensive in statistics than either *MathSciNet* or *Zentralblatt MATH* and thus is needed when supporting a statistics graduate program. Although also available as a CD-ROM, librarians find it helpful to have easy campuswide access via this Web version. At this writing, *CIS-ED* includes coverage of 162 core journals from 1975 to 2002 plus some of 2003; it also includes pre-1975 coverage for a number of core titles, selected articles from about 1,200 additional journals, and about 11,000 books in statistics published since 1975. There are over 250,000 entries.

CIS-ED does not index much of the statistical literature from the early 1900s to 1965 that is covered in Tukey and Ross's **Index to Statistics and Probability** (see below). The Tukey material as a body is found electronically only in *MathSci on Dialog*® (see below). *CIS-ED* did add coverage of some older core journals to fill the gap between the Tukey index and the beginning of **CIS**, but the entire runs of core titles, such as **Annals of Mathematical Statistics**, **JASA, Biometrics**, **Biometrika**, **Sankhya,** or **Applied Statistics,** are not covered. *JSTOR*® (see below) helps to fill this gap by providing indexing and full-text electronic access to a major portion of early core statistical journal literature. *Zentralblatt MATH* and *MathSciNet* (both below) also index core stat materials, but not as far back in time as *JSTOR*®.

CIS records consist of author, title, bibliographic information, and some additional keywords; there are no abstracts or reviews. The search interface is still a work in progress; be sure to read the help files in order to thoroughly understand the options. Librarians have reported difficulties when trying to acquire access to the Web version of *CIS-ED* and in negotiating the license agreement. *CIS-ED* cannot yet be considered a polished product, but the sponsoring societies, American Statistical Association and the Institute of Mathematical Statistics, are giving it more attention and funding. The product is quite affordable.

E *Current Contents Connect*®. Institute for Scientific Information®, 2004. Coverage is current year, backfiles available. Information is available at: http://www.isinet.com/isi/products/cc/ccconnect/cccsitewide/index.html. Subscription: price varies.

Essentially a subset of the *ISI Web of Science*® database (see below), *Current Contents Connect*® indexes new articles from over 8,000 journals and about 2,000 books. Although not comprehensive for either mathematics or statistics, *Current Contents Connect*® does cover nearly 400 of the more highly cited journals in mathematics and statistics. A list of titles covered is available at: http://www.isinet.com/isi/journals/index.html. Records are enriched with author abstracts, additional keywords, and links to the fulltext when available. The ISI® *Current Contents Connect*® Web product is updated daily; updates can be searched separately. Other vendors are updated weekly. Users may set up alerts.

Current Contents Connect® may not be necessary if a library also subscribes to *Web of Science*®. *MathSciNet* (see below) can be used to browse new materials as well, although not automatically. *Current Contents Connect*® may be helpful for statisticians, as *CIS-ED* (see above) is only updated annually and *MathSciNet* is not as comprehensive for statistics.

E *Digital Dissertations*. Proquest®, 2004. Covers 1861– . Information available at: http://www.il.proquest.com/products/pt-product-Dissertations.shtml. Current two years is free. Subscription; price varies.

E **Dissertation Abstracts International. A: The Humanities and Social Sciences; B: The Sciences and Engineering; and C: Worldwide.** Ann Arbor, MI: UMI, 1938– . Covers 1861– . A & B, monthly; C, quarterly. ISSN 0419-4209(A). ISSN 0419-4217(B). ISSN 1042-7279 (C). A & B, $2,490.00/yr.; C, $2,325.00/yr. Also available on CD-ROM.

The Web version of **Dissertation Abstracts** covers U. S. dissertations from 1861 onward, with master's theses and foreign dissertations added over the years. More recent records have searchable author abstracts. Subscribers can get 24-page previews free for dissertations from 1997 onward. Patrons at subscribing institutions may view the entire full text of their own institution's dissertations from 1997 onward.

E *Directory of Mathematics Preprints and e-Print Servers*. American Mathematical Society, 2004. Available at: http://www.ams.org/global-preprints/. Free.

This directory lists all known preprint servers in mathematics with their URLs and an e-mail contact. May be useful for elusive preprints.

E *ERIC, Educational Resources Information Center.* U.S. Department of Education, Institute of Education Sciences, no copyright given. Covers 1966– . Available at: http://www.eric.ed.gov/. Free.

ERIC, the Web version of **Resources in Education** and **Current Index to Journals in Education,** indexes more than 1 million education articles and documents at all levels. Math education is covered from K–12 through the university level. In 2004 the U.S. Department of Education awarded a five-year, $34.6 million contract to an outside contractor, Computer Sciences Corporation (CSC) of Rockville, Md., to develop and operate ERIC beginning in September 2004.

E *EULER*. Euler Consortium, 2001–2002. Available at: http://www.emis.de/projects/EULER/index.html. Free.

EULER, based on Dublin Core metadata, is another ambitious project for mathematics that is being developed by a group of European academic institutions and societies. *EULER* offers full coverage of the mathematics literature worldwide, including bibliographic data, peer reviews and/or abstracts, indexing, classification and search, transparent access to library services, cooperation with commercial information providers (publishers, bookstores). Contents currently include 2.4 milltion entries gathered from three libraries' math holdings (SUB Göttingen, CWI Amsterdam, and Universita degli Studi di Firenze), *Zentralblatt MATH*, and the *Jahrbuch-Project*.

E *Expanded Academic ASAP*™. Gale Group, 2004. Covers 1980– . Information available at: http://www.galegroup.com/pdf/facts/expacad.pdf. Subscription; price varies.

Expanded Academic ASAP™ provides broad coverage at the undergraduate level. It indexes 3,200 journals with 2,000 of these available in full-text. As with *Research Library Complete* (see below), undergraduate students and faculty will find it useful for some of their work. Full-text periodical titles, most not yet available electronically from their publishers, include **American Mathematical Monthly**, **American Statistician**, **Mathematical Intelligencer,** and **Mathematics Magazine**. Full-text coverage may lag several weeks behind publication and may not be stable.

Grinstein, Louise S. **Mathematical Book Review Index, 1800–1940.** New York: Garland, 1992. xxxvi + 448p. (Garland reference library of social science; vol. 527). $86.00. ISBN 0-8240-4114-3.

This useful work indexes book reviews of 3,200 mathematical books published in the United States or Canada from 1800 to 1940.

Index to Translations Selected by the American Mathematical Society. Providence, RI: American Mathematical Society, 1966-73. Vol. 1. iii + 90p. $22.00. ISBN 0-8218-0042-6. Vol. 2. iii + 93p. $35.00 ISBN 0-8218-0059-0.

These two volumes index articles translated from Russian that are included in the book series, **American Mathematical Society Translations—Series 1 and Series 2**, v. 1–100, and **Selected Translations in Mathematical Statistics and Probability**, v. 1–13. Author and subject indexes included. Links to these translated materials can also be found in *MathSciNet* (see below).

E *Ingenta*. Ingenta, 2004. Covers 1988– . Available at: http://www.ingenta.com/. Free searching, other services either fee or subscription; price varies.

Ingenta is a database of over 16 million journal article records taken from over 28,000 journals in all subjects that have appeared since fall 1988. Its services to libraries include authenticated campuswide access to subscribed full-text articles from over 6,000 journals and fax, PDF, or Ariel document delivery for others. *Ingenta*'s *Reveal* current awareness service is available to licensed institutional subscribers. It is particularly useful to have a broadly based index for math and stat researchers in applied and multidisciplinary areas.

E *INSPEC*®. Institution of Electrical Engineers, 2004. Covers 1969– . Updated weekly. Information available at: http://www.iee.org.uk/publish/inspec. Subscription available from various vendors; price varies.

INSPEC® is useful for mathematical physics, applied math and statistics, and computer science. Over 3,400 journals and 2,000 proceedings and other formats are scanned each year for relevant material; there are 7 million records to date.

E *ISI Web of Science*®. Thomson ISI, 2004. Covers current year with backfiles available for additional fees. Updated weekly. Information available at: http://www.isinet.com/isi/products/citation/wos/index.html. Subscription; price varies. Most, but not all, of the sciences portion of *Web of Science*® is available also as **SciSearch**® on CD-ROM or via dial-up on Dialog, STN, or DIMDI.

E **CMCI CompuMath Citation Index.** Philadelphia, PA: Institute for Scientific Information®, 1982– . Formerly in paper, now only on CD-

ROM containing five years, or as part of the larger *Web of Science*. Updated bimonthly. ISSN 0730-6199. Information available at: http://www.isinet.com/presentrep/facts/cmci.pdf. Price varies. Note that **Science Citation Index**® does not cover as many mathematics journals as are covered by **CompuMath Citation Index** and thus is not recommended as a substitute. See http://www.isinet.com/cgi-bin/jrnlst/jloptions.cgi?PC=4 for **CMCI**'s list of journals.

The complete *Web of Science* collectively indexes about 8,500 highly cited journals cover to cover and provides complete bibliographic data, author addresses, and searchable author abstracts when available. Institutions may subscribe to any or all three of the subject collections (Sciences, Social Sciences, and Arts and Humanities), for the current year and a backfile of any size, back to 1945 for sciences, for additional charges. At this writing, approximately 400 math and statistics journals are covered as source titles. You may view the specific titles covered under various mathematical subject categories at http://www.isinet.com/cgi-bin/jrnlst/jlsubcatg.cgi?PC=D. If cost prohibits purchase to the *WOS* backfiles, libraries that subscribed to **CompuMath Citation Index** in paper should retain those back volumes.

Web of Science's most valuable feature is its unique Cited Reference Search that traces the citation of known relevant papers by more recent papers. The Related Records feature leads to a seemingly infinite number of possibly relevant papers. Convenient links from citation to full text are being added to the database. At this time, SIAM, Academic, Elsevier, Kluwer, and Springer are among the relevant publishers available. Users may save queries to run again; current awareness alerting should become available in 2004.

Citation searching on the *Web of Science* is a very powerful feature, but it can be complex to use, interpret, and teach end users. When using it, one should be mindful of a number of nuances that affect citation counts. Carefully read the help and content notes, and consult with experienced searchers. Although also available in other formats, *Web of Science* is definitely the better version for coverage of mathematics and statistics if one can afford it. Though very expensive, this is a faculty favorite.

E *The Jahrbuch-Project, Electronic Research Archive for Mathematics (ERAM)*. European Mathematical Society, 2004. 1868–1942. Available at: http://www.emis.de/MATH/JFM/JFM.html. Database and archive are free. Also fully integrated into *Zentralblatt MATH* database (below).

Jahrbuch über die Fortschritte der Mathematik. Berlin: Georg Reimer, 1871–1944. Covers 1868–1942 in 68 vols. Out of print. ISSN: 0179-2849.

The **Jahrbuch über die Fortschritte der Mathematik** was the first index specifically for mathematics. The reviews were arranged by subject and were usually in German. Today, the *Jahrbuch-Project*, sponsored by the Deutsche Forschungsgemeinschaft, is a wonderful effort in process to digitize and enhance this important print index. It is mounted on the Web, and links have been added to scanned images of abstracts and to selected full-text of articles and books (about 20 percent). There are over 13,000 links to images of original articles.

Jahrbuch-Project Related Resources

E *Cornell University Library Historical Mathematics Monographs.* Cornell University Library, 2004. Available at: http://historical.library.cornell.edu/math/. Free.

For complete entry, see **Chapter 9, Collected and Selected Works, Digital Collections**. *Jahrbuch* records link to some of the 576 math volumes scanned from their originals.

E *DIEPER; Digitised European Periodicals.* [DIEPER], no copyright given. Available at: http://gdz.sub.uni-goettingen.de/dieper/. Free.

For complete entry, see **Chapter 9, Collected and Selected Works, Digital Collections**. The list of digitized journals can be accessed at http://dieper.aib.uni-linz.ac.at/cgi-bin/project2/selbrowse.pl?Select=Periodicals. *Jahrbuch* records link to full-text of **Monatshefte für Mathematik und Physik** articles.

E *Gallica; La Bibliothèque Numérique.* [Bibliothèque Nationale de France], no copyright given. Available at: http://gallica.bnf.fr/. Free.

For complete entry, see **Chapter 9, Collected and Selected Works, Digital Collections**. Some records in the *Jahrbuch* link to full-text images of journals and monographs here. For quick access to the list of nineteenth-century titles available, go to: http://gallica.bnf.fr/periodiques.htm. Titles of interest include: **Catalogue of Scientific Papers** (see Royal Society of London below), **Comptes Rendus Hebdomadaires des Séances de l'Académie des Sciences**, and **Journal des Mathématiques Pures et Appliquées**.

E *GDZ (Göttinger Digitalisierungs Zentrum).* SUB Göttingen, GDZ, 2001–2005. Available at: http://gdz.sub.uni-goettingen.de/en/index.html. Free.

For complete entry, see **Chapter 9, Collected and Selected Works, Digital Collections**. Over 3,000 records in the *Jahrbuch* link to full-text images here. Among the journal titles found here are: **Abhandlungen der Königlichen Gesellschaft der Wissenschaften in Göttingen**, **Inventiones Mathematicae**, **Mathematische Zeitschrift**, and **Mathematische Annalen**.

E *University of Michigan Historical Mathematics Collection*. No copyright given. Available at: http://www.hti.umich.edu/u/umhistmath/. Free.

For complete entry, see **Chapter 9, Collected and Selected Works, Digital Collections**. *Jahrbuch* links to about 400 monographs.

E *JSTOR®*. JSTOR®, 2000–2004. Information available at: http://www.jstor.org/jstor/. Subscription; price varies.

JSTOR® is a vast and growing electronic index and archive of the backfiles of core scholarly journals. Every page of this material has been collected, scanned, and digitized. At present, its coverage includes a sizable collection of core English-language journals in mathematics from 1878– , statistics from 1838– , and general science from 1666– . Not only is *JSTOR®* an archive, it also fills important gaps in the indexing of older mathematics materials. One may perform searches of the full-text of every article, as well as the usual searches of author, title, keywords, or source. Coverage extends back further than any other online subject-specific index in mathematics or statistics, thus making *JSTOR®* another important historical electronic index to these fields.

MAST: Minimum Abbreviations of Serial Titles, Mathematics. Compiled and edited by Mary L. Tompkins. North Hollywood, CA: Western Periodicals, 1969. viii + 427p. Out of print.

Old but still very useful listing of journal title abbreviations in mathematics. Invaluable for translating foreign and unusual title abbreviations into their full entries.

E *MathSciNet*. American Mathematical Society, 2004. Covers 1940– . Updated daily. Information available at: http://www.ams.org/mathscinet. 2004 subscription is $1,998.00 plus annual data access fee ($5,467.00–$6,834.00); consortia pricing available. Includes **Mathematical Reviews** and **Current Mathematical Publications.** A CD-ROM version, **MathSci on SilverPlatter®** and an online dial-up product, *MathSci on Dialog®*, are also available; coverage varies.

Mathematical Reviews. Providence, RI: American Mathematical Society, 1940– . Monthly with annual subject and author indexes. $526.00/yr. plus annual data access fee if not already paid. ISSN 0025-5629.

Current Mathematical Publications. Providence, RI: American Mathematical Society, 1969-. Every three weeks. $494.00–$617.00/yr. ISSN 0361-4794.

MathSciNet is the premier database for mathematical sciences. Now on the Web with additional entries, extensive linking, and cited references, it is the augmented electronic version of the reviews title **Mathematical Reviews** and the current alerts title **Current Mathematical Publications.** It covers books, conferences, and journals in pure and applied mathematics, core statistics, applied statistics (2001+) and computer science (2004+), and related physics and applications at the research level (upper undergraduate and above). Note that only *MathSci on Dialog*® offers electronic access to the early twentieth-century statistical literature as listed in Tukey and Ross's **Index to Statistics and Probability** (see below), a valuable retrospective index covering 1910–1968. *MathSciNet* indexes 1,799 serials and journals in whole or in part and adds about 70,000 bibliographic items with a summary or an evaluative review attached each year. There are over 1.9 million records total as of May 2004 with over 366,000 links to original articles. In a new initiative, *MathSciNet* is retroactively adding bibliographic information for the entirety of two digitized journals: *Annals of Mathematics* (1884–) and *Transactions of the AMS* (1900–). More historical citations will be added as journals are digitized.

MathSciNet is an affordable necessity for faculty and students at North American academic institutions offering a mathematics degree. The AMS's unique pricing structure charges primarily a content fee known as the Data Access Fee, which supports the cost of creating and maintaining the **MR** database, and then an additional fee for each different format. The AMS is very eager to supply *MathSciNet* on a consortial basis so that it becomes quite affordable for all types of institutions worldwide. Under a consortial arrangement, institutions that have not subscribed before can access it for possibly as little as $250 per year. For more pricing information, see the *MathSciNet* home page and contact them directly.

One of the nicest databases around, the *MathSciNet* interface is improved every year. One can easily search for all variants of an author's name (this is particularly useful for common last names, Slavic and Asian names) because **MR** editorial staff has maintained an author authority file for years. Journal names (but *only* those titles in use since the mid-1980s) can be searched by any reasonable journal abbreviation, by journal name or partial name, or by an ISSN. One may also browse an alphabetical list of *current* journal abbreviations. Titles no longer published, such as **Annals of Mathematical Statistics,** are more problematic to search as only title abbreviations (e.g., **Ann. Math. Statistics**) are used in the earlier records. Since space is not really an issue in an electronic database, a useful user enhancement would be to put the full journal title in the record. Then users could go immediately from a *MathSciNet* record to their library catalog or perhaps to the shelf without having to guess at the exact title. Libraries that have invoked OpenURL services can set up links from **MR** records to their own catalog records for quick access. Users can easily download a customized list of records in a variety of formats for further manipulation. French, German, Chinese, and Spanish speakers can set the interface screen in their native language.

MathSciNet records are filled with convenient links to search elements such as author, reviewer, or journal names, as well as links to full-text articles. Records for articles in 100 journals (2000+) include each article's own references (Reference Lists) and, perhaps, later citations to it (Reference Citations) in an effort to provide valuable forward and backward citation linking. Each author is given an institutional code, which links to a departmental mail address. Including a department's Web site address here would be a useful enhancement. If document delivery is needed, users may conveniently order a copy of any item for a fee from the Canada Institute for Scientific and Technical Information (CISTI), a Canadian document delivery organization, by clicking on the Doc. Delivery button.

Links to past and current translated materials is one area where *MathSciNet* had been deficient (Fowler 2000, p. 19). After Sputnik, many Russian journals became available in translation. As mathematics remained one of the Soviet Union's strongest sciences, these articles are often sought. However, because **MR** editors did not want to delay a review long enough to add a reference to the translation citation in the print edition of an **MR** record, most Russian articles that were eventually translated were not so noted in the database. As a result, many *MathSciNet* users may not have realized that a Russian article might be available in translation. *MathSciNet* appears recently to have retroactively added translation information to most affected records.

Mathematicians like *MathSciNet*'s browsing features that can restrict a search to look at specific **MR** or **CMP** issues in their chosen subject area.

As libraries move to electronic-only journal subscriptions, customizable current awareness services, by subject or by journal title, will be vital to help mathematicians methodically scan recent journal issues. Individual AMS members may now set up automated current awareness searches via the e-**CMP** service available at http://www.ams.org/e-cmp/, but *MathSciNet* subscribing institutions need to be able to offer a table of contents alerting service to all mathematics researchers at their institutions. At this writing, *Current Contents*, *ingenta Reveal*, and many publishers provide alerting services.

The **MR**/*MathSciNet* staff has produced an online product that no mathematician wants to be without. *MathSciNet* content is updated daily and is available online ahead of the print version. Informative help pages are available on site, or one may e-mail questions to *MSN* Support. The support desk is responsive to librarian questions and suggestions, and staff make themselves quite available at professional librarian meetings. Upon request, use statistics are sent to subscribing institutions.

Mathematical Reviews/*MathSciNet* Related Resources

Featured Reviews in Mathematical Reviews, 1995–1996 and 1997–1999. Providence, RI: American Mathematical Society, 1998–2000. 2 vols. xvi + 1034p. $90.00, set. ISBN 0-8218-2631-X, set.

Compilations of detailed reviews of some of the best books and articles published in the time period. The second volume includes reviews to classic articles and books published prior to 1970.

E *Featured Reviews in Mathematical Reviews*. Providence, RI: American Mathematical Society, 2002. Available at: http://www.ams.org/msnhtml/featured-reviews/fr.html. Free.

Links to recent Featured Reviews.

E *Mathematical Reviews Database*. Providence, RI: American Mathematical Society, 2004. Available at: http://www.ams.org/mr-database. Free.

This page has a number of links of interest to *MathSciNet* users such as: Mathematics Subject Classification (MSC) 2000, **MR** Serials Abbreviations List, and **MR** Institution Codes.

E *MathSciNet—Mathematical Reviews on the Web: Guiding You through the Literature of Mathematics*. Providence, RI: American Mathematical Society, 2000. Available at: http://www.ams.org/msnhtml/guidebook.pdf or in paper. Free.

This is a helpful booklet that first gives some history and background to the development of Mathematical Reviews from 1931 to the present

MathSciNet product. The remainder of the booklet helps users and librarians explore *MathSciNet* and its many capabilities thoroughly. Librarians may wish to order paper copies to hand out during end-user training sessions.

Reviews in Complex Analysis, 1980–86 (1989); *Reviews in Functional Analysis, 1980–86* (1989); **Reviews in Global Analysis, 1980–86** (1988); **Reviews in Graph Theory, 1940–78** (1980); **Reviews in K-Theory, 1940–84** (1985); **Reviews in Number Theory, 1940–72** (1974); **Reviews in Number Theory, 1973–83** (1984); Reviews in Number Theory, 1984–96 (1998); **Reviews in Numerical Analysis, 1980–86** (1987); **Reviews in Operator Theory, 1980–86** (1989); **Reviews in Partial Differential Equations, 1980–86** (1988); **Reviews in Ring Theory** (1981); **Reviews in Ring Theory, 1980–84** (1986); **Reviews of Papers in Algebraic and Differential Topology, Topological Groups, and Homological Algebra, . . . 1940–1967** (1969); **Reviews on Finite Groups, . . . [1940–1970]** (1974); and **Reviews on Infinite Groups, . . . [1940–1970]** (1974). Providence, RI: American Mathematical Society, 1969–1998.

In the past, the AMS published these subject compilations that served as convenient collections of reviews over time on a subject. Although useful before the advent of *MathSciNet*, one may now construct similar, but more up-to-date searches electronically.

E *MathSearch.* [Jim Richardson], 1999. Available at: http://www.maths.usyd.edu.au:8000/MathSearch.html. Free.

MathSearch searches "a collection of over 200,000 documents on English-language mathematics and statistics servers across the Web." Its particular value is that most of the material searched is university and research level.

E *MPRESS/MathNet.preprints, the Mathematics Preprint Search System).* No copyright given. Available at: http://mathnet.preprints.org/. Free.

MPRESS indexes preprints by retrieving Dublin Core metadata from various distributed servers. *MPRESS* is not a central depository archive for preprints the way *arXiv* (see above) is. Instead, one does a search and then links to the preprints on servers beyond *MPRESS*. *MPRESS* harvests preprints from institutional sites in France, Germany, Italy, Austria, Brazil, Sweden, and Russia. It also draws from subject-specific sites such as the K-Theory Preprints Archives, Algebraic Number Theory Server, and Topology Atlas, and from *arXiv*'s math archive. At this writing, *MPRESS* indexes over 66,000 preprints—almost twice as many as *arXiv* has.

E *PubMed*. National Library of Medicine, National Center for Biotechnology Information (NCBI), 2004. Available at: http://www.ncbi.nlm.nih.gov/PubMed/. Free.

PubMed indexes over 14 million citations in *MEDLINE*, *PreMEDLINE*, and other related databases, with links to participating online journals. Biomathematics and biostatistics materials can be found here.

Rabinowitz, Stanley and Mark Bowron, eds. **Index to Mathematical Problems, 1975–1979**. Westford, MA: MathPro Press, 1999. ix + 518p. (Indexes to Mathematical Problems; 2). $60.00. ISBN 0-9626401-2-3.

Rabinowitz, Stanley, ed. **Index to Mathematical Problems, 1980–1984.** Westford, MA: MathPro Press, 1991. xii + 532p. (Indexes to Mathematical Problems; 1). $49.95. ISBN 0-96264-011-5.

E *20,000 Problems Under the Sea*. No copyright given. Available at: http://problems.math.umr.edu/index.htm. Free.

The books index over 10,000 problems published in various journals' problem columns, 1975–1984. Problems are classified and arranged by topic; references to solutions are given. The Web site provides a search interface to 20,000 problems published in 38 journals and 21 contests, 1877–1990. Each problem's record includes author, title, source, classification keywords, and reference to published solutions.

Referativnyi zhurnal. Matematika. Moscow: Izd-vo Akademii nauk SSSR, 1953–1981. Monthly. $1,701.00/yr. ISSN: 0034-2467.

Referativnyi zhurnal. 13, Matematika. Moscow: VINTI, 1982– . Monthly. $1,701.00/yr. ISSN 0034-2467.

This is an international index in Russian of mathematical journals and books. It can be helpful in finding elusive Russian materials.

E *Research Library*. Proquest®, 2004. Covers 1971– . Information available at: http://www.il.proquest.com/products/pdf/Research.pdf/. Subscription; price varies.

This general college-level database indexes over 2,600 journals and includes links to about 1,700 full-text titles. The full-text titles include some relevant to math and statistics, such as **American Mathematical Monthly, American Statistician, Mathematical Intelligencer, Mathematics Magazine,** and general science titles, such as **Science** and **Nature**.

Like *Expanded Academic ASAP*™ (see above), undergraduate students and faculty will find *Research Library Complete* appropriate for some of their work. Full-text coverage may lag several weeks behind publication and may not be stable.

E Royal Society of London. **Catalogue of Scientific Papers, 1800–1900.** Cambridge: Cambridge University Press, 1914–25. Reprint of 1908–1914 edition. 19 vols. Out of print. Scanned images of these 19 volumes are now available at: http://gallica.bnf.fr/catalog?IdentPerio=NP00188. Free.

Royal Society of London. **Catalogue of Scientific Papers, 1800–1900: Subject Index.** Metuchen, NJ: Scarecrow Reprint Corp., 1968. Reprint of the 1908–1914 edition. Vol. 1. Pure Mathematics. lviii + 666p. Out of print.

This set is an author and classified subject index to nineteenth-century mathematics and other sciences.

Schatz, Joseph A. **A Mathematics Citation Index.** Albuquerque, NM: Sandia Corp., 1970. xi + 580p. (Sandia Laboratories. Research report, SC-RR 70 910.) Price not available.

Early citation index for mathematics. Compiled from 25,000 source papers, 1950–1965. Covers period previous to coverage of **Science Citation Index** (see *ISI Web of Science* above) and its descendents.

E **Statistical Theory and Method Abstracts.** Voorburg, The Netherlands: International Statistical Institute, 2001– . CD-ROM version, updated semi-annually. $120.00/yr. ISSN: 1569-0636. Online version is in development and covers about ten years back. Information available at: http://www.cbs.nl/isi/stma.htm. $93.00/yr. Paper version now ceased: London: Longman, for the International Statistical Institute, 1959–2001. ISSN 0039–0518.

STMA provides reasonably priced worldwide coverage of books and articles on mathematical statistics and probability in a classified arrangement with an author index. About 6,000 records added annually.

Trumbo, Bruce E. and Richard K. Burdick, eds. **Cumulative index to IMS scientific journals, 1960–1989.** Hayward, CA: Institute of Mathematical Statistics, 1990. vii + 555p. Out of print.

This volume indexed IMS journals in the gap between Tukey and Ross's **Index to Statistics and Probability** (see below) and **CIS**. The data is now included in *CIS-ED* (see above).

E Tukey, John W. and Ross, Ian C. **Index to Statistics and Probability.** Los Altos, CA: R & D Press [now distributed by AMS], 1973–1975. 3 vols. in 4. lxxx + 3269p. (Information Access Series, v. 2–5.) Content available electronically only via dial-up in *MathSci on Dialog®*. The intended last volume, subtitled **Permuted Index to Minimum Abbreviations,** was never published.

Index to Statistics and Probability was among the first tools to specifically index the field of statistics. Although never explicitly stated, the dates covered seem to be from the early 1900s up to 1965. The set includes a citation index, a two-volume permuted title (keyword) index, and the Locations and Authors volume that is essentially a table of contents listing by journal and an author bibliography. Tukey and Ross employed their own unique system of bibliographic abbreviation that is difficult to decipher without a fair amount of effort. The never-published fourth volume would have been an index to these abbreviations.

E *Zentralblatt MATH*. European Mathematical Society, FIZ Karlsruhe and Springer-Verlag, copyright not given. Covers 1868– . Updated biweekly. Available at: http://www.emis.de/ZMATH/. In 2003 *Zentralblatt MATH* fully integrated upgraded records from the **Jahrbuch über die Fortschritte der Mathematik.** Free demo access to the full version is available with limited results. €5,300.00/yr. for online access and backup CD; consortia pricing available.

Zentralblatt MATH (formerly **Zentralblatt für Mathematik und ihre Grenzgebiete**). Berlin: Springer, 1931– . 30 vols./yr. Euro 6,200.00/yr. ISSN 1436-3356.

The field of advanced mathematics amazingly still has two high-quality English-language indexes to its worldwide literature. *Zentralblatt MATH* is the integrated Web version of the German-based indexes originally titled **Jahrbuch über die Fortschritte der Mathematik** and **Zentralblatt für Mathematik und Ihre Grenzgebiete.** This paper index, now also titled **Zentralblatt MATH,** provides comprehensive coverage of international mathematical research published from 1931 onward. Mathematics and its applications in physics, mechanics, statistics, computer science, economics, and biology are covered. It indexes books, proceedings, and about 2,300 journals and serials appearing in any language. About 80,000 items are added annually for a total currently of over 2 million records. The database is also available as *MATH* (1972–) via dial-up service from STN International.

Providing access to both of these products is generally beyond most libraries' budgets. European mathematicians and librarians may be more familiar with this database, while North American mathematicians and librarians likely prefer *MathSciNet*. *Zentralblatt MATH* has the advantage over *MathSciNet* of coverage back to 1868 with its recent inclusion of *Jahrbuch-Project* records. Older reviews are in German or other languages, but today most reviews and summaries are in English. The text of some reviews from about 1931 to 1984 are not yet searchable. As *Zentralblatt MATH* kindly allows non-subscribers limited access by showing three records per search, adept non-subscribers can use the demo version as a valuable alternative to *MathSciNet*.

The search interface was greatly upgraded in 2001. One can now easily search by journal name, but as with *MathSciNet's* older journals, titles such as **Annals of Mathematical Statistics** are hard to find with precision. Author searching is less precise than in *MathSciNet* and current issue browsing is not as easy. To *Zentralblatt MATH's* credit, translated articles seem to be listed under both their original and translation sources in *Zentralblatt MATH* (Fowler 2000, p. 19). MSC subject links are better in *Zentralblatt MATH* as they are defined within the article record and thus are searchable, and they link directly to other records with the same code. A link to document delivery from German and Italian libraries is available to all users. The search interface is available in English, French, German, Italian, and Spanish.

It is a luxury for mathematics to have two research-level indexes, but most libraries will only be able to afford one. The primary choice for North American libraries is *MathSciNet*, even though *Zentralblatt MATH* has coverage back to 1868. Perhaps in the future, the two societies could jointly offer an affordable package that would benefit both publishers and subscribers. *Zentralblatt MATH* is a useful complement to *MathSciNet* as, despite the near duplicate coverage, sometimes one has something the other does not.

Search Engines

A listing of finding tools in mathematics today would not be complete without discussing Web search engines. Even though each search engine functions differently, there is no denying the fact that both librarians and researchers use search engines frequently every day. *Google* is most likely the search engine of choice for most. A second choice might be *Alltheweb*. The resources listed below are either search engines themselves or sites to guide search engine users.

E *About: Web Search*. About, Inc., 2003. Available at: http://websearch.about.com. Free.
   Annoyingly commercialized site, but has good, up-to-date information.

E *Alltheweb*. Fast Search & Transfer ASA, 2004. Available at: http://www.alltheweb.com/. Free.
   This large search engine offers advanced and Boolean searching. Includes multimedia, Audio, FTP, PDF, and MS Word® files.

E *Google.com*. Google, 2004. Available at: www.google.com. Free.
   Google searches millions of Web pages and includes PDF, Word, and PS files in its searching. Image files can be searched as well. Search results are ranked according to a page's relevance based on other sites' linkages and authority. Words are ANDed automatically. Boolean searching and nesting is not available, yet *Google* consistently returns great results. Included are cached images of Web pages as they were indexed—useful for pages no longer there. Google also offers machine translation of foreign-language Web pages.

E *Internet Archive Wayback Machine*. Internet Archive, 2001. Available at: http://www.archive.org/. Free.
   Need to see a Web page (from 1996 on) with an Internet address that no longer works? Put the URL in the Wayback Machine to find an archived copy of the page.

E *Tool Kit for the Expert Web Searcher*. American Library Association, 2003. Available at: http://www.lita.org/committe/toptech/toolkit.htm. Free.
   Pat Ensor, an expert information searcher since 1980, developed and maintains this evaluative and informative site.

Reference

Fowler, Kristine K. 2000. Mathematics Sites Compared, Zentralblatt MATH Database and MathSciNet. *The Charleston Advisor* 1, no. 3 (January): 18–21. Available at: http://www.charlestonco.com/comp.cfm?id=5. Text of article is also available at http://math.lib.umn.edu/mathca.html. Free.

3
Selected Journals in Mathematics and Statistics

Journals

The mathematics and statistics titles listed below were chosen from lists of journals indexed by *MathSciNet*, *Current Index to Statistics Extended Database*, or *Web of Science*. The list is a selective, sometimes subjective, list of titles that a math library may want to acquire to support the teaching and research of mathematics, applied math, and statistics. Whereas most are widely used, some were selected as representative of their discipline or category.

These journals are arranged alphabetically by keyword. The citations are composed of the complete title (using cataloged entry), followed by the title abbreviation used in **Mathematical Reviews**, the publisher and place of publication, and the ISSN number (when known). Journals reviewed cover to cover by **Mathematical Reviews** or **Current Index to Statistics** are indicated by **bold type**. A **B** marks bibliographic journals. An **E** marks those journals available electronically. A **T** marks translation journals. An **S** marks a title in statistics. An * marks those journals of interest to an undergraduate audience. Cross references are provided for variant entries and to refer the reader from the original title to the translated title.

> **Abhandlungen aus dem Mathematischen Seminar der Universitat Hamburg.** [Abh. Math. Sem. Univ. Hamburg.] Vandenhoeck & Ruprecht, Göttingen. ISSN: 0025-5858.
> E Acta Applicandae Mathematicae. [Acta. Appl. Math.] Kluwer Acad. Publ.: Boston. ISSN: 0167-8019.

E **Acta Arithmetica.** [Acta Arith.] Polish Acad. Sci., Inst. Math.: Warsaw. ISSN: 0065-1036.

E **Acta Mathematica.** [Acta Math.] Inst. Mittag-Leffler: Djursholm, Sweden. ISSN: 0001-5962.

E **Acta Mathematica Hungarica.** [Acta Math. Hungar.] Akad. Kiadó: Budapest. ISSN: 0236-5294.

Acta Mathematica Scientia. Series B. English Edition. [Acta Math. Sci. (English Ed.)] Science Press, Beijing; Dist. By Baltzer: Basel, Switzerland. ISSN 0252-9602.

E **Acta Mathematica Sinica. English Series.** [Acta Math. Sinica (Engl. Ser.)] Springer: Heidelberg. ISSN: 1000-9574.

E **Advances in Applied Mathematics.** [Adv. in Appl. Math.] Academic Press: Orlando, FL. ISSN: 0196-8858.

S E **Advances in Applied Probability.** [Adv. in Appl. Probab.] Appl. Probab. Trust: Sheffield. ISSN: 0001-8678.

E **Advances in Computational Mathematics.** [Adv. Comput. Math.] Baltzer: Bussum, The Netherlands. ISSN: 1019-7168.

E **Advances in Mathematics.** [Adv. Math.] Academic Press, Duluth, MN. ISSN: 0001-8708.

E **Advances in Theoretical and Mathematical Physics.** [Adv. Theor. Math. Phys.] Internat. Press: Cambridge, MA. ISSN: 1095-0761.

E **Algebra Colloquium.** [Algebra Colloq.] Springer: Singapore. ISSN: 1005-3867.

E **Algebra Universalis.** [Algebra Universalis.] Univ. Manitoba: Winnipeg, MB. ISSN: 0002-5240.

E **Algebraic & Geometric Topology.** [Algebr. Geom. Topol.] Geometry & Topology Publications: Coventry, England. ISSN: 1472-2747.

E **Algebras and Representation Theory.** [Algebr. Represent. Theory] Kluwer Acad. Publ.: Dordrecht, Holland. ISSN: 1386-923X.

E **Algorithmica.** [Algorithmica] Springer: New York. ISSN: 0178-4617.

* **AMATYC Review.** [AMATYC Rev.] Amer. Math. Assoc. of Two-Year Colleges: Garden City, NY. ISSN: 0740-8404.

* E **American Journal of Mathematics.** [Amer. J. Math.] Johns Hopkins Univ. Press: Baltimore, MD. ISSN: 0002-9327.

* **American Mathematical Monthly.** [Amer. Math. Monthly] Math. Assoc. America: Washington, DC. ISSN: 0002-9890.

* S E **American Statistician.** [Amer. Statist.] Amer. Statist. Assoc.: Alexandria, VA. ISSN: 0003-1305.

E **Annales Academiae Scientiarum Fennicae. Mathematica.** [Ann. Acad. Sci. Fenn. Math.]. Acad. Sci. Fennica: Helsinki. ISSN: 1239-629X.

E **Annales Henri Poincaré.** [Ann. Henri Poincaré] Birkhäuser: Berlin. ISSN 1424-0637.

E **Annales de l'Institut Fourier.** [Ann. Inst. Fourier (Grenoble)] Univ. Grenoble I: Saint-Martin-d'Hères, France. ISSN: 0373-0956.

E **Annales de l'Institut Henri Poincaré. Analyse Non Linéaire.** [Ann. Inst. H. Poincaré Anal. Non Linéaire.] Gauthier-Villars, Ed. Sci. Méd. Elsevier: Paris. ISSN: 0294-1449.

S E **Annales de l'Institut Henri Poincaré. Probabilités et Statistiques.** [Ann. Inst. H. Poincaré Probab. Statist.] Gauthier-Villars, Ed. Sci. Méd. Elsevier: Paris. ISSN: 0246-0203.

E **Annales Scientifiques de l'École Normale Superiéure. Quatrième Serie.** [Ann. Sci. Ecole Norm. Sup. (4)] Gauthier-Villars, Ed. Sci. Méd. Elsevier: Paris. ISSN: 0012-9593.

S E **Annals of Applied Probability.** [Ann. Appl. Probab.] Inst. Math. Statist.: Hayward, CA. ISSN: 1050-5164.

E **Annals of Global Analysis and Geometry.** [Ann. Global Anal. Geom.] Kluwer Acad. Publ., Dordrecht: Holland. ISSN: 0232-704X.

S E **Annals of the Institute of Statistical Mathematics.** [Ann. Inst. Statist. Math.] Kluwer Acad. Publ.: Boston. ISSN: 0020-3157.

E **Annals of Mathematics. Second Series.** [Ann of Math. (2)] Princeton Univ. Press: Princeton, NJ. ISSN: 0003-486X.

S E **Annals of Probability.** [Ann. Probab.] Inst. Math. Statist.: Bethesda, MD. ISSN: 0009-1798.

E **Annals of Pure and Applied Logic.** [Ann. Pure Appl. Logic] North-Holland: Amsterdam. ISSN: 0168-0072.

S E **Annals of Statistics.** [Ann. Statist.] Inst. Math. Statist.: Hayward, CA. ISSN: 0090-5364.

E **ANZIAM Journal.** [ANZIAM J.] Austral. Math. Soc.: Canberra. ISSN: 0334-2700.

E **Applied Categorical Structures.** [Appl. Categ. Structures] Kluwer Acad. Publ.: Dordrecht, Holland. ISSN: 0927-2852.

E Applied and Computational Harmonic Analysis. [Appl. Comput. Harmon. Anal.] Academic Press: Orlando, FL. ISSN: 1063-5203.

E Applied Mathematics and Computation. [Appl. Math. Comput.] North-Holland: New York. ISSN: 0096-3003.

E Applied Mathematics and Optimization. [Appl. Math. Optim.] Springer: New York. ISSN: 0095-4616.

Applied Statistics. *See* Journal of the Royal Statistical Society. Series C. Applied Statistics.

E Archiv der Mathematik. [Arch. Math. (Basel)] Birkhäuser: Basel, Switzerland-Boston. ISSN: 0003-889X.

* **E Archive for History of Exact Sciences.** [Arch. Hist. Exact Sci.] Springer: Berlin. ISSN: 0003-9519.

E Archive for Mathematical Logic. [Arch. Math. Logic] Springer: Berlin-New York. ISSN: 0933-5846.

E Archive for Rational Mechanics and Analysis. [Arch. Rational Mech. Anal.] Springer: Heidelberg. ISSN: 0003-9527.

Arkiv för Matematik. [Ark. Mat.] Inst. Mittag-Leffler: Djursholm, Sweden. ISSN: 0004-2080.

Ars Combinatoria. [Ars Combin.] Charles Babbage Res. Centre: Winnipeg, MB. ISSN: 0381-7032.

Astérisque. [Astérisque] Soc. Math. France: Paris. ISSN 0303-1179.

E Asymptotic Analysis. [Asymptotic Anal.] IOS: Amsterdam. ISSN: 0921-7134.

E ATG. Algebraic & Geometric Topology. [ATG Algebr. Geom. Topol.] Geom. Topol.: Coventry, England. ISSN: 1472-2739.

S E Australian & New Zealand Journal of Statistics. [Aust. N. Z. J. Stat.] Blackwell: Oxford. ISSN: 1369-1473.

S E Bernoulli. Official Journal of the Bernoulli Society for Mathematical Statistics and Probability. [Bernoulli] Internat. Statist. Inst.: Voorburg, The Netherlands. ISSN: 1350-7265.

S E Biometrical Journal. [Biometrical J.] VCH: Berlin. ISSN: 0323-3847.

S E Biometrics. [Biometrics] Internat. Biometric Soc.: Alexandria, VA. ISSN: 0006-341X.

S E Biometrika. [Biometrika] Biometrika Trust: London. ISSN: 0006-3444.

S E Biostatistics. [Biostatistics] Oxford University Press: London. ISSN: 1465-4644.

Bollettino della Unione Matematica Italiana. Sezione B. Articoli di Ricerca Matematica Serie VIII. [Boll. Unione Mat. Ital. Sez. B Artic. Mat. (8)] Zanichelli: Bologna.

* **E Bulletin of the American Mathematical Society. New Series.** [Bull. Amer. Math. Soc. (N.S.)] American Mathematical Society: Providence, RI. ISSN: 0273-0979.

Bulletin of the Australian Mathematical Society. [Bull. Austral. Math. Soc.] Austral. Math. Publ. Assoc.: Canberra. ISSN: 0004-9727.

E Bulletin of the Belgian Mathematical Society, Simon Stevin. [Bull Belg. Math. Soc. Simon Stevin] Soc. Math. Belgique: Brussels. ISSN: 1370-1444.

* **E Bulletin of the London Mathematical Society.** [Bull. London Math. Soc.] London Math. Soc.: London. ISSN: 0024-6093.

Bulletin de la Société Mathématique de Belgique. *See* Bulletin of the Belgian Mathematical Society, Simon Stevin.

E Bulletin de la Société Mathématique de France. [Bull. Soc. Math. France] Soc. Math. France: Paris. ISSN: 0037-9484.

E Bulletin of Symbolic Logic. [Bull. Symbolic Logic] Assoc. Symbol. Logic: Champaign, IL. ISSN: 1079-8986.

E Calcolo. [Calcolo] Springer Italia: Milan. ISSN: 0008-0624.

E Calculus of Variations and Partial Differential Equations. [Calc. Var. Partial Differential Equations] Springer: Heidelberg. ISSN: 0001-5903.

E Canadian Applied Mathematics Quarterly. [Canad. Appl. Math. Quart.] University of Alberta: Edmonton. ISSN: 1073-1849.

E Canadian Journal of Mathematics. Journal Canadien de Mathématiques. [Canad. J. Math.] Canadian Math. Soc.: Ottawa, ON. ISSN: 0008-414X.

S Canadian Journal of Statistics. La Revue Canadienne de Statistique. [Canad. J. Statist.] Statist. Soc. Canada: Ottawa, ON. ISSN: 0319-5724.

E Canadian Mathematical Bulletin. Bulletin Canadien de Mathématiques. [Canad. Math. Bull.] Canadian Math. Soc.: Ottawa, ON. ISSN: 0008-4395.

* S **Chance: New Directions for Statistics and Computing.** [Chance] Springer: New York. ISSN: 0933-2480.

Chinese Annals of Mathematics. Series B. Shuxue Niankan. Ji B. [Chinese Ann. Math. Ser. B] Shanghai. Sci. Tech. Lit.: Shanghai. ISSN: 0252-9599.

CMP. *See* Current Mathematical Publications.

* **College Mathematics Journal.** [College Math. J.] Math. Assoc. America: Washington, DC. ISSN: 0746-8342.

E **Combinatorica.** [Combinatorica] János Bolyai Math. Soc.: Budapest. ISSN: 0209-9683.

E **Combinatorics, Probability and Computing.** [Combin. Probab. Comput.] Cambridge Univ. Press: Cambridge. ISSN: 0963-5483.

E **Commentarii Mathematici Helvetici.** [Comment. Math. Helv.] Birkhäuser: Basel, Switzerland. ISSN: 0010-2571.

E **Communications in Algebra.** [Comm. Algebra] Dekker: Monticello, NY. ISSN: 0092-7872.

Communications in Analysis and Geometry. [Comm. Anal. Geom.] Internat. Press: Cambridge, MA. ISSN: 1019-8385.

E **Communications in Contemporary Mathematics.** [Commun. Contemp. Math.] World Sci. Publishing: Singapore. ISSN: 0219-1997.

E **Communications in Mathematical Physics.** [Comm. Math. Phys.] Springer: Berlin. ISSN: 0010-3616.

E **Communications in Partial Differential Equations.** [Comm. Partial Differential Equations] Dekker: Monticello, NY. ISSN: 0360-5302.

E **Communications on Pure and Applied Mathematics.** [Comm. Pure Appl. Math.] Wiley: New York. ISSN: 0010-3640.

S E **Communications in Statistics. Simulation and Computation.** [Comm. Statist. Simulation Comput.] Dekker: Monticello, NY. ISSN: 0361-0918.

S E **Communications in Statistics. Theory and Methods.** [Comm. Statist. Theory Methods] Dekker: Monticello, NY. ISSN: 0361-0926.

E **Compositio Mathematica.** [Compositio Math.] Cambridge University Press: Cambridge. ISSN: 0010-437X.

E **Comptes Rendus Mathématique.** [C. R. Math. Acad. Sci. Paris.] Éd. Elsevier: Paris. ISSN: 1631-073X.

E Computational Complexity. [Comput. Complexity] Birkhäuser: Basel, Switzerland. ISSN: 1016-3328.

E Computational Geometry: Theory and Applications. [Comput. Geom.] Elsevier: Amsterdam. ISSN: 0925-7721.

E Computational Optimization and Applications. [Comput. Optim. Appl.] Kluwer Acad. Publ.: Hingham, MA. ISSN: 0926-6003.

S E **Computational Statistics.** [Comput. Statist.] Physica: Heidelberg. ISSN: 0943-4062.

S E **Computational Statistics & Data Analysis.** [Comput. Statist. Data Anal.] North-Holland: Amsterdam. ISSN: 0167-9473.

E Computers & Mathematics with Applications. [Comput. Math. Appl.] Pergamon: Oxford. ISSN: 0898-1221.

E Conformal Geometry and Dynamics. [Conform. Geom. Dyn.] American Mathematical Society: Providence, RI. ISSN: 1088-4173.

* Consortium. [Consortium] Consortium for Math. and Its Applications: Lexington, MA. ISSN: 0889-5392.

E Constructive Approximation. [Constr. Approx.] Springer: New York. ISSN: 0176-4276.

B S E Current Index to Statistics Extended Database. [Current Index Statist.] Amer. Statist. Assoc.: Alexandria, VA. ISSN: 0364-1228.

* B Current Mathematical Publications. [CMP] American Mathematical Society: Providence, RI. ISSN: 0361-4794. (Published electronically in *MathSciNet*).

E Czechoslovak Mathematical Journal. [Czechoslovak Math. J.] Acad. Sci. Czech Rep.: Prague. ISSN: 0011-4642.

E Designs, Codes and Cryptography. [Des. Codes Cryptogr.] Kluwer Acad. Publ.: Hingham, MA. ISSN: 0925-1022.

T E **Differential Equations.** [Differ. Equ.] MAIK/Interperiod. Publ.: Moscow. ISSN: 0012-2661. (Translation of Differentsial'nye Uravneniia).

E Differential Geometry and Its Applications. [Differential Geom. Appl.] North-Holland: Amsterdam. ISSN: 0926-2245.

Differentsial'nye Uravneniia. *See* Differential Equations.

E Discrete Applied Mathematics. [Discrete Appl. Math.] North-Holland: Amsterdam. ISSN: 0166-218X.

E Discrete & Computational Geometry. [Discrete Comput. Geom.] Springer: New York. ISSN: 0179-5376.

E **Discrete and Continuous Dynamical Systems.** [Discrete Contin. Dynam. Systems] Dept. Math., Southwest Missouri State Univ.: Springfield. ISSN: 1078-0947.

E **Discrete Mathematics.** [Discrete Math.] North-Holland: Amsterdam. ISSN: 0012-365X.

E **Documenta Mathematica.** [Doc. Math.] Doc. Math.: Bielefeld. ISSN: 1431-0643.

T E **Doklady. Mathematics.** [Russian Acad. Sci. Dokl. Math.] "Nauka/Interperiodica": Moscow. ISSN: 1064-5624. (Translation of the mathematics section of Doklady Akademii Nauk).

E **Duke Mathematical Journal.** [Duke Math. J.] Duke Univ. Press: Durham, NC. ISSN: 0012-7094.

Dynamics of Continuous, Discrete and Impulsive Systems. [Dynam. Contin. Discrete Impuls. Systems] Watam Press: Waterloo, ON. ISSN: 1201-3390.

S E **Econometric Theory.** [Econometric Theory] Cambridge Univ. Press: New York. ISSN: 0266-4666.

* E **Educational Studies in Mathematics.** [Ed. Stud. Math.] Kluwer Acad. Publ.: Boston. ISSN: 0013-1954.

S E **Electronic Communications in Probability.** [Electron. Comm. Probab.] Dept. Math., Univ. of Washington: Seattle. ISSN: 1083-589X.

E **Electronic Journal of Combinatorics.** [Electron. J. Combin.] Electron. J. Combin.: Clemson, SC. ISSN: 1077-8926.

E **Electronic Journal of Differential Equations.** [Electron. J. Differential Equations] Southwest Texas State Univ.: San Marcos, TX. ISSN: 1072-6691.

E **Electronic Journal of Linear Algebra.** [Electron. J. Linear Algebra] Internat. Linear Algebra Soc. (ILAS): Haifa, Israel. ISSN: 1081-3810.

S E **Electronic Journal of Probability.** [Electron. J. Probab.] Dept. Math., Univ. of Washington: Seattle. ISSN: 1083-6489.

E **Electronic Journal of Qualitative Theory of Differential Equations.** [Electron. J. Qual. Theory Differ. Equ.] Electron. J. Qual. Theory Differ. Equ.: Szeged, Hungary. ISSN: 1417-3875.

E **Electronic Research Announcements of the American Math-**

ematical Society. [Electron. Res. Announc. Amer. Math. Soc.] American Mathematical Society: Providence, RI. ISSN: 1079-6762.

E Electronic Transactions on Numerical Analysis. [Electron. Trans. Numer. Anal.] Kent State Univ.: Kent, OH. ISSN: 1068-9613.

S E Environmetrics. Wiley: Chichester, England. ISSN 1180-4009.

E Ergodic Theory and Dynamical Systems. [Ergodic Theory Dynam. Systems] Cambridge Univ. Press: New York. ISSN: 0143-3857.

E ESAIM: Control, Optimisation and Calculus of Variations. [ESAIM Control Optim. Calc. Var.] Soc. Math. Appl. Indust.: Paris. ISSN: 1292-8119.

S E ESAIM: Probability and Statistics. [ESAIM Probab. Statist.] Soc. Math. Appl. Indust.: Paris. ISSN: 1292-8100.

E European Journal of Combinatorics. [European J. Combin.] Academic Press: London-New York. ISSN: 0195-6698.

E Experimental Mathematics. [Experiment. Math.] A K Peters: Wellesley, MA. ISSN: 1058-6458.

* Fibonacci Quarterly. [Fibonacci Quart.] Fibonacci Assoc.: Santa Clara, CA. ISSN: 0015-0517.

E Finite Fields and Their Applications. [Finite Fields Appl.] Academic: Orlando, FL. ISSN: 1071-5697.

E Forum Mathematicum. [Forum Math.] de Gruyter: Berlin. ISSN: 0933-7741.

T E Functional Analysis and its Applications. [Functional Anal. Appl.] Consultants Bureau: New York. ISSN: 0016-2663. (Translation of Funktsional'nyi Analiz i ego Prilozheniia).

E Fundamenta Mathematicae. [Fund. Math.] Polish Acad. Sci., Inst. Math.: Warsaw. ISSN: 0016-2736.

Funktsional'nyi Analiz i ego Prilozheniia. *See* Functional Analysis and its Applications.

E Geometriae Dedicata. [Geom. Dedicata] Kluwer Acad. Publ.: Dordrecht, Holland. ISSN: 0046-5755.

E Geometric and Functional Analysis. [Geom. Funct. Anal.] Birkhäuser: Basel, Switzerland. ISSN: 1016-443X.

E Geometry and Topology. [Geom. Topol.] Geometry & Topology Publications: Coventry, England. ISSN: 1465-3060.

E **Glasgow Mathematical Journal.** [Glasgow Math. J.] Cambridge Univ. Press: Cambridge. ISSN: 0017-0895.

E **Graphs and Combinatorics.** [Graphs Combin.] Springer: Tokyo. ISSN: 0911-0119.

* E **Historia Mathematica.** [Historia Math.] Academic Press: Orlando, FL. ISSN: 0315-0860.

E **Houston Journal of Mathematics.** [Houston J. Math.] Univ. Houston: Houston, TX. ISSN: 0362-1588.

E **Illinois Journal of Mathematics**. [Illinois J. Math.] Univ. Illinois Press: Champaign, IL. ISSN: 0019-2082.

E **IMA Journal of Applied Mathematics.** [IMA J. Appl. Math.] Oxford Univ. Press: Oxford. ISSN: 0272-4960.

E **IMA Journal of Numerical Analysis.** [IMA J. Numer. Anal.] Oxford Univ. Press: Oxford. ISSN: 0272-4979.

Indagationes Mathematicae. New Series. [Indag. Math. (N.S.)] North-Holland: Amsterdam. ISSN: 0019-3577.

E **Indian Journal of Pure and Mathematics.** Indian Nat. Sci. Academy: New Delhi. ISSN 0019-5588.

E **Indiana University Mathematics Journal.** [Indiana Univ. Math. J.] Indiana Univ.: Bloomington. ISSN: 0022-2518.

E **Infinite Dimensional Analysis, Quantum Probability and Related Topics.** [Infin. Dimens. Anal. Quantum Probab. Relat. Top.] World Sci. Publishing: Singapore. ISSN: 0219-0257.

E **Information and Computation.** [Inform. and Comput.] Academic Press: Orlando, FL. ISSN: 0890-5401.

Institut des Hautes Etudes Scientifiques. Publications Mathématiques. *See* Publications Mathématiques (Institut des Hautes Etudes Scientifiques).

S E **Insurance: Mathematics & Economics.** [Insurance Math. Econom.] North-Holland: Amsterdam-New York. ISSN: 0167-6687.

Integral Equations and Operator Theory. [Integral Equations Operator Theory] Birkhäuser: Basel, Switzerland. ISSN: 0378-620X.

E **Integral Transforms and Special Functions.** [Integral Transform. Spec. Funct.] Taylor & Francis: London. ISSN: 1065-2469.

E **International Journal of Algebra and Computation.** [Internat. J. Algebra Comput.] World Sci. Publishing: Singapore. ISSN: 0218-1967.

E International Journal of Computational Geometry & Applications. [Internat. J. Comput. Geom. Appl.] World Sci. Publishing: Singapore. ISSN: 0218-1959.

E International Journal of Game Theory. [Int. J. Game Theory] Physica: Heidelberg. ISSN: 0020-7276.

E International Journal of Mathematics. [Intern. J. Math.] World Sci. Publishing: Singapore. ISSN: 0129-167X.

E International Mathematics Research Notices. [Internat. Math. Res. Notices] Hindawi: Cuyahoga Falls, OH. ISSN: 1073-7928.

S E International Statistical Review. [Internat. Statist. Rev.] Longman: London-New York. ISSN: 0306-7734.

E Inventiones Mathematicae. [Invent. Math.] Springer: Berlin-New York. ISSN: 0020-9910.

Israel Journal of Mathematics. [Israel J. Math.] Magnes Press, The Hebrew University: Jerusalem. ISSN: 0021-2172.

Izvestiia Rossiiskaia Nauk. Seriia Matematicheskaia. *See* Izvestiya. Mathematics.

T E Izvestiya. Mathematics. [Izv. Math.] Presidium Russ. Acad. Sci.: Moscow. ISSN: 1064-5632. (Translation of Izvestiia Rossiiskaia Nauk. Seriia Matematicheskaia).

Japan Journal of Industrial and Applied Mathematics. [Japan J. Indust. Appl. Math.] Kinokuniya: Tokyo. ISSN: 0916-7005

E Journal of Algebra. [J. Algebra] Academic Press: Orlando, FL. ISSN: 0021-8693.

E Journal of Algebraic Combinatorics. [J. Algebraic Combin.] Kluwer Acad. Publ.: Hingham, MA. ISSN: 0925-9899.

E Journal of Algebraic Geometry. [J. Algebraic Geom.] Univ. Press: Hong Kong. ISSN: 1056-3911.

* **E Journal of the American Mathematical Society.** [J. Amer. Math. Soc.] American Mathematical Society: Providence, RI. ISSN: 0894-0347.

* **S E Journal of the American Statistical Association.** [J. Amer. Statist. Assoc.] Amer. Statist. Assoc.: Alexandria, VA. ISSN: 0162-1459.

Journal d'Analyse Mathematique. [J. Anal. Math.] Magnes Press, The Hebrew University: Jerusalem. ISSN: 0021-7670.

* S E **Journal of Applied Probability.** [J. Appl. Probab.] Appl. Probab. Trust: Sheffield. ISSN: 0021-9002.

S E **Journal of Applied Statistics.** [J. Appl. Statist.] Carfax: Basingstoke, England. ISSN: 0266-4763.

E **Journal of Approximation Theory.** [J. Approx. Theory] Academic Press: Orlando, FL. ISSN: 0021-9045.

S E **Journal of the Australian Mathematical Society. Series A, Pure Mathematics and Statistics.** [J. Austral. Math. Soc. Ser. A] Austral. Math. Soc.: St. Lucia. ISSN: 0263-6115.

Journal of the Australian Mathematical Society. Series B, Applied Mathematics. *See* ANZIAM Journal.

E **Journal of Combinatorial Designs.** [J. Combin. Des.] Wiley: New York. ISSN: 1063-8539.

E **Journal of Combinatorial Theory. Series A.** [J. Combin. Theory Ser. A] Academic Press: Orlando, FL. ISSN: 0097-3165.

E **Journal of Combinatorial Theory. Series B.** [J. Combin. Theory. Ser. B] Academic Press: Orlando, FL. ISSN: 0095-8956.

E **Journal of Complexity.** [J. Complexity] Academic Press: Duluth, MN. ISSN: 0885-064X.

E **Journal of Computational Analysis and Applications.** [J. Comput. Anal. Appl.] Kluwer/Plenum: New York. ISSN: 1521-1398.

E **Journal of Computational and Applied Mathematics.** [J. Comput. Appl. Math.] North-Holland: Amsterdam. ISSN: 0377-0427.

S E **Journal of Computational and Graphical Statistics.** [J. Comput. Graph. Statist.] Amer. Statist. Assoc.: Alexandria, VA. ISSN: 1061-8600.

Journal of Computational Mathematics. [J. Comput. Math.] VSP: Zeist, The Netherlands. ISSN: 0254-9409.

E **Journal of Convex Analysis.** [J. Convex Analysis] Heldermann: Lemgo, Germany. ISSN: 0944-6532.

E **Journal of Difference Equations and Applications.** [J. Differ. Equations Appl.] Taylor & Francis: London. ISSN: 1023-6198.

E **Journal of Differential Equations.** [J. Differential Equations] Academic Press: Orlando, FL. ISSN: 0022-0396.

E **Journal of Differential Geometry.** [J. Differential Geom.] Lehigh Univ.: Bethlehem, PA. ISSN: 0022-040X.

- **E Journal of the European Mathematical Society.** [J. Eur. Math. Soc. (JEMS)] European Mathematical Society: Berlin. ISSN: 1435-9855.
- **E Journal of Fourier Analysis and Applications.** [J. Fourier Anal. Appl.] Birkhäuser Boston: Cambridge, MA. ISSN: 1069-5869.
- **E Journal of Functional Analysis.** [J. Funct. Anal.] Academic Press: Orlando, FL. ISSN: 0022-1236.
- **E Journal of Geometry and Physics.** [J. Geom. Phys.] Elsevier: Amsterdam. ISSN: 0393-0440.
- **E Journal of Global Optimization.** [J. Global Optim.] Kluwer Acad. Publ.: Dordrecht, Holland. ISSN: 0925-5001.
- **E Journal of Graph Theory.** [J. Graph Theory.] Wiley: New York. ISSN: 0364-9024.
- **E Journal of Group Theory.** [J. Group Theory] de Gruyter: Berlin. ISSN: 1433-5883.
- **E Journal of Inequalities and Applications.** [J. Inequal. Appl.] Taylor & Francis: London. ISSN: 1025-5834.
- **E Journal of Knot Theory and its Ramifications.** [J. Knot Theory Ramifications] World Sci. Publishing: Singapore. ISSN: 0218-2165.
- **E Journal of Lie Theory.** [J. Lie Theory] Heldermann: Lemgo, Germany. ISSN: 0949-5932.
- **E Journal of the London Mathematical Society. Second Series.** [J. London Math. Soc. (2)] London Math. Soc.: London. ISSN: 0024-6107.
- **E Journal of Mathematical Analysis and Applications.** [J. Math. Anal. Appl.] Academic Press: Orlando, FL. ISSN: 0022-247X.
- **E Journal of Mathematical Economics.** [J. Math. Eonom.] North-Holland: Amsterdam-New York. ISSN: 0304-4068.
- **E Journal of Mathematical Physics.** [J. Math. Phys.] Amer. Inst. Physics: Melville, NY. ISSN: 0022-2488.
- **Journal of the Mathematical Society of Japan.** [J. Math. Soc. Japan] Math. Soc. Japan: Tokyo. ISSN: 0025-5645.
- **Journal of Mathematics of Kyoto University.** [J. Math. Kyoto Univ.] Kyoto Univ.: Kyoto. ISSN: 0023-608X.
- **E Journal de Mathématiques Pures et Appliquées. Neuvième Serie.** [J. Math. Pures Appl. (9)] Gauthier-Villars, Ed. Sci. Med. Elsevier: Paris. ISSN: 0021-7824.

- **E Journal of Multivariate Analysis.** [J. Multivariate Anal.] Academic Press: Orlando, FL. ISSN: 0047-259X.
- **E Journal of Nonlinear Mathematical Physics.** [J. Nonlinear Math. Phys.] J. Nonlinear Math. Phys.: Lulea, Sweden. ISSN: 1402-9251.
- **S E Journal of Nonparametric Statistics.** [J. Nonparametric Statist.] Taylor & Francis: London. ISSN: 1048-5252.
- * **E Journal of Number Theory.** [J. Number Theory] Academic Press: Orlando, Fl. ISSN: 0022-314X.
- **Journal of Operator Theory.** [J. Operator Theory] Theta Found.: Bucharest. ISSN: 0379-4024.
- **E Journal of Optimization Theory and Applications.** [J. Optim. Theory Appl.] Kluwer/Plenum: New York. ISSN: 0022-3239.
- **E Journal of Pure and Applied Algebra**. [J. Pure Appl. Algebra] North-Holland: Amsterdam. ISSN: 0022-4049.
- * Journal of Recreational Mathematics. [J. Recreational Math.] Baywood: Amityville, NY. ISSN: 0022-412X.
- **E Journal für die Reine und Angewandte Mathematik.** [J. Reine Angew. Math.] de Gruyter: Berlin-New York. ISSN: 0075-4102.
- **S E Journal of the Royal Statistical Society. Series A. Statistics in Society.** [J. Roy. Statist. Soc. Ser. A] Roy. Statist. Soc.: London. ISSN: 0964-1998.
- **S E Journal of the Royal Statistical Society. Series B. Statistical Methodology.** [J. R. Stat. Soc. Ser. B Stat. Methodol.] Roy. Statist. Soc.: London. ISSN: 1369-7412.
- **S E Journal of the Royal Statistical Society. Series C. Applied Statistics.** [J. Roy. Statist. Soc. Ser. C] Roy. Statist. Soc.: London. ISSN: 0035-9254.
- **S E Journal of the Royal Statistical Society. Series D. The Statistician.** [J. Roy. Stat. Soc. Ser. D Statistician] Carfax: Abingdon, England. ISSN: 0039-0526.
- **S E Journal of Statistical Computation and Simulation.** Taylor & Francis: London. ISSN: 0094-9655.
- **S E Journal of Statistical Planning and Inference.** [J. Statist. Plann. Inference] North-Holland: Amsterdam. ISSN: 0378-3758.
- * **S E Journal of Statistics Education.** Journal of Statistics Education: Raleigh, NC. ISSN: 1069-1898.

E **Journal of Symbolic Computation.** [J. Symbolic Comput.] Academic Press: London. ISSN: 0747-7171.

E **Journal of Symbolic Logic.** [J. Symbolic Logic] Assoc. Symbol. Logic: Champaign, IL. ISSN: 0022-4812.

S E **Journal of Theoretical Probability.** [J. Theoret. Probab.] Kluwer/Plenum: New York. ISSN: 0894-9840.

S E **Journal of Time Series Analysis.** [J. Time Ser. Anal.] Blackwell: Oxford. ISSN: 0143-9782.

* Journal of Undergraduate Mathematics. [J. Undergrad. Math.] Guilford College: Greensboro, NC. ISSN: 0022-5339.

E **K-Theory.** [K-Theory] Kluwer Acad. Publ.: Dordrecht, Holland. ISSN: 0920-3036.

E **Letters in Mathematical Physics.** [Lett. Math. Phys.] Kluwer Acad. Publ.: Dordrecht, Holland. ISSN: 0377-9017.

S E **Lifetime Data Analysis.** [Lifetime Data Analysis] Kluwer Acad. Publ.: Hingham, MA. ISSN: 1380-7870.

E **Linear Algebra and its Applications.** [Linear Algebra Appl.] North-Holland: New York. ISSN: 0024-3795.

E **Linear and Multilinear Algebra.** [Linear and Multilinear Algebra] Taylor & Francis: London. ISSN: 0308-1087.

E **M2AN. Mathematical Modelling and Numerical Analysis.** [M2AN Math. Model. Numer. Anal.] EDP Sci.: Les Ulis, France. ISSN: 0764-583X.

E **Manuscripta Mathematica.** [Manuscripta Math.] Springer: Berlin. ISSN: 0025-2611.

Matematicheskie Zametki. *See* Mathematical Notes.

Matematicheskii Sbornik. *See* Sbornik. Mathematics.

* Math Horizons. [Math Horizons] Math. Assoc. America: Washington, DC. ISSN: 1072-4117.

* E Mathematica in Education and Research. [Math. Ed. Res.] Springer-Verlag: New York. ISSN: 1065-2965.

E **Mathematica Scandinavica.** [Math. Scand.] Aarhus Univ.: Aarhus, Denmark. ISSN: 0025-5521.

Mathematical Inequalities & Applications. [Math. Inequal. Appl.] ELEMENT: Zagreb, Croatia. ISSN: 1331-4343.

* Mathematical Intelligencer. [Math. Intelligencer] Springer: New York. ISSN: 0343-6993.

Mathematical Logic Quarterly. *See* MLQ. Mathematical Logic Quarterly.

E **Mathematical Methods in the Applied Sciences.** [Math. Methods Appl. Sci.] Teubner: Stuttgart. ISSN: 0170-4214.

Mathematical Modelling and Numerical Analysis. *See* M2AN. Mathematical Modelling and Numerical Analysis.

E **Mathematical Models & Methods in Applied Sciences.** [Math. Models Methods Appl. Sci.] World Sci. Publishing: Singapore. ISSN: 0218-2025.

T E Mathematical Notes. [Math. Notes] Consultants Bureau: New York. ISSN: 0001-4346. (Translation of Matematicheskie Zametki).

E **Mathematical Physics, Analysis and Geometry.** [Math. Phys. Anal. Geom.] Kluwer Acad. Publ.: Dordrecht, Holland. ISSN: 1385-0172.

E **Mathematical Physics Electronic Journal.** [Math. Phys. Electron. J.] Math. Phys. Electron. J.: Austin, TX. ISSN: 1086-6655.

E **Mathematical Proceedings of the Cambridge Philosophical Society.** [Math. Proc. Cambridge Philos. Soc.] Cambridge Univ. Press: Cambridge. ISSN: 0305-0041.

E **Mathematical Programming.** [Math. Program.] Springer: Heidelberg. ISSN: 0025-5610.

Mathematical Research Letters. [Math. Res. Lett.] Internat. Press: Cambridge, MA. ISSN: 1073-2780.

* B Mathematical Reviews. [MR] American Mathematical Society: Providence, RI. ISSN: 0025-5629. (Published electronically as *MathSciNet*). Available at: http://www.ams.org/mathscinet.

E **Mathematical Social Sciences.** [Math. Social Sci.] North-Holland: Amsterdam. ISSN: 0165-4896.

* E **Mathematics of Computation.** [Math. Comp.] American Mathematical Society: Providence, RI. ISSN: 0025-5718.

E **Mathematics of Control, Signals, and Systems.** [Math. Control Signals Systems] Springer: Godalming, England. ISSN: 0932-4194.

* Mathematics Magazine. [Math. Mag.] Math. Assoc. America: Washington, DC. ISSN: 0025-570X.

E Mathematics of Operations Research. [Math. Oper. Res.] INFORMS: Linthicum, MD. ISSN: 0364-765X.

* Mathematics Teacher. [Math. Teacher] Nat. Council Teachers Math.: Reston, VA. ISSN: 0025-5769.

Mathematika. [Mathematika] Univ. London: London. ISSN: 0025-5793.

E Mathematische Annalen. [Math. Ann.] Springer: Berlin. ISSN: 0025-5831.

E Mathematische Nachrichten. [Math. Nachr.] Wiley-VCH: Berlin. ISSN: 0025-584X.

E Mathematische Zeitschrift. [Math. Z.] Springer: Berlin, New York. ISSN: 0025-5874.

* **B E** MathSciNet. [MSN] American Mathematical Society: Providence, RI. (Electronic version of **Current Mathematical Publications** and **Mathematical Reviews**).

Memoirs of the American Mathematical Society. [Mem. Amer. Math. Soc.] American Mathematical Society: Providence, RI. ISSN: 0065-9266.

S E Metrika. [Metrika] Physica: Heidelberg. ISSN: 0026-1335.

E Michigan Mathematical Journal. [Michigan Math. J.] Univ. Michigan: Ann Arbor. ISSN: 0026-2285.

E MLQ. Mathematical Logic Quarterly. [MLQ Math. Log. Q.] Wiley-VCH: Berlin. ISSN: 0942-5616.

E Monatshefte für Mathematik. [Monatsh. Math.] Springer: Vienna. ISSN: 0026-9255.

MR. *See* Mathematical Reviews.

E Multiscale Modeling & Simulation. [Multiscale Model. Simul.] SIAM: Philadelphia, PA. ISSN: 1540-3459.

Nagoya Mathematical Journal. [Nagoya Math. J.] Nagoya Univ.: Nagoya, Japan. ISSN: 0027-7630.

E New York Journal of Mathematics. [New York J. Math.] University at Albany, SUNY: Albany, NY. ISSN: 1076-9803.

NoDEA Nonlinear Differential Equations and Applications. *See* Nonlinear Differential Equations and Applications: NoDEA.

E Nonlinear Analysis. Theory, Methods & Applications. [Nonlinear Anal.] Pergamon: Oxford. ISSN: 0362-546X.

E Nonlinear Differential Equations and Applications: NoDEA. [NoDEA Nonlinear Differential Equations Appl.] Birkhäuser: Basel, Switzerland. ISSN: 1021-9722.

E Nonlinearity. [Nonlinearity] Inst. Phys.: Bristol, England. ISSN: 0951-7715.

* **E Notices of the American Mathematical Society.** [Notices Amer. Math. Soc.] American Mathematical Society: Providence, RI. ISSN: 0002-9920.

E Numerical Algorithms. [Numer. Algorithms] Baltzer: Bussum, The Netherlands. ISSN: 1017-1398.

E Numerical Functional Analysis and Optimization. [Numer. Funct. Anal. Optim.] Dekker: Monticello, NY. ISSN: 0163-0563.

E Numerical Linear Algebra with Applications. [Numer. Linear Algebra Appl.] Wiley: Chichester, England. ISSN: 1070-5325.

E Numerische Mathematik. [Numer. Math.] Springer: Heidelberg. ISSN: 0029-599X.

E Optimization Methods and Software. [Optim. Methods Softw] Taylor & Francis: London. ISSN: 1055-6788.

E Order. [Order] Kluwer Acad. Publ.: Dordrecht, Holland. ISSN: 0167-8094.

Osaka Journal of Mathematics. [Osaka J. Math.] Osaka Univ.: Osaka. ISSN: 0030-6126.

E Pacific Journal of Mathematics. [Pacific J. Math.] Pacific J. Math.: Carmel Valley, CA. ISSN: 0030-8730.

* **Pi Mu Epsilon Journal.** [Pi Mu Epsilon J.] Pi Mu Epsilon: St. Paul, MN. ISSN: 0031-952X.

E Positivity. [Positivity] Kluwer Acad. Publ.: Dordrecht, Holland. ISSN: 1385-1292.

E Potential Analysis. [Potential Anal.] Kluwer Acad. Publ.: Dordrecht, Holland. ISSN: 0926-2601.

S E Probability in the Engineering and Informational Sciences. [Probab. Engrg. Inform. Sci.] Cambridge Univ. Press: New York. ISSN: 0269-9648.

S E Probability Theory and Related Fields. [Probab. Theory Related Fields] Springer: Berlin. ISSN: 0178-8051.

* E **Proceedings of the American Mathematical Society.** [Proc. Amer. Math. Soc.] American Mathematical Society: Providence, RI. ISSN: 0002-9939.

E **Proceedings of the Edinburgh Mathematical Society. Series II.** [Proc. Edinburgh Math. Soc. (2)] Oxford Univ. Press: Oxford. ISSN: 0013-0915.

Proceedings of the Japan Academy. Series A, Mathematical Sciences. [Proc. Japan Acad. Ser. A Math. Sci.] Japan Acad.: Tokyo. ISSN: 0386-2194.

E **Proceedings of the London Mathematical Society. Third Series.** [Proc. London Math. Soc. (3)] London Math. Soc.: London. ISSN: 0024-6115.

E **Proceedings of the Royal Society of Edinburgh. Section A. Mathematics.** [Proc. Roy. Soc. Edinburgh Sect. A] Roy. Soc. Edinburgh: Edinburgh. ISSN: 0308-2105.

Publicationes Mathematicae. [Publ. Math. Debrecen] Inst. Math. Univ Debrecen: Debrecen, Hungary. ISSN: 0033-3883.

E **Publications Mathématiques (Institut des Hautes Études Scientifiques).** [Inst. Hautes Etudes Sci. Publ. Math.] Presses Univ. France: Paris. ISSN: 0073-8301.

Publications of the Research Institute for Mathematical Sciences. [Publ. Res. Inst. Math. Sci.] Kyoto Univ.: Kyoto. ISSN: 0034-5318.

Quarterly of Applied Mathematics. [Quart. Appl. Math.] Brown Univ., Div. Appl. Math.: Providence, RI. ISSN: 0033-569X.

E **Quarterly Journal of Mathematics.** [Q. J. Math.] Oxford Univ. Press: Oxford. ISSN: 0033-5606.

E **Ramanujan Journal.** [Ramanujan J.] Kluwer Acad. Publ.: Hingham, MA. ISSN: 1382-4090.

E **Random Structures & Algorithms.** [Random Structures Algorithms] Wiley: New York. ISSN: 1042-9832.

E **Reports on Mathematical Physics.** [Rep. Math. Phys.] Pergamon: Oxford. ISSN: 0034-4877.

E **Representation Theory.** [Represent. Theory] American Mathematical Society: Providence, RI. ISSN: 1088-4165.

E **Reviews in Mathematical Physics.** [Rev. Math. Phys.] World Sci. Publishing: Singapore. ISSN: 0129-055X.

E Revista Matemática Iberoamericana. [Rev. Mat. Iberoamericana] Rev. Mat. Iberoam.: Madrid. ISSN: 0213-2230.

E Rocky Mountain Journal of Mathematics. [Rocky Mountain J. Math.] Rocky Mountain Math. Consortium: Tempe, AZ. ISSN: 0035-7596.

Russian Academy of Sciences. Doklady. Mathematics. *See* Doklady. Mathematics.

Russian Journal of Mathematical Physics. [Russian J. Math. Phys.] Nauka/Interperiodica: Moscow. ISSN: 1061-9208.

T Russian Journal of Numerical Analysis and Mathematical Modelling. [Russian J. Numer. Anal. Math. Modelling] VSP: Zeist, The Netherlands. ISSN: 0927-6467. (Selected translations of Russian mathematical publications).

T E Russian Mathematical Surveys. [Russian Math. Surveys] London Math. Soc.: London. ISSN: 0036-0279. (Translation of Uspekhi Matematicheskikh Nauk).

T St. Petersburg Mathematical Journal. [St. Petersburg Math. J.] American Mathematical Society: Providence, RI. ISSN: 1061-0022. (Translation of Algebra i Analiz).

S E Sankhya. [Sankhya] Indian Statist. Inst.: Calcutta. ISSN: 0972-7671.

T E Sbornik. Mathematics. [Sb. Math.] Presidium Russ. Acad. Sci.: Moscow. ISSN: 1064-5616. (Translation of Matematicheskii Sbornik).

S E Scandinavian Journal of Statistics. Theory and Applications. [Scand. J. Statist.] Blackwell: Oxford. ISSN: 0303-6898.

E Semigroup Forum. [Semigroup Forum] Springer: New York. ISSN: 0037-1912.

E Set-Valued Analysis. [Set-Valued Anal.] Kluwer Acad. Publ.: Dordrecht, Holland. ISSN: 0927-6947.

Shu Hsueh Hsueh Pao. English Series. *See* Acta Mathematica Sinica. English Series.

Shu Hsueh Li Hsueh Pao. English Edition. *See* Acta Mathematica Scientia. Series B. English Edition.

E SIAM Journal on Applied Mathematics. [SIAM J. Appl. Math.] SIAM: Philadelphia, PA. ISSN: 1095-712X.

E SIAM Journal on Applied Dynamics. [Siam J. Appl. Dyn. Sys.] SIAM: Philadelphia, PA. ISSN: 1536-0040.

E SIAM Journal on Computing. [SIAM J. Comput.] SIAM: Philadelphia, PA. ISSN: 1095-7111.

E SIAM Journal on Control and Optimization. [SIAM J. Control Optim.] SIAM: Philadelphia, PA. ISSN: 1095-7138.

E SIAM Journal on Discrete Mathematics. [SIAM J. Discrete Math.] SIAM: Philadelphia, PA. ISSN: 1095-7146.

E SIAM Journal on Mathematical Analysis. [SIAM J. Math. Anal.] SIAM: Philadelphia, PA. ISSN: 1095-7154.

E SIAM Journal on Matrix Analysis and Applications. [SIAM J. Matrix Anal. Appl.] SIAM: Philadelphia, PA. ISSN: 1095-7162.

E SIAM Journal on Numerical Analysis. [SIAM Journal on Numerical Analysis] SIAM: Philadelphia, PA. ISSN: 1095-7170.

E SIAM Journal on Optimization. [SIAM J. Optimization] SIAM: Philadelphia, PA. ISSN: 1095-7189.

E SIAM Journal on Scientific Computing. [SIAM J. Sci. Comput.] SIAM: Philadelphia, PA. ISSN: 1095-7197.

E SIAM News. [SIAM News]. SIAM: Philadelphia, PA.

* E SIAM Review. [SIAM Rev.] SIAM: Philadelphia, PA. ISSN: 1095-7200.

T E Siberian Mathematical Journal. [Siberian Math. J.] Consultants Bureau: New York-London. ISSN: 0037-4466. (Translation of Sibirskii Matematicheskii Zhurnal).

Sibirskii Matematicheskii Zhurnal. *See* Siberian Mathematical Journal.

Simon Stevin. *See* Bulletin of the Belgian Mathematical Society, Simon Stevin.

S E Statistica Neerlandica. [Statist. Neerlandica] Blackwell: Oxford. ISSN: 0039-0402.

S Statistica Sinica. [Statist. Sinica] Statist. Sinica: Taipei. ISSN: 1017-0405.

S E Statistical Papers. [Statist. Papers] Springer: Berlin. ISSN: 0932-5026.

* **S E Statistical Science**. [Statist. Sci.] Inst. Math. Statist.: Bethesda, MD. ISSN: 0883-4237.

B S E Statistical Theory and Method Abstracts. [STMA] Internat. Statist. Inst.: Voorbourg, The Netherlands. ISSN: 0039-0518.

Statistician. *See* Journal of the Royal Statistical Society. Series D. The Statistician.

S E Statistics. [Statistics] Taylor & Francis: London. ISSN: 0233-1888.

S E Statistics and Computing. [Statist. Comput.] Kluwer Acad. Publ.: Dordrecht, Holland. ISSN: 0960-3174.

S E Statistics & Probability Letters. [Statist. Probab. Lett.] North-Holland: Amsterdam. ISSN: 0167-7152.

* **S Stats.** [Stats] Amer. Statist. Assoc.: Alexandria, VA.

S E Stochastic Analysis and Applications. [Stochastic Anal. Appl] Dekker: New York. ISSN: 0736-2994.

S E Stochastic Processes and their Applications. [Stochastic Process. Appl.] North-Holland: Amsterdam. ISSN: 0304-4149.

Studia Mathematica. [Studia Math.] Polish Acad. Sci., Inst. Math.: Warsaw. ISSN: 0039-3223.

Studia Scientiarum Mathematicarum Hungarica. [Studia Sci. Math. Hungar.] Akad. Kiadó: Budapest. ISSN: 0081-6906.

E Studies in Applied Mathematics. [Stud. Appl. Math.] Blackwell: Malden, MA. ISSN: 0022-2526.

E Taiwanese Journal of Mathematics. [Taiwanese J. Math.] Math. Soc. Repub. China (Taiwan), Dept. Math., Nat. Central Univ.: Chung-Li. ISSN: 1027-5487.

* Teaching Children Mathematics. Nat. Council Teachers Math.: Reston, VA. ISSN: 1073-5836.

S E Technometrics. [Technometrics] Amer. Soc. Qual.: Milwaukee, WI. ISSN: 0040-1706.

Teoreticheskaia i Matematicheskaia Fizika. *See* Theoretical and Mathematical Physics.

Teoriia Veroiatnostei i ee Primeneniia. *See* Theory of Probability and its Applications.

T E Theoretical and Mathematical Physics. [Theoret. Math. Phys.] Consultants Bureau: New York. ISSN: 0040-5779. (Translation of Teoreticheskaia i Matematicheskaia Fizika).

E Theory of Computing Systems. [Theory Comput. Systems] Springer: New York. ISSN: 1432-4350.

T E Theory of Probability and its Applications. [Theory Probab. Appl.] SIAM: Philadelphia, PA. ISSN: 0040-585X. (Translation of Teoriia Veroiatnostei i ee Primeneniia).

S T Theory of Probability and Mathematical Statistics. [Theory Probab. Math. Statist.] American Mathematical Society: Providence, RI. ISSN: 0094-9000. (Translation of Teoriia Imovirnostei ta Matematichna Statistika).

Tohoku Mathematical Journal. Second Series. [Tohoku Math. J. (2)] Tohoku Univ.: Sendai, Japan. ISSN: 0040-8735.

E Topology. [Topology] Pergamon: Oxford. ISSN: 0040-9383.

E Topology and its Applications. [Topology Appl.] North-Holland: Amsterdam. ISSN: 0166-8641.

* **E Transactions of the American Mathematical Society.** [Trans. American Mathematical Society.] American Mathematical Society: Providence, RI. ISSN: 0002-9947.

E Transformation Groups. [Transform. Groups] Birkhäuser Boston: Cambridge, MA. ISSN: 1083-4362.

* **E UMAP Journal.** [UMAP J.] Consort. Math. Appl. (COMAP): Lexington, MA. ISSN: 0197-3622.

Uspekhi Matematicheskikh Nauk. *See* Russian Mathematical Surveys.

Utilitas Mathematica. [Utilitas Math.] Univ. Natal: Durban, South Africa. ISSN: 0315-3681.

* What's Happening in the Mathematical Sciences. [What's Happening Math. Sci.] American Mathematical Society: Providence, RI. ISSN: 1065-9358.

E Zeitschrift für Analysis und ihre Anwendungen. [Z. Anal. Anwendungen] Heldermann: Lemgo, Germany. ISSN: 0232-2064.

B E Zentralblatt MATH. [Zbl. MATH] Springer: Berlin. ISSN: 1436-3356. (Electronic version of **Zentralblatt für Mathematik und ihre Grenzgebiete**).

B Zentralblatt für Mathematik und ihre Grenzgebiete. [Zbl. Math.] Springer: Berlin. ISSN: 0044-4235. (Published electronically as *Zentralblatt MATH*).

Journal Resources

E *Abbreviations of Names of Serials*. American Mathematical Society, 2004. Available at: http://www.ams.org/msnhtml/serials.pdf. Free.

This helpful list of abbreviated titles covered by **Mathematical Reviews**/*MathSciNet* includes **MR** coverage type, publisher information, and complete title name.

Ausejo, Elena and Mariano Hormigón, eds. **Messengers of Mathematics: European Mathematical Journals (1800–1946)**. Madrid: Siglo XXI de España Editores, S.A., 1993. xxiv +297p. €15.66. ISBN 84-323-0802-1.

E *Current Index to Statistics [Journal coverage]*. No copyright given. Available at: http://www.statindex.org/CIS/ReleaseInfo/info.html. Free.

This page lists CIS's core journals and has links to lists of all covered journals.

E *DOAJ, Directory of Open Access Journals*. Lund University Libraries, 2003. Available at: http://www.doaj.org/. Free.

This searchable database includes only "open access" scientific and scholarly journals that use some sort of peer review. There are 57 math and stat titles listed to date. The project is supported by the Open Society Institute and SPARC.

E *Elektronische Zeitschriftenbibliothek/ Electronic Journals Library [EZB*. University Library of Regensburg, 1997–2004. Available at: http://rzblx1.uni-regensburg.de/ezeit/index.phtml?bibid=AAAAA&colors=7&lang=en. Free.

This collaboration of over 200 research libraries produced a searchable database of over 14,000 scholarly online journals, both commercial and noncommerical; not all are peer reviewed. There are 723 listed for mathematics.

Liang, Diana E. **Mathematical Journals: An Annotated Guide**. Metuchen, NJ: Scarecrow Press, 1992. x + 235p. ISBN: 0-8108-2585-6. $40.00.

E *New Journals in Mathematics*. American Mathematical Society, 2004. Available at: http://www.ams.org/mathweb/mi-newjs.html. Free.

Listing by year of new journal titles in mathematics.

E *Serials and Journals—covered by Zentralblatt MATH.* Zentralblatt MATH, 2003. Available at: http://www.zblmath.fiz-karlsruhe.de/MATH/serials/index. Free.

Very useful searchable database of titles covered by *Zentralblatt MATH*. Information includes address, publisher, URL if available, *ZM* coverage, and search link.

4
Dictionaries and Encyclopedias

Dictionaries

Aleksandrov, P. S., et al., eds. **Anglo-Russkii Slovar' Matematicheskikh Terminov: okolo 20000 terminov.** Izd. 3. Moscow: "Mir," 2001. 413p. $19.95. ISBN 5-03-003393-9

Reprint of 2nd edition. Alphabetical listings provide in-context translations. One appendix describes units of measure and another is a rather detailed bilingual guide to English grammar and usage.

Aleksandrov, Pavel S., ed. **English-Russian Dictionary of the Mathematical Sciences.** Moscow, 1962. 369p. Out of print.

English to Russian equivalents for some 6,000 mathematical terms plus an outline of English grammar and a table of measurements. No index.

Aleksandrova, N. V. **Matematicheskie Terminy: Spravochnik.** Moscow: Izdat. Vysshaja Shkola, 1978. 189p. Out of print.

Brief entries for origin of various mathematical terms, each with sources. Index includes English-language entries to mathematicians mentioned.

E *Altavista Babel Fish Translation.* Altavista © 2003. Available at: http://babelfish.altavista.com/. Free.

Ever bemoaned a lack of multilingual skills when surfing the Web internationally? Babel Fish is an Altavista Web page translation service for

Chinese, Dutch, French, German, Greek, Italian, Japanese, Korean, Portuguese, Russian, and Spanish to and from English. Simply paste in text or URL and within seconds there is a translation that may not be perfect, but should be helpful. This service may be added to your browser toolbar.

Baker, C. C. T. **Dictionary of Mathematics.** New York: Hart, 1965. v + 338p. Out of print.

Basic dictionary for college and high school students. Includes biographical entries, definitions, processes, formulas, and tables. Illustrated.

Ballentyne, D. W. G. and D. R. Lovett. **Dictionary of Named Effects and Laws in Chemistry, Physics and Mathematics.** 4th ed. London; New York: Chapman & Hall, 1980. viii + 346p. Out of print. ISBN 0-412-22380-5.

Brief explanations of 1,400 effects, laws, formulas, units, definitions, and theorems from mathematics and physical sciences named after individuals.

Bendick, Jeanne. **Mathematics Illustrated Dictionary: Facts, Figures, and People.** Revised edition. New York: Franklin Watts, 1989. 247p. Out of print. ISBN 0-531-10664-0.

Well-designed, easy-to-use dictionary of mathematical terms, concepts, processes, and people. Author organizes formulas in tables at back of book. Other tables cover mathematical symbols, logs, square roots, and the metric system. Revisions include more basic computer terms, additional entries for mathematicians, and improved illustrations.

Berry, John, et al. **Dictionary of Mathematics.** London; Chicago: Fitzroy Dearborn, 1999. 260p. $45.00. ISBN 1-579-58157-9.

A dictionary intended for students. Definitions focus on meaning, significance, and use with each entry beginning with a short definition or explanation; many include detailed explanations.

Boas, R. P., ed. **A. J. Lohwater's Russian-English Dictionary of the Mathematical Sciences.** 2nd edition, revised and expanded. Providence, RI: American Mathematical Society, 1990. xi + 343p. $38.00 pa. ISBN 0-8218-0133-3 pa.

The opening grammar synopsis of this important reference book has been rewritten. Stress marks have been added to Russian words. The vocabulary has been "extensively enlarged" to reflect contemporary Russian writing in the mathematical sciences. Intended only as an aid in translating Russian to English, not vice versa.

Borovkov, K. A. **Russian-English, English-Russian Dictionary on Probability, Statistics, and Combinatorics.** Philadelphia, PA: Society for Industrial and Applied Mathematics, 1994. viii + 154p. + 1 computer disk. $54.00 pa. ISBN 0-89871-316-1 pa.

This well-organized and precise dictionary of current terminology in probability theory, mathematical statistics, combinatorics, and their applications translates from Russian to English and English to Russian in these subject areas. Includes more than 15,000 terms.

Borowski, E. J. and J. M. Borwein, eds. **Dictionary of Mathematics.** London: Collins, 1989. ix + 659p. Out of print. ISBN: 0-00-434347-6.

Containing over 4,000 entries and 400 diagrams, this can be used by people with a wide range of ability levels. It includes worked examples and capsule biographies of major mathematicians. Also known as **The Collins Dictionary of Mathematics**, this edition later became available on a CD-ROM called **MathResource: Interactive Math Dictionary** (see below).

Borowski, E. J. and J. M. Borwein, eds. **The Harper Collins Dictionary of Mathematics.** Revised reprint of the 1988 original. New York: Harper Perennial, 1991. x + 659p. $16.00. ISBN 0-06-461019-5.

Dictionary of some 6,000 terms at the undergraduate level and above. Appendix of symbols and conventions is useful.

Borwein, Jonathan and Peter Borwein. **A Dictionary of Real Numbers.** Pacific Grove, CA: Wadsworth, 1990. viii + 424p. Out of print. ISBN 0-534-12840-8.

Given a number to be understood, this book tells which classical computations have approximately the same outcome. Even with 100,000 entries the book is not complete, but it is the first of its kind. Intended for undergraduate audiences.

Bouvier, Alain and Michel George. **Dictionnaire des Mathématiques.** Paris: Presses Universitaires de France, 1979. xiv + 832p. Out of print. ISBN 2-13-035427-0.

Illustrated French-language mathematical dictionary.

E Bullen, P. S. **A Dictionary of Inequalities.** Essex, England: Addison Wesley Longman, 1998. x + 283p. (Pitman Monographs and Surveys in Pure and Applied Mathematics; 97). $86.95. ISBN 0-582-32748-2. Online supplement available at: http://rgmia.vu.edu.au/monographs/bullen/Dict-Ineq-Supp-Comb.pdf.

Intended to provide an easy way for researchers to locate an inequality either by name or subject. Proofs not given, but references lead one to details and further information. Extensive bibliography updated with additional references.

Burlak, J. **Russian-English Mathematical Vocabulary.** Edinburgh: Oliver & Boyd, 1963. 305p. Out of print.

Includes "Short Guide to Reading Russian" by K. Brooke, which emphasizes grammar. Vocabulary gives English equivalents to some 13,000 Russian (in Cyrillic) mathematical terms.

Cavagnaro, Catherine and William T. Haight II, eds. **Dictionary of Classical and Theoretical Mathematics.** Boca Raton, FL: Chapman & Hall/CRC Press, 2001. 131p. $34.95 pa. ISBN 1-58488-050-3 pa.

One of five volumes in the CRC Comprehensive Dictionary of Mathematics series. Contains more than 1,000 entries, each succinctly defined by professional mathematicians. This single-source reference provides working definitions, meanings of terms, related references, and a list of alternative terms and definitions. Few cross-references.

Chambadal, Lucien. **Dictionnaire de Mathématiques.** Paris: Hachette, 1981. 302 + [10]p. Out of print. ISBN 2-01-007596-X.

Covers terms in algebra, geometry, and differential and integral calculus. Definitions include examples. Index to notations.

E Clapham, Christopher. **The Concise Oxford Dictionary of Mathematics.** 2nd edition. New York: Oxford University Press, 1996. 312p. $10.36. ISBN 0-19-280041-8. Also available online. For information see: http://www.oxfordreference.com/views/GLOBAL.html. Subscription.

Intended as a general undergraduate reference work for mathematics, this book does not include statistics, computing, or applied mathematics terms. It does include entries for names of mathematicians and reference tables.

Clark, Douglas N., ed. **Dictionary of Analysis, Calculus, and Differential Equations.** Boca Raton, FL: CRC Press, 2000. 273p. $29.95 pa. ISBN 0-8493-0320-6 pa.

Contains more than 2,500 detailed entries, written in a clear, readable style and complete with alternative meanings and related references. This is the first volume published in the CRC Comprehensive Dictionary of Mathematics series.

Daintith, John and John Clark, eds. **The Facts on File Dictionary of Mathematics.** 3rd edition. New York: Facts on File, 1999. 241p. $14.36 pa; $40.00 hardbound. ISBN 0-8160-3914-3 pa; 0-8160-3913-5.

Basic definitions for nonspecialists clearly presented and cross-indexed. This edition has been completely revised and expanded. Over 200 new terms have been included with an emphasis on those in applied mathematics.

Daintith, John and R. D. Nelson, eds. **The Penguin Dictionary of Mathematics.** New York: Penguin, 1989. 350p. $13.95 pa. ISBN 0-14-051119-9 pa.

Twenty-eight hundred definitions in pure and applied mathematics for college students; includes 200 biographical entries. Cross-references. For later edition, see Nelson below.

David, H. A. "First (?) Occurrence of Common Terms in Mathematical Statistics." *American Statistician* 49, no. 2 (May 1995): 121–133.

De Francis, John. **Chinese-English Glossary of the Mathematical Sciences.** Providence, RI: American Mathematical Society, 1964. Out of print. 275p.

Contains 16,540 terms from a number of sources, with the majority coming from mathematics dictionaries published in Peking (1956), Taipei (1958), Tokyo (1961), and Moscow (1959).

E Delijska, B. and K. Peeva, comps. **Elsevier's Dictionary of Computer Science and Mathematics: In English, German, French, and Russian.** Amsterdam; New York: Elsevier, 1995. 785 + [3]p. $215.50. ISBN 0-444-81816-2. CD-ROM version, 1997. $247.50. ISBN 0-444-82718-8.

This is an authoritative and well-organized dictionary containing 9,594 entries with some 2,500 cross-references. Covers both computer science and mathematics, including modern developments and contemporary changes, as well as recently established terms. In two parts: the basic table which lists the English terms in alphabetical order with their German, French, and Russian equivalents; and the indexes in which the German, French, and Russian terms are listed separately. Includes a list of the mathematical symbols. Bibliography.

Downing, Douglas. **Dictionary of Mathematics Terms.** 2nd edition. Hauppage, NY: Barron's, 1995. xix + 303p. $8.76. ISBN: 0-8120-3097-4.

Definitions of uneven quality for 600 terms. Includes cross-references. Symbols list, brief tables, and so forth. Useful pocket-sized reference.

Drazil, J. V. **Quantities and Units of Measurement: A Dictionary and Handbook.** London; Wiesbaden: Mansell; O. Brandstetter, 1983. 313p. Out of print. ISBN 0-7201-1665-1.

Originally published as **Dictionary of Quantities and Units** (1971). In two sections: first is a dictionary of units of measurement, symbols, and abbreviations; second is a handbook of quantities and selected constants.

Efimov, Oleg P. **Russian-English Dictionary of Mathematics.** Boca Raton, FL: CRC Press, 1993. viii + 419p. $139.95. ISBN 0-8493-4456-5.

This bilingual dictionary is larger and provides a broader scope than any others now in use. Contains more than 27,000 entries, including many adjectives, verbs, and synonyms. Covers all major branches of mathematics from elementary to advanced topics, including terms from the newest branches of mathematics.

Eisenreich, Günther and Ralf Sube. **Dictionary of Mathematics in Four Languages: English, German, French, Russian.** Amsterdam: Elsevier North-Holland, 1982. 2 vols. 1,459p. Out of print. ISBN 0-444-99706-7.

This is a polyglot mathematical dictionary containing some 35,000 terms. Very thorough coverage. An alphanumeric code and the columnar format help simplify the use of this comprehensive dictionary. Explanatory notes help users with the problems of synonyms and homonyms. **Wörterbuch der Mathematik**, also by Eisenreich and Sube, is the same book, organized in German.

Eisenreich, Günther. **Lexikon der Algebra.** Berlin: Akademie-Verlag, 1989. 677p. Out of print. ISBN 3-05-500231-8.

Comprehensive, one-volume German dictionary of algebra from a recognized authority in mathematical lexicography. Contains many "see" references to longer key entries of up to six pages, most with several references for additional study.

Eiss, Harry Edwin. **Dictionary of Mathematical Games, Puzzles, and Amusements.** Westport, CT: Greenwood, 1988. xvi + 279p. $65.00. ISBN 0-313-24714-5.

Collection of essays on games and puzzles and related mathematical topics such as Euclid's theory of parallels. Includes many historical references.

Engesser, Hermann, ed. **Kleine Duden-Mathematik.** Mannheim, Germany: Bibliographisches Institut, 1986. 480p. Out of print. ISBN 3-411-02180-2.

Intended to aid solution of practical mathematical problems of daily life including data processing and information science terms in this context. Explains abstract mathematical concepts in understandable language with many illustrations and examples.

S Everitt, B. S. **The Cambridge Dictionary of Statistics.** 2nd edition. Cambridge; New York: Cambridge University Press, 2002. ix + 410p. $50.00. ISBN 0-521-81099-X.

A very comprehensive, reliable, and up-to-date sourcebook that provides simple definitions and explanations of statistical concepts. Some 3,500 terms are defined in all areas of statistics, including medical, survey, theoretical, and applied. Most definitions include a reference to where the reader can seek an extended account of the term. In addition, there are over 100 short biographies of leading statisticians from the past.

S Everitt, B. S. **The Cambridge Dictionary of Statistics in the Medical Sciences.** Cambridge; New York: Cambridge University Press, 1995. 274p. $23.95. ISBN 0-521-47928-2.

Definitions of approximately 2,000 terms. Although most are statistical, there are relevant mathematical, computing, and genetic terms. Medical statistics terms have longer entries. Good reference for those in applied statistics.

Feys, R. and F. B. Fitch, eds. **Dictionary of Symbols of Mathematical Logic.** 2nd corrected printing. Amsterdam: North-Holland, 1973. xiv + 171p. Out of print. ISBN 0-7204-2250-7.

Presents concepts and notations of formal deductive systems of symbolic logic employed by most mathematical and philosophical texts. More detailed than Greenstein and Horn's **Dictionary of Logical Terms and Symbols** (see below).

S Freund, John E. and Frank J. Williams. **Dictionary/Outline of Basic Statistics.** New York: Dover, 1991. ix + 195p. $8.05 pa. ISBN 0-486-66796-0 pa.

A slightly corrected but not updated reprint of 1966 original. Divided into two parts: a dictionary of statistical terms and an outline of statistical formulas.

Friedberger, W. F., ed. **International Dictionary of Applied Mathematics.** Princeton, NJ: Van Nostrand Reinhold, 1960. 1,173p. Out of print.

Excellent encyclopedic dictionary defining 8,000 terms and methods for advanced scientists and engineers. Has French, German, Spanish, and Russian indexes. Something of a classic.

García Rodríquez, Mariano. **Diccionario Matemático; Español-Inglés, Inglés-Español. Mathematics Dictionary; Spanish-English, English-Spanish.** New York: Hobbs, Dorman, 1965. vii + 78p. Out of print.

Only word and phrase equivalents in Spanish and English are presented.

Gheorghita, Stefan. **Dictionar Poliglot de Matematica, Mechanica si Astronomie.** Bucharest: Editura Tehnica, 1978. xvi + 664p. Price not available.

This is a polyglot dictionary with listings arranged alphabetically in English. The equivalents in Romanian, German, French, and Russian follow. Indexes in each of the latter four languages direct the user to the appropriate English-language entry.

Gibbs, G. Ian. **Dictionary of Gaming, Modelling & Simulation.** London; Beverly Hills, CA: E & F N Spon; Sage, 1978. xi + 161p. Out of print. ISBN 0-8039-1085-1.

Well illustrated, but dated. Covers statistical tests, mathematical formulas, and related terms.

Glenn, J. A. and G. H. Littler, eds. **Dictionary of Mathematics.** Totowa, NJ: Barnes & Noble, 1984. x + 240p. Out of print. ISBN: 0-389-20451-X.

Definitions of terms gathered from indexes of British college texts are of uneven quality. All technical terms used are also defined.

Glushko, M. M. **Russko-Angliiskii Matematicheskii Slovar'-Minimum.** Moscow: Moskov. Gos. Univ., 1988. 142p. Out of print. ISBN 5-211-00180-X.

Dictionary of 5,000-plus entries based on Lohwater's **Russian-English Dictionary of the Mathematical Sciences** with some updating.

E *Google Web Page Translation.* Google, 2004. Information available at: http://www.google.com/help/features.html#translation. Free.

Google's machine translation service "automatically translates Web pages published in French, German, Italian, Spanish, and Portuguese into English." When Google search results include Web pages in these five languages, then a "translate this page" link is shown. One may also paste text into Google's Language Tools for translation.

Gould, S. H. and P. E. Obreanu. **Romanian-English Dictionary and Grammar for the Mathematical Sciences.** Providence, RI: American Mathematical Society, 1967; 1979. v + 51p. $19.00. ISBN 0-8218-0038-8.

Basic information for readers of mathematical Romanian. It covers basic construction of the language and defines Romanian words commonly appearing in mathematical works.

Greenstein, Carol and Carol Horn. **Dictionary of Logical Terms and Symbols.** New York: Van Nostrand Reinhold, 1978. xiii + 188p. Out of print. ISBN 0-442-22834-1.

Presents notation used in logic, engineering, and computer science with tables for translation from one system to another. Less detailed than Feys and Fitch's **Dictionary of Symbols of Mathematical Logic** (see above).

Herland, Leo Joseph. **Dictionary of Mathematical Sciences.** 2nd edition. New York: Ungar, 1965. 2 vols. Vol. 1. xii + 323p. Out of print. ISBN 0-8044-4393-1. Vol. 2. 349p. Out of print. ISBN 0-8044-4394-7.

German to English and English to German with equivalents given under each term.

Hoffmann, Ludwig. **Mathematisches Wörterbuch: Alphabetische Zusammenstellung sämmtlicher in die mathematischen Wissenschaften** gehörender Gegenstande in erlkärenden und beweisenden synthetisch und analitisch bearbeiteten Abhandlungen. Berlin: v. 1–3, G. Bosselmann; v. 4–7, Wiegandt & Hemple, 1858–1867. 7 vols. in 5. Out of print. Volumes 5–7 edited by L. Natani.

Described once as "the fullest mathematical dictionary ever published" (Bibliotheca Chemico-Mathematica, Second Supplement, 1937, #1700). This work is valuable for its historical interest.

Hyman, Charles, comp. **German-English Mathematics Dictionary.** New York: Interlanguage Dictionaries, 1960. 131p. Out of print.

Drawn from mathematical expressions appearing in textbooks and similar works, 8,500 German terms with English equivalents are included. No definitions are given.

S Inter-American Statistical Institute. **Statistical Vocabulary.** 2nd edition. Washington, DC: Pan American Union, 1960. xi + 83p. Out of print.

Thirteen hundred English-language terms with equivalents in Spanish, Portuguese, and French. Separate word indexes for non-English languages.

S E International Statistical Institute. *ISI Glossary of Statistical Terms.* European Communities, 1995-2002. Available at: http://europa.eu.int/comm/eurostat/research/index.htm?http://www.europa.eu.int/en/comm/eurostat/research/isi/&1. Free.

This multilingual glossary of statistical terms contains over 3,000 terms in 20 languages. Terms are listed with short descriptive text and formulas where appropriate.

Itô, Kiyosi, ed. **Encyclopedic Dictionary of Mathematics.** 2nd edition. See below in **Encyclopedias**.

James, Robert C., ed. **Mathematics Dictionary.** 5th edition New York: Chapman & Hall, 1992. vii + 548p. $77.00 pa. ISBN 0-412-99041-5 pa.

A high-quality general mathematics dictionary of some 8,000 terms, covering arithmetic through calculus into statistics, plus sketches of major contributors. Multilingual index.

Jerrard, H. G. and D. B. McNeil. **Dictionary of Scientific Units Including Dimensionless Numbers and Scales.** 5th edition. London; New York: Chapman & Hall, 1986. ix + 222p. Out of print. ISBN 0-412-28090-6.

Definitions for more than 850 named units and dimensionless numbers. Appendixes for tables of weights and measures, physical constants, and conversion factors for SI (Systeme International) and CGS units. The fifth edition provides more precise values for the fundamental physical constants and more exact definitions of other units (e.g., candela) that have now been approved by the International Committees.

Jordanian Committee for Arabisation, Ministry of Education, Amman, comp. **Mathematics Dictionary: English-Arabic (with an Arabic Index): Covering the Terms (and Definitions) of Traditional and Modern Mathematics, Mechanics and Computers.** Beirut: Librairie du Liban, 1975. 308p. Out of print.
Terms given in English; explanations in Arabic.

Karush, William. **Crescent Dictionary of Mathematics.** Palo Alto, CA: Seymour Publications, 1987. 313p. Out of print. ISBN 0-86651-352-3.
Reprint of book originally published by Macmillan in 1962. Basic dictionary for high school and college with 1,422 entries covering field of mathematics. References in Appendix A.

Karush, William. **Webster's New World Dictionary of Mathematics.** New York: Webster's New World; Distributed by Prentice Hall Trade, 1989. 317p. $9.60 pa. ISBN 0-13-192667-5 pa.
A revised edition of the 1962 edition of **Crescent Dictionary of Mathematics**. Important mathematical advances have been added since then, especially terms related to the field of computers. The list of outside references has also been updated and expanded. Contains more than 1,400 entries and is aimed at the general reader with a curiosity about mathematics as well as students and teachers of high school and college mathematics.

Kerner, Otto, et al. **Vieweg Mathematik Lexikon.** 2nd edition. Braunschweig, Germany: Friedr. Vieweg, 1988. xii + 377p. Out of print. ISBN 3-528-06308-4.
Reference tool for basic mathematics courses at West German universities. Covers analysis, including differential equations and function theory, algebra, topology, probability, and statistics, plus some basic geometry and number theory.

Klaften, E. B. **Mathematisches Vokabular.** Munich: Wilhelm Lampl. 1961. x + 186p. Out of print. ISBN 3-87910-151-5.

English-German and German-English vocabulary of elementary mathematics topically arranged. Covers general terms, arithmetic, algebra, plane geometry, solid geometry, trigonometry, calculus, and coordinates.

Kolaitis, Memas. **English-Greek Dictionary of Pure and Applied Mathematics with Greek and English Appendices.** Athens: Technical Chamber of Greece, 1976. 2 vols. cvi + 1516p. Price not available.

Exhaustive, although now somewhat dated, dictionary of Greek equivalents to English-language mathematical terms. Indexes.

Komatsu, Yusaku. **Sugaku Ei-Wa Wa-Ei Jitten. Mathematics: English-Japanese and Japanese-English Dictionary.** Tokyo: Kyoritsu Shuppan, 1979. vi + 358p. Out of print.

Presents general mathematical terms in Japanese characters with English-language equivalents in the first section and mathematical terms in English with their Japanese equivalents in the second part.

Kornegay, Chris. **Math Dictionary With Solutions.** 2nd edition. Thousand Oaks, CA: SAGE Publications, 1999. v + 570p. $39.95 pa. ISBN 0761917853 pa.

Alphabetically arranged articles cover topics from elementary mathematics through beginning calculus. Each article includes such features as a definition, an explanation, and examples with solutions. Cross-references provide directions to more or less difficult discussions. Appendixes.

S Kotz, Samuel. **Russian-English/English-Russian Glossary of Statistical Terms.** Edinburgh: Oliver & Boyd, 1971. vii + 87p. Out of print. ISBN 0-05-002446-9.

Based on and supplemental to Kendall and Buckland's **Dictionary of Statistical Terms,** 3rd edition, it covers 2,500 terms giving Russian equivalents plus somewhat more in Russian to English.

S Központi Statisztikai Hivatal. **Statisztikai Szótar; 1700 Statisztikao Kifejezes het Nyelven. 3. Kiad.** Budapest: Statisztikai Kiadó Vállalat, 1962. viii + 171p. Out of print.

Statistical dictionary of 1,700 terms in seven languages. Major listing in Russian with equivalents in Hungarian, Bulgarian, Czech, Polish, German, and English.

Kramer, K. **Russko-Angliiskii Matematicheskii Slovar'. Russian-English Mathematical Dictionary.** Trenton, NJ: Published by Author, 1961. iii + 123p. Out of print.

The author writes, "This dictionary more than adequately covers all mathematical terminology likely to be encountered in Russian elementary and advanced scientific and technical literature containing more than 5,000 entries." It does not provide definitions, merely Russian-English equivalents.

Krantz, Steven G., ed. **Dictionary of Algebra, Arithmetic, and Trigonometry.** Boca Raton, FL: Chapman & Hall/CRC Press, 2000. 368p. $39.95. ISBN 1-58488-052-X.

One of five volumes in the CRC Comprehensive Dictionary of Mathematics series. This lexicon offers clear, rigorous working definitions, complete with alternative meanings and related references, for over 2,800 terms associated with arithmetic, algebra, and trigonometry, with natural overlap into geometry, topology, and other related areas. Features self-contained entries that avoid awkward cross-references.

S Kurtz, Albert K. and Harold A. Edgerton. **Statistical Dictionary of Terms and Symbols.** New York: Wiley, 1939; reprint 1967. xiii + 191p. Out of print.

An excellent dictionary with detailed definitions and explanations of symbols.

Lapedes, Daniel, ed. **McGraw-Hill Dictionary of Physics and Mathematics.** New York: McGraw-Hill, 1978. xiv + 1120p. Out of print. ISBN 0-07-045480-9.

Includes some 20,000 definitions of terms in physics, mathematics, and related fields. Some illustrations. Forty-six pages of appendixes.

Lewisch, Ingrid and Alfred S. Posamentier. **Mathematisches Fachwörterbuch: Englisch-Deutsche, Deutsche-Englisch.** Wien, Austria: R. Oldenbourg, 1996. 91p. Price not available. ISBN 3-7029-0708-4.

Includes not only translation sections on German-English and English-German, but also a section of common mathematical expression so the reader can learn "to say it correctly." Takes into account differences between American and British English.

Loh, Shiu-chang, et al., comps. **Glossary of the Mathematical and Computing Sciences (English-Chinese).** Hong Kong: Machine Translation Project, The Chinese University of Hong Kong, 1976. iv + 494p. Out of print.

Contains 30,000 terms used in connection with mathematics and computing science. English with Chinese equivalents in this volume, Chinese to English in other (see below).

Loh, Shiu-chang, et al., comps. **Glossary of the Mathematical and Computing Sciences (Chinese-English).** Hong Kong: Machine Translation Project, The Chinese University of Hong Kong, 1976. iv + 551p. Out of print.

Companion volume to English with Chinese equivalents (see above).

Macintyre, Sheila and Edith Witte. **German-English Mathematical Vocabulary.** 2nd edition. New York: Interscience, 1966. x + 95p. Out of print.

Covers German-English equivalents for pure mathematics and basics of German grammar in one slim volume.

E *Math Forum Internet Mathematics Library [Dictionaries].* The Math Forum@Drexel, 1994–2004. Available at: http://mathforum.org/library/resource_types/dictionaries/. Free.

The *Math Forum* dictionary page lists over 200 links, but most are narrowly focused. It may be worth searching or browsing for special interests.

E **MathResource: Interactive Math Dictionary.** Version 1.0. Halifax, NS: MathResources Inc., 1998. booklet (32 pp.) +1 CD-ROM (Windows only). $125.00. ISBN 1-896977-02-2.

This interactive version of **The Collins Dictionary of Mathematics** by Ephraim Borowski and Jonathan Borwein (above) was augmented by Dr. Carolyn Watters' work with Maple™. It has over 5,000 entries with Maple™ enabled computation, graphing, and plotting. No programming is required of the user. Appropriate for students and teachers.

McDowell, C. H. **Short Dictionary of Mathematics.** New York: Philosophical Library, 1957. xiii + 61p. Out of print.

The first part covers arithmetic and algebra; the second part has plane trigonometry and geometry. Provides definitions (some with illustrations), list of signs and symbols, and very simple tables.

Meschkowski, Herbert. **Mathematisches Begriffswörterbuch.** 4., wesentl. verb. u. erw. Aufl. Mannheim, Germany: Bibliographisches Institut, 1976. 315p. (B. I.-Hochschultaschenbücher; 99). Out of print. ISBN 3-411-05099-3.

This illustrated German-language dictionary includes formulas, examples, graphs, useful "see" and "see also" references, and a bibliography.

Meschkowski, Herbert. **Mehrsprachenwörterbuch Mathematischer Begriffe.** Mannheim, Germany: Bibliographisches Institut, 1972. 131p. Out of print. ISBN 3-411-01409-1.

Multilingual. The first part is a list of German terms with corresponding terms in English, French, Russian, and Italian. The second part has lists of mathematical terms in the four languages with their respective equivalents.

Mikisha, A. M. and V. B. Orlov. **Tolkovyi Matematicheskii Slovar'.** Moscow: Russkii Iazyk, 1988. 240p. Out of print. ISBN 5-2000-0246-X.

Russian-language dictionary of basic mathematical terms.

Millington, T. Alaric and William Millington. **Dictionary of Mathematics.** New York: Barnes and Noble, 1971 (c. 1966). ix + 259p. $8.95. ISBN 0-06-463311-X.

Covers all areas of mathematics with brief definitions suitable for beginning students. Dated.

Milne-Thomson, L. M. **Russian-English Mathematical Dictionary: Words and Phrases in Pure and Applied Mathematics.** Madison: University of Wisconsin Press, 1962. xiv + 191p. (Publication of the Mathematics Research Center, United States Army, the University of Wisconsin; 7). Out of print.

Developed as an aid for translating Russian works in applied mathematics, the dictionary provides English equivalents to some 8,500 Russian terms and is supplemented by a 28-page outline of Russian grammar.

Naas, Josef and Hermann Ludwig Schmid, eds. **Mathematisches Wörterbuch: mit Einbeziehung der theoretischen Physik.** 3rd edition. Berlin: Akademie-Verlag; New York: Pergamon, 1979. 2 vols. $395.67. ISBN 3-519-02400-4 (set). Vol. 1. xv + 1043p. Vol. 2. viii + 952p.

Comprehensive, containing definitions, articles on trends, and 400 biographies. Some articles include reference notes. Appendixes.

Nelson, David. **The Penguin Dictionary of Mathematics.** 2nd edition. London; New York: Penguin Books, 1998. 461p. $11.96 pa. ISBN 0-14-051342-6 pa.

Revised and updated. Over 3,000 words fully cross-referenced and with diagrams where needed, covering all branches of pure and applied mathematics, including topics such as chaos, fractals, and graph theory. Biographies of over 200 key figures in mathematics. For earlier edition, see Daintith above.

Orlov, V. B., N. S. Skorokhod, and A. B. Sosinskii. **Russko-Anglo-Nemetsko-Frantsuzskii Matematicheskii Slovar'.** Moscow: Russkii Iazyk, 1987. 298p. Out of print.

Three thousand basic terms for university students and those utilizing mathematics in their professions. Alphabetical lists of English, German, and French equivalents.

S Paenson, Isaac. **English-French-Spanish-Russian Systematic Glossary of the Terminology of Statistical Methods.** New York: French and European Publications, 1970. xxxviii + 517p. $295.00 pa. ISBN 0-8288-2354-5 pa.

Arranged by topical chapters to place terms in context. Individual terms are defined in all four languages. Separate index for each language.

Parker, Sybil P., ed. **McGraw-Hill Dictionary of Mathematics.** New York: McGraw-Hill, 1997. xi + 306p. $15.96. ISBN 0-07-052433-5.

All text in this dictionary was previously published in the fifth edition of **McGraw-Hill Dictionary of Scientific and Technical Terms.** Includes 4,000 terms with their definitions, pronunciations, synonyms, acronyms, and abbreviations. For all levels of mathematics.

Peeva, K., et al. **Elsevier's Dictionary of Mathematics.** New York: Elsevier, 2000. 996p. $209.50. ISBN 0-444-82953-9.

A very useful dictionary containing 11,652 entries with more than 4,750 cross-references. Each English term is followed by its German, French, and Russian equivalents; a second part lists German, French, and Russian terms indexed to the English equivalent. In the appendix, one may learn how to read and pronounce important math expressions in English, German, French, and Russian.

Pfeil, Trante. **Mathematischer Fachwortschatz: Englisch-Deutsch, Deutsch-Englisch.** Jena, German Democratic Republic: Friederich-Schiller-Universität Jena, 1980. 100p. Price not available.

Hierarchical vocabulary of mathematical terms giving English-German and German-English equivalents.

S Porkess, Roger. **The Harper Collins Dictionary of Statistics.** New York: Harper Perennial, 1991. xi + 267p. $12.80 pa. ISBN 0-06-461020-9 pa.

Intended for use by mathematics or statistics students, this book includes definitions and worked examples.

Rainich, Gabrielle. **Russian-English Vocabulary with Grammatical Sketch: To Be Used in Reading Mathematical Papers.** Providence, RI: American Mathematical Society, 1950, 1980. 66p. $17.00. ISBN 0-8218-0037-X.

This title aids mathematicians in reading Russian mathematical papers. Vocabulary is based on materials supplied by Society members. Short grammatical sketch by A. H. Kuipers.

E Rowlett, Russ. *How Many? A Dictionary of Units of Measurement.* Russ Rowlett and the University of North Carolina at Chapel Hill, 2003. Available at: http://www.unc.edu/~rowlett/units/index.html. Free.

This award-winning list of definitions of units of measurement is simply designed in an alphabetical arrangement. Interesting commentary and explanations are included on topics such as names of large numbers, roman and Arabic numerals, symbols and abbreviations, and the International System of Units (SI).

S Sahai, Hardeo and José Berríos. **Dictionary of Statistical, Scientific and Technical Terms: English-Spanish, Spanish-English.** New York: French and European Publications, 1981. ix + 143p. $35.00. ISBN: 0-8288-2352-9.

English-to-Spanish and Spanish-to-English terms in statistics and related fields. About 3,000 terms per section, including phrases and proper names.

Schwartzman, Steven. **The Words of Mathematics: An Etymological Dictionary of Mathematical Terms Used in English.** Washington, DC: Mathematical Association of America, 1994. vii + 261p. $37.95 pa. ISBN 0-88385-511-9 pa.

A fascinating book that discusses the etymologies of over 1,500 simple to advanced mathematical terms. Whereas other dictionaries define the technical terms, this book concentrates on where those terms came from and their literal meanings.

Selkirk, K. E. **Longman Mathematics Handbook: The Language and Concepts of Mathematics Explained.** Harlow, Essex, England: Longman, 1991. 312p. Price not available. ISBN 0-582-02161-8.

Nearly 3,000 words used in mathematics and arranged by subjects (e.g., analysis, geometry, etc.). Appendixes on SI and number prefixes. Index.

Sjöstedt, C. E. **Vocabularie Mathematic in Interlingue. Con Traductionin Angles (English), Frances (Français) a German (Deutsch).** Stockholm: Natur och Kultur, 1970. 87p. Out of print.

This is a dictionary with equivalent mathematical terms in Interlingua, English, French, and German.

Sneddon, I. N. **Encyclopaedic Dictionary of Mathematics for Engineers and Applied Scientists.**
See below in **Encyclopedias.**

S E StatSoft. *Statistics Glossary*. StatSoft, Inc., 1984–2003. Available at: http://www.statsoft.com/textbook/glosfra.html. Free.

Use the simple alphanumeric list of this extract from StatSoft's *Electronic Manual of STATISTICA* to find short definitions of terms.

S Tietjen, Gary L. **Topical Dictionary of Statistics.** New York: Chapman and Hall, 1986. xii + 171p. Out of print. ISBN 0-412-01201-4.

Topically arranged, it attempts to provide context, applications, and related terms in addition to basic definitions. Definitions of keywords or phrases are located through index.

Tonian, A. O. **Slovar' Matematicheskikh Terminov Na Angliiskom, Russkom, Armianskom, Nemetskom, Frantsuzksom Iazykakh.** Erevan, SSR Armenia: Akademiia Nauk Armianskoi S. S. R., 1965. 237p. Out of print.

The entries in this polyglot mathematical dictionary are listed in English, with equivalents given in Russian, Armenian, German, and French. Indexes in the latter four languages direct the user to the desired English entry. The format—languages in columns, entries in rows—is easy to use.

Tzelekis, C. P. **English-Greek Mathematical Dictionary.** Athens: Athens Pub. Center, 1973. ix + 234p. Out of print.

Seventy-eight hundred entries of English mathematical terms with their Greek equivalents for Greek-speaking students. Appendixes.

S E Upton, Graham J. G, and Ian Cook. **A Dictionary of Statistics.** New York: Oxford University Press, 2002. 420p. $16.95. 0-19-280100-7 pa. Also available online. For information, see: http://www.oxfordreference.com/views/GLOBAL.html. Subscription.

Comprehensive and authoritative work written by experts in the field.

Wells, David. **The Penguin Dictionary of Curious and Interesting Geometry.** London: Penguin Books, 1991. xiv + 285p. $17.56 pa. ISBN 0-14-011813-6 pa.

Brocard points, dragon curves, and Islamic tessellations are just a few of the hundreds of shapes, famous and obscure, ancient and modern, that are illustrated and briefly described. Good for browsing and can provide excellent stimulation for math club projects.

Wells, D. G. **The Penguin Dictionary of Curious and Interesting Numbers.** Revised edition. London; New York: Penguin Books, 1997. xix + 231p. $11.16 pa. ISBN 0-14-026149-4 pa.

Information about interesting numbers—from minus one to Pascal's triangle and more. This edition includes nearly 200 new entries.

Encyclopedias

S Armitage, Peter and Theodore Colton, eds. **Encyclopedia of Biostatistics.** Chichester, England; New York: J. Wiley, 1998. 6 vols. $3,775.00 (set). ISBN 0-471-97576-1.

Over 1,200 articles from leading authorities worldwide provide a broad coverage of topics of specifically biostatistical interest. Extensive references.

Behnke, H., ed. **Fundamentals of Mathematics.** Translated by S. H. Gould. Cambridge, MA: MIT Press, 1984. 3 vols. Vol. 1. x + 549p. Out of print. ISBN 0-262-52093-1. Vol. 2. xi + 685p. $35.00. ISBN 0-262-02069-6. Vol. 3. xiii + 541p. Out of print. ISBN 0-262-02049-1.

Translation of the German **Grundzüge der Mathematik**, which is considered a classic. Provides extensive coverage and is highly recommended for research collections.

Bunch, Bryan and Jenny Tesar. **The Penguin Desk Encyclopedia of Science and Mathematics.** New York: Penguin Books, 2000. viii + 696p. $32.00. ISBN 0-67-088528-2.

The inclusion of mathematics makes this concise all-in-one reference particularly valuable. Contains several hundred capsule biographies, line drawings, and an extensive index.

Dannan, Fozi Mustafa, et al. **Kuwait Science Encyclopedia: Mathematics.** Kuwait: Kuwait Foundation for the Advancement of Sciences, 1984. 4 vols. Price not available.

Text is in modern Arabic with signs in Latin characters. Covers more than 2,100 mathematical words, terms, and names including biographies and major works from different periods. Can be used as Arabic-English dictionary of mathematics as well.

E Encyklopädie der mathematischen Wissenschaften mit Einschluss ihrer Anwendungen. Leipzig: B. G. Teubner, 1898/1904-1904/35. 6 vols. In 23. Out of print. Also available online at: http://134.76.163.65/agora_docs/183743BIBLIOGRAPHIC_DESCRIPTION.html. Free.

E Enzyklopädie der Mathematischen Wissenschaften, mit Einschluss ihrer Anwendungen. 2nd edition. Leipzig: Teubner, 1939– . 13 vols. Out of print. Also available online at: http://134.76.163.65/agora_docs/193536BIBLIOGRAPHIC_DESCRIPTION.html. Free.

Comprehensive and detailed coverage of mathematics and its various applied fields. Authoritative works noted for their accuracy. The 2nd edition was never completed. Its most recent volume was published in 1967.

E Floudas, Christodoulos A. and Panos M. Pardalos. **Encyclopedia of Optimization.** Dordrecht, Holland; London: Kluwer Acad. Publ., 2001. 6 vols. $1,300.00. ISBN 0-7923-6932-7. Also available online at: http://reference.kluweronline.com/?xmlid=0792369327. $1,620.00 + $162.00/yr.

Optimization problems arise in many sciences. Hundreds of authors contributed survey and applications articles. Historical and biographical articles are included as well. Aimed at theorists and users of optimization techniques.

Fried, E., et al. **Malaia Matematicheskaia Entsiklopediia.** Edited by Ju Blagoveshchenskii and B. Kocsis. Budapest: Akademiai Kiado, 1976. 693p. Out of print. ISBN 963-05-0844-3.

Russian translation of Hungarian original. Classified arrangement with eight major headings. Index and references.

Gamkrelidze, R. V., ed. **Encyclopaedia of Mathematical Sciences.** New York: Springer-Verlag, 1988– . Ongoing series. Individual volumes have been published out of order with various prices. Contact publisher for more information.

Comprised of survey articles that include basic definitions, history, examples, and descriptions of the frontiers of research. Authors are mostly from the former USSR and are often among the most influential in their respective fields. Highly recommended.

Gellert, Walter, et al., eds. **Fachlexikon ABC Mathematik.** Frankfurt am Main: Harri Deutsch, 1978. 624p. Out of print. ISBN: 3-87144336-0.

Contains some 700 articles. Not indexed.

Gellert, W., ed. **VNR Concise Encyclopedia of Mathematics.** 2nd edition. New York: Van Nostrand Reinhold, 1989. 776p. + 56p. of plates. Out of print. ISBN 0-442-20590-2.

Based on **Kleine Enzyklopädie der Mathematik,** this English-language version offers comprehensive coverage in three parts (elementary, higher, and contemporary mathematics) with photographs and biographies. General work for educated readers, not just mathematics subject specialists. Excellent source to consult for answering difficult questions posed by nonspecialists.

Göpfert, Alfred, ed. **Lexikon der Optimierung.** Berlin: Akademie-Verlag, 1986. vi + 388p. Price not available. ISBN 3-05-500031-5.

Lexicon of optimization containing definitions, descriptions, numerical procedures from theory of optimization, and optimal control. Has English-French-German-Russian lexicon of equivalent terms.

Gottwald, S., ed. **VNR Concise Encyclopedia of Mathematics.**
See Gellert, W. **VNR Concise Encyclopedia of Mathematics.**

Grattan-Guinness, I., ed. **Companion Encyclopedia of the History and Philosophy of the Mathematical Sciences.**
See complete entry in **Chapter 7, Biographical and Historical Materials.**

Grinstein, Louise S. and Sally I. Lipsey, eds. **Encyclopedia of Mathematics Education.** New York: Routledge Falmer, 2001. xxviii + 879p. $125.00. ISBN 0-815-31647-X.

A quick-reference encyclopedia of over 400 entries, designed for readers and researchers investigating national and international aspects of mathematics education at the elementary, secondary, and post-secondary levels. Includes a comprehensive index, internal cross-referencing, and coverage of all major aspects of mathematics.

Hazewinkel, M., ed. **Encyclopaedia of Mathematics.** Dordrecht, Holland; Norwell, MA: Kluwer Acad. Publ., 1987–1994. 10 vols. $806.00 pa.(set); $2,200.00 (set). ISBN 0-7923-4709-9 pa.(set); 1-556-08010-7 (set).

English-language translation (with editorial updates and annotations) of the Soviet **Matematicheskaia Entsiklopediia** (see Vinogradov, I. M., below). Includes surveys for nonspecialists, articles on results or problems, and definitions. This set is a reference work for all parts of mathematics. The over 7,000 articles are signed mostly by Russian authors and include AMS classification numbers and bibliographies with added current Western sources.

Hazewinkel, M., ed. **Encyclopaedia of Mathematics. Supplement.** Dordrecht, Holland; Boston: Kluwer Acad. Publ., 1997–2001. Vol. I. viii + 587p. $252.00. ISBN 0-7923-47-9-9. Vol. II. 631p. $229.00. ISBN 0-7923-6114-8. Vol. III. viii + 557p. $229.00. ISBN 1-4020-0198-3.

Sixteen hundred new entries, written by experts, cover developments and topics not covered in the original set. Arranged alphabetically with detailed index. Taken together, all of these volumes comprise the most authoritative, comprehensive, and up-to-date mathematics encyclopedia in print.

E Hazewinkel, M., ed. **Encyclopaedia of Mathematics on CD-ROM.** Norwell, MA: Kluwer Acad. Publ., 1997. Contains vols. 1–10, Supplement vol. 1. $235.00, single-user edition; $1,775.00, networked edition. ISBN 0-7923-4807-9.

In the CD-ROM version, one may do full-text, wildcard, proximity, and Boolean searches of text and symbols. Although the initial search interface is simple, presentation of the results is confusing. Articles may be downloaded or printed. The publisher has allowed libraries to mount the single-user edition on a library network as long as it is limited to one user at a time. The CD does not include Supplement, vols. 2–3.

E Hazewinkel, M., ed. *Encyclopaedia of Mathematics.* Dordrecht, The Netherlands. Kluwer Acad. Publ., 2001. Contains vols. 1–10 and Supplement vol. 1–3. Information available at: http://reference.kluweronline.com/?xmlid=1402006098. $1,650.00–$3,300.00 + $330.00/yr.

This Web version covers all printed volumes of this encyclopedia (more than 8,000 entries) and intends to update 10 percent to 15 percent of the material every year. The search interface is simple but the priority of multiple search results is unclear. Articles may be printed, e-mailed, or downloaded. Articles are signed, but not dated; most bibliographic references are from the early 1990s or before. Almost 50,000 mathematical notations, input as PNG image files, are used in the text.

Itô, Kiyosi, ed. **Encyclopedic Dictionary of Mathematics.** 2nd edition. Cambridge, MA: MIT Press, 1987. 4 vols. xvii + 2,148p. $90.00 pa; $425.00 hardbound. ISBN 0-262-59020-4 pa; 0-262-09026-0.

Translation of the respected **Iwanami Sugaku Jiten** published by Mathematical Society of Japan (Nihon Sugakkai Henshu) (see below). Comprehensive with most entries specific rather than general. Includes biographical information. Vol. 4 contains appendixes of formula and mathematical tables, list of mathematical journals, and name and subject indexes.

S Kotz, Samuel, Norman L. Johnson, and Campbell B. Reed, eds. **Encyclopedia of Statistical Sciences.** New York: Wiley, 1982–88. 9 vols. + 1 sup. $315.00/vol. (vol. 1–8); $372.00 (vol. 9); $205.00 (sup.). $2,500.00 (set, vol. 1–9). ISBN 0-471-81274-9 (sup.); 0-471-05544-1 (set).

Quality encyclopedia with many longer signed articles. Short articles are frequently unsigned, but nearly all articles have references. Intended for knowledgeable readers but not the specialist. Includes articles on organizations, journals, contributors to the field, formulas, and so forth. Volume 9 includes an index to vols. 1–9.

S Kotz, Samuel, Campbell B. Reed, and David L. Banks, eds. **Encyclopedia of Statistical Sciences. Update.** New York: Wiley, 1997–1999. 3 vols. Vol. 1. xii + 568p. $315.00. ISBN 0-471-11836-2. Vol. 2. xv + 745p. $315.00. ISBN 0-471-11939-3. Vol. 3. xvii + 898p. $250.00. ISBN 0-471-23883-X.

Updates are designed to bring the encyclopedia in line with the latest topics and advances made in statistical science over the past decade. Written by over 100 world-renowned experts (including the editors), the entries are self-contained and easily understood by readers with a limited statistical background. Up-to-date bibliographies, thorough cross-referencing, and extensive indexing facilitate quick access to specific information. Volume 3 includes a comprehensive index for the nine volumes and supplement of the encyclopedia plus the three update volumes.

S Kruskal, William H. and Judith M. Tanur, eds. **International Encyclopedia of Statistics.** New York: Free Press, 1978. 2 vols. Vol.1. xxi + 666p. Out of print. ISBN 0-02-917970-X. Vol. 2. 684p. Out of print. ISBN 0-02-917980-7.

Updated and expanded version of statistics articles from **International Encyclopedia of the Social Sciences** (Macmillan, 1968). Original 70 articles increased to 75 and biographies from 45 to 57. New or revised material is indicated.

Lerner, Rita G. and George L. Trigg, eds. **Encyclopedia of Physics.** 2nd edition. New York: VCH, 1991. xiv + 1408p. $159.00. ISBN 0-471-18719-4.

Brief articles cover all of physics; written to be useful to nonspecialists as well as mathematicians and scientists. Some articles deal with mathematical subjects such as Lie groups, matrices, and vector and tensor analysis. The second edition has been fully revised, expanded, and updated.

Nihon, Sugakkai Henshu. **Iwanami Sugaku Jiten.** 3rd edition. Toyko: Iwanami Shoten, 1985. 1,609p. + four leaves of plates. Out of print. ISBN 4-00-080016-7.

Highly respected Japanese encyclopedia of mathematics covering 450 topics arranged under 21 divisions. Translated into English as **Encyclopedic Dictionary of Mathematics**, edited by Kiyosi Itô (see above).

E *PlanetMath.Org*. All pages are GNU copyrighted by their respective authors, various dates. Available at: http://planetmath.org/. Free.

This interesting collaborative encyclopedia project began when Eric Weisstein's *Math World* was taken offline by his copyright dispute with CRC Press. Articles are contributed by individuals, peer review occurs via the community's public corrections system, and access is free. One may search by keyword or browse by keyword or MSC classification. There are over 3,000 entries to date.

E *PRIME (Platonic Realms Interactive Mathematics Encyclopedia).* Math Academy Online™/Platonic Realms™, 1997-2004. Available at: http://www.mathacademy.com/pr/prime/index.asp. Free.

This encyclopedia has an easy search interface with over 1,000 hyperlinked entries, mostly at the undergraduate level.

Prokhorov, Iu. V. **Matematicheskii Entsiklopedicheskii Slovar'.** Moscow: Sovetskaia Entsiklopediia, 1988. 845p. Out of print.

Encyclopedic dictionary containing some 3,500 articles based on **Matematicheskaia Entsiklopediia (ME)** (see Vinogradov, I. M., below). Includes a biographical dictionary with 900 entries and many other features. Inexpensive substitute for five-volume **ME** and a useful source of information on terms found in Russian-English dictionaries.

Rota, Gian-Carlo, ed. **Encyclopedia of Mathematics and Its Applications.** Reading, MA: Addison-Wesley, 1976– . ISSN: 0953-4806.

Eighty volumes of this series have been published so far. Individual volumes are extremely well done and are recommended for any research collection. Currently published by Cambridge University Press.

Shapiro, Max S. **Mathematics Encyclopedia.** Garden City, NY: Doubleday, 1977. 289p. Out of print. ISBN 0-385-12427-9.

Useful general work for schools and public libraries; covers all branches of mathematics. Contains tables, formulas, and symbols.

Sloane, Neil J. A. and Simon Plouffe. **The Encyclopedia of Integer Sequences.** San Diego: Academic Press, 1995. xiii + 587p. $59.95. ISBN 0-12-558630-2.

Contains 5,488 integer sequences. Sequences arranged in numerical order; a brief description and reference is given for each. Bibliography. Index.

E Sloane, Neil J. A. *Sloane's On-Line Encyclopedia of Integer Sequences.* AT&T, 2003. Available at: http://www.research.att.com/~njas/sequences/. Free.

Sloane's searchable database has over 83,000 entries at this writing. Each sequence entry has an ID number, the beginning sequence, name, author(s) and keywords, a list of references, links, and its formula and programming in Maple and Mathematica.

Sneddon, I. N. **Encyclopaedic Dictionary of Mathematics for Engineers and Applied Scientists.** Elkins Park, PA: Franklin, 1976. viii + 800p. Out of print. ISBN 0-08-016767-5.

Comprehensive one-volume encyclopedic dictionary. Longer entries are signed and include references. Relates mathematical concepts and techniques most commonly used in engineering to basics of major branches of mathematics through cross-referencing.

Vinogradov, I. M. **Matematicheskaia Entsiklopediia.** Moscow: Sovetskaia Entsiklopediia, 1977–85. 5 vols. Vol. 1: 1,151p. Vol. 2: 1,104p. Vol. 3: 1,184p. Vol. 4: 1,216p. Vol. 5: 1,246p. Out of print.

The original of **Encylopedia of Mathematics** (see Hazewinkel, M., above), this approaches being an alphabetical list of phrases explained in the terminology of its discipline supplemented by longer pieces on key topics. No biographical or historical entries.

E Weisstein, Eric W. **The CRC Concise Encyclopedia of Mathematics.** 2nd edition. Boca Raton, FL: CRC Press/Chapman & Hall, 2003. 3,242p. $99.95. ISBN 1-58488-37-2. Also available in a CD-ROM version, 2nd edition, 2003. $99.95. ISBN 0-8493-1946-3.

This is a fascinating and useful compendium of mathematical definitions, formulas, figures, tabulations, and references. Its informal style makes it accessible to a broad spectrum of readers with a diverse range of mathematical backgrounds and interests. The author draws connections to other areas of mathematics and science and demonstrates its actual implementation. One thousand pages have been added to the 2nd edition.

E Weisstein, Eric W. *Eric Weisstein's World of Mathematics (MathWorld™).* Eric W. Weisstein and Wolfram Research, Inc., 1999–2004. Available at: http://mathworld.wolfram.com/. Free.

Once the object of a yearlong copyright dispute, *CRC Press v. Weisstein and Wolfram Research, MathWorld*, the Web version of Weisstein's encyclopedic dictionary for mathematics, is now a celebrated site. Although not the equivalent in depth and quality to the **Encyclopaedia of Mathematics** (see Hazewinkel, M., above), or the **Encyclopedic Dictionary of**

Mathematics (see Itô, K., above), academic librarians find *MathWorld* to be a very useful site for quick reference, especially for questions from nonspecialists. The Web site has over 11,400 entries contributed by many experts, over 102,000 cross-references, over 5,000 figures, over 200 animated graphics, and 1,000 live Java applets. One can look up words and phrases or browse by subject. Entries, often lengthy, include both internal and external links, "see also" references, and short bibliographies. Mathematics notations are displayed as GIF images. This free site is sponsored by Wolfram Research and is updated continuously.

West, Beverly Henderson. **Prentice-Hall Encyclopedia of Mathematics.** Englewood Cliffs, NJ: Prentice-Hall, 1982. xv + 683p. Out of print. ISBN 0-13-696013-8.

Eighty articles on various aspects of mathematics plus tables of symbols, weights and measures, and logarithms. Includes biographical entries, cross-references, and references for additional reading. This comprehensive resource is perhaps most appropriate for undergraduates or nonprofessionals.

5
Tables, Handbooks, Manuals, Guides

Tables

S Bagui, Subhash C. **CRC Handbook of Percentiles of Non-Central T-Distributions.** Boca Raton, FL: CRC Press, 1993. 391p. $180.00. ISBN 0-8493-8669-1.

Provides critical values of noncentral t-distributions in an easy-to-use format. Bibliographical references.

S Balakrishnan, N. and William W. S. Chen. **CRC Handbook of Tables for Order Statistics from Inverse Gaussian Distributions, With Applications.** Boca Raton, FL: CRC Press, 1997. x + 688p. $104.95. ISBN 0-8493-3118-8.

Describes the models, their properties, shapes, and applications in different fields and the numerical integration methods used to compute the means, variances, and covariances of order statistics.

S Balakrishnan, N. and William W. S. Chen. **Handbook of Tables for Order Statistics from Lognormal Distributions, With Applications.** Dordrecht, Holland; Boston: Kluwer Acad. Publ., 1999. xiii + 868p. $99.00 pa. ISBN 0-7923-5712-4 pa.

Presents elaborate tables of moments of order statistics as well as BLUES based on complete and censored samples for lognormal distributions.

E Brillhart, John, et al. **Factorizations of $b^n \pm 1$, b = 2, 3, 5, 6, 7, 10, 11, 12 up to High Powers.** 2nd edition. Providence, RI: American Mathematical Society, 1988. cii + 236p. (Contemporary Mathematics; 22). $42.00 pa. ISBN 0-8218-5078-4 pa. Available at: http://www.ams.org/online_bks/conm22/conm22-whole.pdf. Free.

Presents known factorizations of numbers given in title plus historical account of hardware and development. Updated and revised. References.

Chen, J. Q., et al. **Tables of the SU(MN) Contains SU(M) X SU(N) Coefficients of Fractional Parentage.** Teaneck, NJ: World Scientific Press, 1991. viii + 447p. $58.00. ISBN 981-02-0113-3.

Contains tables of the Clebsch-Gordan coefficients of interest to mathematical and theoretical physicists.

S Chiang, Chin Long. **Life Table and Its Applications.** Melbourne, FL: Robert E. Krieger, 1984. xix + 316p. $46.50. ISBN 0-89874-570-5.

Complete and abridged tables of age-specific death rates, adjustment of rates, and maximum likelihood estimations. Includes applications.

Erdelyi, A., ed. **Tables of Integral Transforms.** Bateman Manuscript Project. California Institute of Technology. New York: McGraw-Hill, 1954. 2 vols. Out of print. Vol. 1. xx + 391p. Vol. 2. xvi + 451p.

Extensive collection of integral transforms useful in many fields. Indexes of notations.

S Fisher, Ronald Aylmer and Frank Yates. **Statistical Tables for Biological, Agricultural and Medical Research.** 6th edition, revised and enlarged. New York: Hafner, 1963. x + 146p. Out of print. ISBN 0-05-000872-2.

Authoritative collection of tables plus bibliography of sources on statistical method. Similar to Lebedev and Fedorova's **Guide to Mathematical Tables** (below).

Fletcher, Alan. **An Index of Mathematical Tables.** 2nd edition. Reading, MA: Addison-Wesley, 1962. 2 vols. xi + 994p. Out of print.

Classic working index to mathematical tables, international in scope; covers the sixteenth century to 1961.

Gradshteyn, I. S. and I. M. Ryzhik. **Table of Integrals, Series, and Prod-**

ucts. 6th edition. Translated by Alan Jeffrey. San Diego: Academic, 2000. xlvii + 1163p. $85.95. ISBN 0-12-294757-6.

A useful work for collections in need of tables of integrals.

E Gradshteyn, I. S. and I. M. Ryzhik. **Table of Integrals, Series, and Products.** 5th edition, CD-ROM version 1.0. Translated by Alan Jeffrey. San Diego: Academic, 1995. xlvii + 1163p. $99.95. ISBN 0-12-294756-8.

Allows users to do a full-text search. TeX source for formulas can be copied and pasted into TeX documents. Works with PC, Macintosh, and UNIX.

S Greenwood, Joseph Arthur and H.O. Hartley. **Guide to Tables in Mathematical Statistics.** Princeton, NJ: Princeton University Press, 1962. lxii + 1,014p. Out of print.

Classified arrangement supplemented by a list of contents of several books of tables. Author and subject indexes. Remains useful despite age.

S Harter, H. Leon and N. Balakrishnan. **CRC Handbook of Tables for the Use of Order Statistics in Estimation.** Boca Raton, FL: CRC Press, 1996. xvii + 669p. $139.00. ISBN 0-8493-9452-X.

Revision and expansion of Harter's 1970 **Order Statistics and Their Use in Testing and Estimation** (v.2). Provides maximum likelihood estimations of their parameters based on complete plus Type-II censored samples. The method of computation used to construct the tables is described in detail and their usefulness is illustrated with practical examples.

S Kokoska, Stephen and Daniel Zwillinger. **CRC Standard Probability and Statistics Tables and Formulae.** Student edition. Boca Raton, FL: Chapman & Hall/CRC, 2000. 225p. $24.95 pa. ISBN 0-8493-0026-6 pa.

This volume contains all of the standardized statistical tables and formulas typically needed by students and casual users. See also Zwillinger and Kokoska's **CRC Standard Probability and Statistics Tables and Formulae** (below).

S Kokoska, Stephen and Christopher Nevison. **Statistical Tables and Formulae.** New York; Berlin: Springer-Verlag, 1989. 88p. $11.00. ISBN 0-387-96873-3.

Collection of probability and statistics formulas plus standard tables, including tables for nonparametric tests. No index.

Lebedev, Aleksandr Vasil'evich and R.M.A. Fedorova. **Guide to Mathematical Tables.** New York: Pergamon, 1960. 586p. Out of print.

Translation of **Spravochnik po Matematicheskikh Tablits.** Contains some tables difficult to find elsewhere.

S Lindley, D. V. and W. F. Scott. **New Cambridge Statistical Tables.** 2nd edition. Cambridge; New York: Cambridge University Press, 1995. 96p. $15.95 pa. ISBN 0-521-48485-5 pa.

Abridged and updated version of 1953 work. Second edition includes two new tables.

E *Math2.org* (Formerly *"Dave's Math Tables"*). David Manura, 1995–2003. Available at: http://www.math2.org/. Free.

This is a collection of math tables and formulas in general math, algebra, geometry, trigonometry, calculus, and statistics. A multi-user interactive white board to discuss or teach math concepts over the Internet is available.

S Neave, H. R. **Statistics Tables: For Mathematicians, Engineers, Economists and the Behavioral and Management Sciences.** London: Routledge, 1998. 87p. $10.84. ISBN 0-4151-0485-8.

Reprint of 1978 original, a collection of carefully researched and class-tested statistical tables helpful to many users.

E Nipp, Gordon L. **Quaternary Quadratic Forms: Computer Generated Tables.** New York: Springer-Verlag, 1991. vi + 155p. + computer disk. $87.95. ISBN 0-387-97601-9. Electronic data also available at: http://www.research.att.com/~njas/lattices/nipp.html. Free.

Classified arrangement. Included are the number of automorphs for each class and the mass of each genus plus other complex and computer-intensive information. Accompanying disk contains tables that have been condensed from the book, allowing mathematicians to investigate and answer questions about quaternary forms by means of computer searches.

S Odeh, Robert E. and D. B. Owen. **Attribute Sampling Plans, Tables of Tests and Confidence Limits for Proportions.** New York: Dekker, 1983. xi + 368p. $145.00. ISBN 0-8247-7136-2.

Tables for binomial, Poisson, or hypergeometric distributions. For those in quality control or acceptance sampling.

S Odeh, Robert E. **Parts per Million Values for Estimating Quality Levels.** New York: Marcel Dekker, 1988. xiv + 347p. $167.50. ISBN 0-8247-7950-9.

Carefully computed tables for estimating quality levels from 20,000 ppm to 1 ppm.

S Pearson, Egon Sharpe and H. O. Hartley, eds. **Biometrika Tables for Statisticians.** 3rd edition. London: Biometrika Trust, 1976. 2 vols. Vol. 1. xvi + 270p. Out of print. ISBN 0-904653-10-2. Vol. 2. xviii + 385p. $110.00. ISBN 0-904653-11-0.

Corrected reprint of **Tables for Statisticians and Biometricians.** The handbook of choice for statisticians.

Peters, Jean. **Eight-Place Tables of Trigonometric Functions for Every Second of Arc, with an Appendix on the Computation to Twenty Places.** New York: Chelsea, 1968. xi + 954p. Out of print. ISBN 0-8284-0174-8.

This classic is widely accepted as the authoritative tables for the field.

S Rohlf, F. James and Robert R. Sokal. **Statistical Tables.** 3rd edition. New York: Freeman, 1995. xiv + 199p. $26.70 pa. ISBN 0-7167-2412-X pa.

A useful collection of tables.

Royal Society of London. **Royal Society Mathematical Tables.** Cambridge: Cambridge University Press, 1950–64. 11 vols. Out of print.

A well-respected collection of tables; includes Farley series, Riemann zeta function, and Bessel functions.

Salzer, Herbert E. and Norman Levine. **Tables for Converting Polynomials and Power Series into Chebyshev Series.** New York: Applied Science Publications, 1984. x + 65p. $21.00 pa. ISBN 0-915061-01-5 pa.

Title reflects content plus a discussion of Chebyshev series.

Salzer, Herbert E., Norman Levine, and Saul Serben. **Tables for Lagrangian Interpolation Using Chebyshev Points.** New York: Applied Science Publications, 1984. i + 323p. $28.00 pa. ISBN 0-915061-00-7 pa.

Includes a fifty-page introduction with bibliography; discusses use in the economization of the polynomials.

S Selected Tables in Mathematical Statistics. Providence, RI: American Mathematical Society, 1970–1988. 11 vols. Price varies. ISSN 0094-8837.

A scholarly collection of selected tables and accompanying discussion of underlying distributions. Some volumes are collections of lengthy articles; others are monographs. Lacks cumulative indexing.

U.S. National Bureau of Standards. **Applied Mathematics Series.** Washington, DC: Government Printing Office, 1948–69. 63 vols. Out of print. ISSN 1049-4685.

Contains mathematical tables for those engaged in scientific and technical work.

E Zwillinger, Daniel, ed. **CRC Standard Mathematical Tables and Formulae.** 31st edition. Boca Raton, FL: Chapman Hall/CRC Press, 2003. 910p. $39.95. ISBN 1-58488-291-3. Also available online. For information see: http://www.mathnetbase.com/default. Subscription.

Mathematical tables for scientific, engineering, industrial, and educational personnel. A widely used ready reference tool.

S E Zwillinger, Daniel and Stephen Kokoska. **Standard Probability and Statistics Tables and Formulae.** Boca Raton, FL: Chapman & Hall/CRC, 2000. 554p. $49.95. ISBN 1-58488-059-7. Also available online. For information see: http://www.statsnetbase.com/default.asp. Subscription.

An accessible, example-oriented handbook that supplies the basic principles, the most commonly used values, and the information to make them work for the user. Each entry is accompanied by a textual description. See also Kokoska and Zwillinger's **CRC Standard Probability and Statistics Tables and Formulae.** Student edition. (above).

Handbooks, Manuals, Guides

E Abramowitz, Milton and Irene A. Stegun. **Handbook of Mathematical Functions with Formulas, Graphs, and Mathematical Tables.** 10th printing, with corrections. Washington, DC: Government Printing Office, 1984. xiv + 1,046p. (National Bureau of Standards. Applied Mathematics Series, 55). $65.00. 003-003-00279-8. PDF copy available at: http://www.convertit.com/Go/ConvertIt/Reference/AMS55.ASP. $15.95. Also available online. For information see: http://www.knovel.com/knovel2/default.jsp. Subscription.

Standard work containing special functions, formulas, numerical tables, and mathematical properties of tabulated functions. See also National Institute of Standards and Technology, *Digital Library of Mathematical Functions* (below).

Amman, Hans M., David A. Kendrick, and John Rust, eds. **Handbook of Computational Economics.** Amsterdam; New York: Elsevier, 1996. (Handbooks in Economics, v. 13). Vol. I. xxi + 827p. $110.00. ISBN 0-444-89857-3.

An introduction and selective overview of the rapidly emerging field of computational economics. References follow each chapter. Indexes.

Anastassiou, George, ed. **Handbook of Analytic-Computational Methods in Applied Mathematics.** Boca Raton, FL: Chapman & Hall/CRC, 2000. 1,034p. $119.95. ISBN 1-58488-135-6.

Contains 22 survey chapters with topics reflecting title. Articles address problems in a broad range of disciplines. References. Index.

Anderson, E., et al. **LAPACK Users' Guide.** 3rd edition. Philadelphia, PA: Society for Industrial and Applied Mathematics, 1999. xxi + 407p. $39.00 pa. ISBN 0-89871-447-8 pa.

Reference manual for Release 3.0 of LAPACK. This updated edition includes information on accessing LAPACK and related projects via the Web, new routines, and performance results.

Andrews, Larry C. **Special Functions of Mathematics for Engineers.** 2nd edition. Bellingham, WA: SPIE Optical Engineering Press, 1997. xix + 479p. $80.00. ISBN 0-8194-2616-4.

Contains many worked examples with more applications from a number of fields. Useful as a reference book for practitioners or as a textbook in courses that include higher mathematics.

Arganbright, Deane. **Practical Handbook of Spreadsheet Curves and Geometric Constructions.** Boca Raton, FL: CRC Press, 1993. 197pp + 1 computer disk. $74.95. ISBN 0-8493-8938-0.

A user-friendly and hands-on introduction to constructing, plotting, and animating curves and curve families using computer spreadsheets.

Arrow, Kenneth J. and Michael D. Intriligator, eds. **Handbook of Mathematical Economics.** Amsterdam; New York: North-Holland, Elsevier, 1981-1991. 4 vols. (xvii + 2264p.). Vol. 1. xvii + 378p. $110.00. ISBN 0-

444-86126-2. Vol. 2. xx + p.379–1070. $110.00. ISBN 0-444-86127-0. Vol. 3. xviii + p.1071–1520. $110.00. ISBN 0-444-86128-9. Vol. 4. Hildenbrand, Werner and Hugo Sonnenschein, eds. xxx + p.1521–2264. $110.00. ISBN 0-444-86127-0.

Compilation of survey papers written by widely recognized experts for students and teachers of mathematical economics.

Auth, Joanne Buhl. **Deskbook of Math Formulas and Tables.** New York: Van Nostrand Reinhold, 1985. viii + 219p. Out of print. ISBN 0-442-21106-6.

A handy volume with helpful formulas, techniques, and tables of types used daily.

Bagrov, V. G. and D. M. Gitman. **Exact Solutions of Relativistic Wave Equations.** Dordrecht, Holland: Kluwer Acad. Publ., 1990. x + 323p. (Mathematics and Its Applications (Soviet Series); 39). $246.00. ISBN 0-7923-0215-X.

Contains a systematic study of all known exact solutions of the Dirac and Klein-Gordon equations for a charged particle in an external electromagnetic field.

Baker, Louis. **C Mathematical Function Handbook.** New York: McGraw-Hill, 1992. xviii + 757p. + 1 computer disk. Out of print. ISBN 0-07-911158-0.

A collection of tested algorithms that compute all of the functions in Abramowitz and Stegun's classic **Handbook of Mathematical Functions** (above).

S   Balakrishnan, N. and William W. S. Chen. **CRC Handbook of Tables for Order Statistics from Inverse Gaussian Distributions, With Applications.**

See above, in **Tables** section of this chapter.

S   Balakrishnan, N., ed. **Handbook of the Logistic Distribution.** New York: Dekker, 1991. xv + 601p. (Statistics: Textbooks and Monographs; 123). $180.00. ISBN 0-8247-8587-8.

Consolidation of important past research as well as new developments. Useful to students and practitioners alike. Comprehensive bibliography.

S Balakrishnan, N. and William W. S. Chen. **Handbook of Tables for Order Statistics from Lognormal Distributions, With Applications.**
See above, in **Tables** section of this chapter.

S Balding, D. J., M. Bishop, and C. Cannings, eds. **Handbook of Statistical Genetics.** 2nd edition. Chichester, England; New York: Wiley, 2003. 2 vols. 1,308p. $315.00. ISBN 0-470-84829-4.
Comprehensive coverage of pressing statistical issues in genetics with 35 chapters, each written by a leading authority. Contains numerous examples, case studies, and references to useful resources on the Web.

Barbosa, Valmir C. **An Atlas of Edge-Reversal Dynamics.** Boca Raton, FL: Chapman & Hall/CRC, 2001. xi + 372p. (Chapman & Hall/CRC Research Notes in Mathematics Series; 421). $84.95 pa. ISBN 1-58488-209-3 pa.
First in-depth account of the graph dynamics system SER (Scheduling by Edge Reversal). In two parts: a review of the origins of SER and the atlas proper.

S Barnett, V. and T. Lewis. **Outliers in Statistical Data.** 3rd edition. Chichester, England: Wiley, 1994. xiv + 463p. $195.00. ISBN 0-471-93094-6.
This fully revised and extended edition of the standard reference work on outliers provides relevant illustrations and tabulations as well as suggestions for future research. A definite must for any researcher involved in correlation or regression.

Bartsch, Hans Jochen. **Handbook of Mathematical Formulas.** New York: Academic Press, 1974. 528p. $64.00. ISBN 0-12-080050-0.
Collection of formulas covering entire field.

Barwise, Jon, et al., eds. **Handbook of Mathematical Logic.** 8th reprint edition. Amsterdam; New York: North-Holland, 1999, c 1977. xi + 1,165p. (Studies in Logic and the Foundations of Mathematics; 90). $113.00. ISBN 0-444-86388-5.
The most reliable reference in classical logic (except for recursion theory—see Griffor below) reviews contemporary developments in logic for four key areas: model, set, recursion, and proof theories. Incomparable in its breadth of coverage and high standards of expertise and exposition.

Benzecri, J. P. **Correspondence Analysis Handbook.** New York: Dekker, 1992. xii + 665p. $185.00. ISBN 0-8247-8437-5.

Users of data analysis are the intended audience for this handbook. It contains many illustrations and examples as well as a FORTRAN program for correspondence. The index doubles as a glossary.

Beyer, William H., ed. **CRC Handbook of Mathematical Sciences.** 6th edition. Boca Raton, FL: CRC Press, 1987. 860p. Out of print. ISBN 0-8493-0656-6.

Was standard desk reference for integral tables, special functions, probability and statistics, differential equations, analytic geometry, and more. Continued **Handbook of Tables for Mathematics** and **Handbook of Mathematical Tables**.

Blocksma, Mary. **Reading the Numbers: A Survival Guide to the Measurements, Numbers, and Sizes Encountered in Everyday Life.** New York: Viking Penguin, 1989. xv + 224p. Out of print. ISBN 0-14-010654-5.

Useful for answering a variety of questions dealing with numeric data and as a tool to help readers interpret tables and statistics from another source.

Borceux, Francis. **Handbook of Categorical Algebra.** Cambridge; New York: Cambridge University Press, 1994. (Encyclopedia of Mathematics and Its Applications; 50–52 [52 incorrectly marked 53]). Vol. 1. Basic Category Theory. xv + 361p. ISBN 0-521-44178-1. Vol. 2. Categories and Structures. xvii + 443p. $95.00. ISBN 0-521-44179-X. Vol. 3. Categories of Sheaves. xvii + 522p. $105.00. ISBN 0-521-44180-3.

Volumes are written in sequence and are aimed at graduate students preparing to work in category theory.

Borodin, Andrei N. and Paavo Salminen. **Handbook of Brownian Motion: Facts and Formulae.** Boston: Birkhäuser, 1996. xiv + 462p. $142.00. ISBN 0-8176-5463-1.

In two parts: a summary of the theory of linear diffusions and a table of distributions of functionals of Brownian motion and related processes.

Bronshtein, I. N. and K. A. Semendiaev. **Handbook of Mathematics.** 3rd revised edition. Translated by K. A. Hirsch. Berlin; Heidelberg; New York: Springer-Verlag, 1997. xv + 973p. $57.00. ISBN 3-540-62130-X.

Standard reference work. This English translation was based on the 19th German edition, **Taschenbuch der Mathematik**, of the original Russian edition.

Bronshtein, I. N. and K. A. Semendiaev. **Taschenbuch der Mathematik.** 20th edition. Moscow; Leipzig: Nauka; Teubner, 1989. xi + 860p. Price not available. ISBN 3-8714-4492-8.

The English-language translation of same work is titled **Handbook of Mathematics**.

Bronshtein, I. N. and K. A. Semendiaev. **Taschenbuch der Mathematik, Erganzende Kapitel.** 6th edition. Leipzig: Teubner, 1990. v + 234p. Price not available. ISBN 3-322-00782-0.

Supplementary volume discusses analysis, mathematical methods of operations research, and mathematical information processing. Intended as supplement to their work of same title (above).

Burington, Richard S. **Handbook of Mathematical Tables and Formulas.** 5th edition. New York: McGraw-Hill, 1973. x + 500p. $94.80. ISBN 0-07-009015-7.

In two parts: (1) formulas and theorems and (2) tables of logarithms, several functions, powers and roots, probability, annuity, and distributions.

S Burington, Richard Stevens and Donald Curtis May, Jr. **Handbook of Probability and Statistics with Tables.** 2nd edition. New York: McGraw-Hill, 1970. xiv + 462p. Out of print. ISBN 0-07-009030-0.

Ready reference source for basic formulas, definitions, specialized tables, and more.

Buss, Samuel R., ed. **Handbook of Proof Theory.** New York: Elsevier, 1998. 811p. (Studies in Logic and the Foundations of Mathematics; 137). $161.00. ISBN 0-444-89840-9.

Self-contained, in-depth, detailed expository articles cover a broad spectrum of proof theory, with an emphasis on its mathematical aspects. Considered a successor to the proof theory part of Barwise's **Handbook of Mathematical Logic** (above).

E Chambers, Lance, ed. **Practical Handbook of Genetic Algorithms.** Boca Raton, FL: CRC Press, 1995–2001. 3 vols. + 1 computer disk. Vol. I. Applications. 2nd edition. 555p. $79.95. ISBN 1-58488-240-9. Vol. II.

New Frontiers. 435p. $79.95. ISBN 0-8493-2529-3. Vol. III. Complex Coding Systems. 592p. $84.95. ISBN 0-8493-2539-0. Also available online. For information see: http://www.mathnetbase.com/. Subscription.

The first two volumes of this three-volume set deal with new research and an overview of the types of applications that could be taken with genetic algorithms. The final volume concentrates on specific functions in genetic algorithms, thus serving as a compilation of useful and usable computer code (downloadable from the CRC Web site). Bibliography.

Champeney, D. C. **Handbook of Fourier Theorems.** New York: Cambridge University Press, 1989. xi + 185p. $28.95 pa. ISBN 0-521-36688-7 pa.

For professionals familiar with Fourier theory and applications who want more-detailed knowledge.

Ciarlet, P. G. and J. L. Lions, eds. **Handbook of Numerical Analysis.** Amsterdam: North-Holland, 1990– . Vol. I. **Finite Difference Methods (Part 1). Solutions of Equations in Rn (Part 1).** viii + 652p. Out of print. ISBN 0-444-70366-7. Vol. II. **Finite Element Methods (Part 1).** x + 928p. Out of print. ISBN 0-444-70365-9. Vol. III. **Techniques of Scientific Computing (Part 1). Numerical Methods for Solids (Part 1). Solution of Equations in Rn (Part 2).** ix + 778p. $180.00. ISBN 0-444-89928-6. Vol. IV. **Finite Element Methods (Part 2). Numerical Methods for Solids (Part 2).** x + 974p. $348.00. ISBN 0-444-81794-8. Vol. V. **Techniques of Scientific Computing (Part 2).** x + 818p. $315.00. ISBN 0-444-82278-X. Vol. VI. **Numerical Methods for Solids (Part 3). Numerical Methods for Fluids (Part 1).** x + 689p. $164.00. ISBN 0-444-82569-X. Vol. VII. **Solution of Equations in Rn (Part 3). Techniques of Scientific Computing (Part 3).** x + 1020p. $183.50. ISBN 0-444-50350-1. Vol. VIII. **Solution of Equations in Rn (Part 4), Techniques of Scientific Computer (Part 4), Numerical Methods for Fluids (Part 2).** 650p. $131.00. ISBN 0-444-50906-2. Vol. IX: **Numerical Methods for Fluids (Part 3).** 1,080p. $190.00. ISBN: 0-444-51224-1. Vol. X: **Special Volume: Computational Chemistry.** 898p. $170.00. ISBN: 0-444-51248-9. Vol. XI: **Special Volume: Foundations of Computational Mathematics.** 536p. $140.00. ISBN: 0-444-51247-0. Vol. XII: **Computational Models for the Human Body.** 676p. $215.00. ISBN: 0-444-51566-6.

This series thoroughly surveys numerical analysis with mathematical rigor.

S Cohen, A. Clifford. **Truncated and Censored Samples: Theory and Applications.** New York: M. Dekker, 1991. xiv + 312p. (Statistics, Textbooks and Monographs; 119). $150.00. ISBN 0-8247-8447-2.

Intended as a handbook for practitioners who need simple and efficient methods for the analysis of incomplete data. Numerous brief examples and lots of results.

Colbourn, Charles J. and Jeffrey H. Dinitz, eds. **The CRC Handbook of Combinatorial Designs.** Boca Raton, FL: CRC Press, 1996. xviii + 753p. $109.95. ISBN 0-8493-8948-8.

This comprehensive, easy-to-access reference contains over 1,050 tables, 900 theorems, and 850 definitions—everything one needs on combinatorial designs from experimental design to cryptography.

S Coleman, Shirley, et al. **The Pocket Statistician: A Practical Guide to Quality Improvement.** London; New York: Arnold; Wiley, 1996. 252p. + 1 computer disk. $29.95 pa. ISBN 0-34067721-X pa.

A practical guide to the use of statistics in industry, that is, what methods can do and how they do it.

Coleman, Thomas F. and Charles Van Loan. **Handbook for Matrix Computations.** Philadelphia, PA: SIAM, 1988. vii + 264p. $34.00 pa. ISBN 0-89871-227-0 pa.

Technical work for those doing scientific computations using matrices.

E **Collected Algorithms from ACM.** New York: Association for Computing Machinery, 1978– . 4 vols. + quarterly supplements. Looseleaf. $425.00 for four back volumes. $120.00 for each year's quarterly supplements. ISBN 0-89791-017-6 (Vol. 1); 0-89791-026-5 (Vol. 2); 0-89791-103-2 (Vol. 3); 0-89791-297-7 (Vol. 4). ISSN 0149-1989. Also available at: http://www.acm.org/calgo/contents/. Free.

Highly recommended for mathematical research collections, this is a compilation of algorithms published in **ACM Transactions on Mathematical Software** (1975–) and other ACM titles. Entries list identifying title of algorithm, source, author, institutional address, certification status of the algorithm, and remarks. Algorithms numbered 493 and above, plus some earlier ones, can be downloaded from the Web site. Use the browser Find function to search by algorithm name.

Conway, J. H., et al. **Atlas of Finite Groups: Maximal Subgroups and Ordinary Characters for Simple Groups.** Oxford; New York: Clarendon Press, 1985. xxxiii + [252]p. Out of print. ISBN 0-19-853199-0.

An official collection of character tables and related information about many finite simple groups. For a later, related title see Jansen (below).

D'Agostino, Marcello, et al., eds. **Handbook of Tableau Methods.** Dordrecht, Holland; Boston: Kluwer Acad. Publ., 1999. viii + 670p. $297.00. ISBN 0-7923-5627-6.

The first systematization of this expanding field, from the use of tableaux methods in classical logic to extensive discussions on: the uses of the methodology in intuitionistic logics, modal and temporal logics, nonmonotonic and many-valued logics, and substructural logics.

De Boor, Carl. **Practical Guide to Splines.** New York: Springer-Verlag, 2001. xxiv + 392p. (Applied Mathematical Sciences; 27). $59.95. ISBN 0-387-95366-3.

Reprint of 1978 original, which was based on De Boor's experience with calculations involving polynomial splines. Topical arrangement in 17 chapters covering theory to application, with 120-plus example problems and 106 references.

S Der, Geoff and Brian S. Everitt. **A Handbook of Statistical Analyses Using SAS.** Boca Raton, FL: Chapman & Hall/CRC Press, 2002. xi + 360p. 2nd edition. $41.95 pa. ISBN 1-58488-245-X pa.

This introduction to the use of SAS is intended for professionals and students in applied statistics courses. Updated to support SAS Version 8.1. See also Rabe-Hesketh and Everitt's **A Handbook of Statistical Analyses Using Stata.** 2nd edition (below).

Dershowitz, Nachum and Edward M. Reingold. **Calendrical Calculations.** New York: Cambridge University Press, 1997. xxi + 307p. $69.95. ISBN 0-521-56413-1.

Presents in a unified, completely algorithmic form, a description of 14 calendars and how they relate to one another.

Dillen, F. J. E. and L. C. A. Verstraelen, eds. **Handbook of Differential Geometry.** Amsterdam: Elsevier, 2000– . Volume I. xi + 1054p. $177.50. ISBN 0-444-82240-2.

First in a series of volumes intended to give a complete survey of the field of differential geometry, containing both expository papers and self-contained research surveys.

Dodson, C. T. J. and Phillip E. Parker. **A User's Guide to Algebraic Topology.** Dordrecht, Holland; Boston: Kluwer Acad. Publ., 1997. xii + 405p. (Mathematics and Its Applications; 387). $72.50 pa. ISBN 0-7923-4293-3 pa.

Covers extension and lifting problems, homotopy, cohomology, and obstruction theory; many proofs referenced.

Du, Ding-Zhu and Panos M. Pardalos. **Handbook of Combinatorial Optimization.** Boston: Kluwer Acad. Publ., 1998. 3 vols. $1,325.00 (set). ISBN 0-7923-5019-7.

Brings together several algorithmic approaches for discrete problems as well as with many combinatorial problems. Scholarly treatment of expository material in each chapter.

Du, Ding-Zhu and Panos M. Pardalos. **Handbook of Combinatorial Optimization: Supplement. Volume A.** Dordrecht, Holland; Boston: Kluwer Acad. Publ., 1999. viii+ 648p. $262.00. ISBN 0-7923-5924-0.

Nine survey articles on mathematical and algorithmic aspects of several discrete optimization problems.

S Dudewicz, Edward J. and Thomas G. Ralley. **Handbook of Random Number Generation and Testing with TESTRAND Computer Code.** Columbus, OH: American Sciences Press, 1981. xi + 634p. (American Series in Mathematical and Management Sciences; 4). $195.00. ISBN 0-935950-01-X.

Designed as a quality test of random number generators.

Ershov, Yu. L., et al., eds. **Handbook of Recursive Mathematics.** Amsterdam; New York: Elsevier, 1998. 2 vols. xlvi + 1372p. (Studies in Logic and the Foundations of Mathematics; 138-139). $258.50. ISBN 0-444-50107-X (set). Vol. 1. **Recursive Model Theory.** xlvi + 620p. $129.50. ISBN 0-444-50003-0. Vol. 2. **Recursive Algebra, Analysis and Combinatorics.** xlvi + p.623–1372. $158.00. ISBN 0-444-50106-1.

Scholarly overview and up-to-date account. Provides brief summaries of the papers.

Fanchi, John R. **Math Refresher for Scientists and Engineers.** 2nd edition. New York: J. Wiley, 2000. xiii + 308p. $34.95 pa. ISBN 0-471-38457-7 pa.

A concise and practical reference intended for people with technical backgrounds who need to brush up on their math skills.

Fillmore, Peter A. **A User's Guide to Operator Algebras.** New York: Wiley, 1996. xii + 223p. $99.95 pa. ISBN 0-471-31135-9 pa.

This book makes recent developments in operator algebras accessible to the nonspecialist.

E Finch, Steven. *MathSoft Constants.* MathSoft Engineering & Education, 2001–2003. Available at: http://www.mathcad.com/library/constants/index.htm. Free.

This Web site, arranged by broad topics, links to a growing collection of essays on mathematical constants from various mathematical subdisciplines.

Floudas, Christodoulos A., et al. **Handbook of Test Problems in Local and Global Optimization.** Dordrecht, Holland; Boston: Kluwer Acad. Publ., 1999. xv + 441p. (Nonconvex Optimization and Its Applications; 33). $225.00. ISBN 0-7923-58-1-5.

A collection of problems that can be used for benchmarking. Drawn from applications in engineering and applied sciences.

E Furman University. *Mathematical Quotations Server.* No copyright given. Available at: http://math.furman.edu/~mwoodard/mquot.html. Free.

This collection can be searched by keyword, Perl expression, or by author.

Gardiner, C. W. **Handbook of Stochastic Methods for Physics, Chemistry, and the Natural Sciences.** 2nd edition. Berlin; New York: Springer-Verlag, 1996. xx + 442p. (Springer Series in Synergetics; 13). $53.95 pa. ISBN 3-540-61634-9 pa.

Reprint of 1985 original. Covers stochastic methods frequently used by theoretical physicists and chemists. Restricted to Markov processes with diffusions as focus. This edition adds material with recent progress in stochastic methods taken into account.

S Ghosh, B. K. and P. K. Sen, eds. **Handbook of Sequential Analysis.** New York: Dekker, 1991. xv + 637p. (Statistics, Textbooks and Monographs; 118). $215.00. ISBN 0-8247-8408-1.

Over 30 statisticians describe all major developments in sequential analysis through 1990.

Gieck, Kurt and Reiner Gieck. **Engineering Formulas.** 7th edition. Translated by J. Walters. New York: McGraw-Hill, 1997. 1 vol. (in various pagings). $23.96. ISBN 0-07-024572-X.

Engineer's desk reference that is also good for fieldwork because of its small size. Covers most mathematical formulas and tables necessary to the practice of engineering. Highly recommended for any technically oriented collection.

Goodman, Jacob E. and Joseph O'Rourke, eds. **Handbook of Discrete and Computational Geometry.** Boca Raton, FL: CRC Press, 1997. xvi + 991p. $99.95. ISBN 0-8493-8524-5.

Authors gather together into one volume all the major results in both these fields. The material is presented clearly enough to assist the novice, but in enough depth to appeal to the specialist.

Goossens, Michel, Frank Mittelbach, and Alexander Samarin. **The LaTeX Companion.** Reading, MA: Addison-Wesley, 1994. xxx + 528p. $37.95 pa. ISBN 0-201-54199-8 pa.

This advanced guide to LaTeX2e can be used with Lamport's **LaTeX** (below). Essential for serious users of LaTeX.

Goossens, Michel, Sebastian Rahtz, and Frank Mittelbach. **The LaTeX Graphics Companion: Illustrating Documents With TeX and PostScript.** Reading, MA: Addison-Wesley, 1997. xxv + 554p. $39.95 pa. ISBN 0-201-85469-4 pa.

This handy reference describes techniques and tricks needed to illustrate LaTeX documents, and answers common user questions about graphics and PostScript fonts.

Goossens, Michel and Sebastian Rahtz. **The LaTeX Web Companion: Integrating TeX, HTML, and XML.** Reading, MA: Addison Wesley Longman, 1999. xxii + 522p. $36.95 pa. ISBN 0-201-43311-7 pa.

Authors describe tools and techniques for transforming LaTeX sources into Web formats for electronic publication and for transforming Web sources into LaTeX documents for optimal printing.

Gould, Sydney H. and R. P. Boas, eds. **Manual for Translators of Mathematical Russian.** Revised edition. Providence, RI: American Mathematical Society, 1991. ix + 42p. $21.00. ISBN 0-8218-0172-4.

Suggestions on translating Russian mathematics. Applicable to related sciences as well.

Gould, S. H. **Russian for the Mathematician.** New York; Berlin: Springer-Verlag, 1972. xi + 211p. $69.95 pa. ISBN 0-387-05811-7 pa.

A textbook of Russian prepared for mathematicians. It covers alphabet, pronunciation, inflection, aspect, and vocabulary. Includes a generous selection of readings.

Graham, R. L., M. Grötschel, and L. Lovász, eds. **Handbook of Combinatorics.** Cambridge, MA: MIT Press, 1995. 2 vols. $355.00 (set). ISBN 0-262-07169-X. Vol. 1. cii + 1,018p. ISBN 0-262-07170-3. Vol. 2. cii + 1,177p. ISBN 0-262-07171-1.

Comprehensive overview of the present state of combinatorics, organized into sections on structures, methods, and applications.

Griffor, Edward R. **Handbook of Computability Theory.** Amsterdam; New York: Elsevier, 1999. xii + 727p. (Studies in Logic and the Foundations of Mathematics; 140). $149.50. ISBN 0-444-89882-4.

This book selectively reviews recent research directions of computability theory. Each chapter contains articles by recognized authorities.

S Griliches, Zvi and Michael D. Intriligator, eds. **Handbook of Econometrics.** Amsterdam; New York: Elsevier Science, 1983–1994. 4 vols. Vol. I. xxvii + 771p. Out of print. ISBN 0-444-86185-8. Vol. II. xxvi + 686p. Out of print. ISBN 0-444-86186-6. Vol. III. xxv + p.1466–2107. $110.00. ISBN 0-444-86187-4. Vol. IV. xxvi + p.2112–3155. $123.00. ISBN 0-444-88766-0.

Multivolume survey of econometrics is intended to serve as a reference and teaching supplement. The impressive range of topics covered includes mathematical and statistical methods and time series.

Gruber, P. M. and J. M. Wills, eds. **Handbook of Convex Geometry.** Amsterdam; New York: North-Holland, 1993. 2 vols. $359.00 (set). ISBN 0-444-89598-1. Vol. A. ix + 735p. + lxvi. $196.50. ISBN 0-444-89596-5. Vol. B. xi + 699p. + lxvi. $189.50. ISBN 0-444-89597-3.

Experts have written substantial chapters on convex geometry, its many ramifications, and its relations with other areas of mathematics.

S Härdle, W., S. Klinke, and M. Müller. **XploRe—Learning Guide.** Berlin; New York: Springer, 2000. 526p. $48.00. ISBN 3-540-66207-3.

This comprehensive handbook to XploRe is intended for beginners in computer-aided statistical data analysis.

Harris, John W. and Horst Stöcker. **Handbook of Mathematics and Com-**

putational Science. New York: Springer-Verlag, 1998. xxviii + 1,028p. $34.95. ISBN 0-387-94746-9.

This comprehensive collection of commonly used definitions, facts, formulas, tables, and techniques includes numerical and analytic techniques and a brief introduction to several computer-programming languages.

S Harter, H. Leon and N. Balakrishnan. **CRC Handbook of Tables for the Use of Order Statistics in Estimation.**
See above, in **Tables** section of this chapter.

Hastings, Harold M. and George Sugihara. **Fractals: A User's Guide for the Natural Sciences.** New York: Oxford University Press, 1993. xii + 235p. $29.95 pa. ISBN 0-19-854597-5 pa.

This treatment of mathematics of fractals and modeling patterns includes case studies and user-ready programs.

Hazewinkel, M., ed. **Handbook of Algebra.** Amsterdam; New York: Elsevier, 1996– . Vol. 1. xix + 915p. $200.00. ISBN 0-444-82212-7. Vol. 2. xix + 878p. $177.50. ISBN 0-444-50396-X. Vol. 3. 1036p. $195.00. ISBN: 0-444-51264-0.

This multivolume handbook in progress is intended to provide professional mathematicians with information on topics outside their own areas. Each volume covers a number of topics as articles are published and received. Each article includes primary information and refers the reader to relevant articles, books, and lecture notes. Excellent detailed indexing.

Hildenbrand, Werner and Hugo Sonnenschein, eds. **Handbook of Mathematical Economics.**
See Arrow and Intriligator, eds. **Handbook of Mathematical Economics** (above).

Horst, Reiner and Panos M. Pardalos, eds. **Handbook of Global Optimization.** Dordrecht, Holland; Boston: Kluwer Acad. Publ., 1995. xvii + 880p. (Nonconvex Optimization and Its Applications; 2). Out of print. ISBN 0-7923-3120-6.

This comprehensive book covers recent developments in global optimization, including stochastic and deterministic approaches, and suboptimal algorithms. Each contribution in the handbook is essentially expository in nature, but scholarly in its treatment.

Hu, Shouchuan and Nikolas Papageorgiou. **Handbook of Multivalued Analysis.** Dordrecht, Holland; Boston: Kluwer Acad. Publ., 1997–2000. (Mathematics and Its Applications; 419, 500). Vol. I. **Theory.** xv +964p. $395.00. ISBN 0-7923-4682-3. Vol. II. **Applications.** xi + 926p. $395.00. ISBN 0-7923-6164-4.

This two-volume self-contained exposition provides a comprehensive survey on the theory and applications of set-valued maps.

Ibragimov, N. H., ed. **CRC Handbook of Lie Group Analysis of Differential Equations.** Boca Raton, FL: CRC Press, 1994–1995. Vol. 1. **Symmetries, Exact Solutions, and Conservation Laws.** xiii + 429p. $131.95. ISBN 0-8493-4488-3. Vol. 2. **Applications in Engineering and Physical Sciences.** xviii + 546p. $149.50. ISBN 0-8493-2864-0. Vol. 3. **New Trends in Theoretical Developments and Computational Methods.** xvi + 536p. $125.00. ISBN 0-8493-9419-8.

An up-to-date sourcebook on the application of Lie group methods.

Jackson, J. Edward. **A User's Guide to Principal Components.** New York: John Wiley & Sons, 1991. xvii + 569p. $175.00. ISBN 0-471-62267-2.

A practical rather than theoretical text intended primarily for practitioners of multivariate analysis.

James, I. M., ed. **Handbook of Algebraic Topology.** Amsterdam; New York: Elsevier Science, 1995. x + 1,324p. $222.00. ISBN 0-444-81779-4.

For the reader with some prior knowledge who wishes to know more about the research frontiers.

Jansen, Christoph, et al. **An Atlas of Brauer Characters.** Oxford; New York: Clarendon Press; Oxford University Press, 1996. xvii + 327p. (London Mathematical Society Monographs. New Series; 11). $85.00. ISBN 0-19-851481-6.

A major reference resource for pure mathematicians working in group theory and its applications. Considered a sequel to the **Atlas of Finite Groups** (see Conway above).

Jeffrey, Alan. **Handbook of Mathematical Formulas and Integrals.** 2nd edition. San Diego, CA: Academic Press, 2000. xxvi + 433p. $49.95 pa. ISBN 0-12-382251-3 pa.

Covers formulas, functions, relations and methods from trigonometric and exponential functions, and algebra. Provides information that helps simplify the solution of a problem.

Korn, Granino Arthur and Theresa M. Korn. **Mathematical Handbook for Scientists and Engineers: Definitions, Theorems, and Formulas for Reference and Review.** 2nd edition, enlarged and revised. New York: McGraw-Hill, 1968. xvii + 1,130p. $112.00. ISBN 0-07-035370-0.

Covers mathematical definitions, theorems, and formulas for professionals and students. Efficient format: important formulas and definitions are boxed; topical reviews are in large print, and discussion and advanced topics are in smaller print.

Koziol, James A., ed. **CRC Handbook of Percentage Points of the Inverse Gaussian Distribution.** Boca Raton, FL: CRC, 1989. 300p. $159.00. ISBN 0-8493-3626-0.

The handbook has a detailed introduction with references to support the tables that take up the remainder of the book.

Krantz, Steven G. **Handbook of Complex Variables.** Boston: Birkhäuser, 1999. xxiv + 290p. $59.95 pa; $99.00. ISBN 0-8176-4011-8 pa; 3-7643-4011-8.

A self-contained and comprehensive reference work for scientists and engineers who need to know and use essential information and methods involving complex variables and analysis.

Kuipers, L. and R. Timman, eds. **Handbook of Mathematics.** Translated by I. N. Sneddon. New York: Pergamon, 1969. xi + 782p. (International Series of Monographs in Pure and Applied Mathematics; 99). Out of print. ISBN 0-08-011857-7.

This classic handbook of general mathematics includes comprehensive coverage of all major divisions plus history of mathematics.

Kunen, Kenneth and Jerry E. Vaughan, eds. **Handbook of Set-Theoretical Topology.** Amsterdam; New York: North-Holland, 1984. vii + 1,273p. $463.00. ISBN 0-444-86580-2.

Collection of 24 papers reflecting contemporary thought on the subject.

Lamport, Leslie. **LaTeX: A Documentation Preparation System User's Guide and Reference Manual.** 2nd edition. Reading, MA: Addison-Wesley, 1994. xvi + 272p. $36.95 pa. ISBN 0-201-52983-1 pa.

This definitive guide and reference manual to LaTeX has been revised in response to users' suggestions and to document features available in the software release LaTeX2e. See Goossens (above).

Lawrence, J. Dennis. **Catalog of Special Plane Curves.** New York: Dover, 1972. xi + 218p. $9.80 pa. ISBN 0-486-60288-5 pa.

Illustrates some special plane algebraic and transcendental curves with brief descriptions.

Ledermann, Walter, chief ed. **Handbook of Applicable Mathematics.** Chichester, England: Wiley, 1980–1991. 8 vols. Vol. I. **Algebra.** Ledermann, W. and S. Vajda, eds. xix + 524p. $395.00. ISBN 0-471-27704-5. Vol. II. **Probability.** Lloyd, Emlyn, ed. xix + 450p. Out of print. ISBN 0-471-27821-1. Vol. III. **Numerical Methods.** Churchhouse, Robert F., ed. xvii + 565p. Out of print. ISBN 0-471-27947-1. Vol. IV. **Analysis.** Ledermann, W. and S. Vajda, eds. xxiii + 865p. Out of print. ISBN 0-471-10141-9. Vol. V. Part A. **Combinatorics and Geometry.** Ledermann, W. and S. Vajda, eds. xvii + 327pp + xix-xxiii. Out of print. ISBN 0-471-90567-4. Vol. V. Part B. **Combinatorics and Geometry.** Ledermann, W. and S. Vajda, eds. xvii + p.329–732 + xix–xxiii. Out of print. ISBN 0-471-90568-2. Vol. VI. Part A. **Statistics.** Lloyd, Emlyn, ed. xxi + 498p. +A1–43 + xxiii–xviii. Out of print. ISBN 0-471-90274-8. Vol. VI. Part B. **Statistics.** Lloyd, Emlyn, ed. xix + p.499–942 + A1–43 + xxi–xxvi. Out of print. ISBN 0-471-90272-1. [Vol. VII]. **Supplement.** Ledermann, W., et al., eds. xix + 479p. Out of print. ISBN 0-471-91825-3. [Vol. VIII]. **Contents and General Index.** ix + 125p. $129.95. ISBN 0-471-92792-9.

Quality reference set focuses on practical and applied mathematics. Authoritative, readable articles include bibliographies.

E Lide, David R., ed. **CRC Handbook of Chemistry and Physics.** 84th edition. Boca Raton, FL: CRC Press, 2003. 2,664p. $139.95. ISBN 0-8493-0483-0. Also available online. For information see: http://www.hbcpnetbase.com. Subscription.

E Lide, David R., ed. **CRC Handbook of Chemistry and Physics.** CD-ROM version based on 84th edition. Boca Raton, FL: Chapman & Hall/CRC Press, 2003. ISBN 0-8493-1556-5. $199.95.

The essential reference tool for physical data. Every year, material is critically evaluated, new data is added, and existing tables are updated.

S Linton, Marigold and Philip S. Gallo, Jr. **The Practical Statistician: Simplified Handbook of Statistics.** Monterey, CA: Brooks/Cole, 1975. vii + 384p. Out of print. ISBN 0-8185-0127-8.

A useful guide to using statistics as a research tool, this book enables its users to determine what analysis is appropriate and also shows how to do the computations.

E Liu, John and Murray R. Spiegel. **Mathematical Handbook of Formulas and Tables.** New York: McGraw-Hill, 1999. viii + 278p. (Schaum's Outline Series). $12.76 pa. ISBN 0-07-038203-4 pa. Also available online. For information see: http://www.netlibrary.com. $23.17.

A collection of formulas and tables most likely to be needed by the practitioner.

Mackerle, J. and C. A. Brebbia, eds. **Boundary Element Reference Book.** Boston: Computational Mechanics, 1988. viii + 382p. $77.00. ISBN 0-931-21567-6.

Covers topics for previous 10 years.

Maim, Donald G. **A Computer Laboratory Manual for Number Theory.** Wentworth, NH: COMPress, 1980. viii + 256p. Out of print. ISBN 0-933694-13-X.

Should be a standard reference text for every number theory enthusiast.

Marichev, O. I. **Handbook of Integral Transforms of Higher Transcendental Functions.** Chichester, England: Ellis Horwood; New York: John Wiley & Sons, 1983. 336p. Out of print. ISBN 0-85312-528-7.

Presents method of calculating integrals from special functions including theory and tables of formulas.

MathSci User Guide. 2nd edition. Providence, RI: American Mathematical Society, 1990. Various pagings (loose-leaf). Out of print.

This is a manual developed for users of the **MathSci** online (not *MathSciNet*) database. In addition to the usual searching instructions, aids, and appendixes that are somewhat out of date, it contains a handy cross-reference table of Library of Congress call numbers and MSC subject classifications.

E *MathSciNet—Mathematical Reviews on the Web: Guiding You Through the Literature of Mathematics.* Providence, RI: American Mathematical

Society, [2000]. Available in paper from the AMS or on the Web as a PDF file at: http://www.ams.org/msnhtml/guidebook.pdf. Free.
For complete entry, see **Chapter 2, Finding Tools**.

McCleary, John. **User's Guide to Spectral Sequences.** 2nd edition. New York: Cambridge University Press, 2000. xv + 561p. (Cambridge Studies in Advanced Mathematics; 58). $34.95 pa. ISBN 0-521-56759-9 pa.
Divided into three parts: Algebra, Topology, and Sins of Omission. This edition contains a new chapter on the Bockstein spectral sequence and updated treatment of other topological sequences. An excellent reference for researchers in algebra, geometry, and topology.

Micula, Gheorghe and Sandra Micula. **Handbook of Splines.** Dordrecht, Holland; Boston: Kluwer Acad. Publ., 1999. xvi + 604p. (Mathematics and Its Applications; 462). $297.00. ISBN 0-7923-5503-2.
An up-to-date survey of the theory of spline functions and some of their applications.

Mitrinovic, D. S., J. Sándor, and B. Crstici. **Handbook of Number Theory.** Dordrecht, Holland; Boston: Kluwer Acad. Publ., 1996. xxvi + 622p. (Mathematics and Its Applications; 351). $316.00. ISBN 0-7923-3823-5.
This comprehensive handbook covers a wide range of topics, with special attention being given to estimates and inequalities. The most important results are presented, together with their refinements, extensions, or generalizations. Cross-references provide new insight into fundamental research.

Monk, J. Donald and Robert Bonnet, eds. **Handbook of Boolean Algebras.** Amsterdam; New York: North-Holland, 1989. 3 vols. Vol. 1. xix + 323p. $213.00. ISBN 0-444-70261-X. Vol. 2. xix + 415p. $195.75. ISBN 0-444-87152-7. Vol. 3. xix + 650p. Out of print. ISBN 0-444-87153-5.
This treatment of those areas of the theory of Boolean algebras of most interest to pure mathematicians also includes detailed discussions of the major developments in the theory of Boolean algebras that have occurred over the last quarter century since Sikorski's 1964 **Boolean Algebras.**

Moon, P. and D. E. Spencer. **Field Theory Handbook.** 2nd edition, corrected 3rd printing. New York: Springer-Verlag, 1988. viii + 236p. Out of print. ISBN 0-387-18430-9.

Compilation of equations for those working in field. Tabulates properties of 40 coordinate systems with Laplace and Helmholtz equations and separation equations and their solutions.

Moré, Jorge J. and Stephen J. Wright. **Optimization Software Guide.** Philadelphia, PA: Society for Industrial and Applied Mathematics, 1993. xii + 154p. (Frontiers in Applied Mathematics; 14). $31.00 pa. ISBN 0-89971-322-6 pa.

This compact, well-researched guide for graduate students and researchers familiar with optimization problems is divided into two parts: a brief discussion of several algorithms for different classes of optimization problems and exhaustive information on some of the most widely used optimization software, vendors, and individual researchers in the field.

Moritz, Robert Edouard. **Memorabilia Mathematica: The Philomath's Quotation Book.** Washington, DC: Mathematical Association of America, 1993. xiii + 410p. $29.95 pa. ISBN 0-88385-513-5 pa.

Reprint of the 1914 compilation of 1,140 anecdotes, aphorisms, and passages by famous mathematicians, scientists, and writers. Companion volume to **Out of the Mouths of Mathematicians** (see Schmalz, below).

Mortenson, Michael E. **Computer Graphics Handbook: Geometry and Mathematics.** New York: Industrial Press, 1990. xii + 259p. $29.95 pa. ISBN 0-8311-1002-3 pa.

Though there is no discussion of computer hardware and software or even the central issues relating to computer displays, this is a good reference book on geometry and mathematics.

E National Institute of Standards and Technology. *Digital Library of Mathematical Functions*. NIST, no copyright except where marked, under development, 2003. Available at: http://dlmf.nist.gov/. Free.

This site is being developed as an authoritative replacement for Abramowitz and Stegun's **Handbook of Mathematical Functions** (above). Most content will be provided by NIST. The new DLMF intends to "present not only static data but also . . . made-to-order dynamic information such as graphs, tables of numerical values, and symbolic transformations."

E National Institute of Standards and Technology. *Guide to Available Mathematical Software [GAMS]*. Not copyrighted except where marked, NIST, 2003. Available at: http://gams.nist.gov. Free.

This site provides access to computer software for use in mathematical modeling and statistical analysis. An online cross-index of available mathematical software is included, as is transparent access to abstracts, documentation, and source code of software modules in outside repositories.

S Patel, Jagdish K., C. H. Kapadia, and D. B. Owen. **Handbook of Statistical Distributions.** New York: Dekker, 1976. xiv + 302p. Out of print. ISBN 0-318-35010-6.

Source for most frequently used distributions by statisticians. References to most are available but are not necessarily original sources. Emphasis on practical results.

S Patel, Jagdish K. and Campbell B. Read. **Handbook of the Normal Distribution**. 2nd edition, revised and expanded. New York: Dekker, 1996. ix + 431p. (Statistics, Textbooks and Monographs; 150). $150.00. ISBN 0-824-79342-0.

This fully updated second edition presents a comprehensive treatment of the normal and bivariate normal distributions and their sampling statistics—introducing state-of-the-art estimation procedures for normally distributed samples. Intended for research or applications of statistical methodology. References.

Peterson's Math Review for the GRE, GMAT, and MCAT. 2nd edition. Australia; United States: Peterson's, 2003. 314p. $16.95 pa. ISBN 0-7689-1323-3 pa.

A useful, effective, and comprehensive book enables the reader to focus on and improve specific mathematics skills in order to pass any of these three exams.

Polianin, Andrei D. and Alexander V. Manzhirov. **Handbook of Integral Equations.** Boca Raton, FL: CRC Press, 1998. 787p. $109.95. ISBN 0-8493-2876-4.

An in-depth compendium contains more than 2,100 integral equations with solutions as well as exact, approximate analytical and numerical methods for solving linear and nonlinear integral equations.

S Pollard, J. H. **Handbook of Numerical and Statistical Techniques with Examples Mainly from the Life Sciences.** Cambridge; New York: Cambridge University Press, 1981. xvi + 349p. Out of print. ISBN 0-521-21440-8; 0-521-29750-8.

Easily used handbook of statistics and statistical techniques with examples from life sciences.

Prudnikov, A. P., IU. A. Brychkov, and O. I. Marichev. **Integrals and Series.** Translated by N.M. Queen and G. G. Gould. New York: Gordon and Breach Science, 1986–1992. Vol. 1. **Elementary Functions.** 798p. Out of print. ISBN 2-88124-089-5. Vol. 2. **Special Functions.** 750p. Out of print. ISBN 2-88124-090-9. Vol. 3. **More Special Functions.** 800p. $293.00. ISBN 2-88124-682-6. Vol. 4. **Direct Laplace Transforms.** $279.00 ISBN 2-88124-837-3. Vol. 5. **Inverse Laplace Transforms.** $279.00. ISBN 2-88124-838-1.

This is basically a photo-offset of **Integraly i Riady** with a small amount of translation added. Many of the results were obtained by the authors and are being published for the first time. Intended for specialists and students.

S Rabe-Hesketh, Sophia and Brian Everitt. **A Handbook of Statistical Analyses Using Stata.** 2nd edition. Boca Raton, FL: Chapman & Hall/CRC, 2000. 210p. $39.95 pa. ISBN 1-58488-201-8 pa.

Explains the features of the latest version of Stata. Beginners get a head start on using the program and experienced users are provided a quick reference. See also Der and Everitt's **A Handbook of Statistical Analyses Using SAS** (above).

Råde, Lennert and Bertil Westergren. **Mathematics Handbook for Science and Engineering.** 4th edition. Berlin; New York: Springer, 1999. 546p. $49.95. ISBN 3-540-65569-7.

Comprehensive, well-illustrated handbook presents classical areas of mathematics as well as areas of current interest. Concentrates on definitions, results, formulas, graphs, and tables. Extensive, thoroughly cross-referenced index lists over 1,400 terms. Appendix has portraits of famous mathematicians.

S Rao, C. R., general ed. **Handbook of Statistics.** Amsterdam; New York: North-Holland, Elsevier 1980– . Vol. 1. **Analysis of Variance.** Krishnaiah, P. R., ed. xvii + 1002p. $238.55. ISBN 0-444-85335-9. Vol. 2. **Classification, Pattern Recognition, and Reduction of Dimensionality.** Krishnaiah, P. R. and L. N. Kanal, eds. xxii + 903p. $232.00. ISBN 0-444-86217-X. Vol. 3. **Time Series in the Frequency Domain.** Brillinger, D. R. and P. R. Krishnaiah, eds. xiv + 485p. $213.00. ISBN 0-444-86726-0. Vol. 4.

Nonparametic Methods. Krishnaiah, P. R. and P. K. Sen, eds. xx + 968p. $249.50. ISBN 0-444-86871-2. Vol. 5. **Time Series in the Time Domain.** Hannan, E. J., P. R. Krishnaiah, and M. M. Rao, eds. xiv + 490p. $213.00. ISBN 0-444-87629-4. Vol. 6. **Sampling.** Krishnaiah, P. R. and C. R. Rao, eds. xvi + 594p. $231.50. ISBN 0-444-70289-X. Vol. 7. **Quality Control and Reliability.** Krishnaiah, P. R. and C. R. Rao, eds. xiv + 503p. $228.50. ISBN 0-444-70290-3. Vol. 8. **Statistical Methods in Biological and Medical Sciences.** Rao, C. R. and R. Chakraborty, eds. xvi + 554p. $203.00. ISBN 0-444-88095-X. Vol. 9. **Computational Statistics.** Rao, C. R., ed. xix + 1045p. $228.00. ISBN 0-444-88096-8. Vol. 10. **Signal Processing and Its Applications.** Bose, N. K. and C. R. Rao, eds. xvii + 992p. $228.00. ISBN 0-444-89205-2. Vol. 11. **Econometrics.** Maddala, G. S., C. R. Rao, and H. D. Vinod, eds. xx + 783p. $215.50. ISBN 0-444-89577-9. Vol. 12. **Environmental Statistics.** Patil, G. P. and C. R. Rao, eds. xix + 927p. $228.00. ISBN 0-444-89803-4. Vol. 13. **Design and Analysis of Experiments.** Ghosh, S. and C. R. Rao, eds. xviii + 1229p. $217.00. ISBN 0-444-82061-2. Vol. 14. **Statistical Methods in Finance.** Maddala, G. S. and C. R. Rao, eds. xvi + 733p. $196.50. ISBN 0-444-81964-9. Vol. 15. **Robust Inference.** Maddala, G. S. and C. R. Rao, eds. xvii + 698p. $205.00. ISBN 0-444-82172-4. Vol. 16. **Order Statistics: Theory & Methods.** Balakrishnan, N. and C. R. Rao, eds. xviii + 731p. $175.00. ISBN 0-444-82091-4. Vol. 17. **Order Statistics: Applications.** Balakrishnan, N. and C. R. Rao, eds. xviii + 712p. $175.00. ISBN 0-444-82922-9. Vol. 18. **Bioenvironmental and Public Health Statistics.** Sen, P. K. and C. R. Rao, eds. xxiv + 1105p. $190.00. ISBN 0-444-82900-8. Vol. 19. **Stochastic Processes: Theory and Methods.** Shanbhag, D. N. and C. R. Rao, eds. xvii + 967p. $175.00. ISBN 0-444-50014-6. Vol. 20. **Advances in Reliability.** Balakrishnan, N. and C. R. Rao, eds. 886p. $175.00. ISBN: 0-444-50078-2. Vol. 21. **Stochastic Processes: Modeling and Simulation.** Shanbhag, D.N. and C. R. Rao, eds. $175.00. 1,020p. ISBN: 0-444-50013-8. Vol. 22. **Statistics in Industry.** Khattree, R. and C.R. Rao, eds. $175.00. 1,204p. ISBN: 0-444-50614-4. Vol. 23. **Advances in Survival Analysis.** Balakrishnan, N. and C. R. Rao, eds. $175.00. 1,000p. ISBN: 0-444-50079-0.

This excellent series provides comprehensive and up-to-date surveys of recent developments in a broad range of statistics. Articles are written at a level intended for use by professional researchers and advanced graduate students.

Redfern, Darren. **The Maple Handbook: Maple V Release 4.** New York: Springer-Verlag, 1996. 495p. $35.95 pa. ISBN 0-387-94538-5 pa.

A complete and well-referenced listing of every command in the Maple language categorized into logical categories and explained in the context of those categories with pointers to appropriate sections of the official Maple documentation. This approach enhances the material found in its online help files as it provides a much more organized, intuitive resource.

Redfern, Darren and Colin Campbell. **The MATLAB 5 Handbook.** New York: Springer-Verlag, 1998. xi + 488p. $29.95 pa. ISBN 0-387-94200-9 pa.

This reference work is organized by problem category. Entries give command name, parameters, hints, and cross-references.

Ritter, Gerhard X. and Joseph N. Wilson. **Handbook of Computer Vision Algorithms in Image Algebra.** 2nd edition. Boca Raton, FL: CRC Press, 2001. 417p. $99.95. ISBN 0-8493-0075-4.

Describes more than 80 fundamental computer vision techniques, explaining each technique's purpose and methodology, providing the mathematical formulation of each methodology, and introducing the portable iac++ library. The second edition adds two chapters on compression techniques and on geometric manipulation/spatial transformation.

Rosen, Kenneth H., ed. **Handbook of Discrete and Combinatorial Mathematics.** Boca Raton, FL: CRC Press, 2000. 1,232p. $99.95. ISBN 0-8493-0149-1.

A comprehensive reference to all the important areas of discrete mathematics. Features examples of terms and concepts, summary tables, references to print and nonprint resources, and biographical sketches of important figures.

Sachdev, P. L. **A Compendium on Nonlinear Ordinary Differential Equations.** New York: J. Wiley, 1997. xi + 918p. $142.00. ISBN 0-471-53134-0.

Information on closed form solutions, asymptotics, stability, existence, and numerical results.

Sack, J. R. and J. Urrutia, eds. **Handbook of Computational Geometry.** Amsterdam; New York: Elsevier, 2000. x + 1,027p. $190.50. ISBN 0-444-82537-1.

A comprehensive source of information on the fundamental techniques and tools.

Schmalz, Rosemary. **Out of the Mouths of Mathematicians: A Quotation Book for Philomaths.** Washington, DC: Mathematical Association of America, 1993. x + 294p. $34.95 pa. ISBN 0-88385-509-7 pa.

Companion to Moritz's **Memorabilia Mathematica** (above), with up-to-date quotes.

S Sheskin, David J. **Handbook of Parametric and Nonparametric Statistical Procedures.** 2nd edition. Boca Raton, FL: Chapman & Hall/CRC Press, 2000. 982p. $119.95. ISBN 1-58488-133-X.

Practical information on about 100 statistical procedures and tests, showing how to pick the best, interpret the results, and evaluate others' research.

Shikin, Eugene V. **Handbook and Atlas of Curves.** Boca Raton, FL: CRC Press, 1995. xiv + 545p. $94.95. ISBN 0-8493-8963-1.

In-depth description of available analytic and visual properties of plane and spatial curves. Main definitions, formulas, and facts from curve theory are presented in one half of the book and the other half is devoted to the Atlas of Plane Curves, consisting of nearly 200 plane curve classes, more than 700 figures, and nearly 2,000 drawings of specific curves.

Shikin, Eugene V. and Alexander I. Plis. **Handbook on Splines for the User.** Boca Raton, FL: CRC Press, 1996. xii + 221pp + 1 computer disk. $69.95. ISBN 0-8493-9404-X.

This book describes spline functions and geometric splines and provides an excellent introduction to basic concepts and methods as well as simple, but effective algorithms. Also includes the SplineGuide—a computer diskette that allows the reader to practice using programs to build interpolating and smoothing cubic and bicubic splines of all classes.

Sloane, N. J. A. **A Handbook of Integer Sequences.** New York: Academic Press, 1973. xiii + 206p. Out of print. ISBN 0-12-648550-X.

Most of this book is a table of 2,300 sequences, arranged in lexicographic order, each accompanied by a brief description and a reference to the literature. For a later edition, see Sloane's *On-Line Encyclopedia of Integer Sequences* in **Chapter 4, Dictionaries and Encyclopedias**.

Spanier, Jerome and Keith B. Oldham. **Atlas of Functions.** Washington, DC: Hemisphere, 1987. ix + 700p. $105.00. ISBN 0-89116-573-8.

This basic reference tool is a vital rethinking of the old-fashioned handbook of mathematical tables. Presents information on families of functions incorporating definitions, expansions, and computer-generated graphs.

E *Sparknotes: Math Study Guides*. SparkNotes LLC, 1999-2003. Available at: http://www.sparknotes.com/math/. Free.

This site has over 100 study guides to subjects ranging from pre-algebra to calculus. Useful for undergraduates.

Spivak, M. D. **The Joy of TeX: A Gourmet Guide to Typesetting with the AMS-TeX Macro Package.** 2nd edition. Providence, RI: American Mathematical Society, 1990. xxii + 309p. $39.00 pa. ISBN 0-8218-2997-1 pa.

This definitive guide to AMS-TeX is probably a better introduction for novices than Knuth's **TeXbook** (see **Chapter 8, Mathematics Books for Science Collections**), because Spivak does not attempt to explain everything. Corresponds to changes in Version 2.1 of the AMS-TeX macro package.

S Spurrier, John D., Don Edwards, and Lori A. Thombs. **Elementary Statistics Laboratory Manual: MS-DOS Version.** Belmont, MA: Duxbury Press, 1995. ix + 325p. $37.95 pa. ISBN 0-534-23604-9 pa.

Clear, detailed instructions for 17 labs with PC-Minitab. Macintosh version also available.

Sydsæter, Knut, Arne Strøm, and Peter Berck. **Economists' Mathematical Manual.** 3rd revised and enlarged edition. Berlin; New York: Springer-Verlag, 1999. xi + 206p. $29.95. ISBN 3-540-65447-X.

Presents mathematical formulas and theorems common to economics, including those like Roy's identity that are peculiar to economics and those like Leibniz's rule that are common to many areas of applied mathematics.

E Tallarida, Ronald J. **Pocketbook of Integrals and Mathematical Formulas.** 3rd edition. Boca Raton, FL: CRC Press, 1999. 280p. $22.00. ISBN 0-8493-0263-3. Also available online. For information see: http://www.crcpress.com/default.asp. Subscription.

Easy-to-use information on integrals, derivatives, series, and statistics. One of the features is a comprehensive table of integrals arranged and formatted to facilitate the rapid location of the right form. This edition contains a new chapter on business and financial mathematics.

Thompson, William J. **Atlas for Computing Mathematical Functions: An Illustrated Guide for Practitioners, With Programs in C and Mathematica.** New York: Wiley, 1997. xiv + 903p. +1 computer laser optical disk. $180.00. ISBN 0-471-00260-7.

Offers a consistent approach to visualizing and computing over 150 special functions of mathematics. The CD-ROM, readable by both Windows and Macintosh, provides complete C source programs for each function described and parts of the notebooks for generating test values for them and over 700 graphics of the functions from many viewpoints. Another set (not reviewed) does the same for programs in FORTRAN 90 and Mathematica.

Tuma, Jan H. and Ronald A. Walsh. **Engineering Mathematics Handbook.** 4th edition. New York: McGraw-Hill, 1998. ix + 566p. $84.95. ISBN 0-07-065529-4.

Standard desk reference for engineering and mathematics arranged in parts by type of mathematics covered. Individual parts include definitions, basic concepts, and advanced concepts. The fourth edition features new material on cubic and quartic equations, standard curves and their analytical equations, and maxima and minima equations. Glossary of mathematical terms.

Von Seggern, David H. **CRC Handbook of Mathematical Curves and Surfaces.** Boca Raton, FL: CRC, 1990. 286p. Out of print. ISBN 0-8493-0155-6.

Pictures of families of functions on right-hand pages, facing displays of formulas with relevant parameters: algebraic curves, transcendental functions, orthogonal and non-orthogonal polynomials, special functions (e.g., Legendre, Bessel), probability densities, catastrophe curves, spirals and helices, algebraic and transcendental surfaces, and nondifferentiable curves and surfaces (including polygons and polyhedra).

Von Seggern, David. **CRC Standard Curves and Surfaces.** Boca Raton, FL: CRC Press, 1993. 388p. $94.95. ISBN 0-8493-0196-3.

Based on his **Handbook** (above), this is a comprehensive illustrated catalog of curves and surfaces of geometric figures and algebraic, transcendental, and integral equations used in elementary and advanced mathematics. New material on functions of random processes and functions of complex variable surfaces added in this edition.

E Von Seggern, David. **CRC Standard Curves and Surfaces: A Mathematica® Notebook User's Guide.** Boca Raton, FL: CRC Press, 1993. 1 computer disk + 6p. $73.95 pa. ISBN 0-8493-0761-9 pa.

Software designed to be an interactive tool for plotting desired equations or mathematical figures.

Von Seggern, David. **PHB Practical Handbook of Curve Design and Generation.** Boca Raton, FL: CRC Press, 1994. ix + 267p. $89.95. ISBN 0-8493-8916-X.

A ready reference presents the basic mathematics of curves in a complete, clear manner that enables the reader to apply the material with minimum effort. A treatment of the mathematical transformation of curves gives the reader a general approach for modifying known curves. Later chapters introduce complex curves and cover interesting ideas in space curves and in surfaces.

S Wadsworth, Harrison M., Jr., ed. **Handbook of Statistical Methods for Engineers and Scientists.** 2nd edition. New York: McGraw-Hill, 1998. 1 vol. (in various pagings). $99.95. ISBN 0-07-067678-X.

Updated edition is a good first reference for engineers. Emphasis on quality control. Twenty sections begin with basic statistics and include survey sampling, Bayesian analysis, experimental design, robust and nonparametric methods, and time series.

S E *Web Pages That Perform Statistical Calculations! (StatPages.net).* No copyright, updated 1/07/2004. Available at: http://members.aol.com/johnp71/javastat.html. Free.

Also known as *Interactive Statistical Calculation Pages*, this is a lengthy, but searchable, Web site.

Williams, Robert. **The Geometrical Foundation of Natural Structure: A Source Book of Design.** New York: Dover, 1979. xv + 265p. $14.95 pa. ISBN 0-486-23729-X pa.

Corrected reprint of 1972 **Natural Structure.** Provides a detailed resource of theoretical information for tessellations, packings, and arrangements for designers, scientists, and engineers.

Wolfram, Stephen. **The Mathematica Book.** 4th edition. Champaign, IL; New York: Wolfram Media; Cambridge University Press, 1999. xxvi + 1470p. $49.95. ISBN 0-521-64314-7.

E Wolfram, Stephen. *The Mathematica Book*. 4.2 edition. Wolfram Research, Inc., 2004. Available at: http://documents.wolfram.com/v4/index3.html. Free.

Based on Version 4.2 of Mathematica, this edition of the "definitive" user guide provides an extensive example-based survey of Mathematica behavior. Organized so the reader needs to learn only the part needed for a particular calculation. Full reference guide and a thorough explanation of system design. Web version has internal links.

E *Wolfram Research's Mathematical Functions.* Wolfram Research, 1998–2004. Available at: http://functions.wolfram.com/. Free.

This encyclopedic site for over 37,000 mathematical functions is arranged hierarchically and interlinked so one may search by names, formulas, or a unique citation number. Functions are available in Mathematica StandardForm for use within Mathematica documents, in MathML for use in Web documents, and in ASCII form.

Zayed, Ahmed I. **Handbook of Function and Generalized Function Transformations.** Boca Raton, FL: CRC Press, 1996. xxii + 643p. $84.95. ISBN 0-8493-7851-6.

Provides quick and easy access to the most important and widely used properties and formulas of function transforms (classical plus the newer transforms, e.g., wavelets, Zak, and Radon) in applied mathematics and electrical engineering.

E Zwillinger, Daniel. **Handbook of Differential Equations.** 3rd edition. San Diego, CA: Academic Press, 1998. xxiii + 801p. $69.95. ISBN 0-12-784396-5. Book and companion CD-ROM. $99.95. ISBN 0-12-784395-7.

Describes the most widely used techniques for solving and approximating both ordinary and partial differential equations. This compilation is outstanding in terms of comparison and description, number of methods compared, and its organization.

Zwillinger, Daniel. **Handbook of Integration.** Boston: Jones and Bartlett, 1992. xv + 367p. $69.00. ISBN 0-86720-293-9.

Divided into five sections: applications of integration; concepts and definitions; exact techniques; approximate techniques; and numerical techniques. Each method is followed by examples and several current references to the literature.

Writing Guides

Day, Robert A. **How to Write and Publish a Scientific Paper.** 5th edition. Phoenix, AZ: Oryx Press, 1998. xvi + 275p. $24.50 pa. ISBN 1-573-56165-7 pa.

A witty cookbook approach based on the author's experience. This edition has been revised extensively to reflect the impact of the Internet and other electronic resources on the writing and publishing of scientific papers.

Day, Robert A. **Scientific English: A Guide for Scientists and Other Professionals.** 2nd edition. Phoenix, AZ: Oryx Press, 1995. xii + 148p. $23.75 pa. ISBN 0-89774-989-8 pa.

This succinct, practical, and amusing guide shows scientists and technical writers how to clearly, simply, and accurately communicate complex scientific concepts. Highly recommended.

Derricourt, Robin. **An Author's Guide to Scholarly Publishing.** Princeton, NJ: Princeton University Press, 1996. ix + 233p. $15.16 pa. ISBN 0-691-03709-4 pa.

The author uses a series of informal letters to provide much practical advice from information about the ins and outs of scholarly publishing to being the kind of author with whom scholarly publishers enjoy working.

Gillman, Leonard. **Writing Mathematics Well: A Manual for Authors.** Washington, DC: Mathematical Association of America, 1987. ix + 49p. $10.00 pa. ISBN 0-88385-443-0 pa.

Compact manual covers basics of organization, presentation, and usage in preparation of manuscripts. Good outline of fundamentals. Bibliography.

Harnack, Andrew and Eugene Kleppinger. **Online! A Reference Guide to Using Internet Resources**. New York: St. Martin's, 2001. xi + 260p. $12.50 pa. ISBN 0-312-40068-3.

E Harnack, Andrew and Eugene Kleppinger. *Online! A Reference Guide to Using Internet Resources*. Bedford's/St. Martin's, 2003. Available at: http://www.bedfordstmartins.com/online/. Free.

This primer on doing research on the Internet covers finding, using, evaluating, and citing resources. The Web site offers free access to Chapters 5–8 on various citation style guides.

Higham, Nicholas J. **Handbook of Writing for the Mathematical Sciences.** 2nd edition. Philadelphia, PA: Society for Industrial and Applied Mathematics, 1998. xvi + 302p. $34.00 pa. ISBN 0-89871-420-6 pa.

Revision provides more information on the issues involved in writing a technical paper or talk. Author explains such aspects as choosing the right journal in which to publish a technical paper, handling references, writing English as a second language, and revising a draft. New chapters include TeX and LaTeX typesetting software and writing and defending a thesis. An excellent resource.

Knuth, Donald E., Tracy Larrabee, and Paul M. Roberts. **Mathematical Writing.** Washington, DC: Mathematical Association of America, 1989. 128p. (MAA Notes; 14). $21.00 pa. ISBN 0-88385-063-X pa.

Candid lecture notes full of good advice on mathematical writing, literate programming, publication, and refereeing. An indispensable aid for those teaching a course in technical writing or for those who wish to understand the art of mathematical writing.

Krantz, Steven G. **Handbook of Typography for the Mathematical Sciences.** Boca Raton, FL: Chapman & Hall/CRC: 2001. xv + 173p. $39.95 pa. ISBN 1-5848-8149-6 pa.

Explains how to use TeX, LaTeX, and AMS TeX during the typesetting process so the readers can ensure their work is properly represented in print.

Krantz, Steven G. **Primer of Mathematical Writing : Being a Disquisition on Having Your Ideas Recorded, Typeset, Published, Read & Appreciated.** Providence, RI: American Mathematical Society, 1997. xv + 223p. $20.00 pa. ISBN 0-8218-0635-1 pa.

Highly recommended reading on fundamentals of writing in mathematics.

Luey, Beth. **Handbook for Academic Authors.** 3rd edition. Cambridge; New York: Cambridge University Press, 1995. xviii + 312p. $14.36 pa. ISBN 0-521-49892-9.

Common-sense guide covers a variety of subjects, from choosing a publisher to submitting a journal article. Revised and updated throughout to refect the state of new technologies and their meaning to authors. Includes a new chapter on writing nonfiction. Good annotated bibliography on dictionaries, style manuals, grammar guides, and related works.

A Manual for Authors of Mathematical papers. 8th revised edition. Providence, RI: American Mathematical Society, 1990. 21p. Free. ISBN 0-8218-0022-1.

Covers mechanical aspects, not intellectual content. Useful in preparation of papers in form acceptable to the AMS.

Mittelbach, Frank et al. **The LaTeX Companion.** 2nd edition. xxvii + 1,090p. + 1 CD-ROM. Boston: Addision-Wesley, 2004. $59.99. ISBN 0-201-36299-6.

There are nearly 50 books on LaTeX. This is a new edition of one of the more popular ones.

Steenrod, Norman E., et al. **How to Write Mathematics.** Providence, RI: American Mathematical Society, 1981. 64p. $17.00. ISBN 0-8218-0055-8.

Reprint of 1973 guide covers approaches to exposition, specifically for research monographs and textbooks. Three short essays by Paul Halmos Steenrod and Menchen M. Schiffer on how they individually approach writing.

Swanson, Ellen. **Mathematics into Type; Copy Editing and Proofreading of Mathematics for Editorial Assistants and Authors.** Updated edition. Providence, RI: American Mathematical Society, 1999. x + 102p. $24.00 pa. ISBN 0-8218-1961-5 pa.

Technical details of publishing mathematics manuscripts from copy editors' perspectives. Glossary, bibliography, and index.

E Syropoulos, Apostolos, Antonis Tsolomitis, and Nick Sofroniou. **Digital Typography Using LaTeX.** New York: Springer, 2003. xxix + 510p. + 1 CD-ROM. $44.95 pa. ISBN 0-387-95217-9. Also available at: http://www.netLibrary.com/urlapi.asp?action=summary&v=1&bookid=98886. $69.67. ISBN 0-585-47345-5.

Walker, Janice R. and Todd W. Taylor. **The Columbia Guide to Online Style**. New York: Columbia Press, 1998. xv + 218p. $35.00. ISBN 0-231-10788-9. $17.50 pa. ISBN 0-231-10789-7 pa.

E Walker, Janice R. and Todd W. Taylor. *[Columbia Guide to Online Style:] Basic CGOS Style*. Columbia University Press, 2002. Available at: http://www.columbia.edu/cu/cup/cgos/idx_basic.html. Free.

More comprehensive than other style manuals for Internet resources. The Web version offers brief excerpts from the book explaining citation needs and differences for various types of online resources.

6
Directories and Department Guides

E *2000 National Doctoral Program Survey.* Copyright not given. Available at: http://survey.nagps.org/. Free.

The National Association of Graduate-Professional Students, an organization "dedicated to improving the quality of graduate and professional student life and education," released this survey in fall 2001. Results are based on ratings given by 32,000 U.S. graduate students and recent PhDs. Over 50 math, applied math, and statistics departments are rated.

S E *ASA JobWeb.* American Statistical Association, no copyright given. Available at: http://www.amstat.org/jobweb/index.cfm. Free.

Statistics job site for both job seekers and employers.

E *ASA Membership Directory.* American Statistical Association, 2004. Available at: http://www.amstat.org/membersearch/index.cfm. Free.

S E American Statistical Association. **Directory of Members.** Alexandria, VA: American Statistical Association, 1981– . Irregular. xxvii + 413p. $165.00. ISBN 1-8883276-02-0. Also available as a CD-ROM, 1999.

The 1999 paper and CD-ROM versions include the ASA constitution, past and present officers, and membership listings. Only members who have agreed to be in the online directory will be found there.

E Assistantships and Graduate Fellowships in the Mathematical Sciences. Providence, RI: American Mathematical Society, 1988– . Annual. xii + 112p. $21.00/yr. ISSN 1040-7650. PDF version of 2003 available on the Web (without ads) at: http://www.ams.org/employment/asst.pdf. Free.

A source of information on graduate programs in the United States and Canada, this includes addresses of departments, names of chairpersons, and useful facts about graduate programs, including stipends, fees, and service required for assistantships. Departmental URLs are included.

S Bernoulli Society and the Institute of Mathematical Statistics. **1999 Joint Directory of Members**. Hayward, CA: Institute of Mathematical Statistics, 1999. 148p. ISBN 0-940600-45-5.

Includes constitutions, past and present officers, and membership listings for these societies.

Combined Membership List: American Mathematical Society, American Mathematical Association of Two-Year Colleges, Association for Women in Mathematics, Mathematical Association of America, Society for Industrial and Applied Mathematics. Providence, RI: American Mathematical Society. 1956– . Annual. viii + 304p. $68.00/yr. (Nonmembers); $54.00/yr. (Institutional Members). ISSN 0569-6461.

E *Combined Membership List (CML)*. American Mathematical Society, 2004. Updated daily. Available at: http://www.ams.org/cml. Free.

This title includes over 54,000 individual members' listings plus listings for institutions and other categories of members. The Web version is searchable and includes e-mail addresses and home pages.

E American Men & Women of Science. 21st edition. New York: Thomson/Gale, 2003. 8 vols. $975.00 (set). ISBN 0-7876-6523-1. Also available from netLibrary as an e-book. $1,070.00. ISBN: 0-7876-7698-5.

This title has short biographical information on over 129,000 distinguished scientists who live in North America. The eighth volume lists scientists by field and by state under field. Useful for biographical details such as current position and address, field, education, birth date and place, awards and honorary degrees, and professional and career information. Useful for information on lesser-known mathematicians and statisticians. Gale's database, *Biography and Genealogy Master Index,* also cites to entries in present and past editions of **American Men & Women of Science**.

Employment Information in the Mathematical Sciences. Providence, RI: American Mathematical Society, 1978– . 5/yr. $185.00. ISSN 0163-3287.

E *Employment Information in the Mathematical Sciences (EMIS)*. American Mathematical Society, 2004. Updated daily. Available at: https://

www.ams.org/eims/. Free. AMS members may subscribe to free e-mail listings.

This employment register provides information on open positions alphabetically by state/province with an index by name of institution. Most are academic positions. Users may browse the Web version by date posted or search by institution, employer type, type of position, subject, geographical location, or keyword.

Gourman, Jack. **The Gourman Report: A Rating of Graduate and Professional Programs in American and International Universities.** 8th edition, revised. Biennial. New York: Random House, 1997. xii + 302p. $21.95. ISSN 1049-717X.

Out-of-date and often criticized for its lack of identifiable criteria and methodology, this does a comparative rankings of American graduate programs. Mathematics is 1 of 47 American programs rated. Discussion of how rankings were obtained is included.

Guidebook to Departments in the Mathematical Sciences in the United States and Canada. 6th edition. Washington, DC: Mathematical Association of America, 1975. 99p. Out of print.

In three parts, this directory provides summary information on location, size, staff, library facilities, course offerings, and special features for four-year colleges and PhD-granting universities. U.S. departments arranged alphabetically by state; Canadian by institution. Occasionally useful even though very out-of-date. **Assistantships and Graduate Fellowships in the Mathematical Sciences** (above) now provides some of same information.

Jaguszewski, Janice M., ed. **Recognizing Excellence in the Mathematical Sciences: An International Compilation of Awards, Prizes, & Recipients.** Greenwich, CT: JAI Press, 1997. xix + 275p. (Foundations in library and information science, v. 41.) $82.50. ISBN 0-7623-0235-6.

Enlarges and expands Voelker's **Prizes in Mathematics** (below). International in scope, this compilation of over 100 awards, honors, and prizes through 1995 is an essential reference work. Following each entry is a list of sources consulted, many of which refer to Web sites with additional information. Indexes to sponsoring bodies, recipients, and subjects.

Mathematical Sciences Professional Directory. Providence, RI: American Mathematical Society, 1983– . Annual. 233p. $35.00. ISSN 0737-4356.

Covers structure, boards, and committees of AMS and associated professional associations with addresses for organizational officers. Academic institutions are listed by state with key personnel and telephone numbers. Provides addresses of publishers and editors of mathematical journals. Index of colleges and universities.

E *Mathematics Web sites Around the World.* Penn State Mathematics Department, no date given. Available at: http://www.math.psu.edu/MathLists/Contents.html. Free.

This well-kept Web site lists links to academic mathematics departments, societies, and institutes around the world. The site is useful for tracking down researchers, their e-mail addresses, and their papers.

E *MathJobs.Org.* American Mathematical Society, no copyright given. Available at: https://www.mathjobs.org/jobs. Free.

This is an automated job application system for applicants and employers in advanced mathematics. Service is free for job applicants.

E *Math-Net: Persona Mathematica.* University of Cologne, Mathematisches Institut, 2003. Available at: http://www.mi.uni-koeln.de/Math-Net/persona_mathematica/. Free.

Worthwhile project to gather and provide information about mathematicians such as names, addresses, home pages, and fields of interest. Institutions are asked to provide meta-data information to Math-Net. Link to list of societies' membership directories included.

May, Kenneth O. and Laura Roebuck, eds. **World Directory of Historians of Mathematics.** Toronto, ON: Historia Mathematica, 1972– . 2nd edition, 1978. Irregular. Price not available. ISSN 0315-1700.

Alphabetical listing of scholars working in history of mathematics. Entries include names, mailing addresses, and fields of interest. Indexed by subjects and countries.

The National Faculty Directory. Detroit, MI: Gale Research Co., 1970– . $784.00, including supplements. Annual. ISSN 0077-4472.

Alphabetical list of nearly 600,000 teaching faculty at the colleges and universities of North America. An excellent source for locating mathematicians not found in the **Combined Membership List** (above).

E National Research Council. Committee for the Study of Research-Doctorate Programs in the United States. **Research-Doctorate Programs in the United States: Continuity and Change.** Edited by Marvin L. Goldberger, Brendan A. Maher, and Pamela Ebert Flattau. Washington, DC: National Academy of Sciences, 1995. xiv + 740p. $69.95. ISBN 0-309-05094-4. An executive summary and downloadable data tables are available on the Web at: http://www.nap.edu/readingroom/books/researchdoc. Free.

Comprehensive study and ranking of U.S. doctoral programs in all subjects. Rankings can aid students looking for graduate programs or administrators looking for comparative data. Reputation rating data is based on subjective survey.

Peterson's Graduate Programs in the Physical Sciences, Mathematics, Agricultural Sciences, the Environment & Natural Resources. Princeton, NJ: Peterson's Guides, 1998– . Annual. 38th edition, 2003 latest published, vii + 1072p. $49.95. ISBN 0-7689-1144-3.

E *Thomson/Peterson's Graduate Program Search*. Peterson's, 2004. Available at: http://www.petersons.com/GradChannel/code/search.asp? Free.

Peterson's guides provide a general overview of graduate education, a directory of institutions having programs, and details of particular academic and professional programs. The Web version leads one to a listing of departments, but further information is only found in their paper product.

E *PhDs.org Science, Math, and Engineering Career Resources*. PhDs.org, 1998–2004. Available at: http://www2.phds.org/. Free.

This site is packed with links for budding graduate students and beyond. Its *Rank Graduate Programs* page (http://www2.phds.org/rankings/) allows users to customize their searches for a graduate program based on the 1994 National Research Council data. Includes rankings for both mathematics and statistics/biostatistics departments.

S E *StatLib—Web Links*. Carnegie Mellon University, Department of Statistics, no copyright given. Available at: http://lib.stat.cmu.edu/modules.php?op=modload&name=Web_Links&file=index. Free.

Among *StatLib*'s many links are the over 450 links to academic statistics departments and societies around the world. The site is convenient for tracking down researchers, their e-mail addresses, and their papers.

S Statistical Services Directory. 2nd edition. Detroit, MI: Gale, 1984. 461pp. $200.00. ISBN 0-8103-0668-9.

This is a "guide to organizations, corporations, professional and trade associations, research centers, universities, publishers, foundations, and goverment agencies that provide statistical services." There is also information on statistical serial publications.

Voelker, Margie L. **Prizes in Mathematics.** Minneapolis: University of Minnesota, 1986. 24 leaves. (Mathematics Report. University of Minnesota, School of Mathematics. 85–139.) Out of print.

List of awards and their winners. Individual awards entries include sponsor, eligibility, field, type of award, frequency, information source, recipients. Separate index by winners noting award and year. See Jaguszewski (above) for a more up-to-date and expanded version of this work.

E World Directory of Mathematicians. Princeton, NJ: International Mathematical Union 1958–2002). Final volume is 12th edition. Available from American Mathematical Society, Providence, RI. $70.00 (list); $56.00 (members). ISSN 0512-2740. To be superceded by *Electronic World Directory of Mathematicians (EWDM)*. International Mathematical Union, no copyright given. Available at: http://www.mathunion.org/ewdm/. Free.

The final edition includes over 57,000 names of people who have published at least two articles reviewed by **Mathematical Reviews**, **Zentralblatt Math**, or **Referentivnyi Zhurnal** in the preceding five years. Postal addresses, e-mail, fax numbers, and sometimes title and affiliation are included. Geographical listings give names only. The electronic version depends on voluntary submissions. Over 600 names are there currently.

E The World of Learning. London: Europa Publications, 1947– . $598.00. Annual. ISSN 0084-2117. Also available online. Information at: http://www.worldoflearning.com/. Subscription.

The most comprehensive and timely international directory of colleges and universities and other learned institutions. Latest edition has more than 30,000 institutions arranged alphabetically by country. Also listings for 200,000 key academic staff and professors and more than 400 international organizations concerned with education.

S E *World Wide Web Virtual Library: Statistics.* University of Florida, Department of Statistics, no copyright given. Available at: http://www.stat.ufl.edu/vlib/. Free.

Regularly updated list of statistics departments, institutes, and societies around the world.

7
Biographical and Historical Materials

Reference Resources

E Association for Women in Mathematics. *Links for Biographies*. AWM, 2004. Available at: http://www.awm-math.org/biographies.html. Free.

Nice collection of articles on contemporary women mathematicians. Most drawn from AWM materials.

Aull, C. E. and R. Lowen, eds. **Handbook of the History of General Topology.** Dordrecht, Holland; Boston: Kluwer Acad. Publ., 1997–2001. Vol. 1. ix + 397p. $194.50. ISBN 0-7923-4479-0. Vol. 2. ix + p.399–808. $173.00. ISBN 0-7923-5030-8. Vol. 3. ix + p.809–1221. $124.00. ISBN 0-7923-6970-X.

Traces the historical development of the field from personal recollections of the founders of topology at the beginning of the twentieth century. Contributions deal with individual topologists, specific schools of topology, particular periods of development, or specific topics. Index. Bibliography.

Bailey, Martha J. **American Women in Science: A Biographical Dictionary.** Santa Barbara, CA: ABC-CLIO, 1994. xxi + 463p. $73.50. ISBN 0-874-36740-9.

Eighteen of the 400 concise biographies of women scientists who began their careers before 1950 are about mathematicians. Most are relatively obscure.

Biographical Dictionary of Mathematicians: Reference Biographies from the Dictionary of Scientific Biography. New York: Scribner, 1991. 4 vols. vii + 2,696p. Out of print. ISBN 0-684-19282-9 (set).

The set includes the full text (including drawings and bibliographies) of entries of mathematicians in **Dictionary of Scientific Biography** including **Supplements I** and **II**. Articles sketch the life and work of 1,019 mathematicians worldwide from antiquity to modern times. Appendixes: listing of mathematicians by branch, chronology, and index.

E *Biographies of Women Mathematicians.* Agnes Scott College, 1995–2003. Available at: http://www.agnesscott.edu/lriddle/women/women.htm. Free.

This actively developed site covers women in mathematics from its beginnings to current times. Articles usually feature pictures, text, and a list of references. The site also includes a list of other resources on women mathematicians and scientists, a list of prizes won by women mathematicians, and a list of universities and colleges in the United States and Canada that granted the PhD in mathematics to women before 1930.

Bogoliubov, Aleksei Nikolaevich. **Matematiki Mekhaniki: Biograficheskii Spravochnik.** Kiev: Naukova Dumka, 1983. 637p. Out of print.

This contains brief biographies in Russian of 1,500 scholars who contributed to mathematics or mechanics. Photographs, a chronology of major events in both fields, a bibliography, and an index to persons are included.

Boncompagni, B., ed. **Bullettino di Bibliografia e di Storia della Scienze Matematiche e Fisiche.**

For complete entry, see in **Chapter 1, Bibliographic Resources**.

Borodin, A. I. and A. S. Bugai, eds. **Biograficheskii Slovar' Deiatelei v Oblasti Matematiki.** Kiev: Radians'ka Shkola, 1979. 607p. Out of print.

Over 2,000 short biographies in Russian including illustrations, an index, and a bibliography.

Borodin, A. I. and A. S. Bugai. **Vydaiushchiesia Matematiki: Biograficheskii Slovar'-Spravochnik.** Kiev: Radians'ka shkola, 1987. 653p. Out of print.

Short biographies. International coverage, but with emphasis on Soviet mathematicians. Includes bibliographical references and indexes.

Dass, B. K., ed. **Mathematics: Who's Who.** New Delhi: Analytic, 1984. ii + 187p. Out of print.

Collection of some 350 short biographies of "active" mathematicians worldwide. Most of the entries include a photograph.

Dauben, Joseph W. **The History of Mathematics from Antiquity to the Present: A Selective Bibliography.** New York: Garland, 1985. xxxix + 508p. (Bibliographies of the History of Science and Technology, 6). (Garland Reference Library of the Humanities, 313). Out of print. ISBN 0-8240-9284-8.

Annotated bibliography of 2,384 sources in history of mathematics. Arranged by broad categories.

E Dauben, Joseph W., ed. **The History of Mathematics from Antiquity to the Present: A Selective Annotated Bibliography.** Revised edition on CD-ROM. Edited by Albert C. Lewis in cooperation with the International Commission on the History of Mathematics. Providence, RI: American Mathematical Society, 2000. $49.00. ISBN 0-8218-0844-3.

This electronic version updates Dauben's **The History of Mathematics from Antiquity to the Present: A Selective Bibliography** (above). Forty-eight hundred items are listed. This well-done reference work has a user-friendly interface and is well organized. There is a useful section of annotated Web resources; the user can link directly to the Web resource.

De Morgan, Augustus. **Arithmetical Books from the Invention of Printing to the Present Time: Being Brief Notices of a Large Number of Works Drawn Up from Actual Inspection.**

For complete entry, see **Chapter 1, Bibliographic Resources**.

E *ECHO, Exploring and Collecting History Online, Virtual Center, Science & Technology*. [George Mason University], Center for History and New Media, 2001. Available at: http://echo.gmu.edu/center/. Free.

This site has taken over the well-regarded *WWW Virtual Library History of Science, Technology & Medicine* site, refreshed it, and added to its links. The listing for history of mathematics includes 114 annotated descriptions of sites.

E *Erdös Number Project*. 2004. Available at: http://www.oakland.edu/~grossman/erdoshp.html. Free.

This fascinating site is the mathematicians' six degrees of separation project. If a researcher has an Erdös number of one, that person collaborated directly with Paul Erdös on one or more papers. A person with an Erdös number of two collaborated with an Erdös collaborator, but not with Erdös himself and so on.

E *Eric Weisstein's World of Scientific Biography.* Eric W. Weisstein and Wolfram Research, Inc., 2004. Available at: http://scienceworld.wolfram.com/biography/. Free.

Like Weisstein's other sites, this site is handy for quick reference. The majority of the over 1,000 biographies are for mathematicians and physicists. Most are short and link to an explanation of the person's contribution to his or her field. One can search by discipline, gender, minority status, scientific families, historical period, and nationality. References for further reading are listed and linked.

Extrait du Bulletin signalétique. Histoire des sciences et des techniques.

Bulletin signalétique. 22, Histoire des sciences et des techniques.

Bulletin signalétique. 522, Histoire des sciences et des techniques.

Fauvel, John. **Mathematics Through History: A Resource Guide.** York, England; QED Books, 1990. 47p. Price not available. ISBN 0-946544-71-9.

Annotated bibliography of approximately 250 books and a few videos to support the study of history of mathematics at all levels. Includes many British titles not well known in the United States.

Francis bulletin signalétique. 522, Histoire des sciences et des techniques. Nancy, France: Institut de l'information scientifique et technique, 1946?–1994. ISSN 1157-3724.

Indexes a wide range of journals for articles and book reviews on the history of science. Entries have short annotations and are arranged by subject and period. Annual cumulative subject and author indexes.

Friberg, Jöran. **An Annotated Bibliography of Works on Babylonian Mathematics.** Göteburg, Sweden: Department of Mathematics, Chalmers University of Technology, 1980. 18p. Price not available.

A comprehensive work on the subject.

Gottwald, Siegfried, Hans Joachim Ilgauds, and Karl Heinz Schlote, eds. **Lexikon Bedeutender Mathematiker.** Leipzig: Bibliographisches Institut, 1990. 504 + [3]p.; 8p. of plates. $27.35. ISBN 3-8171-1164-9.

Short biographies in German of more than 1,600 mathematicians worldwide from ancient times to the present.

Grattan-Guinness, I., ed. **Companion Encyclopedia of the History and Philosophy of the Mathematical Sciences.** London; New York: Routledge, 1994. 2 vols. xiii + 1806p. $330.00 (set). ISBN 0-415-03785-9 (set).

This is the first comprehensive work to cover the principal developments and themes in the history and philosophy of mathematics from ancient times up to the twentieth century. One hundred seventy-six articles describe and analyze the variety of theories, proofs, techniques, and cultural and practical applications of mathematics. Also covers the history of higher education in mathematics and the growth of institutions and organizations connected with the development of the field. In two parts: mathematics in various ancient and non-Western cultures from antiquity up to medieval and Renaissance times and developments in the main areas of mathematics.

Grinstein, Louise S. and Paul J. Campbell, eds. **Women of Mathematics: A Biobibliographic Sourcebook.** Westport, CT: Greenwood, 1987. xx + 292p. $78.50. ISBN 0-313-24849-4.

A well-done work profiling 43 women born before 1925 who made contributions of note to the field of mathematics. Each entry includes a biography, summary of work, and bibliography of works by and about the individual.

E *History of Mathematics.* Maintained by David E. Joyce, 1994–1998. Available at: http://babbage.clarku.edu/~djoyce/mathhist/. Free.

This site is primarily a series of bibliographies on the history of mathematics by topic and by region. Source books, textbooks, journals, bibliographies, and catalogs are listed.

E *History of Science, Technology, and Medicine.* History of Science Society, Society for the History of Technology, Istituto e Museo di Storia della Scienza, and The Wellcome Trust, 2003. Information available at: http://www.rlg.org/en/page.php?Page_ID=192. Price varies.

The *HST* file indexes articles from over 9,400 journals, conference proceedings, books, book reviews, and dissertations in the history of science (including mathematics), technology, and medicine and allied historical fields. **Isis Current Bibliography of the History of Science** (1975–), **Current Bibliography in the History of Technology (Technology and Culture)** (1987–), **Bibliografia Italiana di Storia della Scienza** (1982–), and **Wellcome Library for the History and Understanding of Medicine** (1991–) were combined to produce *HST.* Results may be limited by date, form/genre, and source. There are over 248,000 records currently. Updated annually.

Honda, Shojo, comp. **Pre-Meiji Works in the Library of Congress.** For complete entry, see **Chapter 1, Bibliographic Resources**.

E *The Jahrbuch-Project, Electronic Research Archive for Mathematics (ERAM)*. European Mathematical Society, 2001. Covers 1868–1942; in progress. Available at: http://www.emis.de/projects/JFM/JFM.html. Free.

Now that the *Jahrbuch über die Fortschritte der Mathematik* database is enhanced with the 2000 Mathematics Subject Classification (MSC) system, one can easily search for historical and biographical items. Combine a MSC search for 01 (history and biography) with a specific topic, person, or other subject classification to find historical or biographical materials. 01A70 is the specific classification for biographies, obituaries, and bibliographies. Search also by -03 subheading, that is, XX-03, to find related historical citations for that subject. For more detailed information, see **Chapter 2, Finding Tools**.

E *JSTOR*®. JSTOR®, 2000–2004. Information available at: http://www.jstor.org/jstor/. Subscription; price varies.

JSTOR is invaluable for searching for biographical items such as death notices and obituaries as well as determining a term's etymology, a historical trend, and so forth. Whereas other indexes may not always index these types of articles, every single word in *JSTOR*'s collection of core math and stat journals is searchable; coverage is from a journal's beginning volume. For more detailed information, see **Chapter 2, Finding Tools**.

Kapur, J. N., ed. **Some Eminent Indian Mathematicians of the Twentieth Century.** 2nd edition. New Delhi: Mathematical Sciences Trust Society, 1989–1993. 5 vols. Out of print.

Short biographies of 48 prominent Indian mathematicians of the twentieth century.

Karpinski, Louis Charles. **Bibliography of Mathematical Works Printed in America through 1850: and Supplement and Second Supplement.** Reprint edition.
For complete entry, see **Chapter 1, Bibliographic Resources**.

Loria, Gino. **Guida allo Studio della Storia delle Matematiche: Generalit'a Didattica, Bibliografia. Appendice: Questioni Storiche Concernenti le Scienze Esatte.** 2nd edition, revised and augmented. Milano: U. Hoepli, 1946. xix + 385p. Price not available.
Guide to the literature of the history of mathematics, covering all periods and countries. Many typographical errors.

E *MacTutor History of Mathematics Archive.* John J. O'Connor and Edmund F. Robertson, 2004. Available at: http://www-history.mcs.st-andrews.ac.uk/history/index.html. Free.
This superb and actively developed site contains over 1,000 biographies, nearly 80 histories on various mathematics topics (from 650 B.C. to the twentieth century), a chronology of important dates, and extensive links to history of mathematics sources elsewhere on the Web. Biographies include a picture, a link to the birthplace map, links from the text to other related items in the *MacTutor* collection, and a list of references with links to those on the Web.

E *Math Archives: History of Mathematics.* Mathematics Archives, 1996–2001. Available at: http://archives.math.utk.edu/topics/history.html. Free.
This very useful list of Web resources in history of mathematics is succinctly annotated with keywords and icons denoting level of mathematical background needed to comprehend site.

E *Math Forum Internet Mathematics Library, History/Biography.* The Math Forum@Drexel, 1994–2004. Available at: http://mathforum.org/library/topics/history/. Free.
A well-annotated list of selected Web resources in the history of mathematics.

E *Mathematics Genealogy Project.* No copyright given. Available at: http://genealogy.math.ndsu.nodak.edu/. Free.

Professors beget students who beget students. This site of over 76,000 records allows one to compile mathematicians' professional family trees. Records give the person's name, birth/death dates, nationality, PhD institution, dissertation title and MSC code, advisor and graduation date, and lists his or her PhD students. Names are linked internally and, in some cases, to biographical entries in the *MacTutor History of Mathematics Archive*.

E *MathSciNet*. American Mathematical Society, 2004. Covers 1940– . Updated daily. Information available at: http://www.ams.org/mathscinet. Subscription.

Use the MSC system (see *Jahrbuch* above) to find historical and biographical materials. For more detailed information, see **Chapter 2, Finding Tools**.

May, Kenneth O. **Bibliography and Research Manual of the History of Mathematics.** Buffalo, NY: University of Toronto Press, 1973. 818p. Out of print. ISBN 0-8020-1764-9.

In two parts: a manual on retrieval, storage, and analysis of information and a bibliography on history of mathematics with more than 30,000 entries arranged under five broad headings. Very useful listings of biographical articles on individuals appear in the biography chapter.

Morrow, Charlene and Teri Pearl, eds. **Notable Women in Mathematics: A Biographical Dictionary.** Westport, CT: Greenwood Press, 1998. xv + 302p. $50.00. ISBN 0-313-29131-4.

Substantive biographical essays cover 59 women worldwide who have made significant contributions to mathematics, from Hypatia to Andrea Bertozzi; the emphasis, however, is on contemporary mathematicians. References and index.

Navia, Luis E. **Pythagoras: An Annotated Bibliography.** New York: Garland, 1990. xviii + 381p. (Garland reference library of the humanities, vol. 1128). Out of print. ISBN 0-8240-4380-4.

A full list of Pythagorean secondary literature. The 1,197 entries are broadly grouped but accessible through narrow internal divisions and author and name indexes. No subject index.

Parkinson, Claire L. **Breakthroughs: A Chronology of Great Achievements in Science and Mathematics, 1200–1930.** Boston, MA: G. K. Hall, 1985. xii + 576p. Out of print. ISBN 0-8161-8706-1.

Over 700 of the 2,800 events are in mathematics. Includes list of sources, name and subject indexes. Telegraphic style.

Poggendorff, J. C. **Biographisch-literarisches Handworterbuch der exakten Naturwissenschaften.** Berlin: Wiley-VCH, 1863– . Irregular. About $60.00 per issue. ISSN 3-527-40231-4.

E Poggendorff, J. C. **Biographisch-literarisches Handworterbuch der exakten Naturwissenschaften.** Berlin: Wiley-VCH, 2001. Edited by the Sächsische Akademie der Wissenschaften zu Leipzig. Vol. I–vol. VIII/1 on 6 CD-ROMs. Information available at: http://www.poggendorff.com/poggendorff-eng.pdf. €1,299.00; €799.00 for print version owners. ISBN 3-527-40306-X. Final 2 CD-ROMs due in 2004. Price not given. ISBN 3-527-40322-1.

Well-known biographical resource issued in many parts contains biographical and bibliographical material on nearly 9,000 mathematicians out of the 29,000 scientists listed from pre-1857 onward. Data given for each person includes birth/death information, degrees, awards, obituaries, and a listing of all their publications. There is a useful chart at: http://scienceworld.wolfram.com/biography/Poggendorff.html that shows which volumes cover what time period and geographical location. This title is scheduled to be complete in 2004 with the final issues of vol. VIII. The CD-ROM version should greatly simplify searching; full text is provided by facsimiles of the original pages.

Porter, Roy and Marilyn Ogilvie. **The Biographical Dictionary of Scientists.** 3rd edition. New York: Oxford University Press, 2000. 2 vols. $125.00 set. ISBN 0-19-521663-6.

The historical reviews of the major sciences section has been updated and 80 new biographies (out of 1,280) added, focusing on contemporary scientists and women not included in the previous edition, for example, Franklin and Kovalevskaya. Of mathematical interest are the list of Fields medalists and a chronology of important events in mathematics.

Revue semestrielle des publications mathématiques. Amsterdam: Delsman en Nolthenius, 1893–1932.

Semiannual index of journal articles. A history section and an index of biographies are included in the cumulated indexes.

Rider, Robin E. **Bibliography of Early Modern Algebra, 1500–1800.** Berkeley: University of California, 1982. 171p. $9.35 pa. ISBN 0-918102-08-1 pa.

Sketches development of algebra and algebraic theory and influence of publication practices during the period. Arranged chronologically with detailed author index.

E *Search Notices of the AMS.* American Mathematical Society, 2003. Covers 1995– . Available at: http://www.ams.org/noticessearch/. Free.

One can find the **Notices'** death notices and memorial articles here. Because **Mathematical Reviews**/*MathSciNet* has not always indexed these types of articles, this site is very useful.

Smith, David Eugene. **Rara Arithmetica: A Catalogue of the Arithmetics Written Before the Year MDCI. . . .** New York: Chelsea, 1970 reprint of 1939 edition. Distributed by the American Mathematical Society. xvii + 725p. $51.00. ISBN 0-8284-0192-6.

Catalog of Columbia University Library's Plimpton collection. Addenda.

Spencer, Donald D. **Key Dates in Number Theory History: From 10,529 B.C. to the Present.** Ormond Beach, FL: Camelot, 1995. 125p. $18.95 pa. ISBN 0-89218-318-7 pa.

An interesting time line of historical snippets, from a Babylonian tablet on reciprocals to Wiles's proof of the Fermat conjecture. Includes biographical sketches, mathematical summaries.

Taylor, Eva Germaine Rimington. **The Mathematical Practitioners of Hanoverian England, 1714–1840.** Irvine, CA: Reprint Services, 1989 reprint of 1966 edition. xv + 503p. $79.00. ISBN 0-7812-0323-6.

Sequel to her work (below) with similar arrangement. All mathematicians mentioned in the biographical section are in one large alphabetical index issued separately and published by Cambridge University Press in 1980.

Taylor, Eva Germaine Rimington. **The Mathematical Practitioners of Tudor and Stuart England.** Irvine, CA: Reprint Services, 1989 reprint of 1954 edition. xi + 442p. $79.00. ISBN 0-685-10499-0.

Includes narrative accounts, biographies of 582 mathematicians, and annotated bibliography of period's mathematical works. List of secondary references.

Terquem, M., ed. **Bulletin de Bibliographie, d'Histoire et de Biographie Mathématiques.** Paris: Mallet-Bachelier, 1855–1862. 8 vols. Out of print.

Useful for referencing the older literature. Reviews and biographies in French. Note that titles of articles have been translated into French. Subject and author indexes in each volume.

S E University of York Department of Mathematics. *Materials for the History of Statistics.* 2004. Available at: http://www.york.ac.uk/depts/maths/histstat/welcome.htm. Free.

This site hosts a *Portraits of Statisticians* page containing over 300 portraits of statisticians ranging from the fifteenth century to the present day and a *Life and Work of Statisticians* page that lists statisticians with links to their primary works and to secondary materials.

E Westfall, Richard S. *Catalog of the Scientific Community in the 16th and 17th Centuries.* Albert Van Helden, 1995. Available at: http://es.rice.edu/ES/humsoc/Galileo/Catalog/catalog.html. Free.

This collection of 631 detailed biographies includes approximately 164 mathematicians currently. There are 20 searchable fields.

E Wilkins, David. R. *The History of Mathematics.* No copyright given. Available at: http://www.maths.tcd.ie/pub/HistMath/. Free.

Large collection of Web links to history of mathematics sites. Has major full-text collection of works by Berkeley, Hamilton, Riemann, Boole, Cantor, and Newton. Also hosts the Web site, *Mathematicians of the Seventeenth and Eighteenth Centuries*, with links to selected biographical articles from Ball's **A Short Account of the History of Mathematics** (below).

E *World Biographical Index.* München: K.G. Saur, 1998–2004. Available at: http://www.saur-wbi.de/. Free.

This index to Saur's biographical microfiche collection contains 3.1 million short biographical entries for eminent individuals from around the world. Each entry contains the name, variations of the name, pseudonyms, birth and death years, occupation, source, and bibliographic information about the sources used. There are over 21,000 in the mathematics occupation category.

Young, Robyn V. and Zoran Minderovic, eds. **Notable Mathematicians: From Ancient Times to the Present.** Detroit, MI: Gale, 1998. xxi + 612p. $112.25. ISBN 0-7876-3071-3.

Alphabetical entries include a biographical essay written for the general reader, followed by a list of selected publications and further readings. Appendixes include a time line of important events in the history of mathematics, a selected list of major mathematical awards and prizes through 1997, and a selected bibliography of books, periodicals, and Web sites of general interest. Indexes include fields of specialization, gender, nationality, and subject.

E *Zentralblatt MATH*. European Mathematical Society, FIZ Karlsruhe and Springer-Verlag, 2004. Covers 1931– . Updated biweekly. Available at: http://www.emis.de/ZMATH/. Limited free access, otherwise subscription.

Use the MSC system (see *Jahrbuch* above) to find historical and biographical materials. For more detailed information on *Zentralblatt MATH*, see **Chapter 2, Finding Tools**.

Biographies

Akivis, M. A. and B. A. Rosenfeld. **Élie Cartan (1869–1951).** Providence, RI: American Mathematical Society, 1993. xii + 317p. (Translations of Mathematical Monographs, 123). $153.00. ISBN 0-8218-4587-X.

This scientific biography describes and evaluates Cartan's most important discoveries.

Albers, Donald J., G. L. Alexanderson, and Constance Reid. **International Mathematical Congresses: An Illustrated History, 1893–1986.** New York: Springer-Verlag, 1987. 63p. $61.95. ISBN 0-387-96479-7.

The essential picture book for twentieth-century mathematicians. Brief descriptions of each International Congress of Mathematicians, photos of Fields medalists, and lists of plenary addresses.

Albers, Donald J., Gerald L. Alexanderson, and Constance Reid, eds. **More Mathematical People: Contemporary Conversations.** San Diego: Academic Press, [1994], c1990. xviii + 375p. $53.00 pa. ISBN 0-12-048251-7 pa.

Eighteen biographical interviews, from Lipman Bers to Robin Wilson, reveal the human face of mathematics.

Arnold, V. I. **Huygens and Barrow, Newton and Hook: Pioneers in Mathematical Analysis and Catastrophe Theory from Evolvents to**

Quasicrystals. Translated by Eric J. F. Primrose. Basel, Switzerland; Boston: Birkhäuser, 1990. 118p. $27.00 pa. ISBN 0-8176-2383-3 pa.

A penetrating historical investigation that reveals contemporary perspectives on the deep mathematical problems explored by Newton and his contemporaries.

Artmann, Benno. **Euclid: The Creation of Mathematics.** New York: Springer-Verlag, 1999. xvi + 343p. $49.95. ISBN 0-387-98423-2.

A sketchpad of notes interpreting selected propositions and constructions from Euclid's **Elements** from the viewpoint of modern mathematics.

Aspray, William. **John von Neumann and the Origins of Modern Computing.** Cambridge, MA: MIT Press, 1990. xvii + 376p. $52.95. ISBN 0-262-01121-2.

This revealing portrait of the many dimensions of von Neumann's pioneering work in computing also shows his close ties to applied mathematics.

Barrow-Green, June. **Poincaré and the Three Body Problem.** Providence, RI; London: American Mathematical Society; London Mathematical Society, 1997. xvi + 272p. (History of Mathematics, 11). $49.00. ISBN 0-8218-0367-0.

Not only a discussion of Poincaré's memoir from a mathematical and historical perspective, this book covers earlier work by other mathematicians, reactions by contemporaries, and influences on later work.

Bashmakova, I. G. **Diophantus and Diophantine Equations.** Washington, DC: Mathematical Association of America, 1997. xiv + 90p. (Dolciani Mathematical Expositions, 20). $21.95 pa. ISBN 0-88385-526-7 pa.

A delightful discussion of Diophantus's work on rational solution of equations and its influence on the development of number theory and algebraic geometry.

Belhoste, Bruno. **Augustin-Louis Cauchy: A Biography.** Translated by Frank Ragland. New York: Springer-Verlag, 1991. xii + 380p. $99.00. ISBN 0-387-97220-X.

A fascinating and carefully researched account of the professional career of Cauchy. The author balances historical and mathematical detail.

Bell, Eric Temple. **Men of Mathematics.** New York: Simon & Schuster, 1986 reprint of 1937 edition. xvii + 590p. $13.60 pa. ISBN 0-671-62818-6 pa.

Accounts of 34 historical figures instrumental in evolution of mathematics. Persons were selected because of importance of their work to modern mathematics and quality of their personal character.

Bölling, Reinhard, ed. **Das Fotoalbum für Weierstrasse. A Photo Album for Weierstrasse.** Brauschweig, Germany: Vieweg, 1994. xii + 44p. $70.00. ISBN 3-528-06602-4.

A reproduction of the album presented to Weierstrasse on his 70th birthday in 1885; contains over 300 portraits of his students, colleagues, and friends, and interesting details of his life.

S Box, Joan Fisher. **R. A. Fisher: The Life of a Scientist.** New York: Wiley, 1978. xii + 512p. Out of print. ISBN 0-471-09300-9.

Box details her father's life and professional work as a pioneer in statistics.

Cannell, D. M. **George Green: Mathematician and Physicist 1793–1841: The Background to his Life and Work.** London: Athlone Press, 1993. xxvi + 265p. $90.00. ISBN 0-485-11433-X.

The complete picture of a man relatively unknown, but whose contributions to mathematical physics are huge.

Chandrasekharan, K., ed. **Hermann Weyl, 1885–1985: Centenary Lectures Delivered by C. N. Yan, R. Penrose, A. Borel at the ETH Zürich.** New York: Springer-Verlag, 1986. 119p. $68.95. ISBN 0-387-16843-5.

In addition to the three lectures on Weyl's contributions to physics, geometry, and Lie groups, this book includes photographs, details of the celebration of the centenary of his birth, and a list of Weyl's publications.

Cooke, Roger. **The Mathematics of Sonya Kovalevskaya.** New York: Springer-Verlag, 1984. xiii + 234p. $52.00. ISBN 0-387-96030-9.

This is a fascinating mathematical biography with extensive quotations from correspondence and a detailed analysis of her major papers.

Cooney, Miriam P., ed. **Celebrating Women in Mathematics and Science.** Reston, VA: National Council of Teachers of Mathematics, 1996. vii + 223p. $22.50 pa. ISBN 0-87353-425-5 pa.

These 22 biographies, from Hypatia to Mary Ellen Rudin, are captivating readings for everyone. Each biography ends with suggested readings.

Dauben, Joseph Warren. **Abraham Robinson: The Creation of Nonstandard Analysis: A Personal and Mathematical Odyssey.** Princeton, NJ: Princeton University Press, 1998. xix + 559p. $26.00 pa. ISBN 0-691-05911-X pa.

This detailed biography combines explanations of Robinson's work in pure and applied mathematics with a chronological story of his life.

David, Philip J. **Mathematical Encounters of the Second Kind.** Boston: Birkhäuser, 1997. viii + 304p. $24.95. ISBN 0-8176-3939-X.

In this case, "second kind" means a person of mathematics. Here Davis gives us meandering reminiscences (plus a little fiction) about a theorem attributed to Napoleon, and about his friendships with mathematician Stefan Bergman and amateur mathematician Lord Victor Rothschild.

Dunham, William. **Euler: The Master of Us All.** Washington, DC: Mathematical Association of America, 1999. xxviii + 185p. (Dolciani Mathematical Expositions, 22). $29.95 pa. ISBN 0-88385-328-0 pa.

Each chapter in this brief sample of Euler's major contributions clearly describes the efforts that preceded Euler, the magnitude of the challenges he faced, and the impact of the contributions he made.

S Gani, J., ed. **The Making of Statisticians**. New York: Springer-Verlag, 1982. xiii + 263p. $76.95. ISBN 0-387-90684-3.

Personal reminiscences of 16 statisticians, most born in the early twentieth century, on their backgrounds and work in statistics. A photograph and short biography is included for each.

Garciadiego, Alejandro R. **Bertrand Russell and the Origins of Set-Theoretic 'Paradoxes.'** Boston: Birkhäuser, 1992. xxix + 264p. $77.50. ISBN 0-8176-2669-7.

This carefully documented scholarly work "reconstructs and reinterprets the role of Russell in the origins of set-theoretic paradoxes." Extensive bibliography.

Gårding, Lars. **Mathematics and Mathematicians: Mathematics in Sweden before 1950.** Providence, RI; London: American Mathematical

Society; London Mathematical Society, 1998. (History of Mathematics, 13). xiii + 288p. $75.00. ISBN 0-8128-0612-2.

A comprehensive exposition of the many mathematical contributions of the Swedes as well as a look into their personal lives. Includes a short biography of Gösta Mittag-Leffler.

Gillispie, Charles Coulston. **Pierre-Simon Laplace, 1749–1827: A Life in Exact Science.** Princeton, NJ: Princeton University Press, 1997. xii + 322p. $15.96 pa. ISBN 00691-05027-9 pa.

A detailed and comprehensive account of the development of Laplace's mathematical and scientific research. Ivor Grattan-Guinness summarizes the history of the scientist's most important single mathematical contribution, the Laplace Transform.

Halmos, Paul R. **I Have a Photographic Memory.** Providence, RI: American Mathematical Society, 1987. vii + 326p. $39.00. ISBN 0-8218-0115-5.

An interesting and valuable compilation, more or less chronologically arranged, of 600 snapshots of mathematicians from Halmos's larger collection. Includes his chatty, informative commentary. Index of names.

S Heyde, C. C. and E. Seneta, eds. **Statisticians of the Centuries.** New York: Springer-Verlag, 2001. xii + 500p. $45.95 pa; $69.95. ISBN 0-387-95283-7 pa; 0-387-95329-9.

This is a collection of 103 short biographies of statisticians from early times to those born before the twentieth century. Each person's statistical work is placed in its historical and social context. A picture and references are included for each.

Hoffman, Paul. **The Man Who Loved Only Numbers: The Story of Paul Erdös and the Search for Mathematical Truth.** New York: Hyperion, 1998. ix + 288p. $22.95. ISBN 0-7868-6362-5.

A biography of Erdös as well as an excursion through the mathematics he loved.

Hollingdale, Stuart. **Makers of Mathematics.** New York: Penguin Books, 1991. xv + 437p. $12.71 pa. ISBN 0-14-014922-8 pa.

An idiosyncratic history of mathematics told through a series of sketches of the lives and accomplishments of famous men of mathematics. This edition adds two new appendixes.

S Johnson, Norman L. and Samuel Kotz, eds. **Leading Personalities in Statistical Sciences: From the Seventeenth Century to the Present.** New York: Wiley, 1997. xxiii + 399p. $49.95 pa. ISBN 0-471-16381-3 pa.

Brief biographies of 118 important contributors to probabilistic and statistical methods from Bernouilli to Deming. Many articles revised from their entries in Kotz, Johnson, and Reed's **Encyclopedia of Statistical Sciences** (see in **Chapter 4**). Some photographs.

Kaluza, Roman. **Through a Reporter's Eyes: The Life of Stefan Banach.** Edited and translated by Ann Kostant and Wojbor Woyczynski. Boston: Birkhäuser, 1996. x + 137p. $24.50. ISBN 0-8176-3772-9.

This book describes Banach and the Polish mathematical community of the first half of the twentieth century.

Kanigel, Robert. **The Man Who Knew Infinity: A Life of the Genius Ramanujan.** New York: Washington Square Press, 1991. ix + 438p. $14.00 pa. ISBN 0-671-75061-5 pa.

Reprint of perhaps one of the best scientific biographies ever written. This is an extraordinarily compelling book, filled with the social, psychological, personal, and mathematical details of Ramanujan and his mentor, Hardy.

Kennedy, Hubert C. **Peano: Life and Works of Giuseppe Peano.** Dordrecht, Holland: Reidel, 1980. xii + 230p. (Studies in the History of Modern Science, 4). $88.00. ISBN 90-277-1067-8.

First full biography of Peano, describing his life, his development of symbolic logic, his mathematics, and his efforts to promote Interlingua. Appendixes.

Koblitz, Ann Hibner. **A Convergence of Lives: Sofia Kovalevskaia, Scientist, Writer, Revolutionary.** New Brunswick, NJ: Rutgers University Press, 1993. xxxviii + 305p. $15.00 pa. ISBN 0-8135-1963-2 pa.

Reprint of 1983 work, a highly readable and popular account of Kovalevskaia's life, emphasizing her scientific and political interests. Extensive bibliography.

Lutzen, Jesper. **Joseph Liouville 1809–1882: Master of Pure and Applied Mathematics.** New York: Springer-Verlag, 1990. xix + 884p. (Studies in the History of Mathematics and Physical Sciences, 15). $131.00. ISBN 0-387-97180-7.

A massive, thoroughly researched biography of Liouville in two parts: six chapters devoted to his scientific and professional career and 11 chapters describing his mathematical contributions. Numerous quotations (in English) from Liouville's extensive unpublished notebooks enliven the account. Extensive notes link text to lengthy bibliography.

Mahoney, Michael Sean. **The Mathematical Career of Pierre de Fermat (1601–1665).** 2nd edition. Princeton, NJ: Princeton University Press, 1994. xx + 432p. $24.95 pa. ISBN 0-691-03666-7 pa.

1973 edition corrected and updated with more recent results from the literature and the author's own subsequent research.

Masani, P. R. **Norbert Wiener, 1894–1964.** Boston: Birkhäuser, 1990. 416p. (Vita Mathematica, 5). $63.00. ISBN 0-8176-2246-2.

This fascinating, well-documented reflection on the intellectual and personal character of Wiener includes a biography, mathematics and other topics, and extensive quotations from his correspondence.

Maz'ya, Vladimir and Tatyana Shaposhnikova. **Jacques Hadamard: A Universal Mathematician.** Providence, RI: American Mathematical Society, 1998. xxv + 574p. (History of Mathematics, 14). $79.00. ISBN 0-8218-0841-9.

A thoroughly researched biography as well as a summary of contributions to analytic function theory, number theory, geometry, and calculus of variations.

Muir, Jean. **Of Men and Numbers: The Story of the Great Mathematicians.** New York: Dover, 1996. 249p. $7.95 pa. ISBN 0-486-28973-7 pa.

Reprint of the 1961 edition.

Murray, Margaret A. M. **Women Becoming Mathematicians: Creating a Professional Identity in Post-World War II America.** Cambridge, MA: MIT Press, 2000. xviii + 277p. $23.95. ISBN 0-262-13369-5.

The author looks at the lives and careers of 36 of the approximately 200 women who earned PhDs in mathematics from American institutions from 1940 to 1959. Photographs. References.

Nasar, Sylvia. **A Beautiful Mind: A Biography of John Forbes Nash, Jr., Winner of the Nobel Prize in Economics, 1994**. New York: Simon & Schuster, 1998. 461p. $26.00, $16.00 pa. ISBN: 0-684-81906-6819066, 0-684-85370-1 pa.

Now an Academy Award-winning movie, this popular title documents the life and times of mathematician and Nobel Prize winner John Nash and his struggle with and recovery from paranoid schizophrenia.

Osen, Lynn M. **Women in Mathematics.** Cambridge, MA: MIT Press, 1974. xii + 185p. $14.90 pa. ISBN 0-262-65009-6 pa.
Written in an agreeable style, chapters in this book range from Hypatia to the Feminine Mathematique. Bibliography.

Pais, Abraham, et al. **Paul Dirac: The Man and His Work.** New York: Cambridge University Press, 1998. xv + 124p. $19.95. ISBN 0-521-58382-9.
Lectures by A. Pais, M. Jacob, D. I. Olive, and M. F. Atiyah, plus a memorial address by Stephen Hawking.

Reid, Constance. **Hilbert-Courant.** New York: Springer-Verlag, 1986. xv + 547p. $44.95 pa. ISBN 0-387-96256-5 pa.
An excellent account of the closely linked intellectual biographies of the two giants who helped to create modern mathematics. This is the combined edition of Reid's 1970 **Hilbert** and 1976 **Courant in Göttingen and New York**.

Reid, Constance. **Julia: A Life in Mathematics.** Washington, DC: Mathematical Association of America, 1996. (MAA Spectum). xii + 124p. $31.95. ISBN 0-88385-520-8.
This remarkable book contains previously published articles on Robinson's life and work as well as pictures and mathematical memorabilia. Constance Reid is Robinson's sister.

Reid, Constance. **The Search for E. T. Bell, Also Known as John Taine.** Washington, DC: Mathematical Association of America, 1993. x + 372p. $24.95. ISBN 0-88385-508-9.
An engaging biography of one of the more colorful "men of mathematics" of the twentieth century.

Rudin, Walter. **The Way I Remember It.** Providence, RI; London: American Mathematical Society; London Mathematical Society, 1997. ix + 191p. (History of Mathematics, 12). $29.00. ISBN 0-8218-0633-5.
Written for the non-analyst, Rudin's memoirs include samples of his work.

Schabas, Margaret. **A World Ruled by Number: William Stanley Jevons and the Rise of Mathematical Economics.** Princeton, NJ: Princeton University Press, 1990. xii + 192p. $37.50. ISBN 0-691-08543-9.

The author provides a readable account of Jevon's role in the nineteenth-century origins of mathematical economics.

Schwartz, Laurent. **A Mathematician Grappling with his Century.** Translated from the French by Leila Schneps. Basel, Switzerland: Birkhäuser, 2001. viii + 490p. $44.95. ISBN 3-7643-6052-6.

This autobiography by Schwartz, 1950 Fields Medal winner for his work on distributions, also details his work for social justice.

Scott, J. F. **The Mathematical Work of John Wallis.** 2nd edition. New York: Chelsea, 1981. xi + 240p. $16.50. ISBN 0-8284-0314-7.

Reprint of the 1938 London original, a thorough and informative analysis of mid-seventeenth-century arithmetic, mechanics, and algebra. Appendix includes brief biographies of Wallis's contemporaries mentioned in the volume.

Smithies, Frank. **Cauchy and the Creation of Complex Function Theory.** New York: Cambridge University Press, 1997. 216p. $84.95. ISBN 0-521-59278-X.

A scholarly and well-documented analysis of Cauchy's contributions to complex analysis from 1814 to 1831.

Stein, Sherman. **Archimedes: What Did He Do Besides Cry Eureka?** Washington, DC: Mathematical Association of America, 1999. x + 155p. $24.95 pa. ISBN 0-88385-718-9 pa.

An engaging account of some of Archimedes's discoveries such as areas within spirals and parabolas, and the surface area and volume of a sphere.

Wang, Hao. **A Logical Journey: From Gödel to Philosophy.** Cambridge, MA: MIT Press, 1996. xiv + 391p. $45.00. ISBN 0-262-23189-1.

Wang reports on his conversations with Gödel on interpretation of his published work. Fascinating chapters on mind vs. machine and on Gödel's Platonism and objectivism. A continuation of Wang's **Reflections on Kurt Gödel** (not listed).

Weil, André. **The Apprenticeship of a Mathematician.** Translated by Jennifer Gage. Boston: Birkhäuser, 1992. 197p. $39.95. ISBN 0-8176-2650-6.

A fascinating memoir of Weil's early life with many sketches of mathematical people.

Westfall, Richard S. **The Life of Isaac Newton.** Cambridge; New York: Cambridge University Press, 1994. xv + 328p. $13.95 pa. ISBN 0-521-47737-9 pa.

A condensed and less technical version of Westfall's award-winning **Never at Rest: A Biography of Isaac Newton.**

Yau, S. T., ed. **S. S. Chern: A Great Geometer of the Twentieth Century.** Expanded edition. Cambridge, MA: International Press, 1998. xxxi + 331p. $42.00. ISBN 1-571-46098-5.

Includes some of the papers delivered at a 1990 Los Angeles conference in honor of the Chern's 79th birthday, plus an essay by Chern on his mathematical education in China. Includes 25 pages of photos.

Yoder, Joella G. **Unrolling Time: Christiaan Huygens and the Mathematization of Nature.** New York: Cambridge University Press, 1988. xi + 238p. $52.95. ISBN 0-521-34140-X.

A case study of the interrelationship between mathematics and physics in the work of Huygens (1629–1695). The original drawings have been supplemented with clearer redrawn versions.

Histories

Alexander, Daniel S. **A History of Complex Dynamics: From Schröder to Fatou and Julia.** Braunschweig, Germany: Vieweg, 1994. viii + 165p. (Aspects of Mathematics: E24). $42.00. ISBN 3-528-06520-6.

Of broad interest, this history of iteration of complex maps ranges from Schröder's 1870 paper through works of Julia, Fatou, and Montel.

Anglin, W. S. **Mathematics: A Concise History and Philosophy.** New York: Springer-Verlag, 1994. xi + 261p. $42.95. ISBN 0-387-94280-7.

In this concise introduction, 40 chapters range from Egyptian mathematics to twentieth-century number theory.

Baron, Margaret E. **The Origins of the Infinitesimal Calculus.** New York: Dover, 1987. viii + 304p. $9.95 pa. ISBN 0-486-65371-4 pa.

Reprint of the 1969 study of the rise of geometric techniques, from the Greeks to the early seventeenth century.

Ball, W. W. Rouse. *A Short Account of the History of Mathematics.* New York: Dover, 1960. Reprint of 4th edition, 1908. xxiv + 522p. $13.95 pa. ISBN 0-486-20630-0.

E *Mathematicians of the Seventeenth and Eighteenth Centuries.* No copyright given. Available at: http://www.maths.tcd.ie/pub/HistMath/People/RBallHist.html. Free.

Older classic history. The biographies on the Web site are transcribed from Ball's book.

Bashmakova, I. G. and G. S. Smirnova. **The Beginnings and Evolution of Algebra.** Washington, DC: Mathematical Association of America, 2000. xvi + 179p. (Dolciani Mathematical Expositions, 23). $24.95 pa. ISBN 0-88385-329-9 pa.

Authors effectively use modern notation in this selective sketch of the evolution of algebra from ancient Babylon to the twentieth century. Documents the role of archetype problems, indeterminate equations, and geometric methods in the evolution of algebra.

Bell, E. T. **The Development of Mathematics.** New York: Dover, 1992. xiii + 637p. $15.16 pa. ISBN 0-486-27239-7 pa.

Reprint of the 1945 second edition. Bell outlines the development of the main ideas and explains the mathematics involved.

Berggren, J. L. **Episodes in the Mathematics of Medieval Islam.** New York: Springer-Verlag, 1986. xiv + 197p. $65.95. ISBN 0-387-96318-9.

The author provides a sampling of Islamic sources dealing with algebra, geometry, and trigonometry as well as commentary on the historical and Islamic context of these ideas.

Berggren, Lennart, Jonathan Borwein, and Peter Borwein. **Pi: A Source Book.** New York: Springer-Verlag, 1997. xix + 716p. $64.95. ISBN 0-387-94924-0.

Seventy carefully selected papers from research literature, historical studies, and lighthearted pieces, document the history of pi.

Bos, Henk J. M. **Lectures in the History of Mathematics.** Providence, RI; London: American Mathematical Society; London Mathematical Society, 1993. x + 197p. (History of Mathematics, 7). $86.00. ISBN 0-8218-9001-8.

Eleven thought-provoking, insightful, and informative lectures on topics from seventeenth- and eighteenth-century mathematics.

Bottazzini, Umberto. **The Higher Calculus: A History of Real and Complex Analysis from Euler to Weierstrass**. New York: Springer-Verlag, 1986. 332p. $67.95. ISBN 0-387-96302-2.

A well-written historical account of nineteenth-century analysis with emphasis on the foundations of complex analysis.

Boyer, Carl B. **A History of Mathematics.** 2nd revised edition. Revised by Uta Merzbach. New York: Wiley, 1991. xx + 715p. $27.95 pa. ISBN 0-471-54397-7 pa.

Chapters on the nineteenth and twentieth centuries have been revised and expanded from 1968 original. Revised reference and bibliography.

Boyer, Carl B. **The History of the Calculus and Its Conceptual Development.** New York: Dover, 1959. v + 346p. $7.95 pa. ISBN 0-486-60509-4 pa.

Reprint of the 1949 original, **The Concepts of the Calculus**, a well-rounded history of the concepts of the subject rather than the theorems and applications of calculus.

Brigaglia, A. and C. Ciliberto. **Italian Algebraic Geometry Between the Two World Wars.** Kingston, ON: Queen's University Printing Services, 1995. vii + 223p. (Queen's Papers in Pure and Applied Mathematics, 100). $50.00 pa. ISBN 0-88911-699-7 pa.

This interesting collection of essays gives a broad historical background.

Burton, David M. **The History of Mathematics: An Introduction.** 4th edition. Boston: WCB McGraw Hill, 1999. x + 710p. $88.40. ISBN 0-07-009468-3.

One of the best textbooks on history of mathematics, this is a well-illustrated work for the undergraduate reader, with some emphasis on personalities. The biggest change in this edition is a more extensive treatment of the mathematics developed in the non-Western world. Numerous references.

Cajori, Florian. **A History of Mathematics.** 5th revised edition. New York: Chelsea, 1991; distributed by the American Mathematical Society. xi + 524p. $39.00. ISBN 0-8284-1303-7.

This edition of the 1919 classic makes a few minor improvements and revises the chapter on Babylonian mathematics in light of new research.

Cajori, Florian. **A History of Mathematical Notations.** New York: Dover, 1993. 2 vols. in 1. $19.95 pa. ISBN 0-486-67766-4 pa. Vol. I. **Notations in Elementary Mathematics.** xvi + 451p. Vol. II. **Notations Mainly in Higher Mathematics.** xii + 367p.

An entertaining and interesting book, detailing the first appearance, origins, spread, and competition of each symbol.

Calinger, Ronald, ed. **Classics of Mathematics.** Englewood Cliffs, NJ: Prentice Hall, 1995. xii + 793p. $35.80 pa. ISBN 0-02-31842-X pa.

Anthology includes Proclus, Oresme, Fermat, and many others. Each chapter is preceded by historical and biographical notes.

Cardano, Girolamo. **Ars Magna or the Rules of Algebra.** Translated by T. Richard Witmer. New York: Dover, 1993. xxiv + 267p. $8.95 pa. ISBN 0-486-67811-3 pa.

Translation of the classic Renaissance text from 1545, using modern algebraic notation.

Chabert, Jean Luc, ed. **A History of Algorithms: From the Pebble to the Microchip.** Translated by Chris Weeks. New York: Springer-Verlag, 1999. ix + 524p. $59.95. ISBN 3-540-63369-3.

By focusing on algorithms, the authors offer a different perspective to the history of mathematics. Gives a historical background to contemporary algorithmic practice.

Clawson, Calvin C. **The Mathematical Traveler: Exploring the Grand History of Numbers.** New York: Plenum Press, 1994. x + 307p. $25.95. ISBN 0-306-44645-6.

The author takes us on a mathematical adventure that reveals the history of numbers as a reflection of the evolution of culture. A clear and compelling presentation for the serious lay reader.

Corry, Leo. **Modern Algebra and the Rise of Mathematical Structures.** Boston: Birkhäuser, 1996. 460p. (Science Networks: Historical Studies, 17). $139.00. ISBN 0-8176-5311-2.

Concentrating on Dedekind, Hilbert, Fraenkel, Noether, Ore, and the Bourbaki group, the author develops the idea of mathematics as a study of structures as exemplified by ideal theory and category theory.

Crowe, Michael J. **A History of Vector Analysis: The Evolution of the Idea of a Vectorial System.** New York: Dover, 1994. xvii + 270p. $8.46 pa. ISBN 0-486-67910-1 pa.

Corrected reprint of 1967 edition.

Curtis, Charles W. **Pioneers of Representation Theory: Frobenius, Burnside, Schur, & Brauer.** Providence, RI: American Mathematical Society, 1999. xvi + 286p. (History of Mathematics, 15). $49.00. ISBN 0-8218-9002-6.

Both a history and an introduction to representation theory. Although focusing on the early twentieth century, the author covers Gauss to the classification to finite simple groups.

S Dale, Andrew I. **A History of Inverse Probability: From Thomas Bayes to Karl Pearson.** 2nd edition. New York: Springer-Verlag, 1999. xxiv + 670p. $94.00. ISBN 0-387-98807-6.

The study encompasses some 150 years of work on inverse probability, but includes little biographical detail and does not attempt to put matters in historical or sociological context. In this edition, the author adds a discussion of the work of a number of authors inadvertently omitted from the first edition in order to shed more light on the use made by nineteenth-century authors of inverse probability.

S David, F. N. **Games, Gods, and Gambling: The Origins and History of Probability and Statistical Ideas from the Earliest Times to the Newtonian Era.** New York: Dover, 1998. Reprint of 1962 original. xvi +275p. $9.95. ISBN 0-486-40023-9.

Classic account of the development of modern probability and statistics.

Densmore, Dana, ed. **Apollonius of Perga. Conics, Books I-III.** New revised edition. Santa Fe, NM: Green Lion Press, 1998. xxxviii + 284p. $23.95 pa. ISBN 1-888009-05-5 pa.

Revision of the Taliaferro translation, with a lengthy and informative introduction, historical notes, and diagrams.

Drucker, Thomas, ed. **Perspectives on the History of Mathematical Logic.** Boston: Birkhäuser, 1991. xxiii + 195p. $86.50. ISBN 0-8176-3444-4.

Thirteen papers "dedicated to unraveling the thoughts and the circumstances that have contributed to the evolution of mathematical logic" over the last century.

Duren, Peter, Richard A. Askey, and Uta C. Merzbach, eds. **A Century of Mathematics in America.** Providence, RI: American Mathematical Society, 1989. (History of Mathematics, 1–3). Part I. viii + 477p. $69.00. ISBN 0-8218-0124-4. Part II. x + 585p. $90.00. ISBN 0-8218-0130-9. Part III. ix + 675p. $93.00. ISBN 0-8218-0136-8.

Rich collection of papers on research, people, teaching, organizations, politics, and education on the history of mathematics in America. The final volume contains historical papers written in honor of the AMS centennial.

Edwards, C. H., Jr. **The Historical Development of the Calculus.** New York: Springer-Verlag, 1994 reprint of 1979 edition. xii + 351p. $44.95 pa. ISBN 0-387-94313-7 pa.

A careful and comprehensive history of calculus, from Babylonian geometry to Robinson's infinitesimals.

Eves, Howard. **Great Moments in Mathematics (After 1650).** Washington, DC: Mathematical Association of America, 1983. xii + 263p. (Dolciani Mathematical Expositions, 7). $28.95. ISBN 0-88385-311-6.

A very readable and non-detailed book of 20 lectures from the modern era covering the discovery of Fourier series, non-Euclidean geometry, noncommutative algebra, transfinite numbers, and abstract spaces.

Eves, Howard. **Great Moments in Mathematics (Before 1650).** Washington, DC: Mathematical Association of America, 1983. xiv + 270p. (Dolciani Mathematical Expositions, 5). $28.95 pa. ISBN 0-88385-310-8 pa.

Another 20 lectures, similar to the companion volume above, on ancient mathematics.

Ewing, John H., ed. **A Century of Mathematics: Through the Eyes of the Monthly.** Washington, DC: Mathematical Association of America, 1994. xi + 323p. $27.95. ISBN 0-88385-457-0.

This wide-ranging and delightful collection of articles, excerpts, photographs, and notes from the **American Mathematical Monthly**'s first 100 years (1894–1994) offers a unique survey of modern American mathematics as a discipline and as a profession.

E *Famous Problems in the History of Mathematics.* Math Forum@Drexel, 1994–2004. Available at: http://mathforum.org/isaac/mathhist.html. Free.

This site presents a small portion of the history of mathematics through an investigation of some of the great problems that have inspired mathematicians throughout the ages. Problems include: The Bridges of Konigsberg, The Value of Pi, Puzzling Primes, Famous Paradoxes, The Problem of Points, A Proof of the Pythagorean Theorem, and A Proof That e is Irrational.

Fauvel, John and Jeremy Gray, eds. **The History of Mathematics: A Reader.** Basingstoke, England; Washington, DC: Macmillan Education in association with the Open University; Mathematical Association of America, 1987. xxiv + 628p. $38.95 pa. ISBN 0-333-42791-2 pa.

This book contains a wide selection of readings in the history of mathematics from earliest times to the twentieth century. Useful in the teaching of mathematics.

Fauvel, John, Raymond Flood, and Robin Wilson, eds. **Möbius and his Band: Mathematics and Astronomy in Nineteenth-Century Germany.** New York: Oxford University Press, 1993. 172p. $35.00. ISBN 0-19-853969-X.

The first five essays of this work describe the flowering of German science from 1810 to 1850, treating Möbius's life and work as archetype. The final essay surveys highlights of modern celestial mechanics and chaotic dynamics.

Fauvel, John, Raymond Flood, and Robin Wilson, eds. **Oxford Figures: 800 Years of the Mathematical Sciences.** New York: Oxford University Press, 2000. 296p. $60.00. ISBN 0-19-852309-2.

This highly readable and beautifully illustrated book reveals the richness and influence of Oxford's mathematical tradition and the fascinating characters who have helped to shape it. It ends with some entertaining reminiscences by Michael Atiyah of the 30 years he spent as an Oxford mathematician.

Federico, P. J. **Descartes on Polyhedra: A Study of the De Solidorum Elementis.** New York: Springer-Verlag, 1982. ix + 145p. (Sources in the

History of Mathematics and the Physical Sciences, 4). $110.00. ISBN 0-387-90760-2.

The first English translation of Descartes' general treatment of polyhedra. This edition includes a facsimile of the manuscript, with transcription and commentary.

Field, J.V. **The Invention of Infinity: Mathematics and Art in the Renaissance.** New York: Oxford University Press, 1997. 384p. $35.00. ISBN 0-19-652394-7.

This entertaining book describes the everyday worlds of art and mathematics in a time when artists were merely "craftsmen" and their practical mathematics were separate from the mathematics of scholars. The story brings together the histories of art and mathematics and shows how the craftsmen's discoveries changed learned mathematics. Infinity at last acquired a precise mathematical meaning. Extensively illustrated with superb color and black-and-white plates. Includes selected extracts from the original mathematical texts.

Gandt, François de. **Force and Geometry in Newton's Principia.** Princeton, NJ: Princeton University Press, 1995. xiv + 296p. $49.50. ISBN 0-691-03367-6.

The clear, careful treatment of Newton's concept of force and its historical antecedents makes this book an essential companion for studying the physics or mathematics of Newton's **Principia.**

Goldman, Jay R. **The Queen of Mathematics: A Historically Motivated Guide to Number Theory.** Wellesley, MA: A.K. Peters, 1998. xxiv + 525p. $59.95. ISBN 1-56881-006-7.

Goldman's fascination with the history of mathematics led him to teach a course in number theory from a historical perspective. His lecture notes will lead readers to an understanding of today's research problems on the basis of their historical evolution.

Hairer, E. and G. Wanner. **Analysis by Its History.** New York: Springer-Verlag, 1996. x + 374p. $49.95. ISBN 0-387-94551-2.

The traditional order of topics (sets, limits, continuity) in this text is reversed to reflect the historical development of the subject. Includes quotations and diagrams from original sources.

S Hald, Anders. **A History of Mathematical Statistics from 1750 to 1930.** New York: Wiley, 1998. xvii + 795 pp. $148.00. ISBN 0-471-17912-4.

This companion volume to his **History of Probability and Statistics and their Applications before 1750** (below) details the history of the two branches of mathematical statistics, direct and inverse probability, and their applications.

S Hald, Anders. **A History of Probability and Statistics and their Applications before 1750.** New York: John Wiley & Sons, 1990. xiii + 586p. $190.00. ISBN 0-471-50230-8.

Hald traces the foundations of probability and statistics through their historical background, personalities, and applications of theories.

Heath, Sir Thomas. **A History of Greek Mathematics.** New York: Dover, 1981. Vol. I. **From Thales to Euclid.** xv + 446p. $11.00 pa. ISBN 0-486-24073-8 pa. Vol. II. **From Aristarchus to Diophantus.** xi + 586p. $11.00 pa. ISBN 0-486-24074-6 pa.

Reprint of Heath's 1921 classic that was noted for its careful scholarship. It is more or less in chronological order. Special chapters on the history of certain important problems and the roles of major figures are included.

Herz-Fischler, Roger. **A Mathematical History of the Golden Number.** New York: Dover, 1998. xxii + 195p. $14.95 pa. ISBN 0-486-40007-7 pa.

Unabridged, but corrected, reprint of the 1987 **Mathematical History of Division in Extreme and Mean Ratio.**

Ifrah, Georges. **The Universal History of Numbers: From Prehistory to the Invention of the Computer.** Translated by David Bellos, et al. New York: J. Wiley, 2000. xxii + 633p. $11.50 pa. ISBN 0-471-39340-1 pa.

Ifrah describes numbers and reckoning systems of many tribes and cultures; organized into 27 chapters by culture. Although widely praised in the popular press, mathematicians have criticized this work for its mistakes and misrepresentations (Dauben 2002, 32–33). This is a revision of his earlier book, **From One to Zero**.

James, I. M., ed. **History of Topology.** Amsterdam; New York: Elsevier, 1999. ix + 1,056p. $190.50. ISBN 0-444-82375-1.

Forty articles survey the history of classical topology from the mid-1800s to the present. Several biographies are included among the papers.

Jesseph, Douglas M. **Squaring the Circle: the War Between Hobbes and Wallis.** Chicago: University of Chicago Press, 1999. xiv + 419p. $28.00 pa. ISBN 0-226-39900-1 pa.

This book details the most significant intellectual dispute of the seventeenth century between philosopher Thomas Hobbes and mathematician John Wallis. The author covers the core questions of mathematics as well as the broader issues of religion, politics, physics, and morals.

Joseph, George Gheverghese. **The Crest of the Peacock: Non-European Roots of Mathematics.** London; New York: Penguin Books, 1991. xv + 371p. $12.00 pa. ISBN 0-14-012529-9 pa.

Joseph makes a well-written and convincing presentation of the crucial importance of transmission of diverse mathematics across cultures.

Joyner, David, ed. **Coding Theory and Cryptography: From Enigma and Geheimschreiber to Quantum Theory.** New York: Springer-Verlag, 2000. vii + 256p. $79.00 pa. ISBN 3-540-66336-3.

Both historical and mathematical papers from a 1998 conference at the U.S. Naval Academy.

Kac, Mark and Stanislaw Ulam. **Mathematics and Logic.** New York: Dover, 1992. ix + 170p. $7.95 pa. ISBN 0-486-67085-6 pa.

Reprint of 1968 original.

Katz, Victor J. **A History of Mathematics: An Introduction.** 2nd edition. Reading, MA: Addison-Wesley, 1998. xiv + 864p. $89.00. ISBN 0-321-01618-1.

"Designed for mathematics majors who intend to teach in college or high school." This edition has new material on combinatorics in the Islamic tradition, Newton's derivation of his system of the world, linear algebra in the nineteenth and twentieth centuries, and statistical ideas in the nineteenth century.

Kellert, Stephen H. **In the Wake of Chaos: Unpredictable Order in Dynamical Systems.** Chicago: University of Chicago Press, 1993. xiv + 176p. $21.00. ISBN 0-226-42974-1.

Written by a philosopher who makes a very readable presentation of mathematics and history of dynamical systems, before moving on to philosophical issues.

Klein, Felix. **Vorlesungen über die Entwicklung der Mathematik im 19. Jahrhundert.** New York: Chelsea, 1956. 2 vols. in 1. xiii + 385p; x + 208p. $12.95. ISBN 0-8284-0074-1.

Reprint of 1926–1927 original. Volume 2 is titled **Die Grundbegriffe der Invariantentheorie und ihr Eindringen in die mathematische Physik**.

Klein, Jacob. **Greek Mathematical Thought and the Origin of Algebra.** Translated by Eva Brann. New York: Dover, 1992. xv + 360p. $12.95 pa. ISBN 0-486-27289-3 pa.

Unabridged reprint of the 1968 MIT Press text.

Kline, Morris. **Mathematical Thought from Ancient to Modern Times.** 2nd edition. New York: Oxford University Press, 1990. Vol. 1. xviii + 390p. + xxii. $15.16 pa. ISBN 0-19-506135-7 pa. Vol. 2. xx + 421p. + xxii. $15.16 pa. ISBN 0-19-506136-5 pa. Vol. 3. xvi + 299p. + xxii. $15.16 pa. ISBN 0-19-506137-3 pa.

Unaltered reprint of the 1972 original. Every library must have this lucid, monumental history of the major themes in mathematics, half of which is devoted to the nineteenth and twentieth centuries.

Kline, Morris. **Mathematics: The Loss of Certainty.** New York: Oxford University Press, 1980. 366p. $11.96. ISBN 0-19-5030850.

A popular historical account of the "rise and decline of the majesty of mathematics." Kline's literate and lucid tale moves beyond the "loss of truth" to suggest two issues for a new foundation of mathematics.

S Koren, John. **History of Statistics, Their Development and Progress in Many Countries.** New York, B. Franklin, 1970 reprint of 1918 ed. xii + 773p. Out of print. ISBN 0-8337-1950-5.

History of official statistical publications.

S Kotz, Samuel and Norman L. Johnson, eds. **Breakthroughs in Statistics**. New York: Springer-Verlag, 1992–1997. 3 vols. Vol. I: **Foundations and Basic Theory**. xxi + 631p. $59.95 pa. ISBN 0-387-94037-5 pa. Vol. II: **Methodology and Distribution**. xxi + 600p. $59.95 pa. ISBN 0-387-94039-1 pa. Vol. III. xxv + 559p. $59.95 pa; $110.00. ISBN 0-387-94989-5pa; 0-387-94988-7.

This collection of significant papers on the development of statistics covers the last 100 years. Each paper is introduced and commented on by a prominent statistician.

Laubenbacher, Reinhard and David Pengelley. **Mathematical Expeditions: Chronicles by the Explorers.** New York: Springer-Verlag, 1998. (Undergraduate texts in mathematics. Readings in mathematics.) $59.95; $34.95 pa. ISBN 0-387-98434-8; 0-387-98433-X pa.

Well-chosen primary sources document the thrill of mathematical discovery for five different problems. Each chapter includes an introduction that summarizes the problem's history and mathematical importance.

Lehto, Olli. **Mathematics Without Borders: A History of the International Mathematical Union.** New York: Springer-Verlag, 1998. xvi + 399p. $35.00. ISBN 0-387-98358-9.

This history of the international mathematical community of the twentieth century covers the development of international cooperation in mathematics over the past decades. Appendix contains various lists: members and General Assemblies of the IMU, International Congresses of Mathematics, and Fields Medals. Complex index.

Lejeune Dirichlet, P. G. **Lectures on Number Theory.** Translated by John Stillwell. Providence, RI: American Mathematical Society, 1999. xx + 275p. (History of Mathematics, 16). $49.00 pa. ISBN 0-8218-2017-6 pa.

Translation of **Vorlesungen über Zahlentheorie**, including supplements I–IX as they fill some gaps in the main text and also showcase some famous results Dirichlet modestly omitted. Stillwell gives the historical context. Thus, this presentation gives an overview of number theory from 1640 to 1840, the period that produced the problems and ideas that are still central to the subject.

Mackey, George W. **The Scope and History of Commutative and Noncommutative Harmonic Analysis.** Providence, RI: American Mathematical Society, 1992. xi + 370p. (History of Mathematics, 5.) $52.00. ISBN 0-8218-9903-1.

Book consists mainly of reprints of six of the author's articles plus final remarks. All are expository in character and all are overlapping presentations of various aspects of the same theme.

Mankiewicz, Richard. **The Story of Mathematics.** Princeton, NJ: Princeton University Press, 2001. 192p. $24.95. ISBN 0-691-08808-X.

A nicely illustrated "coffee-table" book for mathematics, this book examines how mathematics has influenced and been influenced by social and cultural trends.

Maor, Eli. *e*: **The Story of a Number.** Princeton, NJ: Princeton University Press, 1994. xiv + 223p. $35.00. ISBN 0-691-03390-0.

History of *e*, beginning with Napier and logarithms and connections to compound interest and its role in calculus.

E *Mathematical Museum and Exhibitions.* No copyright given. Available at: http://www.math-net.de/links/show?collection=math. museum. Free.

This site, part of the Math-Net service, has annotated links to history of mathematics sites, related museums, image collections, and exhibitions. Many beautiful images here.

S Matthews, J. Rosser. **Quantification and the Quest for Medical Certainty.** Princeton, NJ: Princeton University Press, 1995. x + 195p. $39.50. ISBN 0-691-03794-9.

A history of the debates surrounding the development of medical statistics and the clinical trial.

McArthur, Charles W. **Operations Analysis in the U.S. Army Eighth Air Force in World War II**. Providence, RI: American Mathematical Society, 1990. xxiv + 349p. (History of Mathematics, 4). $36.00. ISBN 0-8218-0158-9.

A story told chronologically, from October 1942 to 1945, of the important role civilian analysts in operations research played in the Eighth Air Force. Fifteen of these men were mathematicians.

Medvedev, Fyodor A. **Scenes from the History of Real Functions.** Translated by Roger Cooke. Basel, Switzerland; Boston: Birkhäuser, 1991. 265p. (Science Networks Historical Studies, 7). $156.00. ISBN 0-8176-2572-0.

A well-documented scholarly analysis of the struggle to crystallize the fundamental ideas of analysis. Extensive references.

Monastyrsky, Michael. **Modern Mathematics in the Light of the Fields Medals.** Wellesley, MA: A. K. Peters, 1998. xv + 160p. $10.00 pa. ISBN 1-56881-083-0 pa.

Expanded English translation of the 1991 Russian original. Monastyrsky provides concise expository surveys of the mathematical work of every Fields medallist since the prize was awarded in 1936, the historical background on Fields, the prize, and the selection process. Updated by two appendixes.

Neugebauer, O. **The Exact Sciences in Antiquity.** 2nd edition. New York: Dover, 1969. xvi + 240p. $7.95 pa. ISBN 0-486-22332-9 pa.

Unabridged, slightly corrected printing of 1957 classic.

Parshall, Karen Hunger and Adrian C. Rice, eds. **Mathematics Unbound: The Evolution of an International Mathematics Research Community.** Providence, RI: American Mathematical Society; London: London Mathematical Society, 2002. xxi + 406p. (History of Mathematics, v. 23). $85.00. ISBN 0-8218-2124-5.

Documents the movement of mathematics and mathematicians from country to country and together as an international community.

Parshall, Karen Hunger and David E. Rowe. **The Emergence of the American Mathematical Research Community, 1876–1900: J. J. Sylvester, Felix Klein, and E. H. Moore.** Providence, RI; London: American Mathematical Society; London Mathematical Society, 1994. xxiv + 500p. (History of Mathematics, 8). $100.00. ISBN 0-8218-9004-2.

A scholarly, well-documented historical "exploration of a dynamic process that stimulated the growth of the discipline in America."

Phillips, Esther R., ed. **Studies in the History of Mathematics.** Washington, DC: Mathematical Association of America, 1987. 320p. (Studies in Mathematics, 26). $5.00. ISBN 0-88385-128-8.

Ten essays on recent research in the history of mathematics, in particular the period 1870–1950.

S Porter, Theodore M. **The Rise of Statistical Thinking, 1820-1900.** Princeton, NJ: Princeton University Press, 1986. xii + 333p. $19.95. ISBN 0-691-02409-X.

A detailed account of the roots of modern statistics in nineteenth-century science.

E *Princeton Mathematics Community in the 1930's: An Oral History Project.* Princeton University Library, 2002. Available at: http://infoshare1. princeton.edu/libraries/firestone/rbsc/finding_aids/mathoral/math.html. Free.

The community of eminent mathematicians and mathematical physicists at Princeton in the 1930s produced an exciting environment for mathematics. Reminiscences of these times were captured in 1985 in an oral history project. Transcripts of those interviews are now mounted on the Web and enhanced with many hyperlinks.

Resnikoff, H. L. and R. O. Wells, Jr. **Mathematics in Civilization.** Enlarged and corrected edition. New York: Dover, 1984. viii + 408p. $11.95 pa. ISBN 0-486-24674-4 pa.

Reprint of the 1973 original, which covered 4,000 years of mathematics, and supplemented with a brief chapter on twentieth-century mathematics and an appendix of solutions.

Rowe, David E., John McCleary, and Eberhard Knobloch, eds. **The History of Modern Mathematics: Proceedings of the Symposium on the History of Modern Mathematics, Vassar College, Poughkeepsie, New York, June 20–24, 1988.** Boston: Academic Press, 1989–1994. Vol. I. **Ideas and Their Reception.** xvi + 453p. $39.50. ISBN 0-12-599661-6. Vol. II. **Institutions and Applications.** xvi + 325p. $71.00. ISBN 0-12-599662-4. Vol. III. **Images, Ideas, and Communities.** xiv + 301p. $61.00. ISBN 0-12-599963-2.

Twenty-four interesting essays compose the first two volumes of this set, volume I on pure mathematics and volume II on mathematical physics and applied mathematics. Volume III is a sequel to these proceedings and a result of outstanding scholarly studies on the mathematics of the nineteenth and twentieth centuries.

Schlissel, Arthur, ed. **Essays in the History of Mathematics.** Providence, RI; London: American Mathematical Society; London Mathematical Society, 1984. v + 73p. (Memoirs of the American Mathematical Society, 298). $16.00 pa. ISBN 0-8218-2298-5 pa.

Mathematicians offer their perspectives on the origins of their fields of specialty in these six papers from a special session of the 1981 annual AMS meeting.

Smith, David Eugene. **History of Mathematics.** New York: Dover, 1958. Vol. I. **General Survey of the History of Elementary Mathematics.** xxii + 596p. $11.86 pa. ISBN 0-486-20429-4 pa. Vol. II. **Special Topics of Elementary Mathematics.** xii + 725p. $11.86 pa. ISBN 0-486-20430-8 pa.

An unaltered and unabridged reprint of the 1951 edition of the 1923–1925 original.

S Stigler, Stephen M. **The History of Statistics: The Measurement of Uncertainty Before 1900.** Cambridge, MA: Harvard University Press, 1990. xvi + 410p. $20.50 pa.; $44.50. ISBN 0-674-40341-X pa; 0-674-40340-1.

An interesting exposition of how modern statistical methods evolved as solutions to intellectual puzzles posed by scientific data.

S Stigler, Stephen M. Statistics on the Table: The History of Statistical Concepts and Methods. Cambridge, MA: Harvard University Press, 1999. ix + 488p. $45.00. ISBN 0-674-83601-4.

A highly readable collection of essays on the topic. Most are revisions of previously published work.

Stillwell, John. **Mathematics and Its History.** New York: Springer-Verlag, 2002. 2nd edition. xviii + 542p. $54.95. ISBN 0-387-95336-1.

Written for an advanced undergraduate course, this updated text aims to give a unified view of mathematics through its history. Excellent references.

Stillwell, John. **Sources of Hyperbolic Geometry.** Providence, RI: American Mathematical Society, 1996. ix + 153p. (History of Mathematics, 10). $39.00. ISBN 0-8218-0529-0.

Introductory commentaries and English translations of papers on hyperbolic geometry by Beltrami, Klein, and Poincaré. Excellent resource for those interested in the development of non-Euclidean geometry. References.

Struik, Dirk J. **A Concise History of Mathematics.** 4th revised edition. New York: Dover, 1987. xii + 228p. $7.61 pa. ISBN 0-486-60255-9 pa.

This edition adds a new chapter on the mathematics of the first half of the twentieth century and extends the bibliographies.

S Studies in the History of Statistics and Probability. Selected and edited by E. S. Pearson and M. G. Kendall. Darien, CT: Harner, 1970. Out of print. ISBN 0-85264-193-1.

S Studies in the History of Statistics and Probability. Vol. 2. Selected and edited by Maurice Kendall and R. L. Plackett. London: Charles Griffin, 1977. Out of print. ISBN 0-85264-232-6.

These collections of previously published articles explore the many facets of the historical development of probability and statistics.

Swetz, Frank J. ed. **From Five Fingers to Infinity: A Journey Through the History of Mathematics.** Chicago: Open Court, 1994. xx + 770p. $34.95 pa. ISBN 0-8126-9194-6 pa.

This anthology features fascinating historical essays (reprinted from various sources), mathematics put into cultural and social contexts, and serious attention paid to non-European mathematics.

Thompson, Thomas M. **From Error-Correcting Codes Through Sphere Packings to Simple Groups.** Washington, DC: Mathematical Association of America, 1983. xiv + 228p. (Carus Mathematical Monographs, 21). $28.50. ISBN 0-88385-023-0.

A fascinating monograph tracing the events leading from Hamming and Golay's discovery of error-correcting codes in 1948 through Conway's explication of the related group "·0" two decades later.

S Todhunter, I. **A History of the Mathematical Theory of Probability from the Time of Pascal to that of Laplace.** Bristol, England: Thoemmes Press, 2001. Reprint of 1865 original. xvi + 624p. $120.00. ISBN 1-85506-884-2.

Oft reprinted classic account of the development of probability as a science and of the men who were involved.

Woodhouse, Robert. **A History of the Calculus of Variations in the Eighteenth Century.** New York: Chelsea, 1964. ix + 154p. $12.50. ISBN 0-8284-0177-2.

A textually unaltered reprint of the 1810 **A Treatise on Isoperimetrical Problems and the Calculus of Variations.**

Wussing, Hans. **The Genesis of the Abstract Group Concept.** Translated by Abe Shenitzer. Cambridge, MA: MIT Press, 1984. 331p. $55.00. ISBN 0-262-23109-3.

In this pioneering work, Wussing traces the evolution of the abstract group concept from implicit group theoretic modes of thought in geometry and number theory through the concept of a group as a permutation group to the axiomatization of the concept.

Zdravkovska, Smilka and Peter L. Duren, eds. **Golden Years of Moscow Mathematics.** Providence, RI: American Mathematical Society, 1993. ix + 271p. (History of Mathematics, 6). $94.00. ISBN 0-8218-9003-4.

Eleven essays or reminiscences offer a fascinating glimpse into the mathematical life at Moscow State University in the 50 years following the Revolution.

Reference

Dauben, Joseph. 2002. Review of **The Universal History of Numbers and The Universal History of Computing** by Georges Ifrah. *Notices of the American Mathematical Society* 49, no. 1 (January): 32–38. Available at: http://www.ams.org/notices/200201/rev-dauben.pdf. Free.

8
Mathematics Books for Science Collections

The monographs selected for this list were culled from the literature (primarily **The American Mathematical Monthly** and **Mathematical Reviews/***MathSciNet*), recommendations from the faculty of the Department of Mathematics at the University of Illinois at Urbana–Champaign (UIUC), and the senior author's 25 years of experience as a mathematics librarian. Each title considered for inclusion was searched on the Web interface to the ILLINET online catalog to determine if holdings were widespread within the academic libraries of the State of Illinois. Generally, if a title was held only at UIUC, it was not selected for inclusion in this chapter. Also, titles were included only if they were in print at the time this book was written. In most cases, paperbound editions were selected for inclusion rather than hardbound because librarians often find them more cost effective.

This list is made up of books that should be part of any science collection and that are relatively easy to acquire; generally they are English-language titles. Each science library should, however, reflect the needs of its users. We leave the selection of specialized titles to the discretion of selectors, responding to the the mathematicians at their institutions who are doing research in those particular areas. This list aims to enable librarians to spend time and effort in acquiring those foreign-language and out-of-print or otherwise difficult to identify or obtain materials that are recommended by the mathematicians who are using their collection.

There are two other excellent sources for collection development in mathematics. One is **Library Recommendations for Undergraduate**

Mathematics (Mathematical Association of America, 1992). This list was developed by mathematicians for libraries with the emphasis on undergraduate mathematics. Books were selected without regard to availability. The other is Anderson's **A Guide to Library Service in Mathematics: The Non-Trivial Mathematics Librarian** (JAI Press, 1993). One of the chapters in this book is a comprehensive annotated bibliography of in-print mathematics books appropriate for academic, public, special libraries, or all three.

Because our page numbers are limited in this book, only monographs in the areas of general mathematics, mathematical recreations, applications of mathematics to other disciplines, and mathematical and statistical computing are included here.

General

Abbott, Edwin. **Flatland: A Romance of Many Dimensions.** New York: New American Library, 1984. 160p. $4.95 pa. ISBN 0-451-52290-7.

A reissue of the 1884 classic with an introduction highlighting issues of interest today.

Anthony, Joby Milo, ed. **In Eve's Circles.** Washington, DC: Mathematical Association of America, 1994. xxvii + 209p. (MAA Notes; 34.) $14.00. ISBN 0-88385-088-5.

Papers on geometry, history, pedagogy, and problem solving from a 1991 conference honoring Howard Eves.

Atiyah, Sir Michael and Daniel Iagolnitzer, eds. **Fields Medallists' Lectures.** 2nd edition. Singapore; River Edge, NJ: Singapore University Press, World Scientific, 2003. xv + 806p. (World Scientific Series in 20th Century Mathematics; 9.) $118.00; $62.00 pa. ISBN 981-238-256-9; ISBN 981-238-259-3.

This volume provides an interesting picture of mathematics over the last 60 years. Each medallist chose his contribution, either a reprint of an already published work or a new article produced for this volume. Every contribution is introduced by the speech given by another mathematician during the prize ceremony, which outlined the basic work of the medallist and the reasons why the prize was awarded. A photograph and an up-to-date biographical note are included as well. The second edition includes six additional medalists.

Bell, E. T. **Mathematics: Queen and Servant of Science.** Washington, DC: Mathematical Association of America, 1987. xxiv + 437p. $8.00. ISBN 0883854473.

Reprint of Bell's 1951 classic, a meandering tour of traditional mathematics.

Bennett, Curtis D. and Annalisa Crannell, eds. **Starting Our Careers: A Collection of Essays and Advice on Professional Development from the Young Mathematicians' Network.** Providence, RI: American Mathematical Society, 1999. xi + 116p. $24.00 pa. ISBN 0-8218-1543-1.

This very helpful guide originated as a weekly e-mail newsletter, *Concerns of Young Mathematicians* (http://youngmath.org/). Articles cover topics on applying for jobs, what it's like in industry and small schools, doing research, what to do with your research once it's done, getting grants, and tenure. References with each chapter. List of authors. Index.

Berlekamp, Elwyn R., John H. Conway, and Richard K. Guy. **Winning Ways for Your Mathematical Plays.** San Diego, CA: Academic Press, 1982. Vol. 1. **Games in General.** xxxii + 437p. Out of print. Vol. 2. **Games in Particular.** xxxi + 423p. + xix. $62.00 pa. ISBN 0-12-091102-7.

Berlekamp, Elwyn R., John H. Conway, and Richard K. Guy. **Winning Ways for Your Mathematical Plays.** 2nd edition. Natick, MA: A. K. Peters, 2001– . 2nd edition to be published in 4 vols. Vol. 1. xix + 276p. $49.95. ISBN 1-56881-130-6.

This whimsical work actually discusses serious mathematics: strategic analyses of games. Casual reading, however, is difficult due to specialized terminology and notations.

Beutelspacher, Albrecht. **Cryptology.** Washington, DC: Mathematical Association of America, 1994. xvi + 156p. $35.95. ISBN 0-88385-504-6.

An extensive revision of the original German edition. "An introduction to the art and science of enciphering . . . without any arcane skullduggery . . . for the delectation and instruction of the general public."

Bollobás, Béla, ed. **Littlewood's Miscellany.** New York: Cambridge University Press, 1986. 200p. $18.95. ISBN 052133702X.

An edited reprinting of Littlewood's **A Mathematician's Miscellany** and **The Mathematician's Art of Work.**

Browder, Felix E., ed. **Mathematics into the Twenty-First Century.** Providence, RI: American Mathematical Society, 1992. xviii + 491p. $165.00. ISBN 0-8218-0167-8.

These proceedings include 16 of the original 18 addresses presented at the AMS's Centennial Symposium held on August 8–12, 1988. Talks by highly respected mathematicians cover much of the most important central directions of contemporary mathematical research, broadly defined.

Bunch, Bryan. **The Kingdom of Infinite Number: A Field Guide.** New York: W. H. Freeman, 2000. xii + 388p. $23.95 pa. ISBN 0-7167-3388-9.

Mathematical tidbits for a general audience.

Campbell, Douglas M. and John C. Higgins, eds. **Mathematics: People, Problems, Results.** Belmont, CA: Wadsworth, 1984. Vol. I. xvi + 304p. Vol. II. iv + 275p. Vol. III. iv + 292p. $64.95 (set). ISBN 053403202-8.

A splendid collection of reprints of 90 expository articles, mostly by distinguished contemporary mathematicians, on all aspects of mathematics. No index.

Casacuberta, C. and M. Castellet, eds. **Mathematical Research Today and Tomorrow: Viewpoints of Seven Fields Medalists.** New York: Springer-Verlag, 1992. 112p. (Lecture Notes in Mathematics; 1525.) $36.95. ISBN 0-387-56011-4.

The text of seven invited lectures by Fields Medalists given in Barcelona, June 1991, at the Institut d'Estudis Catalans' Symposium on the Current State and Prospects of Mathematics. Includes bibliographic references.

Casti, John L. **Five Golden Rules: Great Theories of 20th-Century Mathematics and Why They Matter.** New York: Wiley, 1996. xii + 225p. $14.36 pa. ISBN 0-471-00261-5.

With characteristic flair, Casti discusses five theorems (minimax, Brouwer's fixed point, theorems of Morse and Halting, and the simplex method), their solutions, and their significance. Intended for the non-mathematician. See a later work (below).

Casti, John L. **Five More Golden Rules: Knots, Codes, Chaos and Other Great Theories of 20th-Century Mathematics.** New York: Wiley, 2000. iv + 268p. $13.56 pa. ISBN 0-471-39528-5.

This sequel to **Five Golden Rules: Great Theories of 20th-Century Mathematics and Why They Matter** (above) explores the intricacies of knot theory, functional analysis, control theory, chaotic systems, and information theory.

Casti, John L. **Mathematical Mountaintops: The Five Most Famous Problems of All Time**. New York: Oxford University Press, 2001. 177p. Out of print. ISBN 0-195-14171-7.

This title was recalled by Oxford because of alleged plagiarism.

Changeux, Jean-Pierre and Alain Connes. **Conversations on Mind, Matter, and Mathematics.** Edited and translated by M. B. DeBevoise. Princeton, NJ: Princeton University Press, 1995. xii + 260p. $13.56 pa. ISBN 0-691-00405-6.

A fascinating discussion between two creative individuals on the nature of knowledge and reality, using mathematics (Connes—see his **Noncommutative Geometry** [below]) and neuroscience (Changeux) as the playing field for philosophical jousting.

COMAP, Inc. **Principles and Practice of Mathematics.** New York: Springer-Verlag, 1997. xi + 686p. $64.95. ISBN 0-387-94612-8.

This thoughtful alternative to calculus as an entry point to college mathematics prepares students for more advanced studies in mathematics and complements the calculus sequence. Extensive applications give students a sense of the breadth of mathematics used in scientific and industrial settings.

Coxeter, H. S. M., et al., eds. **M. C. Escher, Art and Science.** New York: Elsevier Science, 1986. xiii + 402p. $50.00. ISBN 0444700110.

Papers from a 1985 international interdisciplinary conference dealing with the links between Escher's work and symmetry and geometry.

Dantzig, Tobias. **Number, the Language of Science.** 4th edition, revised and augmented. New York: Free Press, 1967. ix + 340p. $18.95. ISBN 0-02-906990-4.

Reprint of 1954 original in which the author aimed to restore to mathematics its cultural content and to present the evolution of number as the profoundly human story it is.

Davidoff, Giuliana, et al., eds. **Laboratories in Mathematical Experimentation: A Bridge to Higher Mathematics.** New York: Springer-Verlag, 1997. xix + 278p. $34.95 pa. ISBN 0-387-94922-4.

Sixteen labs help students understand the experimental nature of mathematics before continuing into theoretical courses.

Davis, Donald M. **The Nature and Power of Mathematics.** Princeton, NJ: Princeton University Press, 1993. xi + 389p. $29.95 pa. ISBN 0-691-02562-2.

Main topics covered are non-Euclidean geometry, number theory and cryptography, fractals. Assumes more mathematical maturity than most texts.

Davis, Philip J. and Reuben Hersh. **The Mathematical Experience.** Boston: Birkhäuser, 1980. xix + 440p. $39.50. ISBN 3-8176-3739-7.

A marvelous montage of history, reflection, commentary, and philosophy that reveals the roots and importance of contemporary mathematics to the general reader.

Dean, Nathaniel, Cassandra M. McZeal, and Pamela J. Williams, eds. **African Americans in Mathematics II.** Providence, RI: American Mathematical Society, 1999. xii + 168p. (Contemporary Mathematics; 252.) $35.00. ISBN 0-8218-1195-9.

Proceedings of the fourth Conference for African-American Researchers in the Mathematical Sciences held at Rice University on June 16–19, 1998. The proceedings of the second conference held at Rutgers University in 1996 are still available from the AMS.

Devlin, Keith. **All the Math That's Fit to Print: Articles from the Manchester Guardian.** Washington, DC: Mathematical Association of America, 1994. xvii + 330p. $29.95 pa. ISBN 0-88385-515-1.

A decade of newspaper columns by one of the best mathematics writers. A must for all levels of readers.

Devlin, Keith. **Goodbye, Descartes: The End of Logic and the Search for a New Cosmology.** New York: Wiley, 1997. x + 301p. $14.95 pa. ISBN 0-471-25186-0.

An interesting survey of the rise of logic and Cartesian views of the mind. Devlin concludes that traditional mathematical and scientific views of the mind will not be fruitful and must be replaced.

Devlin, Keith. **The Language of Mathematics: Making the Invisible Visible.** New York: W. H. Freeman, 1998. viii + 344p. $11.96 pa. ISBN 0-7167-3967-4.

This spinoff of his **Mathematics: The Science of Patterns** (below) has added two new chapters on patterns of chance and cosmology. Even though it is intended for a wider audience, it has no references or suggestions for further reading.

Devlin, Keith. **Mathematics: The New Golden Age.** New York: Columbia University Press, 1999. xi + 320p. $19.96. ISBN 0-2311-1638-1.

In this well-written and informative book, Devlin captures all of the power, beauty, and excitement of mathematics. Revised and updated to include developments of the 1980s and1990s, for example, Fermat's Last Theorem, major new sections on knots and topology, and the mathematics of the physical universe.

Devlin, Keith. **Mathematics: The Science of Patterns: The Search for Order in Life, Mind and the Universe.** New York: Scientific American Library, 1997. vii + 216p. $19.95 pa. ISBN 0-7167-6002-3.

Updated to reflect proof of Fermat's Last Theorem.

Devlin, Keith. **The Millennium Problems: The Seven Greatest Unsolved Mathematical Puzzles of Our Time**. New York: Basic Books, 2002. x +237p. $26.00 ISBN 0-465-01729-0.

The Clay Mathematics Institute is offering 1 million dollars to the person or persons who solve each of these seven problems. Devlin's book details each problem's background and description in layman's terms.

Dewdney, A. K. **A Mathematical Mystery Tour: Discovering the Truth and Beauty of the Cosmos.** New York: Wiley, 1999. vi + 218p. $18.36 pa. ISBN 0-471-23847-3.

On a tour of great sites of discovery, from the ruins of ancient Greece to a present-day computer lab, Dewdney tells the stories of the fascinating insights and leaps of imagination that have revealed the astonishing power of mathematics to unveil the beautiful truths that rule the universe.

Dewdney, A. K. **200% of Nothing: An Eye-Opening Tour Through the Twists and Turns of Math Abuse and Innumeracy.** New York: Wiley, 1993. ix + 182p. $12.95 pa. ISBN 0-471-14574-2.

A witty collection of distortions and misrepresentations that advertisers, politicians, and others foist on an innumerate public. Great resource for introductory mathematics and statistics courses.

Dieudonné, Jean. **A Panorama of Pure Mathematics: As Seen by N. Bourbaki.** San Diego, CA: Academic Press, 1982. x + 289p. (Pure and Applied Mathematics; 97.) $68.00. ISBN 0-12-215560-2.

A remarkable survey of those areas of mathematics that have been exposed in the 30-plus years of the Seminaire Bourbaki.

Dudley, Underwood. **Mathematical Cranks.** Washington, DC: Mathematical Association of America, 1992. x + 372p. $33.95 pa. ISBN 0-88385-507-0.

Dudley, who has saved crank submissions over the years, has produced a fascinating book about a variety of strange people obsessed by mathematics.

Dudley, Underwood. **The Trisectors.** 2nd edition. Washington, DC: Mathematical Association of America, 1994. xvii + 184p. $12.50. ISBN 0-88385-514-3.

Lightly revised from **The Budget of Trisections**, this delightful book is a hilarious introduction to trisection, trisectors, and erroneous constructions.

Dunham, William. **Journey Through Genius: The Great Theorems of Mathematics.** New York: Wiley, 1990. xiii + 300p. $29.95. ISBN 0471500305.

Twelve mathematical masterpieces from Hippocrates' quadrature of the lune to Cantor's theorem on nondenumerability, each set in historical context and explained in modern language. Excellent source material for popular audiences.

Dunham, William. **The Mathematical Universe: An Alphabetical Journey Through the Great Proofs, Problems, and Personalities.** New York: Wiley, 1994. vi + 314p. $24.95. ISBN 0-471-53656-3.

A valuable supplement for the undergraduate. In 26 essays the author goes from Arithmetic to Z (the complex variable).

Ekeland, I. **The Broken Dice: And Other Mathematical Tales of Chance.** Translated by Carol Volk. Chicago: University of Chicago Press, 1993. 183p. $19.95. ISBN 0-226-19991-6.

A refreshingly literary look at the mathematics of chance as partly told through Norse myths.

Ekeland, Ivar. **Mathematics and the Unexpected.** Chicago: University of Chicago Press, 1990. xiii + 146p. $9.95 pa. ISBN 022619990-8.

Translation of a popular French monograph explaining to the layman how deterministic mechanics can lead to random motion and relating these two to ancient worldviews as reflected by Homer.

Emmer, Michele, ed. **The Visual Mind: Art and Mathematics.** Cambridge, MA: MIT Press, 1993. xvii + 274p. $55.00. ISBN 0-262-05048-X.

This fascinating approach to both the mathematics of visual art and the visualization of mathematics consists of 35 essays by mathematicians and visual artisits. A valuable resource for a mathematics appreciation course.

Enzensberger, Hans Magnus. **The Number Devil: A Mathematical Adventure.** Translated by Michael Henry Heim. Illustrated by Rotraut Susanne Berner. New York: Henry Holt, 2000. 262p. $14.40 pa. ISBN 0-805-06299-8.

A best-seller that turns numbers into ideas and ideas into thrilling adventures for adults and children alike. Enzensberger brings together the surreal logic of **Alice in Wonderland** with the kind of math everyone would love, if only they had a number devil to teach it to them.

E Ewing, John, ed. **Towards Excellence: Leading a Doctoral Mathematics Department in the 21st Century.** Providence, RI: American Mathematical Society, 1999. xv + 261p. Free. ISBN 0-8218-2033-8. Also available on the Web at: http://www.ams.org/towardsexcellence. Free.

This publication was written by and for mathematicians who work in America's research universities. The AMS Task Force on Excellence has provided examples and essays to show how mathematics departments, through research and the instructional program, should position themselves to receive new and reallocated resources by meeting the needs of their institutions.

Ewing, Richard E., Kenneth I. Gross, and Clyde F. Martin, eds. **The Merging of Disciplines: New Directions in Pure, Applied, and Computational Mathematics.** New York: Springer-Verlag, 1986. xvi + 214p. $64.95. ISBN 0387964142.

An excellent collection of thoughtful papers on all aspects of mathematics from the proceedings of the 1985 symposium honoring Gail Young on the occasion of his 70th birthday.

Fadiman, Clifton, ed. **Fantasia Mathematica.** New York: Springer-Verlag, 1997. xix + 298p. $16.88 pa. ISBN 0-387-94931-3.

This reprint of the 1958 anthology of mathematically oriented short stories, anecdotes, essays, and poems should delight a new generation of readers.

Fadiman, Clifton, ed. **The Mathematical Magpie.** New York: Springer-Verlag, 1997. xviii + 303p. $19.95. ISBN 0-387-94950-X.

A sequel to **Fantasia Mathematica** (above).

Ferguson, Claire. **Helaman Ferguson: Mathematics in Stone and Bronze.** Erie, PA: Meridian Crative Group, 1994. xv + 79p. $29.95. ISBN 0-96391921-0-0.

Gorgeous photographs of 29 striking works by mathematician/sculptor Helaman Ferguson. Mathematical discussions by Helaman and artistic commentaries by his wife, Claire.

Fine, Benjamin and Gerhard Rosenberger. **The Fundamental Theorem of Algebra.** New York: Springer-Verlag, 1997. xi + 208p. $42.95. ISBN 0-387-94657-8.

The purpose of this book is to examine three pairs of proofs of the theorem from three different areas of mathematics: abstract algebra, complex analysis, and topology. Intended for junior/senior level undergraduate mathematics students or first-year graduate students.

E Fischer, Gerd and Ulf Rehmann, eds. **Proceedings of the International Congress of Mathematicians, August 17–18, 1998, Berlin.** Bielefeld, Germany: Deutscher Mathematiker-Vereinigung, 1998. (Documenta Mathematika; Extra Volume ICM 1998.) $140.00 (set). Vol. I: **Plenary Lectures and Ceremonies.** 662p. Vol. II: **Invited Lectures.** 881p. Vol. III: **Invited Lectures.** 825p. Also available at: http://www.mathematik.uni-bielefeld.de/DMV-J/xvol-icm/ICM.html. Free.

These volumes contain well-written expository articles by prominent researchers and lectures by the Fields medalists and the Rolf Nevanlinna Prize winner. These and earlier ICM proceedings are distributed by the American Mathematical Society.

Fomenko, Anatolii T. **Mathematical Impressions.** Providence, RI: American Mathematical Society, 1990. 184p. $19.00. ISBN 0-8218-0162-7.

A collection of nearly 80 starkly beautiful drawings and paintings conveying Fomenko's romantic visions. Mathematical theorems and human emotions serve as inspiration.

Garrity, Thomas A. **All the Mathematics You Missed: But Need to Know for Graduate School.** New York: Cambridge University Press, 2002. xxvii + 347p. $25.00 pa; $55.00. ISBN 0-521-79707-1 pa; 0-521-79285-1.

Useful review and bibliography for graduate students and librarians.

Growney, JoAnne. **Intersections.** Bloomsburg, PA: Kadet Press, 1993. 56p. $6.95 pa. ISBN 0-9637964-0-2.

One-fourth of the spare and sometimes elegant poems in this slim volume are on mathematical subjects.

Gudder, Stanley. **A Mathematical Journey.** 2nd edition. New York: McGraw-Hill, 1994. xvii + 622p. $55.00. ISBN 0-07-025130-4.

This pleasant journal for non-math majors makes stops at art, gambling, and consumer mathematics as well as logic, number theory, and graphs.

Herstein, I. N. and I. Kaplansky. **Matters Mathematical.** 2nd edition. New York: Chelsea, 1978. viii + 246p. $18.95. ISBN 0-8284-0300-7.

Reprint, with minor additions and corrections, of 1974 original: a series of lectures for nonmajors in mathematics.

Higgins, Peter M. **Mathematics for the Imagination**. Oxford: Oxford University Press, 2002. vii +229p. $14.95 pa. ISBN0-19-860460-2.

Enlightening tour of mathematics involved in history, biography, astronomy, geometry, and geography.

Hildebrandt, Stefan and Anthony Tromba. **The Parsimonious Universe: Shape and Form in the Natural World.** New York: Springer-Verlag, 1996. xiii + 330p. $32.00. ISBN 0-387-97991-3.

A lavishly illustrated exploration of the worldly consequences of optimization principles.

Hilton, Peter, Derek Holton, and Jean Pedersen. **Mathematical Reflections In a Room With Many Mirrors.** New York: Springer-Verlag, 1997. xvi + 351p. $37.95. ISBN 0-387-94770-1.

The purpose of this text is twofold: to teach mathematics so that students comprehend how and why mathematics is done by those who do it successfully and to attract readers to mathematics.

Hilton, Peter, Friedrich Hirzebruch, and Reinhold Remmert, eds. **Miscellanea Mathematica.** Berlin; New York: Springer-Verlag, 1991. xiii + 326p. $42.95. ISBN 0-387-54174-8.

A score of world-famous mathematicians such as Atiyah, Cartan, Hironaka, and Weil have contributed papers on a very diverse range of topics.

Hoffman, Paul. **Archimedes' Revenge: The Joys and Perils of Mathematics.** New York: Fawcett, 1989. viii + 285p. $5.99. ISBN 0449-21750-7.

A vivid account of selected challenges in modern mathematics as told through the actions and words of individuals working on these problems.

Honsberger, Ross. **Mathematical Gems III.** Washington, DC: Mathematical Association of America, 1985. 250p. (Dolciani Mathematical Expositions; 9.) $12.00. ISBN 0883853132.

Eighteen vignettes of number theory, combinatorics, and geometry, which will delight anyone who has studied college mathematics.

Iaglom, A. M. and I. M. Iaglom. **Challenging Mathematical Programs with Elementary Solutions.** Translated by James McCawley, Jr. New York: Dover, 1987. Vol. I: **Combinatorial Analysis and Probability Theory.** ix + 231p. $7.16 pa. ISBN 0486655369. Vol. II: **Problems in Various Branches of Mathematics.** ix + 214p. $6.36 pa. ISBN 0486655377.

Reprint of the translation from Russian of **NonElementary Problems in an Elementary Exposition.**

Jacobs, Harold R. **Mathematics, a Human Endeavor: A Book for Those Who Think They Don't Like the Subject.** 3rd edition. New York: W. H. Freeman, 1994. xiii + 678p. $58.95. ISBN 0-7167-2426-X.

Revision of 1971 classic. Graphics and cartoons demonstrate mathematical ideas.

Jacobs, Konrad. **Invitation to Mathematics.** Princeton, NJ: Princeton University Press, 1992. xi + 247p. $24.95 pa. ISBN 0-691-02528-2.

Translation of 1987 **Resultate**, a wide-ranging introduction to mathematical thinking.

Jerison, David, I. M. Singer, and Daniel W. Stroock, eds. **The Legacy of Norbert Wiener.** Providence, RI: American Mathematical Society, 1997. xix + 405p. (Proceedings of Symposia in Pure Mathematics; 60.) $80.00. ISBN 0-8218-0415-4.

Proceedings of a centennial symposium in honor of the 100th anniversary of Norbert Wiener's birth held at MIT in October 1994.

Kac, Mark, Gian-Carlo Rota, and Jacob T. Schwartz. **Discrete Thoughts: Essays on Mathematics, Science, and Philosophy.** Boston: Birkhäuser, 1992. xii + 266p. $32.50 pa. ISBN 0-8176-3636-6.

A collection of essays, some of which are new, by three of the most scholarly and thoughtful mathematicians.

Kahneman, Daniel, Paul Slovic, and Amos Tversky, eds. **Judgment Under Uncertainty: Heuristics and Biases.** New York: Cambridge University Press, 1982. xiii + 555p. $35.95. ISBN 0521284147.

Interesting collection of articles focusing on psychological studies of how people estimate probabilities and the types of biases produced by these heuristic methods. Good set of references.

Kenschaft, Patricia Clark and Sandra Keith. **Winning Women into Mathematics.** Washington, DC: Mathematical Association of America, 1991. ix + 78p. $16.50. ISBN 0-88385-453-8.

This varied collection of materials documents the increasing role of women in mathematics as well as the continuing impediments they face.

Kline, Morris. **Mathematics and the Physical World.** New York: Dover, 1981. 482p. $11.95 pa. ISBN 0-486-24104-1.

Corrected reprint of the 1959 original, a series of surveys on various topics of applied mathematics.

Kline, Morris. **Mathematics in Western Culture.** New York: Oxford University Press, 1982. x + 484p. $17.95. ISBN 0-19-500714-X.

Reprint of 1953 original, which discusses the cultural significance of mathematics in the development of Western civilization.

Lang, Serge. **The Beauty of Doing Mathematics: Three Public Dialogues.** New York: Springer-Verlag, 1985. x + 127p. $29.95 pa. ISBN 0387961496.

English translation of three highly interactive public lectures delivered by Lang at the Palais de la Decouverte in Paris.

Loeb, Arthur L. **Concepts & Images: Visual Mathematics.** Boston: Birkhäuser, 1993. xi + 228p. $58.50. ISBN 0-8176-3620-X.

An informal and inviting introduction to the mathematics of visual figures: symmetry, tessellation, and geometric construction.

Lyons, Louis. **All You Wanted to Know about Mathematics But Were Afraid to Ask: Mathematics for Science Students.** New York: Cambridge University Press, 1995–1998. 2 vols. Vol. 1. xviii + 325p. $27.95 pa. ISBN 0-521-43600-1. Vol. 2. xv + 382p. $29.95 pa. ISBN 0-521-43601-X.

Popular mathematics text for undergraduates in the physical sciences. Questions such as, "Will gazing out of a window at night remind you about boundary conditions for partial differential equations?" help students relate formal mathematical theory and applications to real systems. Appendixes. Index.

Mac Lane, Saunders. **Categories for the Working Mathematician.** 2nd edition. New York: Springer-Verlag, 1998. xii + 314p. (Graduate Texts in Mathematics; 5.) $49.46. ISBN 0-387-98403-8.

Reprint of the 1971 original, an enjoyable and convincing book that shows that categories provide a convenient conceptual language that can be used to illuminate and clarify a wide variety of fields of mathematical research. This edition adds new chapters: one on symmetric monoidal categories and braided monoidal categories and the other on 2-categories and the higher-dimensional categories. Updated and expanded bibliography.

Mermin, N. David. **Boojums All the Way Through: Communicating Science in a Prosaic Age.** New York: Cambridge University Press, 1990. xxi + 308p. $21.95 pa. ISBN 0-521-38880-5.

A collection of warm and lucid essays for laypeople about mathematics and physics, mostly reprinted from **Physics Today**.

Miller, Arthur I. **Insights of Genius: Imagery and Creativity in Science and Art.** New York: Springer-Verlag, 1996. xxii + 482p. $15.16. ISBN 0-387-94671-3.

Includes a fascinating discussion of Poincaré's creativity profile by his contemporary, the psychologist Edouard Toulouse.

Morrison, Philip and Phylis Morrison. **Powers of Ten.** Revised edition. New York: W. H. Freeman, 1994. 150p. $15.96. ISBN 071676008-8.

Stunning re-creation on paper of the famous short film, *Powers of Ten.* Each righthand page contains a view of a picnic in Chicago at different distances, while the lefthand page offers commentary and other illustrations at each scale. Includes an opening essay on matters of size, concluding commentary, and references.

Newton, Sir Isaac. **The Principia: Mathematical Principles of Natural Philosophy.** Translated by I. Barnard Cohen and Anne Whitman; assisted by Julia. Budenz. Berkeley, CA: University of California Press, 1999. xvii + 974p. $35.00 pa. ISBN 0-520-08817-4.

This highly regarded work, the first completely new translation in 270 years, is based on the third (1726) edition, the final revised version approved by Newton. It includes extracts from the earlier editions, corrects errors found in earlier versions, and replaces archaic English with contemporary prose and up-to-date mathematical forms. Includes Cohen's **A Guide to Newton's Principia**, an up-to-date on matters of Newton.

Paulos, John Allen. **Beyond Numeracy: Ruminations of a Numbers Man.** New York: Alfred A. Knopf, 1991. xiii + 285p. $21.50. ISBN 0-394-58640-9.

Seventy brief essays covering mathematical vocabulary from algebra to Zeno plus a list of the "top 40" mathematicians from antiquity to the present.

Paulos, John Allen. **Innumeracy: Mathematical Illiteracy and Its Consequences.** New York: Vintage Books, 1990. 135p. $16.95. ISBN 0809074478.

An outspoken exposé of public obliviousness to quantitative meanings. The author links innumeracy with the spread of pseudoscience.

Paulos, John Allen. **Mathematics and Humor.** Chicago: University of Chicago Press, 1982. 116p. $12.95. ISBN 0226650251.

A serious, though brief, inquiry into common elements in mathematics and humor. The author uses self-reference paradoxes and catastrophe theory as mathematical paradigms of various types of humor.

Peterson, Ivars. **Islands of Truth: A Mathematical Mystery Cruise.** New York: W. H. Freeman, 1990. xvii + 325p. $21.95. ISBN 0-7167-2113-9.

Innovative and pleasure-filled guide reveals to the mathematical tourist many mysteries of modern mathematics.

Peterson, Ivars. **Jungles of Randomness: A Mathematical Safari.** New York: Wiley, 1998. $31.95 pa. ISBN 0-471-16449-6.

Another of Peterson's guided tours of mathematics. Like the others, it's beautifully produced and very readable.

Peterson, Ivars. **The Mathematical Tourist: New and Updated Snapshots of Modern Mathematics.** New York: W. H. Freeman, 1998. xviii + 266p. $11.96. ISBN 071673250-5.

A top-notch example of popular mathematical writing. The author updates and expands his 1988 work to give insight into modern mathematics. New sections include crystal structure, string theory, mathematicians' use of computers, chaos theory, and Fermat's Last Theorem.

Pickover, Clifford A. **Keys to Infinity.** New York: Wiley, 1995. xviii + 331p. $13.56 pa. ISBN 0-471-19334-8.

Pickover compiles a delightful anthology of essays, puzzles, computer code, images, and quotations to explore the patterns emerging from recursion, limits, randomness, and other infinite processes. For the mathematically literate.

Pickover, Clifford A., ed. **The Pattern Book: Fractals, Art, and Nature.** Singapore; River Edge, NJ: World Scientific, 1995. xxxvi + 427p. $51.00. ISBN 981-02-1426-X.

An interesting collection of patterns, many with computational hints and recipes for their creation. Glossary of technical terms.

Reid, Constance. **From Zero to Infinity: What Makes Numbers Interesting.** 4th edition. Washington, DC: Mathematical Association of America, 1992. xiv + 186p. $24.95 pa. ISBN 0-88385-505-4.

Reprint of the 1955 classic.

Roberts, Joe. **Lure of the Integers.** Washington, DC: Mathematical Association of America, 1992. xvii + 310p. $25.00 pa. ISBN 0-88385-502-X.

This collection of interesting facts about the number n for around 75 different values of n is intended for both the beginner and professional. Each section includes a bibliography of relevant reading.

Rucker, Rudy. **Infinity and the Mind: The Science and Philosophy of the Infinite.** Princeton, NJ: Princeton University Press, 1995. x + 342p. $12.76. ISBN 0691001723.

A wideranging discourse on the infinite, mixing traditional mathematical aspects with philosophical roots and pseudoscience. Exposition is both popular and technical.

Ruelle, David. **Chance and Chaos.** Princeton, NJ: Princeton University Press, 1991. xi + 195p. $37.50. ISBN 0-691-08574-9.

This superb, concise monograph explains for lay readers the profound shift of natural philosophy from phenomena ruled by determinism to events determined by chaos.

Schiffer, M. M. and Leon Bowden. **Role of Mathematics in Science.** Washington, DC: Mathematical Association of America, 1984. xi + 207p. (New Mathematical Library; 30.) $8.00. ISBN 0883856301.

A delightful mathematical excursion through classical science (mainly mechanics) to illustrate and teach the role of mathematics as a sixth sense for scientific intuition.

Schroeder, Manfred. **Fractals, Chaos, Power Laws: Minutes from an Infinite Paradise.** New York: W. H. Freeman, 1990. xviii + 429p. $19.96 pa. ISBN 0-7167-2357-3.

Clearly written and inviting exposition of the worldly and mathematical manifestations of self-similarity. For the literate, but not highly scientific, audience.

Smith, Karl J. **Mathematics, Its Power and Utility.** 6th edition. Pacific Grove, CA: Brooks-Cole, 2000. xvi + 616p. $75.95. ISBN 0 534364551.

A beginning-level text emphasizing problem solving and using techniques from arithmetics, algebra, and geometry. Includes bibliography and discussion of math anxiety.

Smith, Karl J. **The Nature of Mathematics.** 9th edition. Pacific Grove, CA: Brooks/Cole, 2001. xxviii + 995p. $85.95 pa. ISBN 0-534-36890-5.

The author emphasizes problem solving and estimation with new problems coupled with numerous in-text study aids. The ninth edition goes further than earlier editions toward helping students master mathematics rather than just get the right answer.

Steinhaus, H. **Mathematical Snapshots.** 3rd American edition, revised and enlarged. New York: Oxford University Press, 1983. 311p. $8.95. ISBN 0195032675.

Reprint of 1969 edition of 1938 classic uses visual reasoning to "stretch the imagination without unduly straining the mind."

Sterrett, Andrew, ed. **101 Careers in Mathematics.** Washington, DC: Mathematical Association of America, 1996. x + 260p. $20.00 pa. ISBN 0-88385-704-9.

A selection of informal personal profiles from Sterrett's "mathematician of the month" series, plus job-seeking advice for the undergraduate reprinted from **Math Horizons.**

Stewart, Ian. **Does God Play Dice? The Mathematics of Chaos.** Cambridge, MA: Basil Blackwell, 1990. 317p. $22.95 pa. ISBN 1-55786-106-4.

Popular, witty, yet mathematically vigorous treatment of chaos theory.

Stillwell, John. **Numbers and Geometry.** New York: Springer-Verlag, 1998. xiv + 339p. $34.95. ISBN 0-387-98289-2.

In an engaging storytelling style, Stillwell weaves together introductory number theory and geometry and algebra. Highly recommended for independent study by undergraduate math students.

Weyl, Hermann. **Symmetry.** Princeton, NJ: Princeton University Press, 1989. 176p. $15.95 pa. ISBN 0-691-02374-3.

Reprint of 1952 classic on symmetry, its manifestations, and its mathematical significance.

White, Alvin M., ed. **Essays in Humanistic Mathematics.** Washington, DC: Mathematical Association of America, 1993. xii + 212p. (MAA Notes; 32.) $12.00 pa. ISBN 0-88385-089-3.

A valuable resource of 22 brief essays, often elegant or provocative, on broadly cultural aspects of mathematics.

Zaslavsky, Claudia. **Africa Counts: Number and Pattern in African Culture.** Revised edition. Brooklyn, NY: Lawrence Hill Books, 1991. 328p. $14.95 pa. ISBN 1-55652-075-1.

A beautiful book, full of pictures and figures illustrating the development of mathematics among the tribes of sub-Saharan Africa: numeration systems, cultural significance of numbers, mathematical games, and geometric form and pattern in architecture and art.

Mathematical Recreations

Andreescu, Titu and Riazvan Galca. **Mathematical Olympiad Challenges.** Boston: Birkhäuser, 2000. xv + 260p. $29.95 pa. ISBN 0-8176-4155-6.

This is a rich collection of problems selected from numerous mathematical competitions and journals and compiled by two of the coaches of the U.S. International Mathematical Olympiad Team. The problems are clustered by topic into self-contained sections with solutions provided separately.

Ball, W. W. Rouse and H. S. M. Coxeter. **Mathematical Recreations and Essays.** 13th edition. New York: Dover, 1987. xvii + 428p. $11.00 pa. ISBN 0486253570.

This edition features the role of the computer in extending the list of Mersenne primes and in the resolution of the problem of "squaring the square."

Barbeau, Edward J., Murray S. Klamkin, and William O. J. Moser. **Five Hundred Mathematical Challenges.** Washington, DC: Mathematical Association of America, 1995. xi + 227p. $36.95. ISBN 0-88385-519-4.

With problems progressing from easy to Olympiad level, this collection provides a solid base for students entering mathematical competitions.

Berlekamp, Elwyn and Tom Rogers, eds. **The Mathemagician and Pied Puzzler: A Collection in Tribute to Martin Gardner.** Wellesley, MA: A. K. Peters, 1999. x + 266p. $34.00 pa. ISBN 1-56881-075-X.

Proceedings of the first "gathering for Gardner" held in 1993. Games, puzzles, and recreational mathematics (all accessible to general readers) contributed by the world's foremost magicians, puzzlists, and mathematicians.

Berzsenyi, George and Stephen B. Maurer. **The Contest Problem Book V.** Washington, DC: Mathematical Association of America, 1997. xx + 286p. (New Mathematical Library; 38.) $27.95 pa. ISBN 0-88385-640-9.

Problems and solutions from the American High School Mathematics Exam (AHSME) and the American Invitational Mathematics Examination (AIME) for the years 1983–1988. A thorough index, comments, and other information are included.

De Souza, Paulo Ney and Jorge-Nuno Silva. **Berkeley Problems in Mathematics.** New York: Springer-Verlag, 2004. 3rd edition. xiv + 591p. $44.95 pa. ISBN 0-387-00892-6.

E De Souza, Paulo Ney and Jorge-Nuno Silva, eds. *Berkeley Preliminary Exams*. No copyright given. Available at: http://math.berkeley.edu/~desouza/pb.html. Free.

Problems and solutions in real and complex analysis, calculus, differential equations, linear and abstract algebra drawn from 20 years, 1977–2000, of Berkeley prelim exams. A good resource for graduate and undergraduate students. The actual exams are posted on the Web site.

Gardiner, Toni. **More Mathematical Challenges.** New York: Cambridge University Press, 1997. 140p. $14.95 pa. ISBN 0-521-58568-6.

Most of the problems in this collection come from the 1989–1995 United Kingdom Junior Mathematical Olympiads.

Gardner, Martin. **Aha! Gotcha: Paradoxes to Puzzle and Delight.** New York: W. H. Freeman, 1982. vii + 164p. $11.95 pa. ISBN 0-7167-1414-0.

Another delightful book by Gardner, in which he explains, in nontechnical language, why each paradox is paradoxical. References and suggested readings appear at end of book.

Gardner, Martin. **The Last Recreations: Hydras, Eggs, and Other Mathematical Recreations.** New York: Copernicus, 1997. x + 392p. $20.00. ISBN 0-387-94929-1.

Gardner's "Mathematical Games" columns from the **Scientific American** for the last seven years before his retirement in 1986. One of the many Gardner books still in print.

Gardner, Martin. **Mathematical Circus: More Puzzles, Games, Paradoxes, and Other Mathematical Entertainments from Scientific**

American. Washington, DC: Mathematical Association of America, 1992. xv + 279p. $10.45 pa. ISBN 0-88385-506-2.

Updated from 1979 edition, with a new bibliography.

Gardner, Martin. **Penrose Tiles to Trapdoor Ciphers ... and the Return of Dr. Matrix.** Revised Edition. Washington, DC: Mathematical Association of America, 1997. ix + 319p. $27.95 pa. ISBN 0-88385-521-6.

This edition features a new bibliography, corrections to the text, and postscript by Gardner.

Gardner, Martin. **Unexpected Hanging and Other Mathematical Diversions.** Chicago: University of Chicago Press, 1991. 263p. $15.95 pa. ISBN 0-226-28256-2.

Augmented, updated edition of a collection of the author's **Scientific American** columns.

Gardner, Martin. **The Universe in a Handkerchief: Lewis Carroll's Mathematical Recreations, Games, Puzzles, and Word Plays.** New York: Copernicus, 1996. x + 158p. $14.67. ISBN 0-387-94673-X.

An entertaining, informative introduction and guide. Bibliographical references.

Gilbert, George T., Mark I. Krusemeyer, and Loren C. Larsen. **The Wohascum County Problem Book.** Washington, DC: Mathematical Association of America, 1993. ix + 233p. (Dolciani Mathematical Expositions; 14.) $24.95 pa. ISBN 0-88385-316-7.

One hundred thirty challenging, original problems with clear, elegant solutions.

Golomb, Solomon W. **Polyominoes: Puzzles, Patterns, Problems, and Packings.** 2nd edition. Princeton, NJ: Princeton University Press, 1994. xii + 184p. $16.95 pa. ISBN 0-691-02444-8.

Invaluable introduction to a fascinating recreation that has inspired volumes of mathematical research. This edition has added two new chapters on recent developments. Bibliography.

Guy, Richard K. and Robert E. Woodrow, eds. **The Lighter Side of Mathematics.** Washington, DC: Mathematical Asociation of America, 1994. viii + 367p. $20.00 pa. ISBN 0-88385-516-X.

Thirty-five papers from the 1986 Eugene Sterns Memorial Conference on Recreational Mathematics & Its History held at the University of Calgary.

Halmos, Paul. **Problems for Mathematicians, Young and Old.** Washington, DC: Mathematical Association of America, 1991. xviii + 318p. (Dolciani Mathematical Expositions; 12.) $35.95 pa. ISBN 0-88385-320-5.

This appealing book arranges the 165 problems by the mathematical subdisciplines into which they most naturally fit. The fascinating problems and commentary stimulate both student and teacher to think and do mathematics.

Hardy, Kenneth and Kenneth S. Williams. **The Green Book of Mathematical Problems.** New York: Dover, 1997. ix + 173p. $6.25 pa. ISBN 0-486-69573-5.

Corrected reprint of their 1985 **Green Book: 100 Practice Problems for Undergraduate Mathematics Competitions.**

Honsberger, Ross. **From Erdös to Kiev: Problems of Olympiad Caliber.** Washington, DC: Mathematical Association of America, 1996. xii + 257p. (Dolciani Mathematical Expositions; 17.) $34.00. ISBN 0-88385-324-8.

The author has made these problems, drawn from **Crux Mathematicorum** 1987–1988, appealing to the general reader. The problems are made interesting by drawing attention to subtleties and solutions are clear, easy to read, and instructive.

Klamkin, Murray S. **International Mathematical Olympiads, 1978–1985 and Forty Supplementary Problems.** Washington, DC: Mathematical Association of America, 1986. xii + 141p. (New Mathematical Library; 31.) $18.00 pa. ISBN 088386631X.

An excellent collection of truly challenging problems from the Olympiads with rewritten and expanded solutions. References and a glossary of uncommon terms.

Klamkin, Murray S. **U.S.A. Mathematical Olympiads, 1972–1986.** Washington, DC: Mathematical Association of America, 1988. xv + 127p. (New Mathematical Library; 33.) $14.50 pa. ISBN 0883856344.

A collection of intriguing problems and elegant solutions, grouped by subject. Comprehensive bibliography and glossary.

Martin, George E. **Polyominoes: A Guide to Puzzles and Problems in Tiling.** Washington, DC: Mathematical Association of America, 1991. ix + 184p. $14.95 pa. ISBN 0-88385-501-1.

A systematic exploration with many examples and problems of the tiling properties of polyominoes.

Mosteller, Frederick. **Fifty Challenging Problems in Probability with Solutions.** New York: Dover, 1987. viii + 88p. $3.95 pa. ISBN 0486653552.

An unabridged reprint of the 1965 work, which demonstrates mathematical thinking at its best.

Shklarsky, D. O., N. N. Chentzov, and I. M. Yaglom. **The USSR Olympiad Problem Book: Selected Problems and Theorems in Elementary Mathematics.** Translated by John Maykovich. New York: Dover, 1993. xvi + 452p. $10.36 pa. ISBN 0-486-27709-7.

Reprint of 1962 edition, which was one of the all-time best problem collections.

Székely, Gábor J. **Contest in Higher Mathematics: Miklós Schweitzer Competitions, 1962–1991.** New York: Springer-Verlag, 1996. vii + 569p. $64.95. ISBN 0-387-94588-1.

Questions and solutions from this prestigious Hungarian take-home exam.

Applications of Mathematics to Other Disciplines

Anderson, Simon P., André de Palma, and Jacques-François Thisse. **Discrete Choice Theory of Product Differentiation.** Cambridge, MA: MIT Press, 1992. xix + 423p. $55.00. ISBN 0-262-01128-X.

In this mathematically sophisticated and rigorous work the authors model consumer demands among undifferentiated products under free market and oligopolistic conditions.

Andresen, Jorgen Ellegaard, et al., eds. **Geometry and Physics.** New York: Dekker, 1997. xxii + 745p. (Lecture Notes in Pure and Applied Mathematics; 184.) $185.00. ISBN 0-8247-9791-4.

Invited papers from a series of workshops, a summer school and a conference held in Denmark in 1995.

Arbib, Michael A. **Brains, Machines, and Mathematics.** 2nd edition. New York: Springer-Verlag, 1987. xvi + 202p. $54.95. ISBN 0387965394.

Revision of innovative 1962 work outlining a theory of automata to explain the processing of information in brainlike machines.

Arnold, V. I. **Catastrophe Theory.** 3rd revised and expanded edition. Translated by G. S. Wassermann and R. K. Thomas. New York: Springer-Verlag, 1992. xiii + 150p. $32.95. ISBN 038754811-4.

A masterful, elementary exposition of catastrophe theory, from Whitney's singularity theory to Dynkin diagrams.

Arnold, V. I. **Mathematical Methods of Classical Mechanics.** 2nd edition. Translated by K. Vogtmann and A. Weinstein. New York: Springer-Verlag, 1989. xvi + 508p. (Graduate Texts in Mathematics; 60.) $49.50. ISBN 0387968903.

Based on a course given by the author in 1966–1968. Includes three new appendixes on work on Poisson structures.

Aston, Philip J., ed. **Nonlinear Mathematics and Its Applications.** New York: Cambridge University Press, 1996. vii + 256p. $26.95. ISBN 0-521-57676-8.

Contains most of the lectures given at a 1995 EPSRC Spring School held at the University of Surrey. Demonstrates applications to engineering, fluid mechanics, materials science, and biology.

Bailey, T. N. and R. J. Baston, eds. **Twistors in Mathematics and Physics.** New York: Cambridge University Press, 1990. (London Mathematical Society Lecture Notes Series; 156.) $49.95 pa. ISBN 0-521-39783-9.

A collection of 18 review articles covering twistors from both the mathematical and physical perspectives. Penrose's introduction surveys the history of twistors and its future.

Baxter, Martin and Andrew Rennie. **Financial Calculus: An Introduction to Derivative Pricing.** New York: Cambridge University Press, 1996. ix + 233p. $44.95. ISBN 0-521-55289-3.

Authors introduce basic ideas in discrete-time setting and then generalize to continuous time.

Bélair, Jacques, et al., eds. **Dynamical Disease: Mathematical Analysis of Human Illness.** Woodbury, NY: AIP Press, 1995. ix + 220p. $53.95. ISBN 1-56396-370-1.

Papers from a 1994 NATO Advanced Research Workshop in Québec.

Berry, Michael W. and Murray Browne. **Understanding Search Engines: Mathematical Modeling and Text Retrieval.** Philadelphia, PA: Society for Industrial and Applied Mathematics, 1999. xiii + 116p. $32.00 pa. ISBN 0-89871-437-0.

Authors focus on the applied mathematics part of search engines, particularly vector space information retrieval models and orthogonal matrix decompositions.

Boas, Mary L. **Mathematical Methods in the Physical Sciences.** 2nd edition. New York: Wiley, 1983. xx + 793p. $93.75. ISBN 0-471-04409-1.

Intended for students who want to quickly develop a basic competence in the areas of mathematics needed in junior- to graduate-level courses in physics, chemistry, and engineering. This edition has more problems.

Callahan, James J. **The Geometry of Spacetime: An Introduction to Special and General Relativity.** New York: Springer-Verlag, 2000. xvi + 451p. $49.95. ISBN 0-387-98641-3.

The author explains special and general relativity with clarity and care.

Çambel, A. B. **Applied Chaos Theory: A Paradigm for Complexity.** Boston: Academic Press, 1993. xviii + 246p. $44.95. ISBN 0-12-155940-8.

An informal and very readable survey of chaos-theoretic approaches to complex systems.

Castillo, Enrique and Maria Reyes Ruiz-Cobo. **Functional Equations and Modelling in Science and Engineering.** New York: Dekker, 1992. xv + 328p. (Monographs and Textbooks in Pure and Applied Mathematics; 161.) $145.00. ISBN 0-8247-8717-X.

The authors aim to "provide engineers and applied scientists with some selected results of functional equations which can be useful in applications." The many examples illustrate how functional equations are "the ideal tool to design mathematical models."

Chandler, David. **Introduction to Modern Statistical Mechanics.** New York: Oxford University Press, 1987. xiv + 274p. $34.95 pa. ISBN 019504277-8.

This text emphasizes major topics such as Monte Carlo sampling, renormalization groups, and the fluctuation-dissipation theorem.

Charlesworth, Brian. **Evolution in Age-Structured Populations.** 2nd edition. New York: Cambridge University Press, 1994. xiii + 306p. (Studies in Mathematical Biology; 1.) $33.95 pa. ISBN 0-521-45967-2.

A mathematically rigorous survey of the topic, including recent developments.

Chui, Charles K. **Wavelets: A Mathematical Tool for Signal Processing.** Philadelphia, PA: Society for Industrial and Applied Mathematics, 1997. xviii + 210p. $36.50 pa. ISBN 0-89871-384-6.

An introduction to the "most basic concepts, techniques, and computational algorithms of the wavelet transform, as well as the implications of this transform to the understanding and solution of various problems in signal processing."

Clark, Colin W. **Mathematical Bioeconomics: The Optimal Management of Renewable Resources.** 2nd edition. New York: Wiley, 1990. xiii + 386p. $120.00 pa. ISBN 0-4715-0883-7.

Revision of 1977 work features economic models of resource management, optimal control, and models.

Crump, Thomas. **The Anthropology of Numbers.** New York: Cambridge University Press, 1992. x + 201p. $20.95 pa. ISBN 0-521-43807-1.

Reprint of the 1990 scholarly work, the first to examine the role of mathematics in culture. This excellent resource contains a thorough bibliography and comprehensive index.

Das, Anadijiban. **The Special Theory of Relativity: A Mathematical Exposition.** New York: Springer-Verlag, 1993. xii + 214p. $44.95 pa. ISBN 0-387-94042-1.

Strong mathematical emphasis makes this a particularly interesting book for mathematicians.

Dempster, M. A. H. and S. R. Pliska, eds. **Mathematics of Derivative Securities.** New York: Cambridge University Press, 1997. xvii + 582p. $90.00. ISBN 0-521-58424-8.

Papers based on lectures on numerical methods in finance presented at the Newton Institute in 1995.

Dennery, Philippe and André Krzywicki. **Mathematics for Physicists.** New York: Dover, 1995. xiii + 384p. $12.95 pa. ISBN 0-486-69193-4.
Corrected reprint of 1967 text.

Fuchs, Jürgen. **Affine Lie Algebras and Quantum Groups: An Introduction with Applications in Conformal Field Theory.** New York: Cambridge University Press, 1992. xiv + 433p. $44.95 pa. ISBN 0-521-48412-X.
Clearly written introduction to these topics and the connection between them.

Gardner, Martin. **The New Ambidextrous Universe: Symmetry and Asymmetry from Mirror Reflections to Superstrings.** 3rd revised edition. New York: W. H. Freeman, 1990. xiv + 392p. $11.95. ISBN 0-7167-2093-0.
The latest revision to Gardner's classic 1964 nontechnical exposition of the fall of parity adds five more chapters on twisters and superstrings.

Gasquet, C. and P. Witomski. **Fourier Analysis and Applications: Filtering, Numerical Computation, Wavelets.** Translated by R. Ryan. New York: Springer-Verlag, 1999. xviii + 442p. (Texts in Applied Mathematics; 30.) $49.95. ISBN 0-387-98485-2.
In this modular presentation, the authors introduce material on signal processing and filters, then discuss convergence of Fourier series, Lebesgue theory, and Hilbert space.

Gerber, Hans U. **Life Insurance Mathematics.** 3rd edition. Berlin; New York: Springer-Verlag, 1997. xvii + 217p. $64.95. ISBN 3-540-62242-X.
A basic introduction into the basic concepts of life insurance mathematics. Good collection of exercises added in the second edition. Minor corrections in this third edition.

Guillemin, Victor and Shlomo Sternberg. **Symplectic Techniques in Physics.** New York: Cambridge University Press, 1990. xi + 468p. $37.95 pa. ISBN 052138990-9.
Reprint of 1984 edition. Applications in physics are an integral part of this introduction to symplectic geometry from a modern point of view.

Harpaz, Amos. **Relativity Theory: Concepts and Basic Principles.** Boston: Jones and Bartlett, 1992. viii + 224p. $44.00. ISBN 0-86720-220-3.

In this impressive introduction the underlying mathematics is simplified, but not eliminated.

Hastings, Alan. **Population Biology: Concepts and Models.** New York: Springer-Verlag, 1997. xvi + 220p. $27.95 pa. ISBN 0-387-94853-8.

Mathematical models for single and interacting species.

Heaviside, Oliver. **Electromagnetic Theory.** 3rd edition. New York: Chelsea, 1971. $69.00 (set). ISBN 0-8284-0237-X. Vol. I. xxxiv + 504p. Vol. II. xvi + 547p. Vol. III. ix + 666p.

This reprint includes Heaviside's writings on vector algebra and analysis, generalized differentiation, and divergent series.

Hilton, Peter J. and Gail S. Young, eds. **New Directions in Applied Mathematics.** New York: Springer-Verlag, 1982. ix + 163p. $69.95. ISBN 0-387-90604-5.

Seven papers presented at Case Western Reserve University in April 1980 on modern topics in applied mathematics. Also an essay on the nature and pedagogy of applied mathematics by Hilton.

Hoppensteadt, Frank C. and Charles S. Peskin. **Mathematics in Medicine and the Life Sciences.** New York: Springer-Verlag, 1992. xii + 252p. (Texts in Applied Mathematics; 10.) $43.95. ISBN 0-387-97639-6.

An exploration of the use of mathematics in a wide variety of settings, for example, demographics, genetics, epidemics, physiology, and neural dynamics.

Islam, J. N. **An Introduction to Mathematical Cosmology.** New York: Cambridge University Press, 1992. xii + 190p. $24.95 pa. ISBN 0-521-37760-9.

A fascinating and lucid text with selected formulas.

Joseph, Anthony. **Quantum Groups and Their Primitive Ideals.** New York: Springer-Verlag, 1995. ix + 383p. (Series of Modern Surveys in Mathematics; 29.) $150.00. ISBN 0-387-57057-8.

A self-contained, thorough, and highly technical text that begins with a basic introduction to Hopf algebras then systematically proceeds through various spectral theorems.

Karatzas, Ioannis and Steven E. Shreve. **Methods of Mathematical Finance.** New York: Springer-Verlag, 1998. xv + 407p. (Applications of Mathematics; 39.) $69.95. ISBN 0-387-94839-2.

Authors establish Brownian motion for financial markets, treat pricing and hedging contingent claims, address problems faced by agents for optimal consumption and investment decisions.

Karger, Adolf and Josef Novak. **Space Kinematics and Lie Groups.** New York: Gordon & Breach, 1985. xv + 422p. $205.00. ISBN 2881240232.

After a beginning chapter introducing differentiable manifolds and Lie groups, this translation divides into two somewhat independent parts, one for those who deal with concrete problems and the other for those who are theoretically oriented.

Keener, James and James Sneyd. **Mathematical Physiology.** New York: Springer-Verlag, 1998. xix + 766p. (Interdisciplinary Applied Mathematics; 8.) $69.95. ISBN 0-387-98381-3.

This introductory survey emphasizing continuous, deterministic approaches is accessible to mathematicians with little knowledge of physiology.

Kellison, Stephen G. **The Theory of Interest.** 2nd edition. Homewood, IL: R. D. Irwin, 1991. xiv + 446p. $90.55. ISBN 0-256-09150-1.

This edition is a substantially revised and expanded treatment of the theory of interest: almost all the material in the first edition has been retained and updated and a significant amount of new material (e.g., an introduction to the economic and financial theory of interest) has been added.

Kreyszig, Erwin. **Advanced Engineering Mathematics.** 8th edition. New York: Wiley, 1999. 1156 + 97 + 20p. $117.95. ISBN 0-471-15496-2.

This edition of the well-known textbook on mathematical topics for engineers has been simplified by rewriting various sections and by placing more emphasis on qualitative methods and applications of the examples and inclusion of team projects.

Krieger, Martin H. **Constitutions of Matter: Mathematical Modeling the Most Everyday of Physical Phenomena.** Chicago: University of Chicago Press, 1998. xxii + 343p. $30.00 pa. ISBN 0-226-45305-7.

Reprint of 1996 original. A solid, scholarly, and lively account of the mathematical description of matter, one of the central problems in modern physics.

Lebedev, N. N., I. P. Skalskaia, and Y. S. Ufliand. **Worked Problems in Applied Mathematics.** Translated by Richard A. Silverman. New York: Dover, 1979. xi + 429p. $11.95 pa. ISBN 0-486637301.

Unabridged reprint of the 1965 English edition with over 600 problems. This is a good sourcebook, even though the bibliography is now dated.

Logan, J. David. **Applied Mathematics.** 2nd edition. New York: Wiley, 1997. xiv + 476p. $74.95. ISBN 0-471-16513-1.

Major changes in this edition of a very good text include additions to perturbation methods and improvements to coverage of integral equations.

Marsden, Jerrold E. and Tudor S. Ratiu. **Introduction to Mechanics and Symmetry: A Basic Exposition of Classical Mechanical Systems.** New York: Springer-Verlag, 1994. xv + 500p. (Texts in Applied Mathematics; 17.) $83.50. ISBN 0-387-97275-7.

A demanding introduction to Hamiltonian and Lagrangian mechanics. References to recent literature.

Marsden, Jerrold E. and Thomas J. R. Hughes. **Mathematical Foundations of Elasticity.** New York: Dover, 1993. xviii + 556p. $16.95 pa. ISBN 0-486-67865-2.

This book treats the mathematical foundations of three-dimensional elasticity using modern differential geometry and functional analysis.

Mestre, Neville de. **Mathematics of Projectiles in Sport.** New York: Cambridge University Press, 1990. xi + 175p. (Australian Mathematical Society Lecture Series; 6.) $31.95 pa. ISBN 0-521-39857-6.

All aspects of projectiles, derived from military sources, but applied to sports projectiles. Extensive references.

Musiala, Marek and Marek Rutkowski. **Martingale Methods in Financial Modelling.** New York: Springer-Verlag, 1997. xii + 512p. (Applications in Mathematics; 36.) $79.95. ISBN 0-387-61477-X.

A comprehensive introduction to the theory of option pricing. Whereas the initial chapters require few mathematical prerequisites, the later chapters demand familiarity with stochastic calculus.

Myers, Dowell. **Analysis with Local Census Data: Portraits of Change.** Boston: Academic Press, 1992. xii + 369p. $59.95 pa. ISBN 0-12-512308-6.

This comprehensive reference attempts to fill the gap between national theories and the practical realities if local researchers.

Naber, Gregory L. **The Geometry of Minkowski Spacetime: An Introduction to the Mathematics of the Special Theory of Relativity.** New York: Springer-Verlag, 1992. xvi + 257p. (Applied Mathematical Sciences; 92.) $65.95. ISBN 0-387-97848-8.

A mathematically rigorous introduction, with standard material and more contemporary results.

Naber, Gregory L. **Spacetime and Singularities: An Introduction.** New York: Cambridge University Press, 1988. ix + 178p. (London Mathematical Society Student Texts; 11.) $25.95. ISBN 0521336120.

A singleminded attempt to explain Hawking's Theorem.

Ostaszewski, Adam. **Advanced Mathematical Methods.** New York: Cambridge University Press, 1990. xiii + 545p. $47.95 pa. ISBN 0-521-28964-5.

This encyclopedic text makes a great reference, introducing linear algebra, real analysis, advanced calculus, and differential equations.

Pless, Vera. **Introduction to the Theory of Error-Correcting Codes.** New York: Wiley, 1998. xii + 207p. $74.95. ISBN 047119047-9.

An introduction to linear block codes for mathematics, computer science, and electrical engineering students, which assumes knowledge of linear algebra. This edition adds some new topics, many new problems, and updates the references.

Pullman, Bernard, ed. **The Emergence of Complexity in Mathematics, Physics, Chemistry and Biology.** Princeton, NJ: Princeton University Press, 1996. xix + 472p. $39.50 pa. ISBN 0-691-01238-5.

Proceedings of the 1992 plenary session of the Pontifical Academy of Sciences.

Riley, K. F., M. P. Hobson, and S. J. Bence. **Mathematical Methods for Physics and Engineering.** New York: Cambridge University Press, 1997. xix + 1,008p. $54.95 pa. ISBN 0-521-55529-9.

Brief expositions of a wide variety of mathematical tools including basic calculus, PDEs, and complex analysis. Each topic is introduced qualitatively, then more rigorously.

Sadovskii, L. E. and A. L. Sadovskii. **Mathematics and Sports.** Translated by S. Makar-Limanov. Providence, RI: American Mathematical Society, 1993. ix + 152p. (Mathematical World; 3.) $26.39 pa. ISBN 0-8218-9500-1.

Translated from the 1985 Russian edition. Introduces many mathematical techniques in discussing the mathematical models for various sports.

Saunders, P. T. **An Introduction to Catastrophe Theory.** New York: Cambridge University Press, 1980. xii + 144p. $24.95 pa. ISBN 0521297826.

A brief elementary exposition designed for those who are competent in calculus. It includes complete descriptions of elementary catastrophes with applications to physics, social science, and biology.

Shone, Ronald. **Economic Dynamics: Phase Diagrams and Their Economic Application.** New York: Cambridge University Press, 1997. xiv + 553p. $39.95 pa. ISBN 0-521-47973-8.

An introduction to applications of dynamical systems in economics, using discrete and continuous dynamics, linear and nonlinear systems.

Sirovich, Lawrence, ed. **Trends and Perspectives in Applied Mathematics.** New York: Springer-Verlag, 1994. xii + 336p. (Applied Mathematical Sciences; 100.) $69.95. ISBN 0-387-94201-7.

Ten papers dedicated to Fritz John on his 80th birthday.

Sternberg, S. **Group Theory and Physics.** New York: Cambridge University Press, 1994. xiii + 429p. $33.95 pa. ISBN 0-521-24870-1.

Group theory motivated by physics.

Stewart, Ian. **Life's Other Secret: The New Mathematics of the Living World.** New York: Wiley, 1999. xiii + 285p. $16.95 pa. ISBN 0-471-29651-1.

A sequel to D'Arcy Thompson's 1942 classic **On Growth and Form**, this very readable monograph explores the structure of living things from the symmetry of DNA to the gate of legged creatures in support of its thesis that life is a partnership between genes and mathematics.

Stigum, Brent P. **Toward a Formal Science of Economics: The Axiomatic Method in Economics and Econometrics.** Cambridge, MA: MIT Press, 1990. xiv + 1033p. $71.50. ISBN 0-262-19284-5.

Encyclopedic treatment of foundations for a formal methodological basis of econometric theory.

Strang, Gilbert. **Introduction to Applied Mathematics.** Wellesley, MA: Wellesley-Cambridge Press, 1986. xii + 758p. $62.50. ISBN 0961408804.

An innovative text, integrating continuous and discrete methods with an algorithmic spirit and links to scientific software packages.

Temam, Roger. **Navier-Stokes Equations and Nonlinear Functional Analysis.** 2nd edition. Philadelphia, PA: Society for Industrial and Applied Mathematics, 1995. xiv + 141p. (CBMS-NSF Regional Conference Series in Applied Mathematics; 66.) $29.00 pa. ISBN 0-89871-340-4.

This edition includes a new appendix on inertial manifolds. Updated bibliography.

Terano, Toshiro, Kiyoji Asai, and Michio Sugeno. **Fuzzy Systems Theory and Its Applications.** Boston: Academic Press, 1992. xi + 268p. $49.95. ISBN 0-12-685245-6.

A well-written monograph focusing on applications: fuzzy regression models and fuzzy mathematical programming.

Tolimieri, Richard and Myoung An. **Time-Frequency Representations.** Boston: Birkhäuser, 1998. xiii + 284p. $65.00. ISBN 0-8176-3918-7.

Authors cover topics in time-frequency analysis over abelian groups.

Wilcox, Calvin H. **Sound Propagation in Stratified Fluids.** New York: Springer-Verlag, 1984. ix + 198p. (Applied Mathematical Sciences; 50.) $36.00. ISBN 0387909869.

A highly mathematical and usually clear work presenting the theory of the propagation of transient sound waves in fluids whose densities and sound speeds are functions of depth.

Wilmott, Paul, Sam Howison, and Jeff Dewynne. **The Mathematics of Financial Derivatives: A Student Introduction.** New York: Cambridge University Press, 1995. xiii + 317p. $29.95 pa. ISBN 0-521-49789-2.

An introduction to the principles and practice of derivative pricing from an applied mathematician's perspective.

Wilson, Edward O. and William H. Bossert. **A Primer of Population Biology.** Sunderland, MA: Sinauer Associates, 1971. 192p. $19.95 pa. ISBN 0-87893-926-1.

An introduction to the methods of population biology, for example, mathematical model building, measurement techniques, and problem solving.

Yeargers, Edward K., Ronald M. Shonkwiler, and James V. Herod. **An Introduction to the Mathematics of Biology: With Computer Algebra Models.** Boston: Birkhäuser, 1996. x + 417p. $64.50. ISBN 0-8176-3809-1.

The mathematics behind problems such as aging, genetics, and HIV with the biological concepts developed as needed. Rich resource of examples.

Mathematical and Statistical Computing

(see also **Chapter 5, Tables, Handbooks, Manuals, Guides**)

Abell, Martha L. and James Braselton. **Maple V by Example.** 2nd edition. San Diego, CA: Academic Press, 1999. xii + 644p. + 1 computer disk. $44.95 pa. ISBN 0-12-041558-5.

An excellent introduction to Maple V for readers of all levels, but beginners in particular. This useful reference covers all the topics needed in calculus, linear algebra, and differential equations.

Blachman, Nancy. **Mathematica: A Practical Approach.** 2nd edition. Englewood Cliffs, NJ: Prentice Hall, 1998. xv + 365p. $58.00. ISBN 0-13-259201-0.

This complete introductory tutorial provides the easiest way for engineers, scientists, and mathematicians to learn Mathematica. Chapters show how to use and extend the program. Appendixes provide answers to exercises.

Gander, Walter and Jiří Hrebícek. **Solving Problems in Scientific Computing Using Maple and MATLAB.** 3rd expanded and revised edition. Berlin; New York: Springer-Verlag, 1997. xvii + 408p. $ 53.95 pa. ISBN 3-540-61793-0.

Teaches by applying Maple and MATLAB to high-level classroom problems such as trajectories of tennis balls and orbits in the three-body problem. An excellent reference on undergraduate mathematical computing. This third edition has been expanded by six chapters; two chapters from the second edition have been considerably revised.

Glynn, Jerry and Theodore Gray. **The Beginner's Guide to Mathematica Version 4.** New York: Cambridge University Press, 2000. viii + 434p. $29.95 pa. ISBN 0-521-77769-0.

Elementary introduction to Mathematica, including features new to Version 4.

Grätzer, George. **Math into LATeX.** Boston; New York: Birkhäuser; Springer-Verlag, 2000. xxxviii + 584p. $24.97 pa. ISBN 0-8176-4131-9.

This well-written guide effectively teaches the novice LaTeX and serves as an excellent reference to the more expereinced user. This edition adds sections pertaining to Internet-related document preparations.

Gray, John. **Mastering Mathematica: Programming Methods and Applications.** Second Edition. San Diego, CA: Academic Press, 1998. xx + 629p. + 1 computer laser optical disc. $44.95 pa. ISBN 0-12-296105-6.

A guide to programming in Mathematica with nice applications to pattern analysis, graph theory, differentiable mappings, and minimal surfaces.

Griffiths, David F. and Desmond J. Higham. **Learning LATeX.** Philadelphia, PA: Society for Industrial and Applied Mathematics, 1997. x + 84pp. $15.50 pa. ISBN 0-89871-383-8.

A clear, simple, brief yet surprisingly comprehensive introduction to LATeX.

Heck, André. **Introduction to Maple**. 2nd edition. New York: Springer-Verlag, 1996. xx + 699p. $39.95. ISBN 0-387-94535-0.

Revised and updated to reflect new mathematical features in Maple V.

Knuth, Donald E. **METAFONT: The Program.** Reading, MA: Addison-Wesley, 1986. xvii + 566p. $51.95. ISBN 0-201-60658-5.

This program epitomizes many kinds of software all at once as the algorithms of METAFONT span a wide range of ideas, from random number generation and trigonometry to combinatorial optimization.

Knuth, Donald E. **The METAFONTbook.** Reading, MA: Addison-Wesley, 1986. xi + 361p. $30.95 pa. ISBN 0-201-13444-6.

This book enables users with only minimal computer science or word processing experience to master basic and advanced features of METAFONT programming.

Knuth, Donald E. **TeX: The Program.** Reading, MA: Addison-Wesley, 1988. xv + 594p. $51.95. ISBN 0201134373.

Corrected reprint of the 1986 complete text of the TeX program, written in WEB. The program consists of 1,377 consecutively numbered single-topic sections, each with commentary.

Knuth, Donald E. **TeXbook.** Spiral edition. Reading, MA: Addison-Wesley, 1988. $41.95. ix + 483p. $41.95 pa. ISBN 0-201-13448-9.

Latest printing of the witty TeX bible. Because it provides layer upon layer of cleverly illustrated examples of TeX behavior, it is not intended for the person who wants to learn the system quickly. See also Spivak in the **Handbooks, Manuals, Guides** section of **Chapter 5**, **Tables, Handbooks, Manuals, Guides**.

Nicolaides, Roy and Noel Walkington. **Maple: A Comprehensive Introduction.** New York: Cambridge University Press, 1996. xix + 466p. $44.95. ISBN 0-521-56230-9.

This "deeper" introduction to Maple V aims to provide the reader with a solid foundation in Maple as a computer algebra system and a programming language.

Salomon, D. **The Advanced TeXbook.** New York: Springer-Verlag, 1995. xx + 490p. $51.95 pa. ISBN 0-387-94556-3.

This excellent book explains the essential workings of TeX and then goes on to cover a wide range of more advanced topics.

Seroul, Raymond and Silvio Levy. **A Beginner's Book of TeX.** New York: Springer-Verlag, 1991. xii + 284p. $39.95 pa. ISBN 0-387-97562-4.

This introductory book to help TeX users get quickly started on their own contains a careful explanation of all fundamental concepts and commands plus a wealth of commented examples and "tricks" based on the authors' long experience with TeX. Last third of the book is devoted to a dictionary-index, summarizing all the material in the text and going into greater detail in many areas.

Shaw, William T. and Jason Tigg. **Applied Mathematica: Getting Started, Getting It Done.** Reading, MA: Addison-Wesley, 1994. xiv + 432p. $36.95 pa. ISBN 0-201-54217-X.

An impressive introduction to Mathematica's power and versatility. Includes basic techniques and detailed coverage of data handling. Well-thought-out examples make this a highly recommended book.

Tierney, Luke. **LISP-STAT: An Object-Oriented Environment for Statistical Computing and Dynamic Graphics.** New York: Wiley, 1990. xiii + 397p. $74.95. ISBN 0-471-50916-7.

Author describes the statistical computing environment Lisp-Stat, based on XLISP language. A well-written book with excellent examples and exercises.

Torrence, Bruce F. and Eve A. Torrence. **The Student's Introduction to Mathematica: A Handbook for Precalculus, Calculus, and Linear Algebra.** New York: Cambridge University Press, 1999. xvii + 280p. $24.95 pa. ISBN 0-521-59461-8.

A compact introduction to Mathematica. A unique feature of this book is that concepts are presented in an order that closely follows a standard mathematics curriculum, rather than structuring the book along features of the software.

Wagon, Stan. **Mathematica in Action**. 2nd edition. New York: Springer-TELOS, 1999. xvi + 592p + computer laser optical disc. $49.95 pa; $69.95. ISBN 0-387-98252-3 pa; 0-387-98684-7.

Intended for the Mathematica novice, this superb resource allows the reader to explore the virtually limitless capabilities of the program. Hundreds of diverse examples are worked in detail.

Walsh, Norman. **Making TeX Work.** Sebastopol, CA: O'Reilly & Associates, 1994. xxxvi + 483p. Out of print. ISBN 1-56592-051-1.

This invaluable book, for midlevel users, is a wide-ranging compendium of TeX-related information.

9
Collected and Selected Works, Digital Collections

Collected and Selected Works
(arranged by individual)

Collected works are a valuable part of an academic mathematics library collection. Although collected works may not always be complete collections of an author's work, they are a convenient source of much of their work and often a source of biographical and bibliographical content. Papers published in obscure or old journals are more easily retrievable from more recently published collected works. There are over 900 titles of collected works and correspondence in mathematics (Rockey 1996). Listed below are some of the more important collections.

Adams, J. Frank. **The Selected Works of J. Frank Adams.** Edited by J. P. May and C. B. Thomas. New York: Cambridge University Press, 1992. Vol. I. xvi + 536p. $90.00. ISBN 0-521-41063-0. Vol. II. xvi + 529p. $90.00. ISBN 0-521-41065-7.

These volumes bring together all of the major research contributions of one of the world's leading topologists. Even though they are organized by subject matter rather than strict chronological order, most fall within the period 1955–1988.

Ahlfors, Lars Valerian. **Collected Papers.** Boston: Birkhäuser, 1982. Vol. 1. xix + 520p. ISBN 0-8176-3075-9. Vol. 2. xix + 515p. ISBN 0-8176-3076-7. $145.00 (set). ISBN 0-8176-3077-5 (set).

Volume 1 covers the years 1929–1955 and volume 2 the years 1954–1979, with bibliographical references.

Albanese, Giacomo. **Collected Papers of Giacomo Albanese.** Edited by Ciro Ciliberto, Paulo Ribenboim and Edoardo Sernesi. Kingston, ON: Queen's University Printing Services, 1996. xii + 182p. (Queen's Papers in Pure and Applied Mathematics; 103). $50.00. ISBN 0-88911-737-3.

This volume contains the papers, including 20 from the period 1915–1934, of one of most highly regarded representatives of the Italian school of algebraic geometry. There is a list of publications, a biography, and an updated bibliography.

Albert, A. Adrian. **Collected Mathematical Papers.** Edited by Richard E. Block. Providence, RI: American Mathematical Society, 1992. Part 1. **Associative Algebras and Riemann Surfaces.** 743p. $100.00. ISBN 0-8218-0005-1. Part 2. **Nonassociative Algebras and Miscellany.** 938p. $117.00. ISBN 0-8218-0007-8. $206.00 (set). ISBN 0-8218-0003-5 (set).

This set contains the collected works of Albert, a leading algebraist of the twentieth century.

Alling, Norman L. **Collected Papers of Norman Alling.** Edited by Paulo Ribenboim. Kingston, ON: Queen's University Printing Services, 1998. xii + 597p. (Queen's Papers in Pure and Applied Mathematics; 107). $45.00. ISBN 088941-796-9.

A brief vita is followed by all of Alling's publications from 1960 to 1997. Topics cover a wide range of mathematics, from the theory of ordered groups to Riemann surfaces.

S Anderson, T. W. **The Collected Papers of T. W. Anderson, 1943–1985.** Edited by George P.H. Styan. New York: Wiley, 1990. Vol. 1. xliii + 825p. Vol. 2. v + 680p. $350.00 (set). ISBN 0-471-62422-5.

These two volumes include 109 research papers by Anderson on probability, statistics, econometrics, and matrix theory, published from 1943 to 1985, 16 commentaries, a list of other publications (i.e., books, book reviews, papers published after 1985, Festschrift, interviews), and a list of his 22 doctoral students. Author and subject indexes.

Artin, Emil. **Collected Papers.** Edited by Serge Lang and John T. Tate. New York: Springer-Verlag, 1988. xvi + 560p. Out of print. ISBN 0-387-90686-X.

Unaltered reprint of 1965 Addison-Wesley original.

Atiyah, Michael. **Collected Works.** New York: Oxford University Press, 1988. Vol. 1. **Early Papers: General Papers.** xxiii + 364p. Out of print. ISBN 0-19-853275-X. Vol. 2. **K-Theory.** xxiii + 829p. Out of print. ISBN 0-19-853276-8. Vol. 3. **Index Theory: 1.** xxiii + 593p. Out of print. ISBN 0-19-853277-6. Vol. 4. **Index Theory: 2.** xxiii + 617p. Out of print. ISBN 0-19-853278-4. Vol. 5. **Gauge Theories.** xxiii + 685p. Out of print. ISBN 0-19-853279-2.

A scholarly record of accomplishment with each section introduced by the author's commentary to document the origins of his ideas.

Aubert, Karl Egil. **Collected Papers of Karl Egil Aubert.** Edited by Paulo Ribenboim. Kingston, ON: Queen's University Printing Services, 1992. xxxviii + 603p. (Queen's Papers in Pure and Applied Mathematics; 89). Out of print. ISSN 0079-8797.

The papers, including his doctoral thesis, of this important Norwegian algebraist are arranged chronologically. Biographical sketch included.

Aumann, Robert J. **Collected Papers.** Cambridge, MA: MIT Press, 2000. Vol. I. xi + 786p. $65.00. ISBN 0-262-01154-9. Vol. II. xii + 792p. $65.00. ISBN 0-262-01155-7.

All 73 of Aumann's papers through 1995 are arranged in several categories. Almost all the papers concern game theory, its applications, and its tools. Indexes: author, journal, citation, name, and subject.

Barrow, Isaac. **The Mathematical Works.** Edited by W. Whewell. Hildesheim, Germany: G. Olms, 1973. xix + 414 + 320p. Price not available. ISBN 3-487-04788-8.

Reprint of 1860 edition. Preface in English; text in Latin.

Bellman, Richard E. **The Bellman Continuum: A Collection of the Works of Richard E. Bellman.** Edited by Robert S. Roth. Teaneck, NJ: World Scientific, 1986. xxii + 868p. $122.00. ISBN 9971-50-090-6.

Collection of some of the works of Bellman in the field of mathematics, including bits of notes left at the time of his death. After an introductory chapter that briefly summarizes his life, the book considers nine general topics from Bellman's more than 600 papers and 30 books written over the past 40 years.

Bernoulli, Daniel. **Die Werke von Daniel Bernoulli.** Edited by David Speiser. Basel, Switzerland; Boston: Birkhäuser, 1982– . Band. 1. **Medizin und Physiologie; Mathematische Jugendschriften; Positionsastronomie.** 528p. $187.20. ISBN 3-7643-5272-8. Band 2. **Analysis Wahrscheinlichkeitsrechnung.** 403p. $63.95. ISBN 3-7643-1084-7. Band 3. **Mechanik.** 484p. $144.00. ISBN 3-7643-1213-0. Band 7. **Magnetismus.** 357p. $169.00. ISBN 0-8176-2808-8.

The first four volumes of a projected eight-volume set of the collected works of Daniel Bernoulli, second son of Johann I. Bernoulli.

Bernoulli, Jakob. **Der Briefwechsel.** Edited by A. Weil. Basel, Switzerland; Boston: Birkhäuser, 1993. xxi + 305p. $77.95. ISBN 3-7643-2950-5.

Bernoulli's correspondence with revision and commentary by André Weil. Contributions from Clifford Truesdell and Fritz Nage. Indexes. Bibliographical references.

Bernoulli, Jakob. **Die Werke von Jakob Bernoulli.** Edited on behalf of the Naturforschende Gesellschaft in Basel. Basel, Switzerland; Boston: Birkhäuser, 1969– . Band 1. **Astronomie, Philosophie Naturalis.** 541p. $158.40. ISBN 3-7643-0028-0. Band 2. **Elementar-mathematik.** xiii + 685p. $187.20. ISBN 3-7643-0028-0. Band 3. **Die Wahrscheinlichkeitstheorie.** x + 585p. $94.08. ISBN 3-7643-0713-7. Band 4. **Reihentheorie.** xxi + 298p. $81.60. ISBN 3-7643-2453-8. Band 5. **Differentialgeometrie.** 472p. $202.18. ISBN 3-7643-5779-7.

The first five volumes of a six-volume set of the first critical edition of the collected works of Jakob Bernoulli, brother of Johann I. Bernoulli. Includes appendixes, bibliography, and indexes.

Bernoulli, Johann. **Der Briefwechsel von Johann Bernoulli.** Edited on behalf of the Naturforschende Gesellschaft in Basel. Basel, Switzerland: Birkhäuser, 1955– . Band 1. **Der Briefwechsel mit Jakob Bernoulli, dem Marquis de l'Hôpital u.a.** 531p. $91.20. ISBN 3-7643-0027-2. Band 2. **Der Briefwechsel mit Pierre Varignon, Teil I: 1692–1702.** 460p. $105.60. ISBN 3-7643-1183-5. Band 3. **Der Briefwechsel mit Pierre Varignon, Teil II: 1703–1714.** 648p. $158.40. ISBN 3-7643-2637-9.

The first three volumes of a projected four-volume set of the correspondence of Johann I. Bernoulli, father of Daniel and brother of Jakob.

Beurling, Arne. **The Collected Works of Arne Beurling.** Edited by Lennart Carleson et al. Boston: Birkhäuser, 1989. Vol. 1. **Complex**

Analysis. xx + 475p. Vol. 2. **Harmonic Analysis.** xx + 389p. $129.00 (set). ISBN 0-8176-3412-6.

Papers and seminar notes by Beurling, who did pioneering work in extremal length, inner functions, and spectral theory. Brief foreword assesses his mathematical contributions.

Bing, R. H. **The Collected Papers of R. H. Bing.** Edited by Sukhjit Singh, Steve Armentrout, and Robert J. Daverman. Providence, RI: American Mathematical Society, 1988. Vol. 1. xix + 886p. Vol. 2. xvii + 759p. $188.00 (set). ISBN 0-8218-0117-1.

This celebration of Bing's mathematical life includes all of his mathematical papers and abstracts, organized, in part, with Bing's help. Singh has prepared an autobiographical essay from tapes made by Bing.

Bishop, Errett. **Selected Papers.** Teaneck, NJ: World Scientific, 1986. xxiv + 414p. $79.00. ISBN 9971-50-127-9.

Papers on complex and functional analysis and constructive mathematics are arranged chronologically. Includes vita and bibliography of Bishop's papers.

Borel, Armand. **Oeuvres: Collected Papers.** New York: Springer-Verlag, 1983–2001. Vol. I. **1948–1958.** viii + 718p. Vol. II. **1959–1968.** iv + 790p. Vol. III. **1969–1982.** iv + 718p. $350.00 (v. 1–3). ISBN 0-387-12126-9 (set). Vol. IV. **1983–1999**. $129.00 (v. 4). ISBN: 3-540-67640-6 (v. 4)

The official record of Borel's work, concentrated in topology, algebraic geometry, and especially algebraic groups.

S Box, George E. P. **The Collected Work of George E. P. Box.** Edited by George C. Tiao et al. Belmont, CA: Wadsworth, 1985. Vol. I. xiv + 657p. $72.95. ISBN 0-534-03307-5. Vol. II. xiv + 710p. $79.95. ISBN 0-534-03308-3.

The set includes a major portion of Box's articles.

Brauer, Richard. **Collected Papers.** Edited by Paul Fong and Warren J. Wong. Cambridge, MA: MIT Press, 1980. (Mathematicians of Our Time; 17-19). Vol. I. **Theory of Algebras and Finite Groups.** liv + 615p. Out of print. ISBN 0-262-02135-8. Vol. II. **Finite Groups.** viii + 586p. Out of print. ISBN 0-262-02148-X. Vol. III. **Finite Groups, Lie Groups, Number Theory, Polynomials and Equations, Geometry, and Biography.** x + 689p. Out of print. ISBN 0-262-02149-8.

All but 29 of Brauer's 129 papers. Vol. I also has a brief recounting by Brauer of his mathematical education, a reprinted biography, and a complete list of his publications.

Cantor, Georg. **Gesammelte Abhandlungen mathematischen und philosophischen Inhalts, mit erläuternden Anmerkungen sowie mit Erganzungen aus dem Briefwechsel Cantor-Dedekind.** Edited by Ernst Zermelo. New York: Springer-Verlag, 1980. vii + 486p. Out of print. ISBN 0-387-09849-6.
Reprint of 1932 edition.

Chandrasekhar, S. (Subrahmanyan). **Selected Papers of S. Chandrasekhar.** Chicago: University of Chicago Press, 1989–1991. Vol. 1. **Stellar Structure and Stellar Atmospheres.** vi + 791p. $39.00 pa. ISBN 0-226-10090-1. Vol. 2. **Radiative Transfer and Negative Ion of Hydrogen.** xvi + 622p. $39.00 pa. ISBN 0-226-10093-6. Vol. 3. **Stochastic, Statistical, and Hydromagnetic Problems in Physics and Astronomy.** xiv + 642p. $39.00 pa. ISBN 0-226-10095-2. Vol. 4. **Plasma Physics, Hydrodynamic and Hydromagnetic Stability, and Applications of the Tensor-Virial Theorem.** xiii + 585p. $39.00 pa. ISBN 0-226-10096-0. Vol. 5. **Relativistic Astrophysics.** xx + 587p. $39.00 pa. ISBN 0-226-10099-5. Vol. 6. **The Mathematical Theory of Black Holes and of Colliding Plane Waves.** xix + 739p. $45.00 pa. ISBN 0-226-10101-0. Vol. 7. **The Non Radial Oscillations of Stars in General Relatitivy and Other Writings.** viii + 295p. $48.00 pa. ISBN 0-226-10104-5.
The seventh volume of 27 reprinted articles was conceived by the distinguished astrophysicist as a supplement to this six-volume collection.

Chen, K.-T. **Collected Papers of K.-T. Chen.** Boston: Birkhäuser, 2001. Edited by Philippe Tondeur. 784p. $189.00. ISBN 0-8176-4005-3.
An article, "The Life and Work of Kuo-Tsai Chen" introduces this comprehensive collection of Chen's mathematical publications.

Chern, Shiing-shen. **Selected Papers.** New York: Springer-Verlag, 1978–1989. Vol. I. xxxi + 476p. $89.95. ISBN 0-387-90339-9. Vol. II. xxx + 444p. $84.95. ISBN 0-387-96816-4. Vol. III. xiv + 504p. $89.95. ISBN 0-387-96817-2. Vol. IV. xiv + 462p. $84.95. ISBN 0-387-96820-2.
Chronological arrangement of Chern's papers with a complete bibliography and recently revised scientific autobiography.

E Clifford, William K. **Mathematical Papers.** New York: Chelsea, 1968. lxx + 658p. $49.50. ISBN 0-8284-0210-8. Original available at: http://www.hti.umich.edu/cgi/t/text/text-idx?c=umhistmath;idno=AAS8031. Free.
   Reprint of 1882 edition. Bibliographical references in preface.

Coxeter, H. S. M. **Kaleidoscopes: Selected Writings of H. S. M. Coxeter.** Edited by F. Arthur Sherk. New York: Wiley & Sons, 1995. xxx + 439p. $125.00. ISBN 0-471-01003-0.
   Coxeter selected 26 of his writings on reflection theory in recognition of the 50th anniversary of the Canadian Mathematical Society. References and an index.

Dickson, Leonard Eugene. **The Collected Mathematical Papers of Leonard Eugene Dickson.** Edited by A. Adrian Albert. New York: Chelsea, 1975-83. Vol. I. xvii + 680p. Vol. II. 766p. Vol. III. 580p. Vol. IV. 636p. Vol. V. 644p. Vol. VI. 714p. $221.00 (set). ISBN 0-8284-0273-6.
   A collection of nearly all of Dickson's research papers and two of his books. Bibliography and index.

Dilworth, Robert P. **The Dilworth Theorems: Selected Papers of Robert P. Dilworth.** Edited by Kenneth P. Bogart, Ralph Freese, and Joseph P. S. Kung. Boston: Birkhäuser, 1990. xxvi + 465p. $80.50. ISBN 0-8176-3434-7.
   A collection of Dilworth's important papers on ordered sets and lattice theory. Each section is preceded by background exposition by Dilworth and followed by articles on later influences. Extensive references.

Dirichlet, P. G. L. See Lejeune Dirichlet, Peter Gustav (below).

Eckmann, Beno. **Selecta.** Edited by Max-Albert Knus, Guido Mislin, and Urs Stammbach. New York: Springer-Verlag, 1987. xii + 835p. $226.95. ISBN 0-387-17518-0.
   A collection of Eckmann's major papers as well as a complete bibliography and a brief biographical note, on the occasion of his 70th birthday.

Einstein, Albert. **The Collected Papers of Albert Einstein.** English translation version. Edited by John Stachel. Princeton, NJ: Princeton University Press, 1987– . Vol. 1. **The Early Years: 1879–1902.** xxii + 196p. $39.50 pa. ISBN 0-691-08475-0. Vol. 2. **The Swiss Years: Writings,**

1900–1909. xxxii + 656p. $42.50 pa. ISBN 0-691-08549-8. Vol. 3. **The Swiss Years: Writings, 1909–1911.** $39.50 pa. ISBN 0-691-10250-3. Vol. 4. **The Swiss Years: Writings, 1912–1914.** xi + 314p. $39.50 pa. ISBN 0-691-02610-6. Vol. 5. **The Swiss Years: Correspondence, 1902–1914.** xxii + 384p. $42.50 pa. ISBN 0-691-00099-9. Vol. 6. **The Berlin Years: Writings, 1914–1916.** xii + 449p. $53.25 pa. ISBN 0-691-01734-4. Vol. 7. **The Berlin Years: Writings, 1918–1921.** 432p. $45.00 pa. ISBN: 0-691-05718-4. Vol. 8. **The Berlin Years: Correspondence, 1914–1918.** 2 vols. $65.00 pa. ISBN 0-691-04841-X.

First eight of an anticipated 30-volume set constituting the definitive, comprehensive edition of all of Einstein's papers, letters, and related documents—an extraordinary achievement. This paperback edition contains typewritten English translations of all original documents in the official edition (but without editorial commentary). It is intended for use in conjunction with the documentary edition of the same title. (In that hardcover edition, each manuscript appears in its original language, typeset in a manner that is faithful to the original German. All editor's notes are in English.) Vol. 2 will likely be the most frequently consulted volume of this set as it contains reprints of 62 papers published by Einstein between 1900 and 1909.

Eisenstein, Gotthold. **Mathematische Werke.** 2nd edition. New York: Chelsea, 1989. Band I. xiii + 502p. Band II. xiii + 434p. $125.00 (set). ISBN 0-8284-1280-4.

First complete collection of Eisenstein's works together with his letters to Hermite, Richelot, Stern, and Gauss as well as a youthful autobiography and Biermann's biographical article.

Elgot, Calvin C. **Calvin C. Elgot: Selected Papers.** Edited by Stephen L. Bloom. New York: Springer-Verlag, 1982. xxiv + 460p. $66.00. ISBN 0-387-90698-3.

Photographic reproductions of 13 original papers on the study of computation in the framework of category theory and algebra.

Erdös, Paul. **Paul Erdös: The Art of Counting. Selected Writings.** Edited by Joel Spencer. Cambridge, MA: MIT Press, 1973. xxiii + 742p. (Mathematicians of Our Time; 5). Out of print. ISBN: 0-262-19116-4.

Selected papers arranged by broad category (e.g., special interest, graph theory, combinatorial analysis, and miscellany). Bibliography of all his papers through 1972.

Euler, Leonhard. **Opera Omnia. Series Prima. Opera Mathematica.** Edited by Ferdinand Rudio, Adolf Krazer, and Paul Stäckel. Boston: Birkhäuser, 1911-1956. Vol. I. **Vollstandige Anleitung zur Algebra.** 651p. ISBN 3-7643-1400-1. Vol. II. **Commentationes Arithmeticae: 1.** 611p. ISBN 3-7643-1401-X. Vol. III. **Commentationes Arithmeticae: 2.** 543p. ISBN 3-7643-1402-8. Vol. IV. **Commentationes Arithmeticae: 3.** 431p. ISBN 3-7643-1403-6. Vol. V. **Commentationes Arithmeticae: 4.** 374p. ISBN 3-7643-1404-4. Vol. VI. **Commentationes Algebraicae ad Theoriam Aequationum Pertinentes.** 509p. ISBN 3-7643-1405-2. Vol. VII. **Commentationes Algebraicae ad Theoriam Combinatorionum et Probabilitatum Pertinentes.** 580p. ISBN 3-7643-1406-0. Vol. VIII. **Introductio in Analysin Infinatorum: 1.** 392p. ISBN 3-7643-1407-9. Vol. IX. **Introductio in Analysin Infinatorum: 2.** 676p. ISBN 3-7643-1408-7. Vol. X. **Institutiones Calculi Differentialis.** 676p. ISBN 3-7643-1409-5. Vol. XI. **Institutiones Calculi Integralis: 1.** 462p. ISBN 3-7643-1410-9. Vol. XII. **Institutiones Calculi Integralis: 2.** 542p. ISBN 3-7643-1411-7. Vol. XIII. **Institutiones Calculi Integralis: 3.** 505p. ISBN 3-7643-1412-5. Vol. XIV. **Commentationes Analyticae ad Theoriam Serierum Infinitarum Pertinentes: 1.** 617p. ISBN 3-7643-1413-3. Vol. XV. **Commentationes Analyticae ad Theoriam Serierum Infinitarum Pertinentes: 2.** 2. Auflg. 1990. 722p. ISBN 3-7643-1414-1. Vol. XVI/1. **Commentationes Analyticae ad Theoriam Serierum Infinitarum Pertinentes: 3.1.** 355p. ISBN 3-7643-1415-X. Vol. XVI/2. **Commentationes Analyticae ad Theoriam Serierum Infinitarum Pertinentes: 3.2.** 332p. ISBN 3-7643-1416-8. Vol. XVII. **Commentationes Analyticae ad Theoriam Integralium Pertinentes: 1.** 457p. ISBN 3-7643-1417-6. Vol. XVIII. **Commentationes Analyticae ad Theoriam Integralium Pertinentes: 2.** 475p. ISBN 3-7643-1418-4. Vol. XIX. **Commentationes Analyticae ad Threoriam Integralium Pertinentes: 3.** 494p. ISBN 3-7643-1419-2. Vol. XX. **Commentationes Analyticae ad Theoriam Integralium Ellipticorum Pertinentes: 1.** 371p. ISBN 3-7643-1420-6. Vol. XXI. **Commentationes Analyticae ad Theoriam Integralium Ellipticorum Pertinentes: 2.** 380p. ISBN 3-7643-1421-4. Vol. XXII. **Commentationes Analyticae ad Theoriam Aequationum Differentialium Pertinentes: 1.** 420p. ISBN 3-7643-1422-2. Vol. XXIII. **Commentationes Analyticae ad Theoriam Aequationum Differentialium Pertinentes: 2.** 455p. ISBN 3-7643-1423-0. Vol. XXIV. **Methodus Inveniendi Lineas Curvas Maximi Minimive Proprietate Gaudentes Sive Solutio Problematis Isoperimetrici Latissimo Sensu Accepti.** 308p. ISBN 3-7643-1424-9. Vol. XXV. **Commentationes**

Analyticae ad Calculum Variationum Pertinentes. 343p. ISBN 3-7643-1425-7. Vol. XXVI. **Commentationes Geometricae: 1.** 362p. ISBN 3-7643-1426-5. Vol. XXVII. **Commentationes Geometricae: 2.** 400p. ISBN 3-7643-1427-3. Vol. XXVIII. **Commentationes Geometricae: 3.** 381p. ISBN 3-7643-1428-1. Vol. XXIX. **Commentationes Geometricae: 4.** 448p. ISBN 3-7643-1429-X. All volumes $176.50 each.

This series of Euler's collected works contains his contributions on mathematics in Latin, French, and German.

Faddeev, L. D. **40 Years in Mathematical Physics.** Singapore; River Edge, NJ: World Scientific, 1995. x + 471p. (Scientific Series in 20th Century Mathematics; 2). $40.00 pa. ISBN 981-02-2199-1.

A very brief vita is followed by 16 of his papers, with commentary by the author. The first paper is his scientific autobiography, written 10 year ago. No index.

S Fisher, R. A. **Collected Papers of R. A. Fisher.** Edited by J. H. Bennett. Adelaide, Australia: University of Adelaide, 1971–1974. Vol. 1. **1912–24.** 604p. Vol. 2. **1925–31.** 558p. Vol. 3. **1932–36.** 560p. Vol. 4. **1937–47.** 668p. Vol. 5. **1948–62.** 575p. Out of print. No ISBN.

Fisher's more than 300 papers on statistics and genetics are published here in chronological order. A bibliography, biography, and name and subject indexes are included.

Frege, Gottlob. **Collected Papers on Mathematics, Logic, and Philosophy.** Edited by Brian McGuinness. Translated by Max Black et al. Cambridge, MA: Basil Blackwell, 1984. viii + 412p. Out of print. ISBN 0-631-12728-3.

Frege's occasional writings are all collected in the present volume, about half of them now first appearing in English. They form a corpus as great and as important as his three systematic works.

Friedrichs, Kurt Otto. **Selecta.** Edited by Cathleen S. Morawetz. Boston: Birkhäuser, 1986. Vol. 1. 427p. $151.50. ISBN 0-8176-3268-9. Vol. 2. 608p. $201.00. ISBN 0-8176-3269-7.

This selection contains reproductions of 34 articles and one report. Papers in the volumes are divided into seven subject groupings together with their commentators-reviewers: Lax, Kato, John, Wasow, Weitzner, Nirenberg, and Isaacson. Biography by Constance Reid. List of degrees and awards received by Freidrichs.

Gallarati, Dionisio. **Collected Papers of Dionisio Gallarati.** Edited by A. V. Geramita. Kingston, ON: Queen's University Printing Services, 2000. xxiv + 472p. (Queen's Papers in Pure and Applied Mathematics; 116). $51.20. ISBN 0-88911-844-2.

Vita and list of students plus 64 papers (all in Italian) from the man who was a major influence on the development of algebra and geometry at the University of Genova.

Gelfand, Izrail M. **Collected Papers.** Edited by S. G. Gindikin et al. New York: Springer-Verlag, 1987–1989. Vol. I. vi + 883p. Out of print. ISBN 0-387-13619-3. Vol. II. x + 1039p. Out of print. ISBN 0-387-19035-X. Vol. III. x + 1075p. $289.00. ISBN 0-387-19399-5.

Gelfand's 450 research papers from Banach algebras to cell biology are collected into three volumes. Complete bibliography.

Gödel, Kurt. **Collected Works.** Edited by Solomon Feferman et al. New York: Oxford University Press, 1986–1995. Vol. I. **Publications 1929–1936.** xvi + 474p. Out of print. ISBN 0-19-503964-5. Vol. II. **Publications 1938–1974.** xiv + 407p. Out of print. ISBN 0-19-503972-6. Vol. III. **Unpublished Essays and Lectures.** xix + 532p. Out of print. ISBN 0-19-507255-3.

Two volumes of published works followed by volumes of unpublished manuscripts and lectures. Each article has a note to elucidate it and place it in proper historical context. Includes English translations and a biographical essay.

E Green, George. **Mathematical Papers of George Green.** Edited by N. M. Ferrers. New York: Chelsea, 1970. x + 336p. $25.00. ISBN 0-8284-0229-9. Original available at: http://www.hti.umich.edu/cgi/t/text/text-idx?c=umhistmath;idno=AAN8197. Free.

Reprint of 1871 original with errata corrected. The curious may amuse themselves by trying to locate something here that looks like Green's theorem.

Hall, Philip. **The Collected Works of Philip Hall.** Compiled by K. W. Gruenberg and J. E. Roseblade. New York: Oxford University Press, 1988. xi + 776p. Out of print. ISBN 0-19-853254-7.

This beautiful book of one of the greatest mathematicians of this century consists of almost 50 years of publications, arranged chronologically. Obituary is by Roseblade.

Halmos, P. R. **Selecta.** New York: Springer-Verlag, 1983. **Expository Writing.** Edited by Donald E. Sarason and Leonard Gillman. xix + 304p. Out of print. ISBN 0-387-90756-4. **Research Contributions.** Edited by Donald E. Sarason and Nathaniel A. Friedman. xxviii + 458p. Out of print. ISBN 0-387-90755-6.

The two volumes present a selection of Halmos's mathematical writings, from research publications to expository and popular writings.

E Hamilton, William Rowan. **The Mathematical Papers of Sir William Rowan Hamilton.** New York: Cambridge University Press, 1931–1967, 2000. (Royal Irish Academy. Cunningham memoir no. 13-16). Vol. 1. **Geometrical Optics.** xxviii + 534p. Out of print. No ISBN. Vol. 2. **Dynamics.** xv + 656p. Out of print. No ISBN. Vol. 3. **Algebra.** xxiv + 672p. $140.00. ISBN 0-521-05183-5. Vol. 4. **Geometry, Analysis, Astronomy, Probability and Finite Differences, Miscellaneous.** 852p. $150.00. ISBN 0-521-59216-X. Papers that were published during his lifetime are also available at: http://www.maths.tcd.ie/pub/HistMath/People/Hamilton/Papers.html. Free.

Papers that have never appeared in print before are included in all volumes. Historical notes.

Hardy, G. H. **Collected Papers of G. H. Hardy; Including Joint Papers with J. E. Littlewood and Others.** Edited by a committee appointed by the London Mathematical Society. New York: Oxford University Press, 1966–1979. Vol. I. x + 700p. Out of print. No ISBN. Vol. II. vii + 702p. Out of print. No ISBN. Vol. III. viii + 748p. Out of print. No ISBN. Vol. IV. ix + 722p. Out of print. No ISBN. Vol. V. xv + 694p. Out of print. No ISBN. Vol. VI. xii + 854p. Out of print. ISBN 0-19-853340-3. Vol. VII. xviii + 897p. Out of print. ISBN 0-19-853347-0.

The complete bibliography of Hardy's mathematical papers, from 1899 to 1949. Titchmarsh's obituary of Hardy and a table showing the arrangement of the papers appears in the first volume.

Harish-Chandra. **Harish-Chandra, Collected Papers.** Edited by V. S. Varadarajan. New York: Springer-Verlag, 1984. Vol. I. **1944–1954.** lxxvii + 566p. Vol. II. **1955–1958.** v + 539p. Vol. III. **1959–1968.** v + 670p. Vol. IV. **1970–1983.** v + 461p. Out of print. ISBN 0-387-90782-3 (set).

All of Harish-Chandra's papers, arranged chronologically to emphasize the evolution of his thinking from theoretical physics to group representations to harmonic analysis on reductive groups. Includes a brief biography, three surveys of his work, and frontispiece photographs in each volume.

Hasse, Helmut. **Mathematische Abhandlungen.** Edited by Heinrich Wolfgang Leopoldt and Peter Roquette. Berlin; New York: de Gruyter, 1975. Band 1. xv + 535p. Band 2. xv + 525p. Band 3. x + 532p. $603.85 (set). ISBN 3-11-005931-2.

These three volumes contain the selected papers of Hasse, arranged by topics. Volume 1 contains Hasse's reflections on the period during which he developed his celebrated local-global principle for quadratic forms. This collection does not include a survey of his work or a biography.

E Hesse, Ludwig Otto. **Gesammelte Werke.** 2nd edition. New York: Chelsea, 1972. xi + 727p. $45.00. ISBN 0-8284-0261-2. Original available at: http://www.hti.umich.edu/cgi/t/text/text-idx?c=umhistmath; idno=ABW0809. Free.

This corrected reprint of the 1897 volume edited by several of his students omits various textbooks by Hesse. Bibliography.

E Hilbert, David. **Gesammelte Abhandlungen.** 4th edition. New York: Chelsea, 1981. Band I. **Zahlentheorie.** Band II. **Algebra. Invariantentheorie. Geometrie.** Band III: **Analysis. Grundlagen der Mathematik, Physik, Verschiedenes, Lebensgeschichte.** Out of print. ISBN 0-8284-0195-0. Original available at: http://134.76.163.65/agora_docs/41998BIBLIOGRAPHIC_DESCRIPTION.html. Free.

Reprint of 1932–1935 original.

E Hill, George William. **The Collected Mathematical Works of George William Hill.** New York: Johnson Reprint, 1965. Vol. 1. xviii + 363p. Vol. 2. v + 339p. Vol. 3. 577p. Vol. 4. vi + 577p. Out of print. ISBN 0-384-23255-8. Original available at: http://historical.library.cornell.edu/cgi-bin/cul.math/docviewer?did=03610002. Free.

Reprint of 1905–1907 Carnegie Institution of Washington original.

Hille, Einar. **Einar Hille: Classical Analysis and Functional Analysis, Selected Papers.** Edited by Robert R. Kallman. Cambridge, MA: MIT Press, 1975. xlvii + 708p. (Mathematicians of Our Time; 11). $82.00. ISBN 0-262-08080-X.

Hille's own selection of his important papers that document the transition from classical to functional analysis.

Hirzebruch, Friedrich. **Gesammelte Abhandlungen, Collected Papers.** New York: Springer-Verlag, 1987. Band I. **1951–1962.** viii + 814p. Band II. **1963–1987.** iv + 818p. $401.00 (set). ISBN 0-387-18087-7.

Virtually all of Hirzebruch's papers, in chronological order, with added commentary by the author to indicate progress since original publication.

S Hsü, Pao-Lu. **Pao-Lu Hsü Collected Papers.** Edited by Kai Lai Chung. New York: Springer-Verlag, 1983. xii + 589p. $160.00. ISBN 0-387-90725-4.

English reprints of all of Hsü's published mathematical papers as well as biographical information and short discussions of Hsü's work in inference, multivariate analysis, and probability.

Hua, Loo-Keng. **Loo-Keng Hua Selected Papers.** Edited by H. Halberstam. New York: Springer-Verlag, 1983. xiv + 889p. $160.00. ISBN 0-387-90744-0.

Selection of about 50 papers, supplemented by topical surveys on number theory, algebra and geometry, and function theory. Brief biography. Complete publication list.

Inkeri, Kustaa. **Collected Papers of Kustaa Inkeri.** Edited by Tauno Metsänkylä and Paulo Ribenboim. Kingston, ON: Queen's University, 1992. xxxi + 566p. (Queen's Papers in Pure and Applied Mathematics; 91). Out of print. ISBN 0-88911-632-6.

Inkeri was the founder of the Finnish school of number theory. This volume includes a biography and 53 papers on number theory, especially those on topics related to Fermat's Last Theorem.

Itô, Kiyosi. **Kyosi Itô: Selected Papers.** Edited by Daniel W. Stroock and S. R. S. Varadhan. New York: Springer-Verlag, 1987. xxi + 647p. $125.00. ISBN 0-387-96326-X.

This collection offers the major part of Itô's work on stochastic integrals and stochastic differential equations. Includes an autobiography.

E Jacobi, C. G. J. **C. G. J. Jacobi's Gesammelte Werke.** 2nd edition. New York: Chelsea, 1969. Erster Band. x + 546p. Zweiter Band. vi + 527p. Dritter Band. viii + 612p. Vierter Band. 541p. Funfter Band. vi + 515p. Sechster Band. viii + 433p. Siebenter Band. viii + 440p. Supplementband (Vol. 8). vi + 300p. $168.00 (set). ISBN 0-8218-0554-1 (set). Original available at: http://www.hti.umich.edu/cgi/t/text/text-idx?c=umhistmath;idno=ABR8803. Free.

Volumes 1–7 of the 1881–1891 edition have been reprinted with minor changes and rearrangements. These were edited by C. W. Borchardt and K. Weierstrasse. Volume 8, consisting of Jacobi's **Vorlesungen über Dynamik**, was first published in 1866 and edited by A. Clebsch. It was then published in a second edition in 1884 edited by K. Weierstrasse. It is this second edition that has been reprinted, unaltered.

Jacobson, Nathan. **Collected Mathematical Papers.** Boston: Birkhäuser, 1989. Vol. 1. **1934–1946**. xviii + 454p. $115.00. ISBN 0-8176-3410-X. Vol. 2. **1947–1965**. xviii + 556p. $115.00. ISBN 0-8176-3411-8. Vol. 3. **1965–1988**. xviii + 596p. $115.00. ISBN 0-8176-3446-0.

Complete collection of Jacobson's papers, both research and expository. He begins each volume with an autobiographical account of the specified period.

Kac, Mark. **Mark Kac: Probability, Number Theory, and Statistical Physics: Selected Papers.** Edited by K. Baclawski and M. D. Donsker. Cambridge, MA: MIT Press, 1979. xxxviii + 529p. (Mathematicians of Our Times; 14). $65.00. ISBN 0-262-11067-9.

Reprints of papers. Bibliography of papers through 1975 and books. Commentary on specific papers by other mathematicians. Autobiographical note.

S Kendall, Maurice. **Statistics, Theory and Practice: Selected Papers by Sir Maurice Kendall (1907–1983)**. Edited by Alan Stuart. New York: Oxford University Press, 1984. xviii + 268p. Out of print. ISBN 0-195-20588-X.

Includes bibliography of his statistical works.

S Kiefer, Jack Carl. **Jack Carl Kiefer Collected Papers.** Edited by Lawrence D. Brown et al. New York: Springer-Verlag, 1985–1986. Vol. I. **Statistical Inference and Probability (1951–1963).** xxxi + 502p. Vol. II. **Statistical Inference and Probability (1964–1984).** xiii + 590p. $240.00 (v.1-2). ISBN 0-387-96003-1 (v.1-2). Vol. III. **Design of Experiments.** xxiv + 718p. $117.00. ISBN 0-387-96004-X. Supplementary Vol. vi + 56p. Out of print. ISBN 0-387-96383-9.

Includes all of Kiefer's papers as well as brief commentaries. Short biography. Complete bibliography.

Kodaira, Kunihiko. **Collected Works.** Princeton, NJ: Princeton University Press, 1975. Vol. I. xx + 647p. Out of print. ISBN 0-691-08158-1. Vol. II.

x + 494p. Out of print. ISBN 0-691-08163-8. Vol. III. x + 480p. Out of print. ISBN 0-691-08164-6.

This set of Kodaira's collected works was issued on the occasion of his 60th birthday and contain 70 articles from the period 1937 through 1971. The first volume includes a brief biography, a detailed survey of his work, and a list of those papers that serve to link Kodaira's main fields of interest.

Kolmogorov, A. N. **Selected Works of A. N. Kolmogorov.** Edited by V. M. Tikhomirov. Dordrecht, Holland: Kluwer Acad. Publ., 1991–1992. (Mathematics and Its Applications [Soviet Series]; 25, 26, 27). Vol. I. **Mathematics and Mechanics.** xix + 551p. $282.50. ISBN 9-0277-2796-1. Vol. II. **Probability Theory and Mathematical Statistics.** xvi + 597p. $282.00. ISBN 9-0277-2797-X. Vol. III. **Information Theory and the Theory of Algorithms.** xxv + 275p. $165.00. ISBN 9-0277-2798-8.

The annotated English translation of Kolmogorov's selected works, originally published in Russian in 1985–1987.

E Kronecker, Leopold. **Leopold Kronecker's Werke.** Edited by K. Hensel. New York: Chelsea, 1968. Vol. I. ix + 483p. Vol. II. viii + 540p. Vol. III, Part I. vii + 473p. Vol. III, Part II. iii + 215p. (Parts I and II bound as one.) Vol. IV. x + 508p. Vol. V. x + 527p. $175.00 (set). ISBN 0-8284-0224-8. Original available at: http://www.hti.umich.edu/cgi/t/text/text-idx?c=umhistmath;idno=AAS8260. Free.

Reprint of 1895–1930 original. Errata have been corrected and half-title pages before each paper have been omitted.

Krull, Wolfgang. **Gesammelte Abhandlungen. Collected Papers.** Edited by Paulo Ribenboim. Berlin; New York: Walter de Gruyter, 1999. Vol. I. xiii + 822p. Vol. II. vii + 907p. $343.00 (set). ISBN 3-11-012771-7.

A two-volume set collecting German-language papers of Krull. In the first volume, Ribenboim records his contacts with Krull. No index.

E Laguerre, E. **Oeuvres de Laguerre, Publiées Sous les Auspices de l'Académie des Sciences.** 2nd edition. Edited by Ch. Hermite, H. Poincaré et E. Rouché. New York: Chelsea, 1972. Tome 1. **Algèbre. Calcul Intégral.** xv + 468p. Tome 2. **Géométrie.** 711p. $69.00 set. ISBN 0-8284-0263-9. Original available at: http://gallica.bnf.fr/document?O=N090210. Free.

Unaltered reprint (except for the correction of errata) of 1898–1905 original.

Lang, Serge. **Collected Papers.** New York: Springer, 2000-2001. Vol. I. **1952–1970.** xxiv + 525p. $79.95. ISBN 0-387-98802-5. Vol. II. **1971–1977.** xvi + 590p. $79.95. ISBN 0-387-98803-3. Vol. III. **1978–1990.** xvi + 393p. $79.95. ISBN 0-387-98800-9. Vol. IV. **1990–1996.** xvi + 471p. $79.95. ISBN 0-387-98804-1. Vol. V. **1993–1999.** With Jay Jorgensen. xvi + 410p. $89.95. ISBN 0-387-95030-3.

Collection of 83 of his research papers, ranging over a variety of topics. Also includes two out-of-print books, the 1966 **Introduction to Transcendental Numbers** and the 1996 **Topics in Cohomology of Groups,** as well as some seminar talks. Very brief vita. Complete bibliography through 1999.

Lawler, Eugene L. **Selected Publications of Eugene L. Lawler.** Edited by K. Aardal. Amsterdam: Stichting Mathematisch Centrum, Centrum voor Wiskunde en Informatica, 1999. x + 318p. (CWI Tracts; 126). Dfl 60 pa. ISBN 90-6196-484-9.

List of all publications plus 26 of Lawler's technical and expository papers on combinatorial optimization.

Lefschetz, S. **Selected Papers.** New York: Chelsea, 1971. 639p. Out of print. ISBN 0-8284-0234-5.

A collection of 18 papers on topology dating from 1921 to 1954 plus a complete Lefschetz bibliography through 1969.

E Leibniz, G. W. **Mathematische Schriften.** Edited by C. I. Gerhardt. Hildesheim, Germany: G. Olms, 1962. Band. I. **Briefwechsel zwischen Leibniz und Oldenbourg, Collins, Newton, Galloys, Vitale Giordano.** viii + 200p. Band. II. **Briefwechsel zwischen Leibniz, Hugens van Zulichem und dem Marquis de l'Hospital.** 343p. Band. III/1. **Briefwechsel zwischen Leibniz, Jacob Bernoulli, Johann Bernoulli und Nicolaus Bernoulli.** 420p. Band. III/2. **Briefwechsel zwischen Leibniz, Jacob Bernoulli, Johann Bernoulli und Nicolaus Bernoulli.** p. [421]–994. Band. IV. **Briefwechsel zwischen Leibniz, Wallis, Varignon, Guido Grandi, Zendrini, Hermann und Freiherrn Tschirnhaus.** 539p. Band. V. **Die mathematischen Abhandlungen.** viii + 418p. Band VI. **Die Mathematischen Abhandlungen.** vi + 514p. Band. VII. **Die Mathematischen Abhandlungen.** vi + 393p. Out of print (v. 1–7). ISBN 3-4870-6451-0 (set). Original available at: http://gallica.bnf.fr/document?O=N021147. Free.

Reprint from the edition published in 1849–1863. Edited by G. H. Pertz from the third volume, **Mathematik,** of Leibniz's collected works.

E Lejeune Dirichlet, Peter Gustav. **G. Lejeune Dirichlet's Werke.** New York: Chelsea, 1969. 2 vols. in 1. (644 + 422pp). Out of print. ISBN 0-8284-0225-6. Original available at: http://gallica.bnf.fr/document?O=N099435. Free.

Reprint of two volumes originally published in 1889–1897 of his papers, a few letters, and commentary.

Leray, Jean. **Selected Papers. Oeuvres Scientifiques.** Edited by Paul Malliavin. Berlin; New York; Paris: Springer; Société Mathématique de France, 1998. Vol. I. **Topology and Fixed Point Theorems. Topologie et Théorème du Point Fixe.** viii + 507p. Vol. II. **Fluid Dynamics and Real Partial Differential Equations. Equations aux Dérivées Partielles Réelles et Méchanique des Fluides.** viii + 587p. Vol. III. **Several Complex Variables and Holomorphic Partial Differential Equations. Fonctions de Plusiers Variables Complexes et Equations aux Dérivées Partielles Holomorphes.** vi + 599p. $325.00 (set). ISBN 3-540-60949-0.

Jean Leray is one of the great French mathematicians of the twentieth century. His life's work divides into three major areas, reflected in these three volumes (mostly in French). Well-known mathematicians introduce each volume: volume 1 by Armand Borel, volume 2 by Peter D. Lax, and volume 3 by G. Henkin. Complete bibliography.

Lesniewski, Stanislaw. **Collected Works.** Edited by Stanislaw J. Surma, Jan T. Srzednicki, and D. I. Barnett. Boston: Kluwer Acad. Publ., 1992. (Nijhoff International Philosophy Series; 44). Vol. I. xvi + 382p. Vol. II. vi + 412p. Out of print. ISBN 0-7923-1512-X (set).

First English-language version of all of Lesniewski's papers on mathematical logic and the foundations of mathematics, originally published in either Polish or German. Annotated bibliography by V. Frederick Rickey. Index.

Littlewood, J. E. **Collected Papers of J. E. Littlewood.** New York: Oxford University Press, 1982. Vol. I. xxxviii + 790p. Out of print. ISBN 0-19-853353-5. Vol. II. xxxviii + 886p. Out of print. ISBN 0-19-853355-1.

All of Littlewood's papers arranged in five groups. Most papers are followed by a brief commentary by the editors to provide modern perspective. Introductory biographical memoir.

Loewner, Charles. **Charles Loewner, Collected Papers.** Edited by Lipman Bers. Boston: Birkhäuser, 1988. xii + 517p. $135.00. ISBN 0-8176-3377-4.

Loewner's published contributions in the areas of complex analysis and differential geometry have been gathered in this work.

Lorentz, George G. **Mathematics from Leningrad to Austin: George G. Lorentz' Selected Works in Real, Functional and Numerical Analysis.** Edited by Rudolph A. Lorentz. Boston: Birkhäuser, 1997. Vol. I. xxxvi + 548p. Vol. II. xxviii + 648p. $189.00 (set). ISBN 0-8176-3923-3.

Volume 1 of this set contains his autobiography, list of doctoral students, a section of unpublished works, "Mathematics in a Broader Setting," papers on summability and number theory, and interpolation. Volume 2 contains papers on real and functional analysis and approximation theory. Bibliography.

Mac Lane, Saunders. **Selected Papers: Saunders Mac Lane.** Edited by I. Kaplansky. New York: Springer-Verlag, 1979. xiii + 556p. Out of print. ISBN 0-387-90394-1.

Twenty-one papers along with a biographical note by Putnam, a personal tribute by Lyndon, and technical reviews of Mac Lane's work by Kaplansky, Eilenberg, and Kelly. Complete bibliography and list of his doctoral students.

MacLaurin, Colin. **The Collected Letters of Colin MacLaurin.** Edited by Stella Mills. Nantwich, Cheshire, England: Shiva Publishing, 1982. xx + 496p. Out of print. ISBN 0-906812-08-9.

One of Scotland's greatest mathematicians, MacLaurin helped to interpret and defend Newton. This volume of letters traces the development of his ideas in exchanges with Newton and Stirling and other eighteenth-century scientists and mathematicians.

MacMahon, Percy Alexander. **Percy Alexander MacMahon: Collected Papers.** Edited by George E. Andrews. Cambridge, MA: MIT Press, 1978–1986. (Mathematicians of Our Time; 13, 24). Vol. I. **Combinatorics.** xxix + 1,438p. $125.00. ISBN 0-262-13121-8. Vol. II. **Number Theory, Invariants, and Applications.** xxv + 952p. $105.00. ISBN 0-262-13214-1.

MacMahon's work on symmetric functions, determinants, number theory, and invariant theory with commentary, references, and summaries.

Magiros, Demetrios C. **Selected Papers of Demetrios C. Magiros: Applied Mathematics, Nonlinear Mechanics, and Dynamical Systems Analysis.** Edited by S. G. Tzafestas. Norwell, MA: Kluwer Acad. Publ., 1985. xv + 518p. $316.00. ISBN 90-277-2003-7.

This book contains 43 of Magiros's 54 papers from 1946 to 1984. An appendix has two papers in Russian and at the end of the book is a list of unpublished works.

Magnus, Wilhelm. **Wilhelm Magnus: Collected Papers.** Edited by Gilbert Baumslag and Bruce Chandler. New York: Springer-Verlag, 1984. xvi + 726p. $105.95. ISBN 0-387-90879-X.

Collected works of one of the few mathematicians who has done significant work in two unrelated fields: combinatorial group theory and diffraction problems and related topics in analysis.

Mandelbrot, Benoit B. **Selecta: Selected Works of Benoit M. Mandelbrot.** Reprinted, translated, or new with annotations and guest contributions. New York: Springer-Verlag, 1997– . Vol. E. **Fractals and Scaling in Finance: Discontinuity, Concentration, Risk.** x + 551p. $39.95. ISBN 0-387-98363-5. Vol. N. **Multifractals and 1/F Noise: Wild Self-Affinity in Physics (1963–1976).** viii + 442p. $42.95. ISBN 0-387-98539-5. Vol. H. **Gaussian Self-Affinity and Fractals: Globality, the Earth, 1/F Noise, R/S.** ix + 654p. $54.95. ISBN 0-387-98993-5.

First three volumes of his selected works. The first volume discusses the fractal nature of price variation The second, a major contribution to an understanding of wild variability and randomness along two new frontiers of physics, consists of a synthesis, historical background, and 20-plus reprints. The third volume focuses on a detailed study of fractal Brownian motions.

Maxwell, James Clerk. **The Scientific Letters and Papers of James Clerk Maxwell.** Edited by P. M. Harman. Cambridge, England; New York: Cambridge University Press, 1990– . Vol. I. **1846–1862.** xxviii + 748p. $245.00. ISBN 0-521-25625-9. Vol. II. **1862–1879.** xxx + 999p. $295.00. ISBN 0-521-25626-7.

First two volumes of a comprehensive edition of Maxwell's letters and manuscripts, with a full historical commentary by Harman. Maxwell's contributions have earned him a special place in the history of physics and mathematics.

Mindlin, Raymond D. **The Collected Papers of Raymond D. Mindlin.** Edited by H. Deresiewicz, M. P. Bieniek, and F. L. DiMaggio. New York: Springer-Verlag, 1989. Vol. I. xxviii + 596p. Vol. II. xxviii + 591p. Out of print (set). ISBN 0-387-96933-0.

One hundred of his research papers in applied mechanics from 1934 to 1986.

E Minkowski, Hermann. **Gesammelte Abhandlungen.** New York: Chelsea, 1967. 2 vols. in 1. $75.00. ISBN 0-8284-0208-6. Original available at: http://www.hti.umich.edu/cgi/t/text/text-idx?c=umhistmath;idno=AAT3434. Free.

Collected works of Minkowski, plus Hilbert's 1909 memorial to Minkowski.

Morishima, Taro. **Collected Papers of Taro Morishima.** Edited by Y. Karamatsu. Kingston, ON: Queen's University, 1990. xii + 227p. (Queen's Papers in Pure and Applied Mathematics; 84). $15.00 pa. ISBN 9-991-42506-3.

All but two of Morishima's publications, mostly on Fermat's Last Theorem and class field theory.

Morse, Marston. **Collected Papers: Marston Morse.** Teaneck, NJ: World Scientific, 1987. Vol. 1. xlix + 532p. Vol. 2. vi + 598p. Vol. 3. vi + 639p. Vol. 4. vi + 602p. Vol. 5. vi + 578p. Vol. 6. vi + 559p. Out of print (set). ISBN 9971-978-94-6.

The collected works of Marston Morse contain over 50 papers on Morse theory.

Newton, Isaac. **The Mathematical Papers of Isaac Newton.** Edited by D. T. Whiteside and M. A. Hoskin. New York: Cambridge University Press, 1967–1981. Vol. 1. **1664–1666.** xlvi + 590p. Out of print. No ISBN. Vol. 2. **1667–1670.** xxii + 520p. Out of print. No ISBN. Vol. 3. **1670–1673.** xxxvii + 576p. Out of print. ISBN 0-521-07119-4. Vol. 4. **1674–1684.** xxxii + 678p. Out of print. ISBN 0-521-07740-0. Vol. 5. **1683–1684.** xxii + 627p. Out of print. ISBN 0-521-08262-5. Vol. 6. **1684–1691.** xxxiv + 614p. Out of print. ISBN 0-521-08719-8. Vol. 7. **1691–1695.** xlvii + 706p. $250.00. ISBN 0-521-08720-1. Vol. 8. **1697–1722.** lv + 704p. $240.00. ISBN 0-521-20103-9.

The first edition of all of Newton's extant mathematical notes and papers has been carefully annotated. Each volume has a general introduction as well as introductions and numerous notes to each section, English translations of Newton's Latin pieces, manuscript facsimiles, appendixes, a detailed analytical table of contents, and an index of names.

S Neyman, J. **A Selection of Early Statistical Papers of J. Neyman.** Berkeley, CA: University of California Press, 1967. ix + 429p. Out of print. ISBN 0-520-00992-4.

This volume of Neyman's selected papers includes 28 contributions published or written before the early1940s. A bibliography lists 144 papers and 12 books and monographs either written or edited by the author. Companion volume to **Joint Statistical Papers of J. Neyman and E. S. Pearson** (below) and **The Selected Papers of E. S. Pearson** (below).

S Neyman, J. and E. S. Pearson. **Joint Statistical Papers of J. Neyman and E. S. Pearson.** Berkeley, CA: University of California Press, 1967. iv + 299p. Out of print. ISBN 0-520-00991-6.

Companion volume to **The Selected Papers of E. S. Pearson** (below) and **A Selection of Early Statistical Papers of J. Neyman** (above). This selection includes 10 joint papers published from 1928 to 1938 and concludes with a paper by Neyman alone.

Noether, Emmy. **Gesammelte Abhandlungen, Collected Papers/Emmy Noether.** Edited by N. Jacobson. New York: Springer-Verlag, 1983. viii + 777p. $165.00. ISBN 0-387-11504-8.

Although the collected papers are in German, Paul Alexandroff's memorial address and Nathan Jacobson's introduction are in English.

Oka, Kiyoshi. **Collected Papers.** Edited by R. Remmert. Translated from the French by R. Narasimhan. New York: Springer-Verlag, 1984. xiv + 223p. $169.00. ISBN 0-387-13240-6.

Ten fundamental papers (1936–1962) followed by H. Cartan's commentaries, and two brief notes by one of the founders of function theory of several complex variables.

Olver, F. W. J. **Selected Papers of F. W. J. Olver.** Edited by Roderick Wong. Singapore; River Edge, NJ: World Scientific, 2000. (World Scientific Series in 20th Century Mathematics; 7). Part I. xvii + 520p. Part II. ix + p.521–1,074. $159.00 (set). ISBN 981-02-4106-2 (set).

Selection of research papers in asymptotic analysis, special functions, and numerical analysis, published from 1949 to 1999.

Ostrowski, Alexander. **Collected Mathematical Papers.** Boston, MA: Birkhäuser, 1983–1985. Vol. 1. **Determinants, Linear Algebra, Algebraic Equations.** 904p. $150.00. ISBN 3-7643-1506-7. Vol. 2. **Multivariate**

Algebra, Formal Algebra. 652p. Out of print. ISBN 3-7643-1507-5. Vol. 3. **Number Theory, Geometry, Topology, Convergence.** 532p. Out of print. ISBN 3-7643-1508-3. Vol. 4. **Real Function Theory, Differential Equations, Differential Transformations.** 632p. $91.00. ISBN 3-7643-1509-1. Vol. 5. **Complex Function Theory.** 544p. $85.00. ISBN 3-7643-1510-5. Vol. 6. **Conformal Mapping, Numerical Analysis, Miscellany.** 718p. $110.00. ISBN 3-7643-1511-3. $688.50 (set). ISBN 0-8176-1512-1.

Papers of one of the twentieth century's leading mathematicians.

S Pearson, E. S. **The Selected Papers of E. S. Pearson.** Berkeley, CA: University of California Press, 1966. vi + 327p. Out of print.

Reprinting of 21 articles, from 1928 to 1963 plus the text of a 1962 address. The volume includes a bibliography of 112 items published between 1922 and 1966. Companion volume to **Joint Statistical Papers of J. Neyman and E. S. Pearson** (above) and **A Selection of Early Statistical Papers of J. Neyman** (above).

Peirce, Charles S. **Writings of Charles S. Peirce: A Chronological Edition.** Edited by Christian J. W. Kloesel. Bloomington: Indiana University Press, 1982– . Vol. 1. **1857–1866.** xxxv + 698p. $57.50. ISBN 0-253-37201-1. Vol. 2. **1967–1871.** xlviii + 649p. $57.50. ISBN 0-253-37202-X. Vol. 3. **1872–1878.** xxxvii + 633p. $57.50. ISBN 0-253-37203-8. Vol. 4. **1879–1884.** lxx + 698p. $67.50. ISBN 0-253-37204-6. Vol. 5. **1884–1886.** xlviii + 623p. $75.00. ISBN 0-253-37205-4. Vol. 6. **1886–1890.** lxxxiv + 698p. $49.95. ISBN 0-253-37206-2.

First six volumes of a monumental work containing numerous manuscripts never before published and extensive scholarly and editorial notes.

Polya, George. **Collected Papers.** Edited by R. P. Boas. Cambridge, MA: MIT Press, 1974–1984. (Mathematicians of Our Time; 7, 8, 21, 22). Vol. I. **Singularities of Analytic Functions.** xiv + 808p. $75.00. ISBN 0-262-02104-8. Vol. II. **Location of Zeros.** x + 444p. Out of print. ISBN 0-262-02103-X. Vol. III. **Analysis.** x + 536p. $65.00. ISBN 0-262-16096-X. Vol. IV. **Probability: Combinatorics; Teaching and Learning in Mathematics.** ix + 642p. Out of print. ISBN 0-262-16097-8.

Each volume concludes with brief commentaries on the papers and a complete Polya bibliography keyed to the four volumes.

Rademacher, Hans. **Collected Papers of Hans Rademacher.** Edited by Emil Grosswald. Cambridge, MA: MIT Press, 1974. Vol. I. xix + 692p.

$70.00. ISBN 0-262-07054-5. Vol. II. xxi + 638p. $70.00. ISBN 0-262-07055-3. $135.00 (set). ISBN 0-685-03383-X.

These two volumes contain all the papers published by Rademacher, either alone or as a joint author, essentially in chronological order. Volume 2 includes a list of his writings that are not included in this present collection and a list of dissertations directed by Rademacher. The editor has provided notes for each paper and contributed a biographical sketch.

Ramanujan, Srinivasa. **Ramanujan: Letters and Commentary.** Compiled by and with commentary by Bruce C. Berndt and Robert Rankin. Providence, RI: American Mathematical Society, 1995. xiv + 347p. (History of Mathematics; 9). $59.00 pa. ISBN 0-8218-0287-9.

Among this collection of letters written by, to, or about Ramanujan, there are the first letter he wrote to G. H. Hardy and Hardy's response. Commentaries accompanying each letter provide biographical sketches, cultural background, and mathematical notes.

Ramanujan, Srinivasa. **Ramanujan's Notebooks.** Edited by Bruce C. Berndt. New York: Springer-Verlag, 1985–1998. Part I. x + 537p. $107.95. ISBN 0-387-96110-0. Part II. xi + 359p. $107.95. ISBN 0-387-96794-X. Part III. xiii + 510p. $98.95. ISBN 0-387-97503-9. Part IV. xii + 451p. $107.95. ISBN 0-387-94109-6. Part V. xiii + 624p. $97.95. ISBN 0-387-94941-0.

During the years 1903–1914, Ramanujan recorded many of his mathematical discoveries in notebooks without providing proofs and many of his results were not in the literature. In the 1930s, Watson and Wilson began to edit the notebooks, but never completed the task. In 1957, a photostatic edition was published in Bombay. This five-volume set devoted to the editing of Ramanujan's notebooks is both a tribute to Ramanujan's genius and Berndt's perseverance.

Ramanujan, Srinivasa. **The Lost Notebook and Other Unpublished Papers.** New York: Springer-Verlag, 1988. xxv + 419p. Out of print. ISBN 0-387-18726-X.

This book contains reproductions of the "Lost Notebook," several letters between Ramanujan and his colleagues, "Loose Papers," and 117 pages of unpublished work related to various papers.

S Rao, C. R. **Selected Papers of C. R. Rao.** Edited by S. Das Gupta et al. New York: Wiley, 1994– . Vol. 1. ix + 506p. ISBN 0-470-22091-0. Vol.

2. ix + 504p. ISBN 0-470-22092-9. Vol. 3. x + 437p. ISBN 0-470-22093-7. $151.00 each volume.

First three volumes of a projected five-volume set of selected works by the founder of the Indian Statistical Institute. Volume 1 is a reprint of the 1989 ISI original and contains 31 papers from 1945–1954, Volume 2 contains 37 papers from 1955–1965, and volume 3 contains 38 papers from 1966–1974.

Reissner, Eric. **Selected Works in Applied Mechanics and Mathematics.** Boston, MA: Jones and Bartlett, 1996. xviii + 601p. $82.95. ISBN 0-86720-968-2.

A collection of 71 papers (out of 283) in a wide range of fields in applied mechanics and mathematics. Papers are arranged chronologically in each section and preceded by historical comments. Includes a biographical sketch, a bibliography,

Ribenboim, Paulo. **Collected Papers of Paulo Ribenboim.** Kingston, ON: Queen's University Printing Services, 1997. (Queen's Papers in Pure and Applied Mathematics; 104). Vol. 1. xlviii + 506p. ISBN 0-88911-783-7. Vol. 2. ii + 532p. ISBN 0-88911-785-3. Vol. 3. ii + 550p. ISBN 0-88911-787-X. Vol. 4. ii + 580p. 0-88911-789-6. Vol. 5. ii + 573p. ISBN 0-88911-791-8. Vol. 6. xviii + 581p. ISBN 0-88911-793-4. Vol. 7. ii + 570p. ISBN 0-88911-795-0. $495.00 pa (set). ISBN 0-88911-735-7 (set).

In addition to all of Ribenboim's papers, there are a list of his doctoral students and a bibliography of works from 1949 to 1996, plus a listing of publications to appear.

E Riemann, Bernhard. **Gesammelte mathematische Werke, wissenschaftlicher Nachlass und Nachtrage.** Edited by Raghavan Narasimhan. Berlin: Springer-Verlag, 1990. vi + 911p. $175.00. ISBN 0-354-050033-2. 1876 Weber and Dedekind edition available at: http://www.hti.umich.edu/cgi/t/text/text-idx?c=umhistmath;idno=ABS3163. Free.

Based on the edition by H. Weber and R. Dedekind, this present work reproduces these collected works and adds extensive comments by Narasimhan on Riemann's influence in mathematics and other interesting reports on special aspects. Bibliography and secondary literature on Riemann.

Riesz, Marcel. **Collected Papers.** Edited by Lars Gårding and Lars Hörmander. New York: Springer-Verlag, 1988. vi + 897p. $171.00. ISBN 0-387-18115-6.

Almost all of the published papers, largely in French and German.

S Robbins, Herbert. **Selected Papers.** Edited by T. L. Lai and D. Siegmund. New York: Springer-Verlag, 1985. xli + 518p. $109.00. ISBN 0-387-96137-2.

A selection of nearly half of Robbins's 133 publications arranged in three groups: empirical Bayes methodology, sequential experimentation, and probability and inference. Complete list of his publications.

Robinson, Abraham. **Selected Papers of Abraham Robinson.** Edited by H. J. Keisler et al. New Haven, CT: Yale University Press, 1979. Vol. 1. **Model Theory and Algebra.** xxxvii + 694p. Out of print. ISBN 0-300-02071-6. Vol. 2. **Nonstandard Analysis and Philosophy.** xlv + 582p. Out of print. ISBN 0-300-02072-4. Vol. 3. **Aeronautics.** xxxii + 270p. Out of print. ISBN 0-300-02073-2.

This selection contains Robinson's most important papers (98 out of 134). Each volume begins with a superbly written biography by George Seligman, a topical introduction by one of the editors, and frontispiece photographs. Each concludes with a complete bibliography and a list of Robinson's doctoral students.

Sachs, Gerald E. **Selected Logic Papers.** Singapore; River Edge, NJ: 1999. xviii + 431p. (World Scientific Series in 20th Century Mathematics; 6). $90.00. ISBN 981-02-3267-5.

Twenty-three papers arranged chronologically and spanning the years 1963 to 1996, selected by the author.

Samuel, Pierre. **Collected Papers of Pierre Samuel.** Edited by A. J. Coleman and Paulo Ribenboim. Kingston, ON: Queen's University, 1995. (Queen's Papers in Pure and Applied Mathematics; 99). Vol. I. xxix + 558p. Out of print. ISBN 0-88911-693-8. Vol. II. Vi + 531p. Out of print. ISBN 0-88911-695-4.

Volumes contain a curriculum vita, a eulogy, and lists of his publications, his students and his mathematical and nonmathematical publications.

Schläfli, Ludwig. **Gesammelte mathematische Abhandlungen.** Boston: Birkhäuser, 1950–1956. Band I. 392p. Out of print. ISBN 0-8176-0328-

X. Band II. 381p. Out of print. ISBN 0-8176-0329-8. Band III. 402p. Out of print. ISBN 0-8176-0330-1.

Schäfli, a great Swiss mathematician, rediscovered the foundations of n-dimensional Euclidean and spherical geometry and developed it in a manner that was not approached by anyone else for half a century. These collected works, which could be improved if arranged more systematically, are profusely annotated by Burkhardt and others.

Schoenberg, I. J. **I. J. Schoenberg: Selected Papers.** Edited by Carl de Boor. Boston: Birkhäuser, 1988. Vol. 1. xviii + 405p. $134.50. ISBN 0-8176-3404-5. Vol. 2. xvi + 441p. $134.50. ISBN 0-8176-3405-3. $150.00 (set). ISBN 0-8176-3378-2.

A sampling of 45 of Schoenberg's 173 papers, spanning the period 1928–1987, and covering number theory, geometry, real analysis, complex analysis (all in volume 1), and aspects of spline theory (volume 2). Interspersed are brief commentaries by experts who summarize his contributions.

Schrödinger, E. **Collected Papers on Wave Mechanics.** New York: Chelsea, 1982. xiii + 207p. Out of print. ISBN 0-8284-1302-9.

Third English edition of the 1927 German original along with the text of the 1928 **Four Lectures on Wave Mechanics**.

E Schwarz, Hermann Amandus. **Gesammelte Mathematische Abhandlungen.** 2nd edition. New York: Chelsea, 1972. xiv + 338 + vii + 370p. $49.50. ISBN 0-8284-0260-4. Original available at: http://www.hti.umich.edu/cgi/t/text/text-idx?c=umhistmath;idno=AAT0607. Free.

A reprint with corrections of the two 1890 volumes, which were themselves revisions by Schwarz himself of earlier papers.

Schwinger, Julian. **Selected Papers (1937–1976) of Julian Schwinger.** Edited by M. Flato, C. Fronsdal, and K. A. Milton. Dordrecht, Holland: D. Reidel, 1979. xxvii + 413p. Out of print. ISBN 90-277-0974-2.

A 60th birthday retrospective selection (by Schwinger) of some 50 papers; many important papers omitted. Complete bibliography and brief comments on the importance of the papers included.

Seidel, J. J. **Geometry and Combinatorics: Selected Works of J. J. Seidel.** Edited by D. G. Corneil and R. Mathon. San Diego, CA: Academic Press, 1991. xix + 410p. $88.00. ISBN 0-12-189420-7.

Twenty-eight research and survey papers highlight Seidel's work on the interplay of geometry, combinatorics, and algebra.

Selberg, Atle. **Collected Papers.** New York: Springer-Verlag, 1989-1991. Vol. I. vi + 711p. $215.00. ISBN 0-387-18389-2. Vol. II. viii + 251p. $118.00. ISBN 0-387-50626-8.

Volume 1 ranges from Selberg's early work in analysis to number theory to his later work that enlarged and transfigured the whole concept and structure of arithmetic. Volume 2 contains material (e.g., sieve methods, Eisenstein series, automorphic forms) on which Selberg has lectured recently, but which had not so far appeared in print. Bibliography. Autobiographical note.

Serre, Jean Pierre. **Oeuvres, Collected Papers.** Berlin; New York: Springer-Verlag, 1986–2000. Vol. I. **1949–1959.** xviii + 596p. Out of print. Vol. II. **1960–1971.** iv + 740p. Out of print. Vol. III. **1972–1984.** iv + 728p. Out of print. Vol. IV. **1985–1998.** $159.00. ISBN 3-540-65683-9.

Almost all (132) of Serre's published papers, arranged chronologically, plus a selection of his seminar notes and summaries of his courses at the Collège de France since 1956 constitute the first three volumes. The fourth volume contains those published between 1985 and 1998 and some unpublished letters.

Shafarevich, Igor R. **Collected Mathematical Papers.** New York: Springer-Verlag, 1989. vi + 769p. $128.00. ISBN 0-387-13618-5.

Contains 43 papers, most in English translation, published between 1943 and 1984.

Smale, Stephen. **The Collected Papers of Stephen Smale.** Edited by F. Cucker and R. Wong. Singapore; River Edge, NJ: Singapore University Press, World Scientific, 2000. Vol. I. xxxiv + 488p. ISBN 981-024991-8. Vol. II. xi + p.491–1,031. ISBN 981-02-4992-6. Vol. III. xi + p.1,035–1,677. ISBN 981-02-4993-4. $260.00 (set). ISBN 981-02-4307-3.

Contents of the volumes reflect the breadth of his contributions, including papers on topology, economics, calculus of variations, dynamics, mechanics, biology, electric circuits, mathematical programming, and theory of computation. Papers within each part are arranged chronologically. Volume 1 also contains papers by close friends and colleagues describing different aspects of Smale's work plus a paper by Smale written specifically for this collection in which he gives a retrospective of his own work.

Smarandache, Florentin. **Collected Papers.** Bucharest, Romania: Editura Societatii Tempus, 1996. Vol. I. ii + 301p. Out of print. ISBN 973-9205-02-X. Chisinau, Moldova: Universitatea de Stat din Moldova, 1997. Vol. II. 200p. Price not available. No ISBN.

A collection of articles, notes, generalizations, paradoxes from mathematics, linguistics, and education.

E Smith, Henry John Stephen. **Collected Mathematical Papers.** Edited by J. W. L. Glaisher. New York: Chelsea, 1965. Vol. I. xcv + 603p. Vol. II. vii + 719p. $99.50 set. ISBN 0-8284-0187-X. Original available at: http://www.hti.umich.edu/cgi/t/text/text-idx?c=umhistmath;idno= AAT2237. Free.

Reprint of 1894 edition. Includes a biographical sketch, recollections, and all of his papers published or in preparation at the time of his death, arranged chronologically.

Spencer, Donald C. **Selecta.** Teaneck, NJ: World Scientific, 1985. Vol. 1. xii + 656p. Vol. 2. viii + 657p. Vol. 3. viii + 441p. $197.00 (set). ISBN 9971-97-802-4.

This set includes most of Spencer's 90 papers, arranged into 10 subject areas, a brief biography by J. J. Kohn, a complete bibliography of his work, and a list of the PhD theses supervised by Spencer.

Steiner, Jacob. **Gesammelte Werke.** 2nd edition. New York: Chelsea, 1971. Vol. I. viii + 527p. Vol. II. x + 743p. $75.00 (set). ISBN 0-8284-0233-7.

Virtually unaltered reprinting of the collected works of the famous geometer that were originally published in 1881–1882 and edited by Weierstrasse.

Su, Buchin. **Su Buchin: Selected mathematical papers/Su Buchin.** New York: Gordon & Breach, 1983. xviii + 411p. $226.00. ISBN 0-677-31300-4.

Twenty-six papers of Su's work on affine and projective differential geometry are reprinted here, along with a tribute by S. S. Chern, a brief biography by his Chinese colleagues, and a bibliography of his publications.

Suzuki, Satoshi. **Collected Papers of Satoshi Suzuki.** Edited by Paulo Ribenboim. Kingston, ON: Kingston University, 1994. xxii + 369p. (Queen's Papers in Pure and Applied Mathematics; 97). Out of print. ISBN 0-88911-675-X.

Professor Suzuki's papers span a period of more than 30 years, from his fundamental work on the module of differentials associated to algebra over a ring to his later work in higher derivations and the associated modules of higher differentials. Included are 18 papers from 1958 to 1989 on the algebraic theory of differentials, a list of Suzuki's publications, his vita, and reminiscences from three colleagues.

E Sylvester, James Joseph. **The Collected Mathematical Papers of James Joseph Sylvester.** Edited by H. F. Baker. New York: Chelsea, 1973. Vol. I. **1837–1853.** xii + 659p. Vol. II. **1854–1873.** xvi + 746p. Vol. III. **1870–1883.** xv + 697p. Vol. IV. **1882–1897.** xxxvii + 756p. $195.00 (set). ISBN 0-8284-0253-1. Original available at: http://www.hti.umich.edu/cgi/t/text/text-idx?c=umhistmath;idno=AAS8085. Free.

Corrected reprint of the 1904–1912 edition. General index and biographical notice appear in volume 4.

Szegö, Gabor. **Collected Papers.** Edited by Richard Askey. Boston: Birkhäuser, 1982. Vol. 1. **1915–1927.** xx + 857p. Out of print. ISBN 3-7643-3056-2. Vol. 2. **1927–1943.** x + 869p. Out of print. ISBN 3-7643-3060-0. Vol. 3. **1945–1972.** x + 880p. Out of print. ISBN 3-7643-3061-9.

All of Szegö's papers introduced with a short biography, plus a commentary on Szegö's life and work, reviews of three of his books, and two mathematical commentaries.

Tarski, Alfred. **Alfred Tarski: Collected Papers.** Edited by Steven R. Givant and Ralph N. McKenzie. Boston: Birkhäuser, 1986. Vol. 1. **1921–1934.** 659p. Out of print. ISBN 0-8176-3280-8. Vol. 2. **1935–1944.** 699p. $253.00. ISBN 0-8176-3281-6. Vol. 3. **1945–1957.** 682p. $253.00. ISBN 0-8176-3282-4. Vol. 4. **1958–1979.** 757p. $253.00. ISBN 0-8176-3283-2.

A complete collection of all Tarski papers, abstracts, and reviews forming the "bedrock" of modern logic. Comprehensive scholarly bibliography.

Torelli, Ruggiero. **Collected papers of Ruggiero Torelli.** Edited by Ciro Ciliberto, Paulo Ribenboim, and Edoardo Sernesi. Kingston, ON: Queen's University Printing Services, 1995. xii + 224p. (Queen's Papers in Pure and Applied Mathematics; 101). $50.00 pa. ISBN 0-88911-707-1.

This volume contains 17 papers on algebraic geometry of Torelli. Includes an introduction by Ciliberto and Sernesi, outlining his life and describing how his work continues to influence the present-day researcher.

S Tukey, John W. **The Collected Works of John W. Tukey.** Edited by David R. Brillinger et al. Boca Raton, FL: Chapman & Hall/CRC, 1994. Vol. I. **Time Series: 1949–1964.** lxv + 689p. $91.95. ISBN 0-412-74240-3. Vol. III. **Philosophy and Principles of Data Analysis: 1949–1964.** lxviii + 569p. $91.95. ISBN 0-412-74250-0. Vol. V. **Graphics: 1965–1985.** lxiv + 464p. $91.95. ISBN 0-412-99261-2. Vol. VI. **More Mathematical: 1938–1984.** lxxii + 661p. $91.95. ISBN 0-412-06271-2. Vol. VII. **Factorial and ANOVA.** $91.95. ISBN 0-412-06321-2. Vol. VIII. **Multiple Comparisons: 1948–1983.** lxi + 475p. $91.95. ISBN 0-412-05121-4.

Volumes 1 and 3–7 are reprints (see below for original). Volume 8 is originally published by Chapman & Hall/CRC Press.

S Tukey, John W. **The Collected Works of John W. Tukey.** Edited by David Brillinger et al. vols. 1–7: Pacific Grove, CA: Wadsworth & Brooks-Cole, 1984-1990. Vol. I. **Time Series: 1949–1964.** lxv + 689p. Out of print. ISBN 0-534-03303-2. Vol. II. **Time Series: 1965–1984.** lxvii + 582p. Out of print. ISBN 0-534-03304-0. Vol. III. **Philosophy and Principles of Data Analysis: 1949–1964.** lxviii + 569p. Out of print. ISBN 0-534-03305-9. Vol. IV. **Philosophy and Principles of Data Analysis: 1965–1986.** lxviii + 553p. $91.95. ISBN 0-534-05101-4. Vol. V. **Graphics: 1965–1985.** lxiv + 464p. Out of print. ISBN 0-534-05102-2. Vol. VI. **More Mathematical: 1938–1984.** lxxii + 661p. Out of print. ISBN 0-534-05103-0. Vol. VII. **Factorial and ANOVA: 1949–1962.** Out of print. ISBN 0-534-05104-9.

The first seven volumes of Tukey's many contributions to statistics. Includes some unpublished papers. Biography, bibliography, and an index in volume 8.

Turán, Paul. **Collected Papers of Paul Turán.** Edited by Paul Erdös. Budapest: Akadémiai Kiadó, 1990. Vol. 1. xxxviii + 837p. Vol. 2. xii + p. 847-1749. Vol. 3. xii + p. 751-2665. $199.00 (set). ISBN 9-6305-4298-6.

These volumes include Erdös's personal reminiscences, lists of publications, papers by topics, and publications dealing with Turán's work as well as all the significant publications. Hungarian papers have been translated into English.

Tutte, W. T. **Selected Papers of W. T. Tutte.** Edited by D. McCarthy and R. G. Stanton. St. Pierre, MB: Charles Babbage Research Centre, 1979. 2 vols. 878p. Out of print (set). ISBN 0-9690778-0-7.

Fifty-three of the most influential papers from the work of one of the world's most prolific and profound graph theorists, honoring him on his 60th birthday. Tutte wrote the introductions, giving historical and insightful perspectives.

Ulam, Stanislaw. **Stanislaw Ulam: Sets, Numbers, and Universes: Selected Works.** Edited by W. A. Beyer, J. Mycielski, and G.-C. Rota. Cambridge, MA: MIT Press, 1974. xxiii + 709p. (Mathematicians of Our Time; 9). Out of print. ISBN 0-262-13094-7.

This work contains 52 articles by the author on mathematical topics in pure mathematics and the application of computers to game theory and physics, together with commentaries by a number of distinguished specialists in these fields. Also included are a 108-item bibliography and a complete reprinting of his book, **A Collection of Mathematical Problems**.

Varadarajan, V. S. **The Selected Works of V. S. Varadarajan.** Providence, RI: American Mathematical Society, 1999. xvi + 630p. $125.00. ISBN 0-8218-1068-5.

Reprints of 22 articles, from 1963 to 1997, selected to highlight his contributions in probability theory, various mathematical aspects of quantum mechanics, harmonic analysis on reductive groups and symmetric spaces, and the modern theory of meromorphic differential equations. Index.

Vinogradov, Ivan Matveevic. **Selected Works.** Edited by L. D. Faddeev et al. New York: Springer-Verlag, 1985. xiii + 401p. $235.00. ISBN 0-387-12788-7.

Sixteen articles plus two monographs on the "method of trigonometric sums."

Von Neumann, John. **Collected Works.** Edited by A. H. Taub. Elmsford, NY: Pergamon, 1961–1963. Vol. 1. **Logic, Theory of Sets, and Quantum Mechanics.** x + 654p. Vol. 2. **Operators, Ergodic Theory and Almost Periodic Functions in a Group.** ix + 568p. Vol. 3. **Rings of Operators.** ix + 574p. Vol. 4. **Continuous Geometry and Other Topics.** x + 516p. Vol. 5. **Design of Computers, Theory of Automata and Numerical Analysis.** viii + 784p. Vol. 6. **Theory of Games, Astrophysics, Hydrodynamics, and Meteorology.** viii + 538p. $2,140.00 set. ISBN 0-08-009566-6.

These six volumes contain all the articles published by Von Neumann as well as some of his reports to government agencies and other groups. A useful feature of these well-edited volumes is their indication of unpublished manuscripts found in his files. Although papers are generally arranged in chronological order, exceptions have been made in order to preserve a certain unity in some fields.

Von Neumann, John. **The Neumann Compendium.** Edited by F. Bródy and T. Vámos. Singapore; River Edge, NJ: World Scientific, 1995. lix + 699p. (World Scientific Series in 20th Century Mathematics; 1). $86.00. ISBN 981-02-2201-7.

Thirty years after the publication of Von Neumann's collected works, the editors have chosen some basic papers that are still very relevant today. The book is divided into seven subject sections. A complete bibliography includes much that is unpublished, his "Lebensrauf," a facsimile of a letter he wrote to Féjer, and a radio "Voice of America" transcript.

S Wald, Abraham. **Selected Papers in Statistics and Probability.** Stanford, CA: Stanford University Press, 1969. ix + 702p. $72.50. ISBN 0-8047-0493-7.

Reprint of 1957 edition.

Whitehead, J. H. C. **Mathematical Works of J. H. C. Whitehead.** Edited by I. M. James. Elkins Park, PA: Franklin Books, 1991. Vol. I. **Differential Geometry.** xxxiii + 361p. ISBN 0-08-009869-X. Vol. II. **Complexes and Manifolds.** xiii + 435p. ISBN 0-08-009870-3. Vol. III. **Homotopy Theory.** xiii + 451p. ISBN 0-08-009871-1. Vol. IV. **Algebraic and Classical Topology.** xiii + 347p. ISBN 0-08-009872-X. Out of print (set). ISBN 0-08-009873-8.

Photocopy reproduction of the 1963 original. These volumes are believed to contain all the published mathematical work of Whitehead, excluding reviews and lecture notes.

Whitney, Hassler. **Hassler Whitney: Collected Papers.** Edited by James Eells and Domingo Toledo. Boston: Birkhäuser, 1992. Vol. I. xiv + 590p. $161.00. ISBN 0-8176-3558-0 Vol. II. xv + 596p.$161.00. ISBN 0-8176-3559-9.

Nearly all of Whitney's influential papers, with the exception of his work in school education, arranged by subject. Introduced by his own recent retrospective, "Moscow 1935: Topology Moves Toward America."

Wielandt, Helmut. **Mathematische Werke.** Edited by Bertram Huppert and Hans Schneider. Berlin; New York: Walter de Gruyter, 1996. Vol. 1.

Group Theory. xix + 802p. $209.95. ISB 3-11-012452-1. Vol. 2. **Linear Algebra and Analysis.** xx + 802p. $209.95. ISBN 3-11-012453-X

Collected papers, lecture notes, and reports in German and English. Volume 1 contains group theory, and volume 2 contains all other mathematical works, most of which are on matrix theory. Extensive bibliography in volume 2.

Wiener, Norbert. **Collected Works with Commentaries.** Edited by P. Masani. Cambridge, MA: MIT Press, 1976–1985. (Mathematicians of Our Time; 10, 15, 20, 23). Vol. I. xi + 761p. Out of print. ISBN 0-262-23070-4. Vol. II. xiii + 969p. Out of print. ISBN 0-262-23092-5. Vol. III. xiii + 753p. Out of print. ISBN 0-262-23107-7. Vol. IV. xx + 1083p. Out of print. ISBN 0-262-23123-9.

A four-volume opus with papers ranging from cybernetics to harmonic analysis to the Hopf-Wiener integral equation. Papers are grouped by topic and introduced by commentaries linking them to contemporary research.

S Wolfowitz, Jacob. **Selected Papers.** Edited by J. Kiefer, with the assistance of U. Augustin and L. Weiss. New York: Springer-Verlag, 1980. xxiii + 642p. $79.00. ISBN 0-387-90463-8.

This volume, published to honor Wolfowitz on his 70th birthday, contains 50 of his papers from 1939 to 1979 and covers a wide range of problems in statistics. A biographical sketch is followed by a 13-page discussion of his work. Complete bibliography.

Yamabe, Hidehiko. **Collected Works.** New York: Gordon & Breach, 1967. xii + 142p. Out of print. ISBN 0-677-00610-1.

Eighteen articles written or co-authored by Yamabe from 1950 to 1960.

Yano, Kentaro. **Selected Papers of Kentaro Yano.** Edited by Morio Obata. New York: Elsevier, 1982. liii + 145p. (North-Holland Mathematics Studies; 70). $102.50. ISBN 0-444-86495-4.

Yano has selected many of his research papers in differential geometry for this volume and provided a mathematical autobiography.

Zadeh, L. A. **Fuzzy Sets and Applications: Selected Papers by L. A. Zadeh.** Edited by R. R. Yager, et al. New York: Wiley, 1987. 684p. Out of print. ISBN 0-471-85710-6.

This volume contains 17 papers by Zadeh on the subject he created, fuzzy sets, beginning with his 1965 paper.

Zariski, Oscar. **Collected Papers.** Edited by H. Hironaka et al. Cambridge, MA: MIT Press, 1972–1979. (Mathematicians of Our Time; 2, 6, 12, 16). Vol. I. **Foundations of Algebraic Geometry and Resolution of Singularities.** xxi + 543p. $70.00. ISBN 0-262-08049-4. Vol. II. **Holomorphic Functions and Linear Systems.** xxiii + 505p. $70.00. ISBN 0-262-01038-0. Vol. III. **Topology of Curves and Surfaces, and Special Topics in the Theory of Algebraic Varieties.** xxvi + 480p. Out of print. ISBN 0-262-24021-1. Vol. IV. **Equisingularity on Algebraic Varieties.** xxvi + 651p. $92.25. ISBN 0-262-24022-4.

These volumes present Zariski's collected papers, arranged by fields, with editorial introductions that set his work in the entire field of algebraic geometry. Excluded are his four books, two sets of lecture notes, and four early expository articles on other fields of mathematics. Bibliography.

Zhong, Jia Qing. **Contemporary Geometry: J. Q. Zhong Memorial Volume.** Edited by Hung-Hsi Wu. New York: Plenum Press, 1991. xi + 483p. $110.00. ISBN 0-306-43742-2.

This tribute includes a biography, a publications list, and 14 papers of Zhong's, plus three surveys of areas of interest to him: eigenvalue techniques in geometry, the work in several complex variables in China, and uniformization in several complex variables.

Digital Collections

In the past few years a number of projects have begun to digitize vast quantities of mathematics and statistics online. Some of these can be accessed freely, some are subscription products provided by nonprofit organizations, and some are commercial projects. Monographs, journals, and preprints are available from these collections.

E *[American Mathematical Society Journals]*. American Mathematical Society, 2004. Available at: http://www.ams.org/journals/. Subscription mostly.

The AMS has nine titles available online from the mid-1990s onward. Some have complete backfiles available here; some have their backfiles on *JSTOR*. Starting with the 1996 volumes, the AMS will make their mathematics journals available free online five years after publication. TOC and abstracts free. TOC notification available.

E *arXiv.org* (also known as xxx.lanl.gov or e-Print archive). No copyright given. Covers 1991– . Available at: http://arxiv.org or http://front.math.ucdavis.edu. Free.

There are over 35,500 mathematics preprints from 1991 onward in this fully automated electronic archive. For complete entry, see **Chapter 2, Finding Tools**.

E *Blackwell Publishing*. Blackwell Publishers, no date given. Information available at: http://www.blackwellpublishing.com/cservices/journal_online.asp?site=1. Subscription.

Blackwell has 16 mathematics and statistics journal titles available.

E *Cambridge Journals*. Cambridge University Press, 2003. Available at: http://titles.cambridge.org/journals/journal_subject.asp?subj =22&legend =Mathematics. Subscription.

Cambridge has 17 journals available online, most from 1997 onward. TOC and abstracts free. TOC notification available.

E *Cornell University Library Historical Mathematics Monographs*. Cornell University Library, 2004. Available at: http://library5.library.cornell.edu/math.html. Free.

"From 1990 through 1992 Cornell University and Xerox Corporation, with the support of the Commission on Preservation and Access, collaborated on a pilot project to test advanced technology for scanning deteriorating books as digital images, optical storage, and production of high quality paper copies." Fortunately for mathematicians, a collection of 512 out-of-print titles from before 1914 was digitized for this project. These books, representing important research in mathematics, are now available online as GIF files or as paperbound copies for purchase at a minimal cost. Titles have records in OCLC and RLIN. *Jahrbuch* records link directly to some of these titles. Cornell is participating with the University of Michigan Library and the State and University Library Göttingen (SUB Göttingen) in the *Distributed Digital Library of Mathematical Monographs* project (below) funded by the National Science Foundation (NSF) and Deutsche Forshungsgemeinschaft (DFG) to assure interoperability between these three digital collections of mathematics.

E *De Gruyter*. Walter de Gruyter, 2002. Available at: http://www.degruyter.com/rs/278_ENU_h.htm. Subscription.

De Gruyter has four mathematics journals available from the late 1990s onward. TOC and abstracts free.

E *Dekker.com*. Marcel Dekker, 1997–2004. Available at: http://www.dekker.com/catalog/list.jsp?action=newList&document Types=journal. Free.

Dekker publishes 10 math and stat journals. TOC notification and pay-per-view available.

E *Distributed Digital Library of Mathematical Monographs.* No copyright given. Available at: http://mathbooks.library.cornell.edu:8085/Dienst/UIMATH/2.0/Search. Free.

This interface lets users search bibliographic information and the full text of digitized mathematics books from three collections: *Cornell University Library Historical Mathematics Monographs, University of Michigan Historical Mathematics Collection*, and *GDZ Mathematica.*

E *DML: Digital Mathematics Library, Retrodigitized Mathematics Journals and Monographs.* Ulf Rehmann, 2003. Available at: http://www.mathematik.uni-bielefeld.de/~rehmann/DML/dml_links.html. Free.

Useful, sortable bibliographical list of digitized mathematics from many sources. Links to 124 journals and 1,794 monographs.

E *Electronic Library of Mathematics*. ELibM, 1997–2003. Available at: http://www.emis.ams.org/ELibM.html. Free.

At present, the Electronic Library of Mathematics lists over 60 refereed journals, a collection of proceedings, and 14 monographs in the field of mathematics. All material is in electronic form and access is free. Most of these journals are online only.

E *Gallica; La Bibliothèque Numérique*. Bibliothèque Nationale de France, no copyright given. Available at: http://gallica.bnf.fr/. Free.

Gallica has digitized some 80,000 documents published from the nineteenth century and earlier. Over 240 mathematics journals, multivolume works, and monographs are available at present. Some have records in OCLC. For quick access to the list of periodical titles available, go to: http://gallica.bnf.fr/periodiques.htm. Journals of interest include: **Catalogue of Scientific Papers, Comptes Rendus Hebdomadaires des Séances de l'Académie des Sciences, Journal des Mathématiques Pures et**

Appliquées, Philosophical Transactions of the Royal Society of London, and **Proceedings of the Royal Society of London.** Some records in the *Jahrbuch* link to full-text images here.

E *GDZ (Göttinger Digitalisierungs Zentrum).* SUB Göttingen, GDZ, 2001–2005. Available at: http://gdz.sub.uni-goettingen.de/en/index.html. Free.

The *GDZ Mathematica* collection contains a growing collection of over 370 monographs, 13 multivolume titles (some collected works), and 22 journal titles from the eighteenth and nineteenth centuries. Among the journal titles found here are: **Abhandlungen der Königlichen Gesellschaft der Wissenschaften in Göttingen, Inventiones Mathematicae, Mathematische Zeitschrift,** and **Mathematische Annalen.** Some records in the *Jahrbuch* link to full-text images here. GDZ partners with Cornell and the University of Michigan in the *Distributed Digital Library of Mathematical Monographs* project funded to assure interoperability between the three digital collections.

E *Hindawi.* Hindawi Publishing Corporation, 2004. Available at: http://www.hindawi.com/. Subscription.

Hindawi has 10 mathematics journals and several monographs. The entire runs of each journal are available to subscribers. The monographs are free. TOC and abstracts free. TOC notification available.

E *The Jahrbuch-Project, Electronic Research Archive for Mathematics (ERAM).* European Mathematical Society, 2004. Covers 1868–1942; in progress. Available at: http://www.emis.de/projects/JFM/JFM.html. Free.

The *Jahrbuch-Project,* sponsored by the Deutsche Forschungsgemeinschaft, is an effort in progress to digitize and enhance this early print index and to create an archive of about 20 percent of the items' full texts. To date, over 13,000 links to full text are now included.

E *JSTOR®.* JSTOR®, 2000–2004. Information available at: http://www.jstor.org/jstor/. Subscription; price varies.

JSTOR® is a vast and growing electronic index and archive of the backfiles of core scholarly journals. At present, its mathematics and statistics coverage includes core English-language journals, 11 in mathematics dating from 1878, 12 in statistics dating from 1838, and several of interest in general science dating from 1666. For more complete information, see **Chapter 2, Finding Tools.**

E *Kluwer Online.* Kluwer Online, 2004. Available at: http://www.kluweronline.com/. Subscription.

Kluwer Online includes approximately 60 journal titles and an encyclopedia in mathematics and statistics. Many of the titles have only recent issues on line but some titles are available as far back as 1995. TOC and abstracts free. TOC notification available. Pay-per-view offered.

E *Mathematics on the Web: Mathematical Books.* American Mathematical Society, 2004. Available at: http://www.ams.org/mathweb/mi-books.html. Free.

This is a fairly comprehensive site for online math books. Includes a link to University of Pennsylvania's *Online Books Page* (http://onlinebooks.library.upenn.edu/), which lists nearly 400 books in QA classification, mostly computer science. Also includes links to lists of proceedings and individual books. Does not list various retrospective projects except Cornell's.

E *Multi-Repository Mathematics Collections.* No copyright given. Available at: http://www.hti.umich.edu/m/mathall/. Free.

This interface lets users search bibliographic information and the full text of digitized mathematics books from three collections: *Cornell University Library Historical Mathematics Monographs, University of Michigan Historical Mathematics Collection*, and *GDZ Mathematica.*

E *NUMDAM, Digitization of Ancient Mathematics Documents.* Cellule MathDoc, 2002. Available at: http://www.numdam.org/en/. Free.

This project's first phase digitized four French mathematical journals: **Annales de l'Institut Fourier** (1949–1997), **Bulletin de la Société Mathématique de France** (1872–1992), **Journées Équations aux Dérivées Partielles** (1974–2000), and **Publications Mathématiques de l'Institut des Hautes Études Scientifiques** (1959–1997). Much like *JSTOR*, there will be a five-year moving wall. **Mémoires de la Société Mathématiques de France** (1964–1992) and **Annales Scientifiques de l'Ecole Normale Supérieure** (1864–2000) have since followed.

E *Oxford Journals.* Oxford University Press, 2004. Available at: http://www3.oup.co.uk/jnls/fields/mathematics/list.html. Subscription.

Oxford publishes 16 mathematics and statistics journals online from the late 1990s onward, including some published for the Institute of Mathematics and its Applications (IMA). TOC and abstracts free. TOC notification available.

E *Project Euclid.* Project Euclid, 2004. Available at: http://projecteuclid.org/Dienst/UI/1.0/TitleShort. Some titles are free, some subscription only. Prices vary.

Project Euclid, supported by the Mellon Foundation and SPARC (Scholarly Publishing and Academic Resources Coalition), helps society and independent publishers of math and stat journals transition to the electronic environment. Euclid has posted online content for 25 journals in mathematics and statistics. Some titles may digitize their backfiles. Further partnerships are being negotiated. TOC and abstracts free. Pay-per-view offered.

E *ScienceDirect.* ScienceDirect, 2004. Available at: http://www.sciencedirect.com/science/journals/mathematics. Subscription.

This is Elsevier Science's site for its *ScienceDirect* subscribers (current year plus five years or more backfiles). Elsevier hosts nearly 100 mathematics or statistics titles here. Complete backfiles for 38 mathematics titles are available for a one-time fee. TOC and abstracts free. TOC notification available. Pay-per-view offered.

E *SIAM Journals Online.* Society for Industrial and Applied Mathematics, 2003. Available at: http://epubs.siam.org/. Subscription.

SIAM has 13 journals available online from the mid-1990s onward. Some SIAM titles have their entire runs up between JSTOR and SIAM. TOC and abstracts free.

E *SpringerLINK, Mathematics Online Library.* Springer, 1998–2004. Available at: http://link.springer.de/ol/mathol/index.shtm. Subscription.

LINK has approximately 90 journal titles and two book series published by Springer or Birkhäuser in their mathematics library from the mid-1990s onward. TOC and abstracts free. TOC notification available.

E *Turpion Limited.* Turpion Ltd., 2004. Available at: http://www.turpion.org/. Subscription.

Turpion publishes four Russian mathematics journals in translation. TOC and abstracts free. TOC notification available.

E *University of Michigan Historical Mathematics Collection.* University of Michigan, 2004. Available at: http://www.hti.umich.edu/u/umhistmath/. Free.

The University of Michigan is digitizing hundreds of math books and short series published in the nineteenth and twentieth centuries and making them available on the Web. One may search the full text and go directly to the pages with hits. Pages can be viewed as text, image, or PDF files. This collection is also part of the *Distributed Digital Library of Mathematical Monographs* effort to coordinate access to the digital monographs collections of Cornell University Library and SUB Göttingen.

E *Wiley Interscience®*. John Wiley & Sons, 1999–2004. Available at: http://www3.interscience.wiley.com/cgi-bin browsebysubject?code=MAST&type=1&initial=. Subscription.

Wiley has approximately 26 mathematics and statistics journal titles available from the mid-1990s onward. TOC and abstracts free. TOC notification and pay-per-view available.

E *World Scientific*. World Scientific Publishing, 2003. Available at: http://www.worldscinet.com/maths.shtml. Subscription.

World Scientific has 22 math and stat titles available from the late 1990s onward. TOC and abstracts free. TOC notification and pay-per-view available.

Digital Library Projects

There are a growing number of proposals to preserve mathematics from the past, present, and future in digital form. Mathematics lends itself to such a far-fetched-sounding proposal, as it is a fairly well-defined subject that makes heavy use of its past literature. The international mathematics community understands well the benefits of having its literature in digital form and is ready to cooperate on these kinds of projects. It is thought that all of mathematics (not precisely defined yet) consists of 50 million pages or so. Cost estimates for properly digitizing this material is estimated at $2.00 per page (Ewing 2002, 772). As one can see in the section above, a number of digital collections are already underway. The need is to coordinate efforts, set up standards that will stand the test of time, and solve various problems such as document structure, copyright, and archiving. The projects below have obtained funding to begin the process.

Digital Mathematics Library (DML): http://www.library.cornell.edu/dmlib/.

This effort has NSF funding for two years to plan for a comprehensive digital library of mathematics. Mathematician Keith Dennis and others from Cornell University Library are coordinating this effort. The digitizing process is expected to take about 10 years (Ewing 2002, 773).

Distributed Digital Library of Mathematical Monographs (NSF/DFG): http://mathbooks.library.cornell.edu:8085/Dienst/UIMATH/2.0/Search.

This NSF/DFG funded project is a collaboration of the University of Michigan Libraries, Cornell University Library, and the State and University Library Göttingen. Its NSF award abstract (https://www.fastlane.nsf.gov/servlet/showaward?award=0085853) states, "The requested funding will be used primarily to develop an interoperability layer with the three strong digital library systems at these institutions. In doing so, the participants will focus on many of the issues central to the advancement of digital libraries, including distributed repositories and integration of digital resources, advanced access and retrieval, high levels of interoperability, and models for dissemination and use."

Electronic Mathematical Archives Network Initiative (EMANI): http://www.emani.org/.

This collaboration between Springer-Verlag and the libraries of Cornell, Göttingen, and Tsinghua, is focused on properly archiving Springer mathematical literature in digital format and making it openly accessible within a few years after publication. The partners hope this effort will provide an archiving model that other publishers will be willing to follow.

Distributed Digital Mathematics Archive Library: http://www.library.cornell.edu/digital/math-projects.html (limited info only).

This is a proposal to develop software for scanning print to electronic with automatic extraction of bibliographic data matched and linked to entries in *MathSciNet* and *Zentralblatt MATH*. Led by Keith Dennis and Gerhard Michler of the University of Essen, the project has received funding from the Deutsche Forschungsgemeinschaft (DFG) and awaits NSF funding (Workshop 2002).

References

Ewing, John. 2002. Twenty Centuries of Mathematics: Digitizing and Disseminating the Past Mathematical Literature. *Notices of the American Mathematical Society* 49, no. 7 (August): 771–777. Available at: http://www.ams.org/notices/200207/fea-ewing.pdf. Free.

Rockey, Steven W. 1996– . *A Bibliography of Collected Works and Correspondence of Mathematicians*. Available at: http://www.library.cornell.edu/math/collectedworks.php. Free.

Workshop on Linking and Searching in Distributed Digital Libraries. 2002. University of Michigan–Ann Arbor, University Library, March 18–20, 2002. Available at: http://www.exp-math.uni-essen.de/algebra/veranstaltungen/program4.htm. Free.

10
Monographic Series

Because books are more important to mathematicians than to researchers in engineering and other physical sciences, it follows that monographic series are an important item in the culture. Mathematicians often come to the library for a book with only the series title and volume number in hand. Many publishers allow authors to cite books only by their series title and volume number and not include the individual monograph title. Publishers find it easy to maintain these series and sometimes offer better discounts if the series is ordered as a subscription. In addition to this savings, librarians find it easier to place standing orders for series considered essential to their institutions. Claiming is easier and more efficient than ordering each volume separately.

Only numbered monographic series are included in this chapter. Unnumbered monographic series are a nightmare to order and claim, and the mathematical researcher rarely remembers the names of these series. This is not to say that unnumbered monographic series are not important. For example, many excellent books have been published in the Springer's **Undergraduate Texts in Mathematics** and the **Wiley Series in Probability and Statistics**.

Note that a **T** preceding an entry indicates that this is a translation series. The series abbreviation as listed by *MathSciNet* is in brackets.

Algorithms and Computation in Mathematics. [Algorithms Comput. Math.] Berlin: Springer. ISSN: 1431-1550.

American Mathematical Society Colloquium Publications. *See* **Colloquium Publications**.

AMS/IP Studies in Advanced Mathematics. [AMS/IP Stud. Adv. Math.] Providence, RI: American Mathematical Society. ISSN: 1089-3288.

Annals of Mathematics Studies. [Ann. of Math. Stud.] Princeton, NJ: Princeton University Press. **ISSN:** 0066-2313.

Applications of Mathematics. [Appl. Math.] New York: Springer-Verlag. ISSN: 0172-4568.

Applied Mathematical Sciences. [Appl. Math. Sci.] New York: Springer-Verlag.

Applied Optimization. [Appl. Optim.] Dordrecht, Holland: Kluwer Acad. Publ.

Astérisque. [Astérisque] Paris: Soc. Math. France. ISSN: 0303-1179.

Berkeley Mathematics Lecture Notes. [Berkeley Math. Lect. Notes] Providence RI: American Mathematical Society. ISSN: 1092-9371.

Bolyai Society Mathematical Studies. [Bolyai Soc. Math. Stud.] Budapest, Hungary: János Bolyai Math. Soc. ISSN: 1217-4696.

Cambridge Monographs on Applied and Computational Mathematics. [Cambridge Monogr. Appl. Comput. Math.] Cambridge: Cambridge University Press.

Cambridge Studies in Advanced Mathematics. [Cambridge Stud. Adv. Math.] Cambridge: Cambridge University Press.

Cambridge Texts in Applied Mathematics. [Cambridge Texts Appl. Math.] Cambridge: Cambridge University Press.

Cambridge Tracts in Mathematics. [Cambridge Tracts in Math.] Cambridge: Cambridge University Press.

Carus Mathematical Monographs. [Carus Math. Monogr.] Washington, DC: Mathematical Association America.

CBMS-NSF Regional Conference Series in Applied Mathematics. [CBMS-NSF Regional Conf. Ser. in Appl. Math.] Philadelphia, PA: SIAM.

CBMS Regional Conference Series in Mathematics. [CBMS Reg. Conf. Ser. Math.] Providence, RI: American Mathematical Society. ISSN: 0160-7642.

Chapman & Hall/CRC Monographs and Surveys in Pure and

Applied Mathematics. [Chapman & Hall/CRC Monogr. Surv. Pure Appl. Math.] Boca Raton, FL: Chapman & Hall/CRC.

Chapman & Hall/CRC Research Notes in Mathematics Series. [Chapman & Hall/CRC Res. Notes Math.] Boca Raton, FL: Chapman & Hall/CRC.

Classics in Applied Mathematics. [Classics Appl. Math.] Philadelphia, PA: SIAM.

Colloquium Publications. [Amer. Math. Soc. Colloq. Publ.] Providence, RI: American Mathematical Society. ISSN: 0065-9258.

S **Compstat Lectures**. [Compstat Lectures.] Physica, Heidelberg, Germany.

Contemporary Mathematics. [Contemp. Math.] Providence, RI: American Mathematical Society. ISSN: 0271-4132.

Courant Lecture Notes in Mathematics. [Courant Lect. Notes Math.] New York: New York University, Courant Inst. Math. Sci.

CRM Monograph Series. [CRM Monogr. Ser.] Providence, RI: American Mathematical Society. ISSN: 1065-8599.

CRM Proceedings and Lecture Notes. [CRM Proc. Lecture Notes] Providence, RI: American Mathematical Society. ISSN: 1065-8580.

de Gruyter Expositions in Mathematics. [de Gruyter Exp. Math.] Berlin: de Gruyter. ISSN: 0938-6572.

de Gruyter Studies in Mathematics. [de Gruyter Stud. Math.] Berlin: de Gruyter.

DIMACS Series in Discrete Mathematics and Theoretical Computer Science. [DIMACS Ser. Discrete Math. Theoret. Comput. Sci.] Providence, RI: American Mathematical Society. ISSN: 1052-1798.

Dolciani Mathematical Expositions. [Dolciani Math. Exp.] Washington, DC: Mathematical Association of America.

T **Encyclopaedia of Mathematical Sciences.** [Encyclopaedia Math. Sci.] Berlin: Springer. ISSN: 0938-0396.

Encyclopedia of Mathematics and Its Applications. [Encyclopedia Math. Appl.] Cambridge: Cambridge University Press.

Ergebnisse der Mathematik und ihrer Grenzgebiete. 3 Folge. [Ergeb. Math. Grenzgeb. (3)] Berlin: Springer. ISSN: 0071-1136.

Fields Institute Communications. [Fields Inst. Commun.] Providence, RI: American Mathematical Society. ISSN: 1069-5265.

Fields Institute Monographs. [Fields Inst. Monogr.] Providence, RI: American Mathematical Society. ISSN: 1069-5273.

Frontiers in Applied Mathematics. [Frontiers Appl. Math.] Philadelphia, PA: SIAM.

Graduate Studies in Mathematics. [Grad. Stud. Math.] Providence, RI: American Mathematical Society. ISSN: 1065-7339.

Graduate Texts in Mathematics. [Grad. Texts in Math.] New York: Springer-Verlag.

Grundlehren der Mathematischen Wissenschaften. [Grundlehren Math. Wiss.] New York: Springer-Verlag. ISSN: 0072-7830.

History of Mathematics. [Hist. Math.] Providence, RI: American Mathematical Society.

IAS/Park City Mathematics Series. [IAS/Park City Math. Ser.] Providence, RI: American Mathematical Society.

S **Institute of Mathematical Statistics Lecture Notes—Monograph Series.** [IMS Lecture Notes Monogr. Ser.] Hayward, CA: Institute of Mathematical Statistics.

Interdisciplinary Applied Mathematics. [Interdiscip. Appl. Math.] New York: Springer-Verlag.

Kluwer Texts in the Mathematical Sciences. [Kluwer Texts Math. Sci.] Dordrecht, Holland: Kluwer Acad. Publ.

Lecture Notes in Economics and Mathematical Systems. [Lecture Notes in Econom. and Math. Systems] New York: Springer. ISSN: 0075-8442.

Lecture Notes in Mathematics. [Lecture Notes in Math.] New York: Springer-Verlag. ISSN: 0075-8434.

Lecture Notes in Pure and Applied Mathematics. [Lecture Notes in Pure and Appl. Math.] New York: Dekker.

S **Lecture Notes in Statistics.** [Lecture Notes in Statist.] New York: Springer-Verlag.

London Mathematical Society Lecture Note Series. [London Math. Soc. Lecture Note Series] Cambridge: Cambridge University Press.

London Mathematical Society Monographs. New Series. [London Math. Soc. Mongr. (N.S.)] New York: Oxford University Press.

London Mathematical Society Student Texts. [London Math. Soc. Stud. Texts] Cambridge: Cambridge University Press.

MAA Notes. [MAA Notes] Washington, DC: Mathematical Association of America.

Mathematical Sciences Research Institute Publication. [Math. Sci. Res. Inst. Publ.] Cambridge: Cambridge University Press.

Mathematical Surveys and Monographs. [Math. Surveys Monogr.] Providence, RI: American Mathematical Society. ISSN: 0076-5376.

Mathematical World. [Math. World] Providence, RI: American Mathematical Society. ISSN: 1055-9426.

Mathematics and Its Applications. [Math. Appl.] Dordrecht, Holland: Kluwer Acad. Publ. (Including all subseries.)

Mathematics Education Library. [Math. Ed. Lib.] Dordrecht, Holland: Kluwer Acad. Publ.

Mathematics in Science and Engineering. [Math. Sci. Engrg.] San Diego, CA: Academic Press.

Memoirs of the American Mathematical Society. [Mem. Amer. Math. Soc.] Providence, RI: American Mathematical Society. ISSN: 0065-9266.

Monographs and Textbooks in Pure and Applied Mathematics. [Monogr. Textbooks Pure Appl. Math.] New York: Dekker.

New ICMI Studies Series. [New ICMI Stud. Ser.] Dordrecht, Holland: Kluwer Acad. Publ.

New Mathematical Library. [New Math. Library] Washington, DC: Mathematical Association of America.

Nonconvex Optimization and Its Applications. [Nonconvex Optim. Appl.] Dordrecht, Holland: Kluwer Acad. Publ.

North-Holland Mathematical Library. [North-Holland Math. Library] Amsterdam: North-Holland.

North-Holland Mathematics Studies. [North-Holland Math. Stud.] Amsterdam: North-Holland.

S **NSF-CBMS Regional Conference Series in Probability and Statistics.** [NSF-CBMS Regional Conf. Ser. Probab. Statist.] Hayward, CA: Institute of Mathematical Statistics.

Ohio State University Mathematical Research Institute Publications. [Ohio State Univ. Math. Res. Inst. Publ.] Berlin: de Gruyter. ISSN: 0942-0363.

Operator Theory: Advances and Applications. [Operator Theory Adv. Appl.] Basel, Switzerland: Birkhäuser.

Oxford Lecture Series in Mathematics and its Applications. [Oxford Lecture Ser. Math. Appl.] New York: Oxford University Press.

S **Oxford Statistical Science Series.** [Oxford Statist. Sci. Ser.] New York: Oxford University Press.

Princeton Mathematical Series. [Princeton Math. Ser.] Princeton, NJ: Princeton University Press.

S **Probability and Mathematical Statistics.** [Probab. Math. Statist.] Boston: Academic Press.

Proceedings of Symposia in Applied Mathematics. [Proc. Sympos. Appl. Math.] Providence, RI: American Mathematical Society.

Proceedings of Symposia in Pure Mathematics. [Proc. Sympos. Pure Math.] Providence, RI: American Mathematical Society. ISSN: 0082-0717.

Proceedings of the Steklov Institute of Mathematics. [Proc. Steklov. Inst. Math.] Moscow: MAIK "Nauka"/Interperiodica Publishing. ISSN: 0081-5438.

Progress in Mathematics. [Progr. Math.] Boston: Birkhäuser.

Progress in Nonlinear Differential Equations and Their Applications. [Progr. Nonlinear Differential Equations Appl.] Boston: Birkhäuser.

Progress in Probability. [Progr. Probab.] Boston: Birkhäuser.

Queen's Papers in Pure & Applied Mathematics. [Queen's Papers in Pure and Appl. Math.] Kingston, ON: Queen's University.

Series in Approximations and Decompositions. [Ser. Approx. Decompos.] River Edge, NJ: World Scientific.

Series on Advances in Mathematics for Applied Sciences. [Ser. Adv. Math. Appl. Sci.] River Edge, NJ: World Scientific.

SIAM Studies in Applied Mathematics. [SIAM Stud. Appl. Math.] Philadelphia, PA: SIAM.

Sources and Studies in the History of Mathematics and Physical Sciences. [Sources Stud. Hist. Math. Phys. Sci.] New York: Springer-Verlag.

Sources in the History of Mathematics and the Physical Sciences. [Sources Hist. Math. Phys. Sci.] New York: Springer-Verlag.

Springer Series in Computational Mathematics. [Springer Ser. Comput. Math.] New York: Springer-Verlag.

S Statistics: Textbooks and Monographs. [Statist. Textbooks Monogr.] New York: Dekker.

Student Mathematical Library. [Stud. Math. Libr.] Providence, RI: American Mathematical Society. ISSN: 1520-9121.

Studies in Logic and the Foundations of Mathematics. [Stud. Logic Found. Math.] Amsterdam: North-Holland.

Texts in Applied Mathematics. [Texts Appl. Math.] New York: Springer-Verlag.

T Translations of Mathematical Monographs. [Transl. Math. Monogr.] Providence, RI: American Mathematical Society.

University Lecture Series. [Univ. Lecture Ser.] Providence, RI: American Mathematical Society.

Vita Mathematica. [Vita Math.] Basel, Switzerland: Birkhäuser.

World Scientific Series in 20th Century Mathematics. [World Sci. Ser. 20th Century Math.] River Edge, NJ: World Scientific.

11
Major Societies and Publishers

Societies

Below is a listing of major U.S., Canadian, and international mathematical and statistical societies. Often, academic societies offer institutional memberships to departments and/or the library that are of benefit to the departmental library. Discounts for books and journals are some of the benefits enjoyed by an institutional membership.

American Mathematical Society
201 Charles Street
Providence, RI 02940-6248 USA
Telephone: 800-321-4267, 401-455-4000, 401-331-3842 (fax)
E-mail: ams@ams.org
URL: http://www.ams.org/

Institutional membership includes subscriptions to *Notices*, *Abstracts*, *Combined Membership List*, *Mathematical Sciences Professional Directory*, *Assistantships and Graduate Fellowship in the Mathematical Sciences*, and discounts on books and journals, including the Data Access Fee for *Mathematical Reviews/MathSciNet*.

S American Statistical Association
1429 Duke Street
Alexandria, VA 22314-3415, USA
Telephone: 888-231-3473, 703-684-1221, 703-684-2037 (fax)

E-mail: asainfo@amstat.org
URL: http://www.amstat.org/

Institutional membership benefits include print subscriptions to ASA's 11 journals and magazines and a complete set of ASA Proceedings. Strangely, access to the electronic versions of their journals is not possible via the institutional membership.

Association for Women in Mathematics
4114 Computer & Space Sciences Building
University of Maryland College Park, MD 20742-2461, USA
Telephone: 301-405-7892, 301-314-9363 (fax)
E-mail: awm@math.umd.edu
URL: http://www.awm-math.org/

Canadian Mathematical Society
577 King Edward, Suite 109
POB 450, Station A Ottawa, Ontario K1N 6N5, Canada
Telephone: 613-562-5702, 613-565-1539 (fax)
E-mail: office@cms.math.ca
URL: http://www.cms.math.ca/

Institutional membership benefits include subscriptions to CMS's two journals, a magazine, and a newsletter, as well as discounts on their books.

European Mathematical Society
Ms. T. Mäkeläinen, EMS Secretariat
Department of Mathematics
POB 4 (Yliopistonkatu 5)
00014 University of Helsinki, Finland
Telephone: +358-9-1912 2883, +358-9-1912 3213 (fax)
E-mail: tuulikki.makelainen@helsinki.fi
URL: http://www.emis.de

S Institute of Mathematical Statistics
Business Office
POB 22718
Beachwood, OH 44122, USA
Telephone: 216-295-2340, 216-921-6703 (fax)
E-mail: ims@imstat.org
URL: http://www.imstat.org/

Institutional benefits include two copies of IMS's five journal titles plus discounts on their other publications.

International Mathematical Union
IMU Secretariat
Institute for Advanced Study
Einstein Drive
Princeton, New Jersey 08540, USA
Telephone: 609-683-7605 (fax)
E-mail: imu@ias.edu
URL: http://www.mathunion.org

S International Statistical Institute
Permanent Office
POB 950
2270 AZ Voorburg, The Netherlands
Telephone: 31-70-3375737, 31-70-3860025 (fax)
E-mail: isi@cbs.nl
URL: http://www.cbs.nl/isi/

London Mathematical Society
De Morgan House
57-58 Russell Square
London WC1B 4HS, UK
Telephone: 020-7637-3686, 020-7323-3655 (fax)
E-mail: lms@lms.ac.uk
URL: http://www.lms.ac.uk/

Mathematical Association of America
1529 Eighteenth Street, NW
Washington, DC 20036-1385, USA
Telephone: 800-741-9415, 202-387-5200, 202-265-2384 (fax)
E-mail: maahq@maa.org
URL: http://www.maa.org/

Institutional benefits include copies of MAA's three journals plus discounts on their other publications.

S Royal Statistical Society
12 Errol Street
London, EC1Y 8LX, UK
Telephone: +44(0)20-7638-8998, +44(0)20-7614-3905 (fax)
E-mail: rss@rss.org.uk
URL: http://www.rss.org.uk/

Society for Industrial and Applied Mathematics
3600 University City Science Center
Philadelphia, PA 19104-2688, USA
Telephone: 800-447-7426, 215-382-9800, 215-386-7999 (fax)
E-Mail: service@siam.org
URL: http://www.siam.org/

Institutional membership benefits include a choice of packages of SIAM's 12 journals plus discounts on books.

S Statistical Society of Canada
1485 Laperrière Street
Ottawa, Ontario K1Z 7S8, Canada
Telephone: 613 725-2253, 613 729-6206 (fax)
E-mail: info@ssc.ca
URL: http://www.ssc.ca/

To find societies not listed here, check one of these Web sites listing mathematical and statistical societies:

E *Societies and Associations*. Penn State University, Mathematics Department, no date given. Available at: http://www.math.psu.edu/MathLists/Societies.html. Free.

E *Scholarly Societies Project*. University of Waterloo, 2003. Available at: http://www.scholarly-societies.org. Free.

Publishers

A K Peters, Ltd.: http://www.akpeters.com/

Academic Press, see Elsevier Science

Addison-Wesley/Benjamin Cummings: http://www.aw.com/

American Institute of Physics (AIP) Publications: http://www.aip.org/

American Mathematical Society (AMS): www.ams.org

S American Statistical Association: www.amstat.org

Association for Computing Machinery (ACM) Publications: http://www.acm.org/

Baltzer Science Publishers: see Kluwer Academic Publishing

B. G. Teubner: http://www.teubner.de/

Birkhäuser Boston: http://www.birkhauser.com/

Major Societies and Publishers

Blackwell Publishers: http://www.blackwellpublishing.com/

Brooks/Cole Publishing: http://www.brookscole.com/

Cambridge University Press: http://www.cup.org/

Carfax Publishing Ltd.: see Taylor & Francis

Centre de Recherches Mathématiques: http://www.crm.umontreal.ca/pub/pub_an.html

CRC Press: http://www.crcpress.com/

Dover Publications, Inc.: http://store.doverpublications.com/doverpublications/

Duke University Press: http://www.dukeupress.edu/

Elsevier Science: http://www.elsevier.com/

Gale Research: http://www.gale.com/

Gauthiers-Villars: see Elsevier Science

Gordon and Breach: see Taylor & Francis

Heldermann Verlag: http://www.heldermann.de/

Hindawi Publishing Corporation: http://www.hindawi.com/

IEEE: http://www.ieee.org/prod_svcs.html

Institute of Mathematics and its Applications (IMA): http://www.ima.org.uk/

S Institute of Mathematical Statistics (IMS): http://www.imstat.org/

Institute of Physics (IOP): http://www.ioppublishing.com/

S International Biometric Society: http://www.tibs.org/

International Press: http://www.intlpress.com/

S International Statistical Institute (ISI): http://www.cbs.nl/isi/

IOS Press: http://www.iospress.nl/

Jones and Bartlett Publishers: http://math.jbpub.com/

Kluwer Academic Publishing: http://www.wkap.nl/

Marcel Dekker, Inc.: http://www.dekker.com/index.jsp

Mathematical Association of America (MAA): https://www.maa.org/

MIT Press: http://www-mitpress.mit.edu

North-Holland: see Elsevier Science

Oxford University Press: http://www.oup-usa.org/

Plenum Publishing Corporation: see Kluwer Academic Publishing

Prentice-Hall: http://vig.prenhall.com/

Princeton University Press: http://pup.princeton.edu/
S Royal Statistical Society: http://www.rss.org.uk/
Society for Industrial and Applied Mathematics (SIAM): www.siam.org
Springer-Verlag: http://www.springer-ny.com/
Taylor & Francis: http://www.tandf.co.uk/
Turpion Ltd.: http://www.turpion.org/
University of Chicago Press: http://www.press.uchicago.edu/
Vieweg: http://www.vieweg.de/
VSP International Science Publishers: http://www.vsppub.com/
Walter de Gruyter, Inc: http://www.degruyter.de/
Wiley: http://www.wiley.com/WileyCDA/
World Scientific: http://www.wspc.com.sg/

12
Additional Resources for Mathematics Librarianship

Readings of Interest

E American Mathematical Society Task Force on Excellence, John Ewing, ed. **Towards Excellence: Leading Doctoral Mathematics Department in the 21st Century**. Providence, RI: American Mathematical Society, 2000. xv + 261p. $5.00. ISBN 0-8218-2003-8. Also available at: http://www.ams.org/towardsexcellence/. Free.

E Anderson, N. D., K. Dilcher, and J. Rovnyak. "Mathematics Research Libraries at the End of the Twentieth Century." *Notices of the American Mathematical Society* 44, no. 11 (December 1997): 1469–1472. Also available at: http://www.ams.org/notices/199711/comm-rovnyak.pdf. The complete report with appendixes and budget data is available at: http://wsrv.clas.virginia.edu/~jlr5m/survey/survey.html. Free.

Anderson, Nancy D., and James L. Rovnyak. "Mathematics Research Libraries: A 1990 Snapshot." *Notices of the American Mathematical Society* 38, no. 10 (December 1991): 1258–1262.

Barrat, P., G. Sureau, and L. Zweig, organizers. "Mathematical Libraries in Europe." In **First European Congress of Mathematics, Paris, July 6–10, 1992**, Vol. III: *Round Table L*: July 9, 1992: 397–430. Basel, Switzerland: Birkhäuser, 1994.

E Brown, Cecelia M. "Information Seeking Behavior of Scientists in the Electronic Information Age: Astronomers, Chemists, Mathematicians, and Physicists." *Journal of the American Society for Information Science* 50, no. 10 (August 1999): 929–937. Available at: http://www3.interscience.wiley.com/cgi-bin/fulltext/62502161/PDFSTART. Subscription.

E Cole, Timothy W. "Publishing Mathematics on the Web." *Science & Technology Libraries* 20, no. 2/3 (2002): 27–44. Available at: https://www.haworthpress.com/store/E-Text/FilesU/J122v20n02_04.pdf. Subscription.

E Cole, Timothy W. "Thoughts about Publishing Mathematics on the Web." Participant statement at DML meeting, July 23, 2002, Washington, DC. Available at: http://www.library.cornell.edu/dmlib/cole.pdf Free.

E DeCarlo, Mary. "Mathematics Education Resources on the Internet." *Issues in Science and Technology Librarianship,* no. 38 (Summer 2003). Available at: http://www.istl.org/03-summer/internet.html. Free.

E De Robbio, Antonella. "Online Resources for Mathematics in the Scientific Virtual Reference Desk." *HEP Libraries Webzine,* no. 3 (March 2001), 12p. Available at: http://library.cern.ch/HEPLW/3/papers/4/. Free.

E Dominy, Margaret and Jay Bhatt. "MathSciNet: Mathematical Reviews on the Web: A Review." *Issues in Science and Technology Librarianship* 31 (Summer 2001): 8p. Available at: http://www.istl.org/istl/01-summer/databases2.html. Free.

E Ebersole, W. Dale, Jr. "Using Online Catalogs to Evaluate Science Collections for a Group of Institutions." *Science and Technology Libraries* 18, no. 1 (1999): 105–113. Available at: https://www.haworthpress.com/store/E-Text/FilesU/J122v18n01_07.pdf. Subscription.

E Ewing, John. "State of AMS 2004." To be published in *Notices of the American Mathematical Society*, ([August?] 2004). Available at: http://www.ams.org/ams/state-of-ams2004.pdf. Free.

The 2004 report includes an interesting accounting of **Mathematical Reviews**/*MathSciNet*, its past, present, and future.

E Figa, Jan. "So Many Problems, So Little Time: Maps and Mathematics." *Information Outlook* 6, no. 3 (March 2002), 18–22. Available at: http://www.sla.org/content/memberonly/infoonline/2002/mar02/figa.cfm. SLA members only.

E Fosmire, Michael and Elizabeth Young. "Free Scholarly Electronic Journals: An Annotated Webliography." *Issues in Science and Technology Librarianship* 28 (Fall 2000): 8p. Available at: http://www.library.ucsb.edu/istl/00-fall/internet.html. Free.

E Fosmire, Michael and Song Yu. "Free Scholarly Electronic Journals: How Good Are They?" *Issues in Science and Technology Librarianship*, no. 27 (Summer 2000): 14p. Available at: http://www.library.ucsb.edu/istl/00-summer/refereed.html. Free.

E Fowler, Kristine K. "Mathematics Sites Compared: Zentralblatt MATH Database and MathSciNet." *Charleston Advisor* (January 2000): 18–21. Available at: http://www.charlestonco.com/comp.cfm?id=5. Subscription. Also available at: http://math.lib.umn.edu/mathtca.html. Free.

E Froumentin, Max. "Mathematics on the Web with MathML." *ERCIM News*, no. 50 (July 2002): 2p. Available at: http://www.ercim.org/publication/Ercim_News/enw50/froumentin.html. Free.

E Goodman, David. "A Year Without Print at Princeton, and What We Plan Next." *Learned Publishing* 15, no. 1 (2002): 43–50. Available at: http://www.catchword.com/cgi-bin/linker?ini=alpsp&reqidx=/catchword/alpsp/09531513/v15n1/s6/p43. Free.

E Hill, J. B., Cherie Madarash Hill, and Nancy Hayes. "Monitoring Serials Use in a Science and Technology Library: Results of a Ten Year Study." *Science and Technology Libraries* 18, no. 1 (1999): 89–103. Available at: https://www.haworthpress.com/store/E-Text/FilesU/J122v18n01_06.pdf. Subscription.

E Jackson, Allyn. "Chinese Acrobatics, an Old-Time Brewery, and the 'Much Needed Gap': The Life of *Mathematical Reviews*." *Notices of the American Mathematical Society* 44, no. 3 (March 1997): 330–337. Available at: http://www.ams.org/notices/199703/comm-mr.pdf. Free.

E Jost, Michael and Hans J. Becker. "EULER—A Real Virtual Library for Mathematics." *HEP Libraries Webzine*, no. 9 (February 2004): 8p. Available at: http://library.cern.ch/HEPLW/9/papers/5/. Free.

Kaufmann-Buehler, Walter, Alice Peters, and Klaus Peters. "Mathematicians Love Books." In **Mathematics Tomorrow**, p. 121–126. New York: Springer-Verlag, 1981.

E Kessinger, Pam. "WEBWATCH: Innumeracy." *Library Journal* 127, no. 4 (March 1, 2002): 32–36. Available at: http://www.libraryjournal.com/article/CA197733?display=searchResults&stt=001&text=innumeracy. Free.

S E Kristick, Laurel. "A Bibiliographic Resource for Statistical Theory: Current Index to Statistics." *Issues in Science and Technology Librarianship* 34 (Spring 2002): 8p. Available at: http://www.istl.org/02-spring/databases1.html. Free.

E Luce, Richard E. "E-prints Intersect the Digital Library: Inside the Los Alamos arXiv." *Issues in Science and Technology Librarianship* 29 (Winter 2001): 7p. Available at: http://www.istl.org/istl/01-winter/article3.html. Free.

E McMahon, Timothy E. "Google.com." *The Charleston Advisor* 1, no. 4 (2000): 31–32. Available at: http://www.charlestonco.com/review.cfm?id=44. Subscription. Free.

E McMahon, Timothy E. "This Science Isn't Just for Mathematicians Anymore: Mathematics Resources on the Internet." *College & Research Libraries News* (May 2000): 395–398. Available at: http://www.ala.org/ala/acrl/acrlpubs/crlnews/backissues2000/may4/scienceisntjust.htm. Free.

E Pinfield, Stephen, Mike Gardner, and John MacColl. "Setting Up an Instituitional E-Print Archive." *Ariadne* 31 (March–April 2002): 10p. Available at: http://www.ariadne.ac.uk/issue31/eprint-archives/. Free.

E Roberts, Beth A. "Mathematics Resources on the Internet." *Issues in Science and Technology Librarianship* 35 (Summer 2002): 11p. Available at: http://www.istl.org/02-summer/internet.html. Free.

E Robertson, Kathleen. "Mergers, Acquisitions, and Access: STM Publishing Today." In Corbin, Brenda G., Elizabeth P. Bryson, and Marek

Wolf, eds. **Library and Information Services in Astronomy IV (LISA IV)**, p. 95–102. U.S. Naval Observatory, 2003. Also available at: http://www.eso.org/gen-fac/libraries/lisa4/Robertson.pdf. Free.

E Rowland, Fytton. "The Peer-Review Process." *Learned Publishing* 15, no. 4 (October 2002): 247–258. Available at: http://hermia.ingentaselect.com/vl=5152591/cl=48/nw=1/rpsv/cgi-bin/linker?ini=alpsp&reqidx=/catchword/alpsp/09531513/v15n4/s2/p247. Free.

E Rutter, Sara. "Mathematicians and the Mathematics Library: A Librarian's Perspective." *Notices of the American Mathematical Society* 49, no. 9 (October 2002): 1078–1081. Available at: http://www.ams.org/notices/200209/comm-rutter.pdf. Free.

E Seeds, Robert S. "Impact of a Digital Archive (JSTOR) on Print Collection Use." *Collection Building* 21, no.3 (2002): 120-122. Available at: http://ceres.emeraldinsight.com/vl=5306667/cl=80/nw=1/rpsv/cgi-bin/linker?ini=emerald&reqidx=/cw/mcb/01604953/v21n3/s3/p120. Subscription.

E Seeds, Robert S. "Impact of Remote Library Storage on Information Consumers: 'Sophie's Choice'?" *Collection Building* 19, no. 3 (2000): 105–108. Available at: http://ceres.emeraldinsight.com/vl=5306667/cl=80/nw=1/rpsv/cgi-bin/linker?ini=emerald&reqidx=/cw/mcb/01604953/v19n3/s3/p105. Subscription.

E TePaske-King, Bert and Norman Richert. "The Identification of Authors in the Mathematical Reviews Database." *Issues in Science and Technology Librarianship* 31 (Summer 2001): 9p. Available at: http://www.library.ucsb.edu/istl/01-summer/databases.html. Free.

E Wegner, Bernd and Michael Jost. "EMIS 2001—A Portal to Mathematics in Progress." *HEP Libraries Webzine* No. 6 (March 2002): 8p. Available at: http://library.cern.ch/HEPLW/6/papers/4/. Free.

E Willinsky, John. "Scholarly Associations and the Economic Viability of Open Access Publishing." *Journal of Digital Information* 4, no. 2 (April 9, 2003): 19p. Available at: http://jodi.ecs.soton.ac.uk/Articles/v04/i02/Willinsky/. Free.

Surveys of Journal Prices in Mathematics

E American Mathematical Society. *Journal Price Survey (1994–2002)*. Available at: http://www.ams.org/membership/journal-survey.html. Free.

E Kirby, Rob. *Comparative Prices of Math Journals*. May 27, 1997. Available at: http://math.berkeley.edu/~kirby/journals.html. Jan. 2000 update. Available at: http://math.berkeley.edu/~kirby/jp00.html. Free.

Moline, Sandra R. "Mathematics Journal: Impact Factors and cents per thousand characters." *Serials Librarian* 20, no. 4 (1991): 65–71.

E Rehmann, Ulf. *Math Journal Price Survey based on AMS 2001 data*. Available at: http://www.mathematik.uni-bielefeld.de/~rehmann/BIB/AMS/Publisher.html. Free.

E University of Wisconsin—Madison Libraries. *Journal Value Project*. Available at: http://math.library.wisc.edu./JVP. Free.

Assesses the value of math journals by calculating the title's ratio of the cost per 1,000 characters to its impact factor, (Cost/1000 Char($))/Impact Factor.

Newsletters/Listservs/Journals to Scan

The titles listed below frequently contain articles concerning trends, problems, and outlooks for the scholarly communications system in general or mathematics specifically. Most are electronic themselves, and readers can subscribe to get alerts of new issues.

E *Ariadne*. UKOLN. ISSN: 1361-3200. Available at: http://www.ariadne.ac.uk/. Free.

The focus is on digital library initiatives for academic information professionals, from a UK point of view.

E *College & Research Libraries News*. ACRL/ALA. ISSN: 0099-0086. Available at: http://www.ala.org/ala/acrl/acrlpubs/crlnews/collegeresearch.htm. Subscription. "Internet Reviews" columns are also available at: http://www.bowdoin.edu/~samato/IRA/. Free.

Includes a regular monthly review column on Internet resources in a particular subject.

E *The Charleston Advisor.* The Charleston Advisor. ISSN: 1525-4011. Available at: http://www.charlestonco.com/. Some articles on Web are free, otherwise $295.00/yr.

TCA contains evaluative, and sometimes comparative, review articles of library resources such as databases, journal packages, and library-related services in addition to other topical articles. Some articles are free, but most are not.

E *Current Cites.* Regents of the University of California. ISSN: 1060-2356. Available at: http://sunsite.berkeley.edu/CurrentCites/. Free.

Reviews current information technology and libraries literature.

E *D-Lib Magazine.* Corporation for National Research Initiatives (CNRI). ISSN: 1082-9873. Available at: http://www.dlib.org/. Free.

This title focuses on digital library research and development, such as new technologies, applications, and contextual social and economic issues. Many math-related articles have been published here.

E *EMJ Mailing List Archives.* Available at: http://math.albany.edu:8800/hm/emj/about.html. Free.

The *EMJ* listserv (Electronic Mathematics Journals listserv) is an interesting forum where mathematicians discuss issues relating to scholarly communications in mathematics and its future. Not very active currently.

E *HEP Libraries Webzine.* HEPLW. ISSN: 1424-2729. Available at: http://library.cern.ch/HEPLW/. Free.

Informative articles from innovative, high-energy physics librarians.

E *Issues in Science & Technology Librarianship.* Association of College and Research Libraries, Science and Technology Section. ISSN: 1092-1206. Available at: http://www.library.ucsb.edu/istl/. Free.

Informative quarterly on issues of interest to science and technology librarians.

E *Journal of Electronic Publishing.* University of Michigan Press. ISSN: 1080-2711. Currently available at: http://www.press.umich.edu/jep, but expected to move to: http://www.columbia.edu/cu/cup/index.html. Free.

High-quality online journal on issues relating to scholarly electronic publishing.

E *Learned Publishing*. Association of Learned and Professional Society Publishers. ISSN: 0953-1513. 1997–2002, available at: http://www.alpsp.org.uk/volcont.htm. 1997–2002, free. 2004– , subscription.

This title includes well-written and timely articles of interest to academic not-for-profit publishers, their authors, and subscribers.

E *Math Forum Internet News*. The Math Forum. Available at: http://mathforum.org/electronic.newsletter/. Free.

This weekly newsletter highlights Web resources in mathematics at all levels.

E *NewJour*. NewJour. Available at: http://gort.ucsd.edu/newjour/. Free.

Frequent announcements of new online and new to online journals and newsletters.

E *Newsletter on Serials Pricing Issues*. Marcia Tuttle, 1989–2001. ISSN: 1046-3410. Available at: http://www.lib.unc.edu/prices/. Free.

This title has now ceased. Edited by serials librarian Marcia Tuttle, it arose in response to the serials crisis in academic libraries. There were a number of interesting contributions concerning mathematics journals specifically. The archives remain available.

E *Notices of the American Mathematical Society*. American Mathematical Society. ISSN: 0002-9920. Available at: http://www.ams.org/notices/. Free.

Membership bulletin of the AMS frequently has well-written articles relating to scholarly communications in mathematics or mathematics libraries. Book reviews and mathematical articles also of interest to librarians. Search interface is at: http://www.ams.org/noticessearch/.

E *NSDL Scout Report for Math, Engineering, & Technology*. Internet Scout Project. Available at: http://scout.cs.wisc.edu/Reports/ScoutReport/Current/. Free.

This title is part of NSF's NSDL project (National Science, Technology, Engineering, and Mathematics Education Digital Library). Professional librarians and content experts review online resources in math, engineering, and technology suitable for K–12 and above.

E *PAM Bulletin*. Physics-Astronomy-Mathematics Division, Special Libraries Association. ISSN: 1063-9136. Available at: http://www.sla.org/division/dpam/pam-bulletin/. Free.

The *PAM Bulletin* notes news and issues of interest to SLA members in math, physics, and astronomy.

E *PAM Electronic Discussion List [PAMnet]*. Special Libraries Association, Physics-Astronomy-Mathematics Division. Information available at: http://www.sla.org/division/dpam/manual/pamnet_bulletin/pamnet.html. Free.

Established in 1988, *PAMnet* has become a highly popular online forum for discussion of library issues relevant to the fields of physics, astronomy, and mathematics. Librarians, publishers, and academics use *PAMnet* for discussions, reference questions, and help in obtaining materials not readily available or when timing is critical. Messages to *PAMnet* are archived at: http://listserv.nd.edu/archives/pamnet.html. The list is not moderated, but one must subscribe in order to participate. One may subscribe without being a SLA or PAM member.

E *Public Discussions at The Math Forum*. Math Forum. Available at: http://mathforum.org/discussions/. Free.

Useful linked listing of mathematics and math education-related newsgroups, mailing lists, and Web-based discussions.

E *Sci-Tech Library Newsletter*. Stephanie Bianchi. Available at: http://gill.stanford.edu/depts/swain/nsflibnews/. Free.

Stephanie Bianchi compiles this bimonthly newsletter from a variety of sources for her library users at the National Science Foundation Library and then posts it on the Web for outside consumption. Each issue is full of interesting tips and linked sites for science librarians. Annotations, sometimes lengthy, are present. New electronic journals and interesting Web sites are included.

E *SPARC Open Access Newsletter*. (Formerly the *Free Online Scholarship Newsletter*.) Peter Suber. ISSN: 1535-7848 Available at: http://www.earlham.edu/~peters/fos/. Free.

Peter Suber is an active advocate of free online scholarly literature.

Sources for Mathematical Multimedia

Sometimes a picture or video presentation is worth a thousand words. There are an increasing number of video products available for college-level mathematics and statistics and above. Below are some sources for posters, videos, DVDs, and streaming video to acquire for the library.

American Mathematical Society Bookstore
201 Charles Street
Providence, RI 02904-2294
Telephone: 800-321-4AMS, 401-331-3842 (fax)
URL: http://www.ams.org/bookstore/videos. Free.

   The AMS has a substantial list of videotaped lectures, workshops, and presentations available for sale. Also available are posters by Anatolii Fomenko. *Mathematical Moments* posters are available for downloading at: http://www.ams.org/ams/mathmoments.html.

American Statistical Association
1429 Duke Street
Alexandria, VA 22314-3415
Telephone: 888-231-3473, 703-684-2037 (fax)
URL: http://www.amstat.org/education/lecturevideo.html. Free.

   At present, ASA has over 50 videotapes for sale in their Distinguished Statistician Video Series.

Mathematical Sciences Research Institute (MSRI)
1000 Centennial Drive, #5070 Berkeley, CA 94720-5070
Telephone: 510-642-0143, 510-642-8609 (fax)
URL: http://www.msri.org/publications/video/index.html. Free.

   Streaming video of MSRI lectures can be accessed online for free. MSRI events such as the 1993 *FermatFest*, the Tom Stoppard/Robert Osserman *Mathematics in Arcadia* event, and the *Galileo—A Dialog on Science, Mathematics, History and Drama* event are available for purchase on tape, CD, or DVD.

Project MATHEMATICS!
Caltech Bookstore
Mail Code 1-51 Pasadena, CA 91125
Telephone: 800-514-BOOK, 626-795-3156 (Fax)
URL: http://www.projectmathematics.com/. Free.

   "Project MATHEMATICS! produces videotape-and-workbook modules that explore basic topics in high school mathematics in ways that cannot be done at the chalkboard or in a textbook. The tapes use live action, music, special effects, and imaginative computer animation."

WORLD MATHEMATICAL YEAR 2000
URL: http://wmy2000.math.jussieu.fr/posters.html. Free.

The European Mathematical Society sponsored a mathematics poster competition for the World Mathematical Year 2000 celebration. This Web page links to posters submitted. Some posters are available for purchase.

Miscellany

E *AMS Book & Journal Donation Program.* AMS, 2003. Available at: http://www.ams.org/careers-edu/bookdonation.html. Free.

This is a wonderful program that tries to match donors with libraries and institutions in currency-poor or developing countries needing math-related books and journals. Donors provide the AMS with a list of gifts. If appropriate, the lists are posted on the Web site for review by potential recipients. If a match is made, the AMS reimburses the donor for shipping costs.

AUTHOR/TITLE INDEX

Note: Print titles and electronic resources in fixed format (e.g., CD-ROMs) are indicated by **bold** type. Electronic resources on the Web are indicated by *italic* type.

Abbott, Edwin, 192
Abbreviations of Names of Serials, 76
Abell, Martha L., 224
Abhandlungen aus dem Mathematischen Seminar der Universitat Hamburg, 53
Abhandlungen der Königlichen Gesellschaft der Wissenschaften in Göttingen, 43
About: Web Search, 52
Abraham Robinson: The Creation of Nonstandard Analysis: A Personal and Mathematical Odyssey (Dauben), 167
Abramowitz, Milton, 112, 114, 131
ACM Transactions on Mathematical Software, 119
AcqWeb's Directory of Publishers and Vendors (AcqWeb), 32
Acta Applicandae Mathematicae, 53
Acta Arithmetica, 54
Acta Mathematica, 54
Acta Mathematica Hungarica, 54
Acta Mathematica Scientia. Series B. English Edition, 54
Acta Mathematica Sinica. English Series, 54
Adams, J. Frank, 229
Advanced Engineering Mathematics (Kreyszig), 219
Advanced Mathematical Methods (Ostaszewski), 221
The Advanced TeXbook (Salomon), 226
Advances in Applied Mathematics, 54
Advances in Applied Probability, 54
Advances in Computational Mathematics, 54
Advances in Mathematics, 54
Advances in Theoretical and Mathematical Physics, 54
Affine Lie Algebras and Quantum Groups: An Introduction with Applications in Conformal Field Theory (Fuchs), 217
Africa Counts: Number and Pattern in African Culture (Zaslavsky), 209
African Americans in Mathematics II (Dean, McZeal, and Williams), 196
Aha! Gotcha: Paradoxes to Puzzle and Delight (Gardner), 210
Ahlfors, Lars Valerian, 229
A. J. Lohwater's Russian-English Dictionary of the Mathematical Sciences (Boas), 80
Akivis, M. A., 164
Albanese, Giacomo, 230
Albers, Donald J., 164
Albert, A. Adrian, 230
Aleksandrov, P. S., 79
Aleksandrova, N. V., 79
Alexander, Daniel S., 173
Alexanderson, G. L., 164
Alfred Tarski: Collected Papers (Tarski), 258
Algebraic & Geometric Topology, 54
Algebras and Representation Theory, 54
Algebra Universalis, 54
Algebra Colloquium, 54
Algorithmica, 54
Algorithms and Computation in Mathematics, 273
Alling, Norman L., 230
All the Mathematics You Missed: But Need to Know for Graduate School (Garrity), 201
All the Math That's Fit to Print: Articles from the Manchester Guardian (Devlin), 196
Alltheweb, 52
All You Wanted to Know about Mathematics But Were Afraid to Ask: Mathematics for Science Students (Lyons), 204
Alspach, Dale, 12

299

Altavista Babel Fish Translation, 79
AMATYC Review, 54
Amazon.com, 32
American Journal of Mathematics, 54
American Mathematical Monthly, 48, 54, 178
American Mathematical Society (AMS), 29, 38, 40, 43, 44–47, 57, 61, 68, 69, 70, 71, 75, 129, 162, 263, 274, 275, 277, 281, 292, 294, 296
[American Mathematical Society Journals], 263
American Mathematical Society Task Force on Excellence, 287
American Men & Women of Science, 146
American Statistical Association, 36, 145, 281, 296
American Statistician, 48, 55
American Women in Science: A Biographical Dictionary (Bailey), 153
Amman, Hans M., 113
AMS. *See* American Mathematical Society
AMS Book & Journal Donation Program, 297
AMS/IP Studies in Advanced Mathematics, 274
An, Myoung, 223
Analysis by Its History (Hairer and Wanner), 180
Analysis with Local Census Data: Portraits of Change (Myers), 221
Anastassiou, George, 113
Anderson, E., 113
Anderson, Nancy D., 19, 21, 287
Anderson, Simon P., 213
Anderson, T. W., 22, 230
Andreescu, Titu, 209
Andresen, Jorgen Ellegaard, 213
Andrews, Larry C., 113
Anglin, W. S., 173
Anglo-Russkii Slovar' Matematicheskikh Terminov: okolo 20000 terminov (Aleksandrov, et al.), 79
Annales Academiae Scientiarum Fennicae. Mathematica, 55
Annales de l'Institut Fourier, 55
Annales de l'Institut Henri Poincaré. Analyse Non Linéaire, 55
Annales de l'Institut Henri Poincaré. Probabilités et Statistiques, 55
Annales Henri Poincaré, 55
Annales Scientifiques de l'Ecole Normale Superiéure. Quatrieme Serie, 55
Annals of Applied Probability, 55
Annals of Global Analysis and Geometry, 55
Annals of Mathematical Statistics, 45, 51
Annals of Mathematics, 7
Annals of Mathematics, 44
Annals of Mathematics. Second Series, 55
Annals of Mathematics Studies, 274
Annals of Probability, 55
Annals of Pure and Applied Logic, 55
Annals of Statistics, 55
Annals of the Institute of Statistical Mathematics, 55
Annotated Bibliographies in Combinatorial Optimization (Dell'Amico, Maffioli, and Martello), 22
Annotated Bibliography of Expository Writing in the Mathematical Sciences (Gaffney and Steen), 23
An Annotated Bibliography of Works on Babylonian Mathematics (Friberg), 156
"Another Opinion: Mathematics Journals Should Be Electronic and Free(ly Accessible)" (Kuperberg, Morrison, and Palais), 15
Anthony, Joby Milo, 192
The Anthropology of Numbers (Crump), 216
ANZIAM Journal, 55
Apollonius of Perga. Conics, Books I-III (Densmore), 177
Applications of Mathematics, 274
Applied and Computational Harmonic Analysis, 56
Applied Categorical Structures, 55
Applied Chaos Theory: A Paradigm for Complexity (Çambel), 215

Applied Mathematica: Getting Started, Getting It Done (Shaw and Tigg), 227
Applied Mathematical Sciences, 274
Applied Mathematics (Logan), 220
Applied Mathematics and Computation, 56
Applied Mathematics and Optimization, 56
Applied Mathematics Series (U.S. National Bureau of Standards), 112
Applied Optimization, 274
Applied Statistics. *See* **Journal of the Royal Statistical Society. Series C. Applied Statistics**
The Apprenticeship of a Mathematician (Weil), 173
Apt, Krzysztof, 13
Arbib, Michael A., 214
Archimedes' Revenge: The Joys and Perils of Mathematics (Hoffman), 202
Archimedes: What Did He Do Besides Cry Eureka? (Stein), 172
Archiv der Mathematik, 56
Archive for History of Exact Sciences, 56
Archive for Mathematical Logic, 56
Archive for Rational Mechanics and Analysis, 56
Arganbright, Deane, 113
Ariadne, 292
Arithmetical Books from the Invention of Printing to the Present Time: Being Brief Notices of a Large Number of Works Drawn Up from Actual Inspection (De Morgan), 23
Arkiv för Matematik, 56
Armitage, Peter, 97
Arnold, V. I., 164, 214
Arrow, Kenneth J., 113
Ars Combinatoria, 56
Ars Magna or the Rules of Algebra (Cardano), 176
Artin, Emil, 230
Artmann, Benno, 165
arXiv.org (Cornell University), 36, 264

Asai, Kiyoji, 223
ASA JobWeb, 145
ASA Membership Directory, 145
Askey, Richard A., 178
Aspray, William, 165
Assistantships and Graduate Fellowships in the Mathematical Sciences, 145
Association for Women in Mathematics, 153, 282
Astérisque, 56, 274
Aston, Philip J., 214
Asymptotic Analysis, 56
ATG. Algebraic & Geometric Topology, 56
Atiyah, Michael, 192, 231
Atlas for Computing Mathematical Functions: An Illustrated Guide for Practitioners, With Programs in C and Mathematica (Thompson), 138
An Atlas of Brauer Characters (Jansen), 126
An Atlas of Edge-Reversal Dynamics (Barbosa), 115
Atlas of Finite Groups: Maximal Subgroups and Ordinary Characters for Simple Groups (Conway, et al.), 119
Atlas of Functions (Spanier and Oldham), 136
Attribute Sampling Plans, Tables of Tests and Confidence Limits for Proportions (Odeh and Owen), 110
Aubert, Karl Egil, 231
Augustin-Louis Cauchy: A Biography (Belhoste), 165
Aull, C. E., 153
Aumann, Robert J., 231
Ausejo, Elena, 76
Australian & New Zealand Journal of Statistics, 56
Auth, Joanne Buhl, 114
An Author's Guide to Scholarly Publishing (Derricourt), 141

Babbitt, Donald, 13

Bagrov, V. G., 114
Bagui, Subhash C., 107
Bailey, Martha J., 153
Bailey, T. N., 214
Baker, C. C. T., 80
Baker, Louis, 114
Balakrishnan, N., 107, 109, 114
Balding, D. J., 115
Ball, W. W. Rouse, 174, 209
Ballentyne, D. W. G., 80
Banks, David L., 102
Barbeau, Edward J., 209
Barbosa, Valmir C., 115
Barnett V., 115
Baron, Margaret E., 174
Barr, Michael, 13
Barrat, P., 287
Barrow, Isaac, 231
Barrow-Green, June, 165
Bartsch, Hans Jochen, 115
Barwise, Jon, 115, 117
Bashmakova, I. G., 165, 174
Basic Library List for Four-Year Colleges, 27
Basic Library List for Two-Year Colleges, 27
Baston, R. J., 214
Baxter, Martin, 214
A Beautiful Mind: A Biography of John Forbes Nash, Jr., Winner of the Nobel Prize in Economics, 1994 (Nasar), 170
The Beauty of Doing Mathematics: Three Public Dialogues (Lang), 204
Becker, Hans J., 289
A Beginner's Book of TeX (Seroul and Levy), 226
The Beginner's Guide to Mathematica Version 4 (Glynn and Gray), 225
The Beginnings and Evolution of Algebra (Bashmakova), 174
Behnke, H., 98
Bélair, Jacques, 215
Belhoste, Bruno, 165
Bell, Eric Temple, 166
Bell, E. T., 174, 193
Bellman, Richard E., 231

The Bellman Continuum: A Collection of the Works of Richard E. Bellman (Bellman), 231
Bence, S. J., 221
Bendick, Jeanne, 80
Bennett, Curtis D., 193
Benzecri, J. P., 116
Berck, Peter, 137
Berggren, J. L., 174
Berggren, Lennart, 174
Berkeley Mathematics Lecture Notes, 274
Berkeley Preliminary Exams (De Souza and Silva), 210
Berkeley Problems in Mathematics (De Souza and Silva), 210
Berlekamp, Elwyn, 193, 209
Bernoulli, 56
Bernoulli, Daniel, 232
Bernoulli, Jakob, 232
Bernoulli, Johann, 232
Bernoulli Numbers: Bibliography (Dilcher, Skula, and Slavutskii), 23
Bernoulli Society and the Institute of Mathematical Statistics, 146
Berríos, José, 95
Berry, John, 80
Berry, Michael W., 215
Bertrand Russell and the Origins of Set-Theoretic 'Paradoxes' (Garciadiego), 167
Berzsenyi, George, 210
Beschler, Edwin F., 13
Best Current Practices: Recommendations on Electronic Information Communication (2002) (International Mathematical Union), 14
Beurling, Arne, 232
Beutelspacher, Albrecht, 193
Beyer, William H., 116
Beyond Numeracy: Ruminations of a Numbers Man (Paulos), 205
Bhatt, Jay, 288
Bibliografia Italiana di Storia della Scienza, 158
"A Bibliographic Resource for Statistical Theory: Current Index to Statistics" (Kristick), 290

Bibliography and Research Manual of the History of Mathematics (May), 25, 160
Bibliography of Early Modern Algebra, 1500–1800 (Rider), 26, 161
Bibliography of Mathematical Works Printed in America through 1850 (Karpinski), 24
Bibliography of Mathematics Published in Communist China, 1949–1960 (Tsao), 28
Bibliography of Mathematical Works Printed in America through 1850, Supplement and Second Supplement (Karpinski), 24
Bibliography of Multivariate Statistical Analysis (Anderson, et al.), 22
Bibliography of Non-Euclidean Geometry (Sommerville), 27
Bibliography of Quaternions and Allied Systems of Mathematics (Macfarlane), 25
Bibliography of Recreational Mathematics (Schaaf), 26
Bibliography of Russian Mathematics Books (Forsythe), 23
Bibliography of Statistical Bibliographies (Lancaster), 25
Bibliography of Statistical Literature (Kendall and Doig), 25
Bibliography on Chaos (Zhang), 28
A Bibliography on Continued Fractions, Padé Approximation, Sequence Transformation and Related Subjects (Brezinski), 22
Bibliography on Time Series and Stochastic Processes: An International Team Project (Wold), 28
Bing, R. H., 233
Biograficheskii Slovar' Deiatelei v Oblasti Matematiki (Borodin and Bugai), 154
Biographical Dictionary of Mathematicians: Reference Biographies from the Dictionary of Scientific Biography, 154

The Biographical Dictionary of Scientists (Porter and Ogilvie), 161
Biographies of Women Mathematicians, 154
Biographisch-literarisches Handworterbuch der exakten Naturwissenschaften (Poggendorff), 161
Biometrical Journal, 56
Biometrics, 56
Biometrika, 56
Biometrika Tables for Statisticians (Pearson and Hartley), 111
Biostatistics, 57
Birman, Joan S., 13
Bishop, Errett, 233
Bishop, M., 115
Blachman, Nancy, 224
Blackwell Publishing, 264
Blocksma, Mary, 116
Boas, Mary L., 215
Boas, R. P., 80, 123
Bogoliubov, Aleksei Nikolaevich, 154
Bollettino della Unione Matematica Italiana. Sezione B. Articoli di Ricerca Matematica Serie VIII, 57
Bölling, Reinhard, 166
Bollobás, Béla, 193
Bolyai Society Mathematical Studies, 274
Bonnet, Robert, 130
Boojums All the Way Through: Communicating Science in a Prosaic Age (Mermin), 204
Books In Print (R.R. Bowker), 32
Borceux, Francis, 116
Borel, Armand, 233
Borodin, A. I., 154
Borodin, Andrei N., 116
Borovkov, K. A., 81
Borowski, E. J., 81, 92
Borwein, J. M., 81, 92
Borwein, Jonathan, 174
Borwein, Peter, 81, 174
Bos, Henk J. M., 175
Bossert, William H., 224

Bottazzini, Umberto, 175
Boundary Element Reference Book
  (Mackerle and Brebbia), 129
Bouvier, Alain, 81
Bowden, Leon, 207
Bowron, Mark, 48
Box, George E. P., 233
Box, Joan Fisher, 166
Boyer, Carl B., 175
Brains, Machines, and Mathematics
  (Arbib), 214
Branin, Joseph J., 13
Braselton, James, 224
Brauer, Richard, 233
Breakthroughs: A Chronology of Great Achievements in Science and Mathematics, 1200–1930
  (Parkinson), 160
Breakthroughs in Statistics (Kotz and Johnson), 183
Brebbia, C. A., 129
Brezinski, Claude, 22
Brigaglia, A., 175
Brillhart, John, 108
The Broken Dice: And Other Mathematical Tales of Chance
  (Ekeland), 198
Bronshtein, I. N., 116, 117
Browder, Felix E., 194
Brown, Cecelia M., 288
Browne, Murray, 215
Brychkov, IU. A., 133
The Budget of Trisections (Dudley), 198
Bugai, A. S., 154
Bullen, P. S., 82
Bulletin (AMS), 4
Bulletin de Bibliographie, d'Histoire et de Biographie Mathématiques
  (Terquem), 27, 162
Bulletin de la Société Mathématique de Belgique, 57
Bulletin de la Société Mathématique de France, 57
Bulletin of Symbolic Logic, 57
Bulletin of the American Mathematical Society. New Series, 57
Bulletin of the Australian Mathematical Society, 57
Bulletin of the Belgian Mathematical Society, Simon Stevin, 57
Bulletin of the London Mathematical Society, 57
Bullettino di Bibliografia e di Storia della Scienze Matematische e Fisiche (Boncompagni), 22
Bunch, Bryan, 98, 194
Burdick, Richard K., 49
Burdzy, Krzysztof, 13
Burington, Richard S., 117
Burlak, J., 82
Burton, David M., 175
"The Business of Scientific Communication" (Gilbert), 14
Buss, Samuel R., 117

Cajori, Florian, 176
Calcolo, 57
Calculus of Variations and Partial Differential Equations, 57
Calendrical Calculations (Dershowitz and Reingold), 120
California Digital Library, 31
Calinger, Ronald, 176
Callahan, James J., 215
Calvin C. Elgot: Selected Papers (Elgot), 236
Çambel, A. B., 215
The Cambridge Dictionary of Statistics (Everitt), 85
The Cambridge Dictionary of Statistics in the Medical Sciences (Everitt), 85
Cambridge Journals, 264
Cambridge Monographs on Applied and Computational Mathematics, 274
Cambridge Studies in Advanced Mathematics, 274
Cambridge Texts in Applied Mathematics, 274
Cambridge Tracts in Mathematics, 274
Campbell, Colin, 135
Campbell, Douglas M., 194
Campbell, Paul J., 22, 157
Canadian Applied Mathematics Quarterly, 57

Canadian Journal of Mathematics.
  Journal Canadien de Mathématiques, 57
Canadian Journal of Statistics. La Revue
  Canadienne de Statistique, 57
Canadian Mathematical Bulletin.
  Bulletin Canadien de Mathématiques, 57
Canadian Mathematical Society, 282
Cannell, D. M., 166
Cannings, C., 115
Cantor, Georg, 234
Cardano, Girolamo, 176
Carnegie Mellon University, 30
Carroll, Raymond J., 13
Carus Mathematical Monographs, 274
Casacuberta, C., 194
Case, Mary, 13
Casselman, Bill, 13
Castellet, M., 194
Casti, John L., 194, 195
Castillo, Enrique, 215
Catalog of Special Plane Curves
  (Lawrence), 128
*Catalog of the Scientific Community in
  the 16th and 17th Centuries*
  (Westfall), 163
Catalogue of Scientific Papers, 1800–
  1900 (Royal Society of London),
  49
Catalogue of Scientific Papers, 1800–
  1900: Subject Index (Royal
  Society of London), 49
Catalogue of Scientific Papers (Royal
  Society of London), 42
Catastrophe Theory (Arnold), 214
Categories for the Working Mathematician (Mac Lane), 204
Cauchy and the Creation of Complex
  Function Theory (Smithies), 172
Cavagnaro, Catherine, 82
CBMS-NSF Regional Conference
  Series in Applied Mathematics,
  274
CBMS Regional Conference Series in
  Mathematics, 274
Celebrating Women in Mathematics
  and Science (Cooney), 166

A Century of Mathematics in America, 178
A Century of Mathematics: Through
  the Eyes of the Monthly (Ewing),
  178
C. G. J. Jacobi's Gesammelte Werke
  (Jacobi), 242
Chabert, Jean Luc, 176
Challenging Mathematical Programs
  with Elementary Solutions
  (Iaglom and Iaglom), 202
Chambadal, Lucien, 82
Chambers, Lance, 117
Champeney, D. C., 118
Chance and Chaos (Ruelle), 207
Chance: New Directions for Statistics
  and Computing, 58
Chandler, David, 216
Chandrasekhar, S. (Subrahmanyan), 234
Chandrasekharan, K., 166
Changeux, Jean-Pierre, 195
Chapman & Hall/CRC Monographs
  and Surveys in Pure and Applied
  Mathematics, 274
Chapman & Hall/CRC Research Notes
  in Mathematics, 275
Charles Loewner, Collected Papers
  (Loewner), 246
The Charleston Advisor, 293
Charlesworth, Brian, 216
Chen, J. Q., 108
Chen, K.-T., 234
Chen, William W. S., 107
Chentzov, N. N., 213
Chern, Shiing-shen, 234
Chiang, Chin Long, 108
"Chinese Acrobatics, an Old-Time
  Brewery, and the 'Much Needed
  Gap': The Life of *Mathematical
  Reviews*" (Jackson), 289
Chinese Annals of Mathematics. Series
  B. Shuxue Niankan. Ji B, 58
Chinese-English Glossary of the
  Mathematical Sciences (De
  Francis), 83
Chronological Annotated Bibliography
  of Order Statistics (Harter), 23
Chui, Charles K., 216

Ciarlet, P. G., 118
Ciliberto, C., 175
CISTI (Canada Institute for Scientific and Technical Information) (NRC-CNRC), 33
citebase Search [Open Archives], 36
Clapham, Christopher, 82
Clark, Colin W., 216
Clark, Douglas N., 83
Clark, John, 83
Classics in Applied Mathematics, 275
Classics of Mathematics (Calinger), 176
Clawson, Calvin C., 176
Clifford, William K., 235
CMCI CompuMath Citation Index, 2, 40
Coding Theory and Cryptography: From Enigma and Geheimschreiber to Quantum Theory (Joyner), 182
Cohen, A. Clifford, 118
Colbourn, Charles, 119
Cole, Timothy W., 288
Coleman, Shirley, 119
Coleman, Thomas F., 119
Collected Algorithms from ACM, 119
The Collected Letters of Colin MacLaurin (MacLaurin), 247
Collected Mathematical Papers (Albert), 230
Collected Mathematical Papers (Jacobson), 243
The Collected Mathematical Papers of James Joseph Sylvester (Sylvester), 258
The Collected Mathematical Papers of Leonard Eugene Dickson (Dickson), 235
Collected Mathematical Papers (Ostrowski), 250
Collected Mathematical Papers (Shafarevich), 256
Collected Mathematical Papers (Smith), 257
The Collected Mathematical Works of George William Hill (Hill), 241
Collected Papers (Ahlfors), 229
Collected Papers (Artin), 230

Collected Papers (Aumann), 231
Collected Papers (Brauer), 233
Collected Papers (Gelfand), 239
Collected Papers (Lang), 245
Collected Papers: Marston Morse (Morse), 249
The Collected Papers of Albert Einstein (Einstein), 235
Collected Papers of Dionisio Gallarati (Gallarati), 239
Collected Papers of G. H. Hardy; Including Joint Papers with J. E. Littlewood and Others (Hardy), 240
Collected Papers of Giacomo Albanese (Albanese), 230
Collected Papers of Hans Rademacher (Rademacher), 251
Collected Papers of J. E. Littlewood (Littlewood), 246
Collected Papers of Karl Egil Aubert (Aubert), 231
Collected Papers of K. T. Chen (Chen), 234
Collected Papers of Kustaa Inkeri (Inkeri), 242
Collected Papers of Norman Alling (Alling), 230
Collected Papers of Paulo Ribenboim (Ribenboim), 253
Collected Papers of Paul Turán (Turán), 259
Collected Papers of Pierre Samuel (Samuel), 254
Collected Papers of R. A. Fisher (Fisher), 238
The Collected Papers of Raymond D. Mindlin (Mindlin), 248
The Collected Papers of R. H. Bing (Bing), 233
Collected Papers of Ruggiero Torelli (Torelli), 258
Collected Papers of Satoshi Suzuki (Suzuki), 257
The Collected Papers of Stephen Smale (Smale), 256
Collected Papers of Taro Morishima (Morishima), 249

The Collected Papers of T. W. Anderson, 1943–1985 (Anderson), 230
Collected Papers (Oka), 250
Collected Papers on Mathematics, Logic, and Philosophy (Frege), 238
Collected Papers on Wave Mechanics (Schrödinger), 255
Collected Papers (Polya), 251
Collected Papers (Riesz), 254
Collected Papers (Selberg), 256
Collected Papers (Smarandache), 257
Collected Papers (Szegö), 258
Collected Papers (Zariski), 263
The Collected Work of George E. P. Box (Box), 233
Collected Works (Atiyah), 231
Collected Works (Gödel), 239
Collected Works (Kodaira), 243
Collected Works (Lesniewski), 246
The Collected Works of Arne Beurling (Beurling), 232
The Collected Works of John W. Tukey (Tukey), 259
The Collected Works of Philip Hall (Hall), 239
Collected Works (Von Neumann), 260
Collected Works with Commentaries (Wiener), 262
Collected Works (Yamabe), 262
A Collection of Mathematical Problems (Ulam), 260
College & Research Libraries News, 292
College Mathematics Journal, 58
The Collins Dictionary of Mathematics (Borowski and Borwein), 81, 92
Colloquium Publications, 275
Colton, Theodore, 97
The Columbia Guide to Online Style (Walker and Taylor), 143
[Columbia Guide to Online Style:] Basic CGOS Style (Walker and Taylor), 143
COMAP, Inc., 195
Combinatorial Optimization: Annotated Bibliographies (O'Heigeartaigh and Rinnooy Kan), 26
Combinatorica, 58
Combinatorics, Probability and Computing, 58
Combined Membership List: American Mathematical Society, American Mathematical Association of Two-Year Colleges, Association for Women in Mathematics, Mathematical Association of America, Society for Industrial and Applied Mathematics, 146
Combined Membership List (CML). American Mathematical Society, 2004, 146
Commentarii Mathematici Helvetici, 58
Communications in Algebra, 58
Communications in Analysis and Geometry, 58
Communications in Contemporary Mathematics, 58
Communications in Mathematical Physics, 58
Communications in Partial Differential Equations, 58
Communications in Statistics. Simulation and Computation, 58
Communications in Statistics. Theory and Methods, 58
Communications on Pure and Applied Mathematics, 58
CompactMath, 2
Companion Encyclopedia of the History and Philosophy of the Mathematical Sciences (Grattan-Guinness), 157
Comparative Prices of Math Journals (Kirby), 292
A Compendium on Nonlinear Ordinary Differential Equations (Sachdev), 135
"Competition and Cooperation: Libraries and Publishers in Transition to Electronic Scholarly Journals" (Odlyzko), 15
Complete Categorized Guide to Statistical Selection and Ranking Procedures (Dudewicz and Joo Ok Koo), 19
Compositio Mathematica, 58

Compstat Lectures, 275
Comptes Rendus Hebdomadaires des Séances de l'Académie des Sciences, 42
Comptes Rendus Mathématique, 58
Computational Geometry: Theory and Applications, 59
Computational Optimization and Applications, 59
Computational Statistics, 59
Computational Statistics & Data Analysis, 59
Computer Graphics Handbook: Geometry and Mathematics (Mortenson), 131
A Computer Laboratory Manual for Number Theory (Maim), 129
Computers & Mathematics with Applications, 59
Concepts & Images: Visual Mathematics (Loeb), 204
The Concepts of the Calculus (Boyer), 175
A Concise History of Mathematics (Struik), 188
The Concise Oxford Dictionary of Mathematics (Clapham), 82
Concompagni, B., 22
Conference on Electronic Communication in Mathematics, 6
Conformal Geometry and Dynamics, 59
Connes, Alain, 195
Consortium, 59
Constitutions of Matter: Mathematical Modeling the Most Everyday of Physical Phenomena (Krieger), 219
Constructive Approximation, 59
Contemporary Geometry: J. Q. Zhong Memorial Volume (Zhong), 263
Contemporary Mathematics, 275
Contest in Higher Mathematics: Miklós Schweitzer Competitions, 1962–1991 (Székely), 213
The Contest Problem Book V (Berzsenyi and Maurer), 210
A Convergence of Lives: Sofia Kovalevskaia, Scientist, Writer, Revolutionary (Koblitz), 169

Conversations on Mind, Matter, and Mathematics (Changeux and Connes), 195
Conway, J. H., 119
Conway, John H., 193
Cook, Ian, 97
Cooke, Roger, 166
Cooney, Miriam P., 166
[Cornell] University Faculty Forum, 13
Cornell University, 36, 264
Cornell University Library Historical Mathematics Monographs, 9, 42, 264, 265
Correspondence Analysis Handbook (Benzecri), 116
Corry, Leo, 176
Courant Lecture Notes in Mathematics, 275
Coxeter, H. S. M., 195, 209, 235
Crannell, Annalisa, 193
Crawford, Walt, 13
The CRC Concise Encyclopedia of Mathematics (Weisstein), 104
CRC Handbook of Chemistry and Physics (Lide), 128
The CRC Handbook of Combinatorial Designs (Colbourn and Dinitz), 119
CRC Handbook of Lie Group Analysis of Differential Equations (Ibragimov), 126
CRC Handbook of Mathematical Curves and Surfaces (Von Seggern), 138
CRC Handbook of Mathematical Sciences (Beyer), 116
CRC Handbook of Percentage Points of the Inverse Gaussian Distribution (Koziol), 127
CRC Handbook of Percentiles of Non-Central T-Distributions (Bagui), 107
CRC Handbook of Tables for Order Statistics from Inverse Gaussian Distributions, With Applications (Balakrishnan and Chen), 107
CRC Handbook of Tables for the Use of Order Statistics in Estimation (Harter and Balakrishnan), 109

CRC Standard Curves and Surfaces: A Mathematica Notebook User's Guide (Von Seggern), 139
CRC Standard Curves and Surfaces (Von Seggern), 138
CRC Standard Mathematical Tables and Formulae (Zwillinger), 112
CRC Standard Probability and Statistics Tables and Formulae (Kokoska and Zwillinger), 109
Crescent Dictionary of Mathematics (Karush), 89
The Crest of the Peacock: Non-European Roots of Mathematics (Joseph), 182
CRM Monograph Series, 275
CRM Proceedings and Lecture Notes, 275
Crowe, Michael J., 177
Crstici, B., 130
Crump, Thomas, 216
Crux Mathematicorum, 212
Cryptology (Beutelspacher), 193
Cumulative index to IMS scientific journals, 1960–1989 (Trumbo and Burdick), 49
Current Bibliography in the History of Technology (Technology and Culture), 158
Current Cites, 293
Current Contents, 8
Current Contents Connect (Institute for Scientific Information), 37
Current Index to Journals in Education (U.S. Department of Education), 39
Current Index to Statistics, 4, 8, 76
Current Index to Statistics (American Statistical Association and Institute of Mathematical Statistics), 35, 37
Current Index to Statistics–Extended Database, 36
Current Index to Statistics–Extended Database (American Statistical Association and Institute of Mathematical Statistics), 36, 59
Current Information Sources in Mathematics: An Annotated Guide to Books and Periodicals, 1960-72 (Dick), 19

Current Mathematical Publications (AMS), 2, 44
Curtis, Charles W., 177
Czechoslovak Mathematical Journal, 59

D'Agostino, Marcello, 120
Daintith, John, 83
Dale, Andrew I., 177
Dannan, Fozi Mustafa, 98
Dantzig, Tobias, 195
Das, Anadijiban, 216
Das Fotoalbum für Weierstrasse. A Photo Album for Weierstrasse (Bölling), 166
Dass, B. K., 155
Dauben, Joseph W., 22, 155, 167
David, F. N., 177
David, H. A., 83
David, Philip J., 167
Davidoff, Giuliana, 196
Davis, Donald M., 196
Davis, Philip J., 196
Day, Robert A., 141
Dean, Nathaniel, 196
De Boor, Carl, 120
DeCarlo, Mary, 288
De Francis, John, 83
De Gruyter, 264
De Gruyter Expositions in Mathematics, 275
De Gruyter Studies in Mathematics, 275
Dekker.com, 265
Delijska, B., 83
Dell'Amico, Mauro, 22
"The Demands on Electronic Journals in the Mathematical Sciences" (Steinberger), 16
De Morgan, Augustus, 23
Dempster, M. A. H., 216
Dennery, Philippe, 217
Dennis, Keith, 10
Densmore, Dana, 177
De Palma, André, 213
Der, Geoff, 120
Der Briefwechsel (Bernoulli), 232
Der Briefwechsel von Johann Bernoulli (Bernoulli), 232
De Robbio, Antonella, 288
Derricourt, Robin, 141

Dershowitz, Nachum, 120
Descartes on Polyhedra: A Study of the De Solidorum Elementis (Federico), 179
Designs, Codes and Cryptography, 59
Deskbook of Math Formulas and Tables (Auth), 114
De Souza, Paulo Ney, 210
The Development of Mathematics (Bell), 174
Devlin, Keith, 196, 197
Dewdney, A. K., 197
Dewynne, Jeff, 223
Diccionario Matemático; Español-Inglés, Inglés-Español. Mathematics Dictionary; Spanish-English, English-Spanish (García-Rodríquez), 86
Dick, Elie M., 19
Dickson, Leonard Eugene, 235
Dictionar Poliglot de Matematica, Mechanica si Astronomie (Gheorghita), 86
Dictionary and Bibliography of Discrete Distributions (Patil and Joshi), 26
Dictionary of Algebra, Arithmetic, and Trigonometry (Krantz), 91
Dictionary of Analysis, Calculus, and Differential Equations (Clark), 83
Dictionary of Classical and Theoretical Mathematics (Cavagnaro and Haight), 82
Dictionary of Gaming, Modelling & Simulation (Gibbs), 86
A Dictionary of Inequalities (Bullen), 82
Dictionary of Logical Terms and Symbols (Greenstein and Horn), 87
Dictionary of Mathematical Games, Puzzles, and Amusements (Eiss), 85
Dictionary of Mathematical Sciences (Herland), 87
Dictionary of Mathematics (Baker), 80
Dictionary of Mathematics (Berry, et al.), 80
Dictionary of Mathematics (Borowski and Borwein), 81
Dictionary of Mathematics (Glenn and Littler), 86
Dictionary of Mathematics in Four Languages: English, German, French, Russian (Eisenreich and Sube), 84
Dictionary of Mathematics (Millington and Millington), 93
Dictionary of Mathematics Terms (Downing), 84
Dictionary of Named Effects and Laws in Chemistry, Physics and Mathematics (Ballentyne and Lovett), 80
Dictionary of Quantities and Units (Drazil), 84
A Dictionary of Real Numbers (Borwein and Borwein), 81
Dictionary of Scientific Biography, 154
Dictionary of Scientific Units Including Dimensionless Numbers and Scales (Jerrard and McNeil), 88
Dictionary of Statistical, Scientific and Technical Terms: English-Spanish, Spanish-English (Sahai and Berríos), 95
Dictionary of Statistical Terms (Kendall and Buckland), 90
A Dictionary of Statistics (Upton and Cook), 97
Dictionary of Symbols of Mathematical Logic (Feys and Fitch), 85, 87
Dictionary/Outline of Basic Statistics (Freund and Williams), 86
Dictionnaire des Mathématiques (Bouvier and George), 81
Dictionnaire des Mathématiques (Chambadal), 82
DIEPER, Digitised European Periodicals, 9, 42
Dieudonné, Jean, 198
Die Werke von Daniel Bernoulli (Bernoulli), 232
Die Werke von Jakob Bernoulli (Bernoulli), 232
Differential Equations, 59
Differential Geometry and Its Applications, 59

Differentsial'nye Uravneniia, 59
"A Digital Archive for Mathematics" (Quinn), 16
Digital Dissertations (Proquest), 38
Digital Library of Mathematical Functions (National Institute of Standards and Technology), 131
Digital Mathematics Library, 10
Digital Mathematics Library (DML), 269
Digital Typography Using LaTeX (Syropoulos, Tsolomitis, and Sofroniou), 143
Dilcher, K., 287
Dilcher, Karl, 23
Dillen, F. J. E., 120
Dilworth, Robert P., 235
The Dilworth Theorems: Selected Papers of Robert P. Dilworth (Dilworth), 235
DIMACS Series in Discrete Mathematics and Theoretical Computer Science, 275
Dinitz, Jeffrey H., 119
Diophantus and Diophantine Equations (Bashmakova), 165
Directory of Mathematics Preprints and e-Print Servers (AMS), 38
Directory of Members (American Statistical Association), 145
Discrete & Computational Geometry, 59
Discrete and Continuous Dynamical Systems, 60
Discrete Applied Mathematics, 59
Discrete Choice Theory of Product Differentiation (Anderson, De Palma, and Thisse), 213
Discrete Mathematics, 60
Discrete Thoughts: Essays on Mathematics, Science, and Philosophy (Kac, Rota, and Schwartz), 203
Dissertation Abstracts International (UMI), 38
Distributed Digital Library of Mathematical Monographs, 265
Distributed Digital Library of Mathematical Monographs, 270

Distributed Digital Mathematics Archive Library, 270
D-Lib Magazine, 293
DML: Digital Mathematics Library, Retrodigitized Mathematics Journals and Monographs, 265
DOAJ, Directory of Open Access Journals, 76
Documenta Mathematica, 4, 60
"Documenta Mathematica, A Community-Driven Scientific Journal" (Rehmann), 16
Dodson, C. T. J., 120
Does God Play Dice? The Mathematics of Chaos (Stewart), 208
Doig, Alison G., 25
Doklady. Mathematics, 60
Dolciani Mathematical Expositions, 275
Dominy, Margaret, 288
Dowling, Thomas, 31
Downing, Douglas, 84
Drazil, J. V., 84
Drucker, Thomas, 178
Du, Ding-Zhu, 121
Dudewicz, Edward J., 19, 121
Dudley, Underwood, 198
Duke Mathematical Journal, 60
Dunham, William, 167, 198
Duren, Peter, 178
Duren, Peter L., 189
Dynamical Disease: Mathematical Analysis of Human Illness (Bélair), 215
Dynamics of Continuous, Discrete and Impulsive Systems, 60

Ebersole, W. Dale, Jr., 288
ECHO, Exploring and Collecting History Online, Virtual Center, Science & Technology, 155
Eckmann, Beno, 235
Econometric Theory, 60
Economic Dynamics: Phase Diagrams and Their Economic Application (Shone), 222
"The Economics of Electronic Journals" (Odlyzko), 15

Economists' Mathematical Manual
(Sydsæter, Strøm, and Berck), 137
Edgerton, Harold A., 91
Educational Studies in Mathematics, 60
Edwards, C. H., Jr., 178
Edwards, Don, 137
EEVL: The Internet Guide to Engineering, Mathematics and Computing: [Mathematics], 28
Efimov, Oleg P., 84
Eight-Place Tables of Trigonometric Functions for Every Second of Arc, with an Appendix on the Computation to Twenty Places (Peters), 111
Einar Hille: Classical Analysis and Functional Analysis, Selected Papers (Hille), 241
Einstein, Albert, 235
Eisenreich, Günther, 84
Eisenstein, Gotthold, 236
Eiss, Harry Edwin, 85
Ekeland, Ivar, 198, 199
Electromagnetic Theory (Heaviside), 218
Electronic Communications in Probability, 60
Electronic Journal of Combinatorics, 4, 60
Electronic Journal of Differential Equations, 4, 60
Electronic Journal of Linear Algebra, 60
Electronic Journal of Probability, 60
Electronic Journal of Qualitative Theory of Differential Equations, 60
Electronic Library of Mathematics, 265
Electronic Mathematical Archives Network Initiative (EMANI), 270
"Electronic Mathematics Journals" (Steinberger), 16
"Electronic Publishing and Electronic Publications in Mathematics" (Wegner), 17
Electronic Research Announcements of the American Mathematical Society, 60
Electronic Transactions on Numerical Analysis, 4, 61

Elektronische Zeitschriftenbibliothek/ Electronic Journals Library, 76
Elementary Statistics Laboratory Manual: MS-DOS Version (Spurrier, Edwards, and Thombs), 137
Elgot, Calvin C., 236
Élie Cartan (Akivis and Rosenfeld), 164
Elsevier's Dictionary of Computer Science and Mathematics: In English, German, French, and Russian (Delijska and Peeva), 83
Elsevier's Dictionary of Mathematics (Peeva, et al.), 94
The Emergence of Complexity in Mathematics, Physics, Chemistry and Biology (Pullman), 221
The Emergence of the American Mathematical Research Community, 1876–1900: J. J. Sylvester, Felix Klein, and E. H. Moore (Parshall and Rowe), 186
"EMIS 2001–A Portal to Mathematics in Progress" (Wegner and Jost), 291
EMJ Mailing List Archives, 293
Emmer, Michele, 199
Employment Information in the Mathematical Sciences, 146
Employment Information in the Mathematical Sciences (EMIS), 146
Encyclopaedia of Mathematical Sciences (Gamkrelidze), 99
Encyclopaedia of Mathematics (Hazewinkel), 100, 104
Encyclopaedia of Mathematics (Hazewinkel), 101
Encyclopaedia of Mathematics on CD-ROM (Hazewinkel), 100
Encyclopaedia of Mathematics. Supplement (Hazewinkel), 100
Encyclopaedic Dictionary of Mathematics for Engineers and Applied Scientists (Sneddon), 104
Encyclopedia of Biostatistics (Armitage and Colton), 97
The Encyclopedia of Integer Sequences (Sloane and Plouffe), 103
Encyclopedia of Mathematical Sciences, 275

Encyclopedia of Mathematics and Its
    Applications, 275
Encyclopedia of Mathematics and Its
    Applications (Rota), 103
Encyclopedia of Mathematics Education
    (Grinstein and Lipsey), 100
Encyclopedia of Optimization (Floudas
    and Padalos), 98
Encyclopedia of Physics (Lerner and
    Trigg), 102
Encyclopedia of Statistical Sciences
    (Kotz, Johnson, and Reed), 101
Encyclopedia of Statistical Sciences.
    Update (Kotz, Reed, and Banks),
    102
Encyclopedic Dictionary of Mathematics
    (Itô), 88, 101
Encyklopädie der Mathematischen
    Wissenschaften mit Einschluss
    ihrer Anwendungen, 98
Engesser, Hermann, 85
Engineering Formulas (Gieck and
    Gieck), 122
Engineering Mathematics Handbook
    (Tuma and Walsh), 138
English-French-Spanish-Russian
    Systematic Glossary of the
    Terminology of Statistical
    Methods (Paenson), 94
English-Greek Dictionary of Pure and
    Applied Mathematics with Greek
    and English Appendices
    (Kolaitis), 90
English-Greek Mathematical Dictionary
    (Tzelekis), 97
English-Russian Dictionary of the Math-
    ematical Sciences (Aleksandrov),
    79
Environmetrics, 61
Enzensberger, Hans Magnus, 199
Episodes in the Mathematics of
    Medieval Islam (Berggren), 174
E-Print Archive. See arXiv.org
"E-prints Intersect the Digital Library:
    Inside the Los Alamos arXiv"
    (Luce), 290
Erdelyi, A., 108
Erdös, Paul, 236

Erdös Number Project, 155
Ergebnisse der Mathematik und ihrer
    Grenzgebiete. 3 Folge, 275
Ergodic Theory and Dynamical
    Systems, 61
ERIC, Educational Resources Information
    Center, 38
Eric Weisstein's World of Mathematics
    (MathWorld) (Weisstein), 104
Eric Weisstein's World of Scientific
    Biography (Weisstein and Wolfram
    Research), 156
Ershov, Yu. L., 121
ESAIM: Control, Optimisation and
    Calculus of Variations, 61
ESAIM: Probability and Statistics, 61
Essays in Humanistic Mathematics
    (White), 208
Essays in the History of Mathematics
    (Schlissel), 187
e: The Story of a Number (Maor), 185
Euclid: The Creation of Mathematics
    (Artmann), 165
EULER, 39
Euler, Leonhard, 237
"EULER–A Real Virtual Library for
    Mathematics" (Jost and Becker),
    290
Euler: The Master of Us All (Dunham),
    167
European Journal of Combinatorics, 61
European Mathematical Society, 41, 282
Everitt, Brian, 133
Everitt, B. S., 85, 120
Eves, Howard, 178
Evolution in Age-Structured Populations
    (Charlesworth), 216
Ewing, John, 7, 13, 14, 178, 199, 287,
    288
Ewing, Richard E., 199
The Exact Sciences in Antiquity
    (Neugebauer), 186
Exact Solutions of Relativistic Wave
    Equations (Bagrov and Gitman),
    114
Expanded Academic ASAP (Gale Group),
    39
Experimental Mathematics, 61

Extrait du Bulletin signalétique. Histoire des sciences et des techniques, 156

Fachlexikon ABC Mathematik (Gellert, et al.), 99
Factorizations of $b^n \pm 1$, b = 2, 3, 5, 6, 7, 10, 11, 12 up to High Powers (Brillhart, et al.), 108
The Facts on File Dictionary of Mathematics (Daintith and Clark), 83
Faddeev, L. D., 238
Fadiman, Clifton, 200
Famous Problems in the History of Mathematics, 179
Fanchi, John R., 121
Fang, Joong, 20
Fantasia Mathematica (Fadiman), 200
Fauvel, John, 20, 156, 179
Featured Reviews in Mathematical Reviews, 1995–1996 and 1997–1999 (AMS), 46
Featured Reviews in Mathematical Reviews (AMS), 46
Federico, P. J., 179
Fedorova, R. M. A., 110
Ferguson, Claire, 200
Feys, R., 85, 87
Fibonacci Quarterly, 61
Field, J. V., 180
Fields Institute Communications, 276
Fields Institute Monographs, 276
Fields Medallists' Lectures (Atiyah and Iagolnitzer), 192
Field Theory Handbook (Moon and Spencer), 130
Fifty Challenging Problems in Probability with Solutions (Mosteller), 213
Figa, Jan, 289
Fillmore, Peter A., 121
Financial Calculus: An Introduction to Derivative Pricing (Baxter and Rennie), 214
Finch, Steven, 122
Fine, Benjamin, 200
Finite Fields and Their Applications, 61

First European Congress of Mathematics, Paris, July 6–10, 1992, 287
"First Occurrence of Common Terms in Mathematical Statistics" (David), 83
Fischer, Gerd, 200
Fisher, R. A., 238
Fisher, Ronald Aylmer, 108
Fitch, F. B., 85, 87
Five Golden Rules: Great Theories of 20th-Century Mathematics and Why They Matter (Casti), 194
Five Hundred Mathematical Challenges (Barbeau, Klamkin, and Moser), 209
Five More Golden Rules: Knots, Codes, Chaos and Other Great Theories of 20th-Century Mathematics (Casti), 194
Flatland: A Romance of Many Dimensions (Abbott), 192
Fletcher, Alan, 108
Flood, Raymond, 179
Floudas, Christodoulos A., 98, 122
Fomenko, Anatolii T., 201
Force and Geometry in Newton's Principia (Gandt), 180
Forsythe, George Elmer, 23
40 Years in Mathematical Physics (Faddeev), 238
Forum Mathematicum, 61
Fosmire, Michael, 289
Fourier Analysis and Applications: Filtering, Numerical Computation, Wavelets (Gasquet and Witomski), 217
Four Lectures on Wave Mechanics (Schrödinger), 255
Fowler, Kristine K., 20, 289
Fractals, Chaos, Power Laws: Minutes from an Infinite Paradise (Schroeder), 207
Fractals: A User's Guide for the Natural Sciences (Hastings and Sugihara), 125
Franks, John, 14
Free Online Scholarship Newsletter. See *SPARC Open Access Newsletter*
"Free Publishing" (Kolman), 15

"Free Scholarly Electronic Journals: An Annotated Webliography" (Fosmire and Young), 289
"Free Scholarly Electronic Journals: How Good Are They?" (Fosmire and Yu), 289
Frege, Gottlob, 238
French Mathematical Seminars: A Union List (Anderson), 21
Freund, John E., 86
Friberg, Jöran, 156
Fried, E., 99
Friedberger, W. F., 86
Friedrichs, Kurt Otto, 238
From Aristarchus to Diophantus (Heath), 181
From Erdös to Kiev: Problems of Olympiad Caliber (Honsberger), 212
From Error-Correcting Codes Through Sphere Packings to Simple Groups (Thompson), 189
From Five Fingers to Infinity: A Journey Through the History of Mathematics (Swetz), 188
From One to Zero (Ifrah), 181
From Thales to Euclid (Heath), 181
"From the AMS Secretary: Report of the Executive Director, State of the AMS, 2003" (AMS), 14
From Zero to Infinity: What Makes Numbers Interesting (Reid), 206
Frontiers in Applied Mathematics, 276
Froumentin, Max, 289
Fuchs, Jürgen, 217
Führer durch did Mathematische Literatur (Müller), 21
Functional Analysis and its Applications, 61
Functional Equations and Modelling in Science and Engineering (Castillo and Ruiz-Cobo), 215
Fundamentals of Mathematics (Behnke), 98
The Fundamental Theorem of Algebra (Fine and Rosenberger), 200
Fundamenta Mathematicae, 61
Funktsional'nyi Analiz i ego Prilozheniia. *See* **Functional Analysis and its Applications**
Furman University, 122
Future of Mathematical Communication, 5, 6
"The Future of Scientific Journals" (Schaffner), 16
Fuzzy Sets and Applications: Selected Papers by L. A. Zadeh (Zadeh), 262
Fuzzy Systems Theory and Its Applications (Terano, Asai, and Sugeno), 223

Gaffney, Matthew P., 23
Galca, Riazvan, 209
Gale Group, 39
Gallarati, Dionisio, 239
Gallica; La Bibliothèque Numérique [Bibliothèque Nationale de France], 9, 42, 265
Gallo, Philip S., Jr., 129
Games, Gods, and Gambling: The Origins and History of Probability and Statistical Ideas from the Earliest Times to the Newtonian Era (David), 177
Gamkrelidze, R. V., 99
Gander, Walter, 224
Gandt, François de, 180
Gani, J., 167
Garciadiego, Alejandro R., 167
García Rodríquez, Mariano, 86
Gardiner, C. W., 122
Gardiner, Toni, 210
Gårding, Lars, 167
Gardner, Martin, 210, 211, 217
Gardner, Mike, 290
Garrity, Thomas A., 201
Gasquet, C., 217
GDZ (Göttinger Digitalisierungs-Zentrum) (SUB Göttingen), 9, 42, 265, 266
Gelfand, Izrail M., 239
Gellert, Walter, 99
The Genesis of the Abstract Group Concept (Wussing), 189
Geometriae Dedicata, 61

The Geometrical Foundation of Natural Structure: A Source Book of Design (Williams), 139
Geometric and Functional Analysis, 61
Geometry and Combinatorics: Selected Works of J. J. Seidel (Seidel), 255
Geometry and Physics (Andresen, et al.), 213
Geometry and Topology, 61
The Geometry of Minkowski Spacetime: An Introduction to the Mathematics of the Special Theory of Relativity (Naber), 221
The Geometry of Spacetime: An Introduction to Special and General Relativity (Callahan), 215
George, Michel, 81
George Green: Mathematician and Physicist 1793–1841: The Background to his Life and Work (Cannell), 166
Gerber, Hans U., 217
German-English Mathematical Vocabulary (Macintyre and Witte), 92
German-English Mathematics Dictionary (Hyman), 88
Gesammelte Abhandlungen, Collected Papers/Emmy Noether (Noether), 250
Gesammelte Abhandlungen, Collected Papers (Hirzebruch), 242
Gesammelte Abhandlungen. Collected Papers (Krull), 244
Gesammelte Abhandlungen (Hilbert), 241
Gesammelte Abhandlungen mathematischen und philosophischen Inhalts, mit erläuternden Anmerkungen sowie mit Ergänzungen aus dem Briefwechsel Cantor-Dedekind (Cantor), 234
Gesammelte Abhandlungen (Minkowski), 249
Gesammelte mathematische Abhandlungen (Schläfli), 254

Gesammelte Mathematische Abhandlungen (Schwarz), 255
Gesammelte mathematische Werke, wissenschaftlicher Nachlass und Nachtrage (Riemann), 253
Gesammelte Werke (Hesse), 241
Gesammelte Werke (Steiner), 257
Gheorghita, Stefan, 86
Ghosh, B. K., 122
Gibbs, G. Ian, 86
Gieck, Kurt, 122
Gieck, Reiner, 122
Gilbert, George T., 211
Gilbert, John D., 14
Gillispie, Charles Coulston, 168
Gillman, Leonard, 141
Ginsparg, Paul, 5, 6
Gitman, D. M., 114
Glasgow Mathematical Journal, 62
G. Lejeune Dirichlet's Werke (Lejeune Dirichlet), 246
Glenn, J. A., 86
Glossary of the Mathematical and Computing Sciences (Chinese-English) (Loh, et al.), 92
Glossary of the Mathematical and Computing Sciences (English-Chinese) (Loh, et al.), 92
Glushko, M. M., 87
Glynn, Jerry, 225
Gödel, Kurt, 239
Golden Years of Moscow Mathematics (Zdravkovska and Duren), 189
Goldman, Jay R., 180
Golomb, Solomon W., 211
Goodbye Descartes: The End of Logic and the Search for a New Cosmology (Devlin), 196
Goodman, David, 289
Goodman, Jacob E., 123
Google.com, 52
"Google.com" (McMahon), 290
Google Web Page Translation, 87
Goossens, Michael, 123
Göpfert, Alfred, 99
Gottwald, Siegfried, 157
Gould, S. H., 87, 123
Gourman, Jack, 147

The Gourman Report: A Rating of Graduate and Professional Programs in American and International Universities (Gourman), 147
Gradshteyn, I. S., 108–9
Graduate Studies in Mathematics, 276
Graduate Texts in Mathematics, 276
Graham, R. L., 124
Graphs and Combinatorics, 62
Grattan-Guinness, I., 157
Grätzer, George, 225
Gray, Jeremy, 179
Gray, John, 225
Gray, Theodore, 225
Great Moments in Mathematics (After 1650) (Eves), 178
Great Moments in Mathematics (Before 1650) (Eves), 178
Greek Mathematical Thought and the Origin of Algebra (Klein), 183
Green, George, 239
Green Book: 100 Practice Problems for Undergraduate Mathematics Competitions (Hardy and Williams), 212
The Green Book of Mathematical Problems (Hardy and Williams), 212
Greenstein, Carol, 87
Greenwood, Joseph Arthur, 109
Griffiths, David F., 225
Griffor, Edward R., 124
Griliches, Zvi, 124
Grinstein, Louise S., 22, 39, 100, 157
Gross, Kenneth I., 199
Grötschel, M., 124
Group Theory and Physics (Sternberg), 222
Growney, JoAnne, 201
Gruber, P. M., 124
Grundlehren der Mathematischen Wissenschaften, 276
Grundzüge der Mathematik (Behnke), 98
Gudder, Stanley, 201
Guida allo Studio della Storia delle Matematiche: Generalit'a Didattica, Bibliografia.
Appendice: Questioni Storiche Concernenti le Scienze Esatte (Loria), 21, 159
Guidebook to Departments in the Mathematical Sciences in the United States and Canada, 147
Guide to Available Mathematical Software [GAMS] (National Institute of Standards and Technology), 131
A Guide to Library Service in Mathematics: The Non-Trivial Mathematics Librarian (Anderson and Pausch), 19, 192
Guide to Mathematical Tables (Lebedev and Fedorova), 110
A Guide to Newton's Principa (Cohen), 205
Guide to Statistical Methods and to the Pertinent Literature (Sachs), 21
Guide to Tables in Mathematical Statistics (Greenwood and Hartley), 109
Guide to the Literature of Mathematics and Physics Including Related Works on Engineering Science (Parke), 21
Guide to the Literature of Mathematics Today (Fang), 20
Guillemin, Victor, 217
Guy, Richard K., 193, 211

Haight, William T., II, 82
Hairer, E., 180
Hald, Anders, 180, 181
Hall, Philip, 239
Halmos, Paul, 212
Halmos, Paul R., 168
Halmos, P. R., 240
Hamilton, William Rowan, 240
Handbook and Atlas of Curves (Shikin), 136
Handbook for Academic Authors (Luey), 142
Handbook for Matrix Computations (Coleman and Van Loan), 119
Handbook of Algebra (Hazewinkel), 125

Handbook of Algebraic Topology
(James), 126
Handbook of Analytic-Computational Methods in Applied Mathematics
(Anastassiou), 113
Handbook of Applicable Mathematics
(Ledermann), 128
Handbook of Boolean Algebras (Monk and Bonnet), 130
Handbook of Brownian Motion: Facts and Formulae (Borodin and Salminen), 116
Handbook of Categorical Algebra
(Borceux), 116
Handbook of Combinatorial Optimization (Du and Paradalos), 121
Handbook of Combinatorial Optimization: Supplement. Volume A (Du and Paradalos), 121
Handbook of Combinatorics (Graham, Grötschel, and Lovász), 124
Handbook of Complex Variables
(Krantz), 127
Handbook of Computability Theory
(Griffor), 124
Handbook of Computational Economics
(Amman, Kendrick, and Rust), 113
Handbook of Computational Geometry
(Sack and Urrutia), 135
Handbook of Computer Vision Algorithms in Image Algebra
(Ritter and Wilson), 135
Handbook of Convex Geometry
(Gruber and Wills), 124
Handbook of Differential Equations
(Zwillinger), 140
Handbook of Differential Geometry
(Dillen and Verstraelen), 120
Handbook of Discrete and Combinatorial Mathematics (Rosen), 135
Handbook of Discrete and Computational Geometry (Goodman and O'Rourke), 123
Handbook of Econometrics (Griliches and Intriligator), 124
Handbook of Fourier Theorems
(Champeney), 118

Handbook of Function and Generalized Function Transformations
(Zayed), 140
Handbook of Global Optimization
(Horst and Pardalos), 125
A Handbook of Integer Sequences
(Sloane), 136
Handbook of Integral Equations
(Polianin and Manzhirov), 132
Handbook of Integral Transforms of Higher Transcendental Functions (Marichev), 129
Handbook of Integration (Zwillinger), 140
Handbook of Mathematical Economics
(Arrow and Intriligator), 113
Handbook of Mathematical Economics
(Hildenbrand and Sonnenschein). See **Handbook of Mathematical Economics** (Arrow and Intriligator)
Handbook of Mathematical Formulas and Integrals (Jeffrey), 126
Handbook of Mathematical Formulas
(Bartsch), 115
Handbook of Mathematical Functions with Formulas, Graphs, and Mathematical Tables
(Abramowitz and Stegun), 112, 114, 131
Handbook of Mathematical Logic
(Barwise, et al.), 115, 117
Handbook of Mathematical Tables, 116
Handbook of Mathematical Tables and Formulas (Burington), 117
Handbook of Mathematics and Computational Science (Harris and Stöcker), 124
Handbook of Mathematics (Bronshtein and Semendiaev), 116
Handbook of Mathematics (Kuipers and Timman), 127
Handbook of Multivalued Analysis (Hu and Papageorgiou), 126
Handbook of Number Theory (Mitrinovic, Sándor, and Crstici), 130
Handbook of Numerical Analysis
(Ciarlet and Lions), 118

Handbook of Numerical and Statistical Techniques with Examples Mainly from the Life Sciences (Pollard), 132
Handbook of Parametric and Nonparametric Statistical Procedures (Sheskin), 136
Handbook of Probability and Statistics with Tables (Burington and May), 117
Handbook of Proof Theory (Buss), 117
Handbook of Random Number Generation and Testing with TESTRAND Computer Code (Dudewicz and Ralley), 121
Handbook of Recursive Mathematics (Ershov), 121
Handbook of Sequential Analysis (Ghosh and Sen), 122
Handbook of Set-Theoretical Topology (Kunen and Vaughan), 127
Handbook of Splines (Micula and Micula), 130
A Handbook of Statistical Analyses Using SAS (Der and Everitt), 120
A Handbook of Statistical Analyses Using Stata (Rabe-Hesketh and Everitt), 133
Handbook of Statistical Distributions (Patel, Kapadia, and Owen), 132
Handbook of Statistical Genetics (Balding, Bishop, and Cannings), 115
Handbook of Statistical Methods for Engineers and Scientists (Wadsworth), 139
Handbook of Statistics (Rao), 133
Handbook of Stochastic Methods for Physics, Chemistry, and the Natural Sciences (Gardiner), 122
Handbook of Tableau Methods (D'Agostino, et al.), 120
Handbook of Tables for Mathematics, 116
Handbook of Tables for Order Statistics from Lognormal Distributions, With Applications (Balakrishnan and Chen), 107

Handbook of Test Problems in Local and Global Optimization (Floudas, et al.), 122
Handbook of the History of General Topology (Aull and Lowen), 153
Handbook of the Logistic Distribution (Balakrishnan), 114
Handbook of the Normal Distribution (Patel and Reed), 132
Handbook of Typography for the Mathematical Sciences (Krantz), 142
Handbook of Writing for the Mathematical Sciences (Higham), 142
Handbook on Splines for the User (Shikin and Plis), 136
Handbooks and Tables in Science and Technology (Powell), 26
Härdle, W., 124
Hardy, G. H., 240
Hardy, Kenneth, 212
Harish-Chandra, 240
Harish-Chandra, Collected Papers (Harish-Chandra), 240
Harnack, Andrew, 141
Harnad, Steven, 7
Harpaz, Amos, 218
The Harper Collins Dictionary of Mathematics (Borowski and Borwein), 81
The Harper Collins Dictionary of Statistics (Porkess), 95
Harris, John W., 124
Harter, H. Leon, 23, 109
Hartley, H. O., 109, 111
Hasse, Helmut, 241
Hassler Whitney: Collected Papers (Whitney), 261
Hastings, Alan, 218
Hastings, Harold M., 125
Hayes, Nancy, 289
Hazewinkel, M., 100, 125
Heath, Sir Thomas, 181
Heaviside, Oliver, 218
Heck, André, 225
Helaman Ferguson: Mathematics in Stone and Bronze (Ferguson), 200

HEP Libraries Webzine, 293
Herland, Leo Joseph, 87
Hermann Weyl, 1885–1985: Centenary Lectures Delivered by C. N. Yan, R. Penrose, A. Borel at the ETH Zürich (Chandrasekharan), 166
Herod, James V., 224
Hersh, Reuben, 196
Herstein, I. N., 201
Herz-Fischler, Roger, 181
Hesse, Ludwig Otto, 241
Heyde, C. C., 168
Higgins, John C., 194
Higgins, Peter M., 201
Higham, Desmond J., 225
Higham, Nicholas J., 142
The Higher Calculus: A History of Real and Complex Analysis from Euler to Weierstrass (Bottazzini), 175
Hilbert, David, 241
Hilbert-Courant (Reid), 171
Hildebrandt, Stefan, 201
Hildenbrand, Werner, 125
Hill, Cherie Madarash, 289
Hill, George William, 241
Hill, J. B., 289
Hille, Einar, 241
Hilton, Peter J., 201, 202, 218
Hindawi, 266
Hirzebruch, Friedrich, 202, 242
Historia Mathematica, 62
The Historical Development of the Calculus (Edwards), 178
A History of Algorithms: From the Pebble to the Microchip (Chabert), 176
A History of Complex Dynamics: From Schröder to Fatou and Julia (Alexander), 173
A History of Greek Mathematics (Heath), 181
A History of Inverse Probability: From Thomas Bayes to Karl Pearson (Dale), 177
A History of Mathematical Notations (Cajori), 176
A History of Mathematical Statistics from 1750 to 1930 (Hald), 180

History of Mathematics, 157
History of Mathematics, 276
The History of Mathematics: An Introduction (Burton), 175
A History of Mathematics: An Introduction (Katz), 182
The History of Mathematics: A Reader (Fauvel and Gray), 179
A History of Mathematics (Cajori), 176
History of Mathematics from Antiquity to the Present: A Selective Annotated Bibliography (Dauben), 22
The History of Mathematics from Antiquity to the Present: A Selective Bibliography (Dauben), 155
History of Mathematics (Smith), 187
The History of Mathematics (Wilkins), 163
The History of Modern Mathematics: Proceedings of the Symposium on the History of Modern Mathematics, Vassar College, Poughkeepsie, New York, June 20–24, 1988 (Rowe, McCleary, and Knobloch), 187
A History of Probability and Statistics and their Applications before 1750 (Hald), 181
History of Science, Technology, and Medicine, 157
History of Statistics, Their Development and Progress in Many Countries (Koren), 20, 183
The History of Statistics: The Measurement of Uncertainty Before 1900 (Stigler), 187
"History of the Banach Space Archive and Implications for Electronic Archives of Publications" (Alspach), 12
A History of the Calculus and Its Conceptual Development (Boyer), 175
A History of the Calculus of Variations in the Eighteenth Century (Woodhouse), 189

A History of the Mathematical Theory
 of Probability from the Time of
 Pascal to that of Laplace
 (Todhunter), 189
History of Topology (James), 181
A History of Vector Analysis: The
 Evolution of the Idea of a
 Vectorial System (Crowe), 177
Hobson, M. P., 221
Hoffman, Paul, 168, 202
Hoffmann, Ludwig, 87
Hollingdale, Stuart, 168
Holton, Derek, 201
Honda, Shojo, 24
Honsberger, Ross, 202, 212
Hoppensteadt, Frank C., 218
Hormigón, Mariano, 76
Horn, Carol, 87
Horst, Reiner, 125
Houston Journal of Mathematics, 62
Howison, Sam, 223
*How Many? A Dictionary of Units of
 Measurement* (Rowlett), 95
How to Find Out in Mathematics
 (Pemberton), 21
**How to Write and Publish a Scientific
 Paper** (Day), 141
How to Write Mathematics (Steenrod), 143
Høyrup, Else, 24
Hrebícek, Jirí, 224
Hsü, Pao-Lu, 242
Hu, Shouchuan, 126
Hua, Loo-Keng, 242
Hughes, Thomas J. R., 220
Hurt, Charlie Deuel, 20
**Huygens and Barrow, Newton and
 Hook: Pioneers in Mathematical
 Analysis and Catastrophe
 Theory from Evolvents to
 Quasicrystals** (Arnol'd), 164
Hyman, Charles, 88

Iaglom, A. M., 202
Iaglom, I. M., 202
Iagolnitzer, Daniel, 192
IAS/Park City Mathematics Series, 276
Ibragimov, N. H., 126
"The Identification of Authors in the
 Mathematical Reviews Database"
 (TePaske-King and Richert), 291
Ifrah, Georges, 181
I Have a Photographic Memory (Halmos),
 168
I. J. Schoenberg: Selected Papers
 (Schoenberg), 255
Ilgauds, Hans Joachim, 157
Illinois Journal of Mathematics, 62
IMA Journal of Applied Mathematics, 62
IMA Journal of Numerical Analysis, 62
"Impact of a Digital Archive (JSTOR) on
 Print Collection Use" (Seeds), 291
"The Impact of Electronic Publication on
 Scholarly Journals" (Franks), 14
"Impact of Remote Library Storage on
 Information Consumers: 'Sophie's
 Choice'?" (Seeds), 291
Indagationes Mathematicae. New Series,
 62
"In Defense of Caution" (Ewing), 14
An Index of Mathematical Tables
 (Fletcher), 108
**Index to Mathematical Problems,
 1980–1984** (Rabinowitz), 48
**Index to Mathematical Problems,
 1975–1979** (Rabinowitz and
 Bowron), 48
Index to Statistics and Probability
 (Tukey and Ross), 50
**Index to Translations Selected by the
 American Mathematical Society**, 40
Indiana University Mathematics Journal,
 62
Indian Journal of Pure and Mathematics,
 62
In Eve's Circles (Anthony), 192
**Infinite Dimensional Analysis, Quantum
 Probability and Related Topics**, 62
**Infinity and the Mind: The Science and
 Philosophy of the Infinite**
 (Rucker), 207
Information and Computation, 62
"Information Seeking Behavior of
 Scientists in the Electronic
 Information Age: Astronomers,
 Chemists, Mathematicians, and
 Physicists" (Brown), 288

Information Sources in Science and Technology (Hurt), 20
Ingenta, 8, 33, 40
Inkeri, Kustaa, 242
Innumeracy: Mathematical Illiteracy and Its Consequences (Paulos), 205
Insights of Genius: Imagery and Creativity in Science and Art (Miller), 204
INSPEC (Institution of Electrical Engineers), 40
Institut des Hautes Études Scientifiques. Publications Mathématiques, 62
Institute for Scientific Information, 37
Institute of Mathematical Statistics, 36, 282
Institute of Mathematical Statistics Lecture Notes–Monograph Series, 276
Institution of Electrical Engineers, 40
Insurance: Mathematics & Economics, 62
Integral Equations and Operator Theory, 62
Integrals and Series (Prudnikov, Brychkov, and Marichev), 133
Integral Transforms and Special Functions, 62
Integraly i Riady (Prudnikov, Brychkov, and Marichev), 133
Interactive Statistical Calculation Pages, 139
Inter-American Statistical Institute, 88
Interdisciplinary Applied Mathematics, 276
International Dictionary of Applied Mathematics (Friedberger), 86
International Encyclopedia of Statistics (Kruskal and Tanur), 102
International Encyclopedia of the Social Sciences, 102
International Journal of Algebra and Computation, 62
International Journal of Computational Geometry & Applications, 63
International Journal of Game Theory, 63
International Journal of Mathematics, 63
International Mathematical Congresses: An Illustrated History (Albers, Alexanderson, and Reid), 164
International Mathematical Olympiads, 1978–1985 and Forty Supplementary Problems (Klamkin), 212
International Mathematical Union, 283
International Mathematical Union, Committee on Electronic Information Communication, 14
International Mathematics Research Notices, 63
International Statistical Institute, 49, 88, 283
International Statistical Review, 63
Internet Archive Wayback Machine, 52
Internet Publishing and Beyond: The Economics of Digital Information and Intellectual Property (Kahin and Varian), 14
Intersections (Growney), 201
In the Wake of Chaos: Unpredictable Order in Dynamical Systems (Kellert), 182
Intriligator, Michael D., 113, 124
Introduction to Applied Mathematics (Strang), 223
An Introduction to Catastrophe Theory (Saunders), 222
Introduction to Maple (Heck), 225
An Introduction to Mathematical Cosmology (Islam), 218
Introduction to Mechanics and Symmetry: A Basic Exposition of Classical Mechanical Systems (Marsden and Ratiu), 220
Introduction to Modern Statistical Mechanics (Chandler), 216
An Introduction to the Mathematics of Biology: With Computer Algebra Models (Yeargers, Shonkweiler, and Herod), 224
Introduction to the Theory of Error-Correcting Codes (Pless), 221
Introduction to Transcendental Numbers (Lang), 245

Inventiones Mathematicae, 43, 63
The Invention of Infinity: Mathematics and Art in the Renaissance (Field), 180
Invitation to Mathematics (Jacobs), 202
ISI Glossary of Statistical Terms (International Statistical Institute), 88
Isis Current Bibliography of the History of Science, 158
ISI Web of Science (Thomson ISI), 40–41, 41–42
Islam, J. N., 218
Islands of Truth: A Mathematical Mystery Cruise (Peterson), 206
Israel Journal of Mathematics, 63
Issues in Science & Technology Librarianship, 293
Italian Algebraic Geometry Between the Two World Wars (Brigaglia and Ciliberto), 175
Itô, Kiyosi, 88, 101, 242
Iwanami Sugaku Jiten (Nihon Sugakkai Henshu), 102
Izvestiya. Mathematics, 63

Jack Carl Kiefer Collected Papers (Kiefer), 243
Jackson, Allyn, 14, 289
Jackson, J. Edward, 126
Jacobi, C. G. J., 242
Jacobs, Harold R., 202
Jacobs, Konrad, 202
Jacobson, Nathan, 243
Jacques Hadamard: A Universal Mathematician (Maz'ya and Shaposhnikova), 170
Jaguszewski, Janice M., 147
Jahrbuch Project
Jahrbuch Project, Electronic Research Archive for Mathematics (ERAM) (European Mathematical Society), 10, 41, 51, 158, 266
Jahrbuch über die Fortschritte der Mathematik, 42, 50
James, I. M., 126, 181
James, Robert C., 88
Jansen, Christoph, 126

Japan Journal of Industrial and Applied Mathematics, 63
Jeffrey, Alan, 126
Jerison, David, 203
Jerrard, H. G., 88
Jesseph, Douglas, 182
Johnson, Norman L., 101, 169, 183
John von Neumann and the Origins of Modern Computing (Aspray), 165
Joint Statistical Papers of J. Neyman and E. S. Pearson (Neyman and Pearson), 250
Joo Ok Koo, 19
Jordanian Committee for Arabisation, Ministry of Education, Amman, 89
Joseph, Anthony, 218
Joseph, George Gheverghese, 182
Joseph Liouville 1809–1882: Master of Pure and Applied Mathematics (Lutzen), 169
Joshi, Sharadchandrea W., 26
Jost, Michael, 289, 291
Journal d'Analyse Mathematique, 63
Journal de Mathématiques Pures et Appliquées. Neuviéme Serie, 65
Journal des Mathématiques Pures et Appliquées, 42
Journal für die Reine und Angewandte Mathematik, 66
Journal of Algebra, 63
Journal of Algebraic Combinatorics, 63
Journal of Algebraic Geometry, 63
Journal of Algorithms, 63
Journal of Applied Probability, 64
Journal of Applied Statistics, 64
Journal of Approximation Theory, 64
Journal of Combinatorial Designs, 64
Journal of Combinatorial Theory. Series A, 64
Journal of Combinatorial Theory. Series B, 64
Journal of Complexity, 64
Journal of Computational Analysis and Applications, 64
Journal of Computational and Applied Mathematics, 64
Journal of Computational and Graphical Statistics, 64

Journal of Computational Mathematics, 64
Journal of Convex Analysis, 64
Journal of Difference Equations and Applications, 64
Journal of Differential Equations, 64
Journal of Differential Geometry, 64
Journal of Electronic Publishing, 293
Journal of Fourier Analysis and Applications, 65
Journal of Functional Analysis, 65
Journal of Geometry and Physics, 65
Journal of Global Optimization, 65
Journal of Graph Theory, 65
Journal of Group Theory, 65
Journal of Inequalities and Applications, 65
Journal of Knot Theory and its Ramifications, 65
Journal of Lie Theory, 65
Journal of Mathematical Analysis and Applications, 65
Journal of Mathematical Economics, 65
Journal of Mathematical Physics, 65
Journal of Mathematics of Kyoto University, 65
Journal of Multivariate Analysis, 66
Journal of Nonlinear Mathematical Physics, 66
Journal of Nonparametric Statistics, 66
Journal of Number Theory, 66
Journal of Operator Theory, 66
Journal of Optimization Theory and Applications, 66
Journal of Pure and Applied Algebra, 66
Journal of Recreational Mathematics, 66
Journal of Statistical Computation and Simulation, 66
Journal of Statistical Planning and Inference, 66
Journal of Statistics Education, 4, 66
Journal of Symbolic Computation, 67
Journal of Symbolic Logic, 67
Journal of the American Mathematical Society, 63
Journal of the American Statistical Association, 63
Journal of the Australian Mathematical Society. Series A, Pure Mathematics and Statistics, 64
Journal of the Australian Mathematical Society. Series B, Applied Mathematics, 64
Journal of the European Mathematical Society, 65
Journal of the London Mathematical Society. Second Series, 65
Journal of the Mathematical Society of Japan, 65
Journal of Theoretical Probability, 67
Journal of the Royal Statistical Society. Series A. Statistics in Society, 66
Journal of the Royal Statistical Society. Series B. Statistical Methodology, 66
Journal of the Royal Statistical Society. Series C. Applied Statistics, 66
Journal of the Royal Statistical Society. Series D. The Statistican, 66
Journal of Time Series Analysis, 67
Journal of Undergraduate Mathematics, 67
Journal Price Survey (AMS), 292
Journal Value Project (University of Wisconsin–Madison Libraries), 292
Journey Through Genius: The Great Theorems of Mathematics (Dunham), 198
Joyner, David, 182
The Joy of TeX: A Gourmet Guide to Typesetting with the AMS-TeX Macro Package (Spivak), 137
JSTOR, 9, 43, 158, 266
Judgment Under Uncertainty: Heuristics and Biases (Kahneman, Slovic, and Tversky), 203
Julia: A Life in Mathematics (Reid), 171
Jungles of Randomness: A Mathematical Safari (Peterson), 206

Kac, Mark, 182, 203, 243
Kahin, Brian, 14
Kahneman, Daniel, 203

Kaleidoscopes: Selected Writings of H. S. M. Coxeter (Coxeter), 235
Kaluza, Roman, 169
Kanigel, Robert, 169
Kapadia, C. H., 132
Kaplansky, I., 201
Kapur, J. N., 158
Karatzas, Ioannis, 219
Karger, Adolf, 219
Karpinski, Louis Charles, 24
Karush, William, 89
Katz, Victor J., 182
Kaufmann-Buehler, Walter, 290
Keener, James, 219
Keith, Sandra, 203
Kellert, Stephen H., 182
Kellison, Stephen G., 219
Kendall, Maurice, 25, 243
Kendrick, David A., 113
Kennedy, Hubert C., 169
Kenschaft, Patricia Clark, 203
Kerner, Otto, 89
Kessinger, Pam, 290
Key Dates in Number Theory History: From 10,529 B. C. to the Present (Spencer), 162
Keys to Infinity (Pickover), 206
Kiefer, Jack Carl, 243
The Kingdom of Infinite Number: A Field Guide (Bunch), 194
Kirby, Rob, 14, 292
"Kirby Letter to Elsevier Officers" (Kirby), 14
Klaften, E. B., 89
Klamkin, Murray S., 209, 212
Klein, Felix, 183
Klein, Jacob, 183
Kleine Duden-Mathematik (Engesser), 85
Kleine Enzyklopädie der Mathematik, 99
Kleppinger, Eugene, 141
Kline, Morris, 183, 203
Klinke, S., 124
Kluwer Online, 267
Kluwer Texts in the Mathematical Sciences, 276
Knobloch, Eberhard, 187

Knuth, Donald, 14, 142, 225, 226
Knuth letter to Editorial Board (Knuth), 14
Koblitz, Ann Hibner, 169
Kodaira, Kunihiko, 243
Kokoska, Stephen, 109, 112
Kolaitis, Memas, 90
Kolman, Michiel, 15
Kolmogorov, A. N., 244
Komatsu, Yusaku, 90
Koren, John, 20, 183
Korn, Granino Arthur, 127
Korn, Theresa M., 127
Kornegay, Chris, 90
Kotz, Samuel, 90, 101, 102, 169, 183
Koziol, James A., 127
Központi Statisztikai Hivatal, 90
Kramer, K., 91
Krantz, Stephen, 15
Krantz, Steven G., 91, 127, 142
Kreyszig, Erwin, 219
Krieger, Martin H., 219
Kristick, Laurel, 290
Kronecker, Leopold, 244
Krull, Wolfgang, 244
Krusemeyer, Mark I., 211
Kruskal, William H., 102
Krzywicki, André, 217
K-Theory, 67
Kuipers, A. H., 95
Kuipers, L., 127
Kunen, Kenneth, 127
Kuperberg, Greg, 15
Kurtz, Albert K., 91
Kuwait Science Encyclopedia: Mathematics (Dannan, et al.), 98
Kyosi Itô: Selected Papers (Itô), 242

Laboratories in Mathematical Experimentation: A Bridge to Higher Mathematics (Davidoff, et al.), 196
Laguerre, E., 244
Lamport, Leslie, 127
Lancaster, Henry Oliver, 25
Lang, Serge, 204, 245
The Language of Mathematics: Making the Invisible Visible (Devlin), 197
LAPACK Users' Guide (Anderson, et al.), 113

Lapedes, Daniel, 91
Larrabee, Tracy, 142
Larsen, Loren C., 211
The Last Recreations: Hydras, Eggs, and Other Mathematical Recreations (Gardner), 210
LaTeX: A Documentation Preparation System User's Guide and Reference Manual (Lamport), 127
The LaTeX Companion (Goossens, Mittelbach, and Samarin), 123
The LaTeX Companion (Mittelbach), 143
The LaTeX Graphics Companion: Illustrating Documents With TeX and Post-Script (Goossens, Rahtz, and Mittelbach), 123
The LaTeX Web Companion: Integrating TeX, HTML, and XML (Goossens and Rahtz), 123
Laubenbacher, Reinhard, 184
Lawler, Eugene L., 245
Lawrence, J. Dennis, 128
Leading Personalities in Statistical Sciences: From the Seventeenth Century to the Present (Johnson and Kotz), 169
Learned Publishing, 294
Learning LATeX (Griffiths and Higham), 225
Lebedev, Aleksandr Vasil'evich, 110
Lebedev, N. N., 220
Lecture Notes in Economics and Mathematical Systems, 276
Lecture Notes in Mathematics, 276
Lecture Notes in Pure and Applied Mathematics, 276
Lecture Notes in Statistics, 276
Lectures in the History of Mathematics (Bos), 175
Lectures on Number Theory (Lejeune Dirichlet), 184
Ledermann, Walter, 128
Lefschetz, S., 245
The Legacy of Norbert Wiener (Jerison, Singer, and Stroock), 203
Lehto, Olli, 184
Leibniz, G. W., 245
Lejeune Dirichlet, Peter Gustav, 184, 246
Lenski, Wolfgang, 25
Lenstra, J. K., 26
Leopold Kronecker's Werke (Kronecker), 244
Leray, Jean, 246
Lerner, Rita G., 102
Lesniewski, Stanislaw, 246
Letters in Mathematical Physics, 67
Levine, Norman, 111
Levy, Silvio, 15, 226
Lewis, T., 115
Lewisch, Ingrid, 91
Lexikon Bedeutender Mathematiker (Gottwald, Ilgauds, and Schlote), 157
Lexikon der Algebra (Eisenreich), 84
Lexikon der Optimierung (Göpfert), 99
Liang, Diana E., 76
Library Recommendations for Undergraduate Mathematics (Steen), 27, 191
LIBWEB; Library Servers via WWW (Dowling), 31
Lide, David R., 128
Life Insurance Mathematics (Gerber), 217
The Life of Isaac Newton (Westfall), 173
Life's Other Secret: The New Mathematics of the Living World (Stewart), 222
Life Table and Its Applications (Chiang), 108
Lifetime Data Analysis, 67
The Lighter Side of Mathematics (Guy and Woodrow), 211
Linda Hall Library Document Services, 33
Lindley, D. V., 110
Linear Algebra and its Applications, 67
Linear and Multilinear Algebra, 67
Links for Biographies (Association for Women in Mathematics), 153
Linton, Marigold, 129
Lions, J. L., 118
Lipsey, Sally I., 100
LISP-STAT: An Object-Oriented Environment for Statistical Computing and Dynamic Graphics (Tierney), 227

Littler, G. H., 86
Littlewood, J. E., 246
Littlewood's Miscellany (Bollobás), 193
Liu, John, 129
Loeb, Arthur L., 204
Loewner, Charles, 246
Logan, J. David, 220
A Logical Journey: From Gödel to Philosophy (Wang), 172
Loh, Shiu-chang, 92
London Mathematical Society, 283
London Mathematical Society Lecture Note Series, 276
London Mathematical Society Monographs. New Series, 276
London Mathematical Society Student Texts, 277
Longman Mathematics Handbook: The Language and Concepts of Mathematics Explained (Selkirk), 96
Loo-Keng Hua Selected Papers (Hua), 242
Lorentz, George G., 247
Loria, Gino, 21, 159
The Lost Notebook and Other Unpublished Papers (Ramanujan), 252
Lovász, L., 124
Lovett, D. R., 80
Lowen, R., 153
Luce, Richard E., 290
Luey, Beth, 142
Lure of the Integers (Roberts), 207
Lutzen, Jesper, 169
Lyons, Louis, 204

M2AN. Mathematical Modelling and Numerical Analysis, 67
MAA Notes, 277
MacColl, John, 290
Macfarlane, Alexander, 25
Macintyre, Sheila, 92
Mackerle, J., 129
Mackey, George, 184
Mac Lane, Saunders, 204, 247
MacLaurin, Colin, 247
MacMahon, Percy Alexander, 247

MacTutor History of Mathematics Archive (O'Connor and Robertson), 159
Maffioli, Francesco, 22
Magiros, Demetrios C., 247
Magnus, Wilhelm, 248
Mathematics for Physicists (Dennery and Krzywicki), 217
Mahoney, Michael Sean, 170
Maim, Donald G., 129
Makers of Mathematics (Hollingdale), 168
The Making of Statisticians (Gani), 167
Making TeX Work (Walsh), 227
Malaia Matematicheskaia Entsiklopediia (Fried, et al.), 99
Mandelbrot, Benoit B., 248
Mankiewicz, Richard, 184
A Manual for Authors of Mathematical Papers, 143
Manual for Translators of Mathematical Russian (Gould and Boas), 123
Manura, David, 110
Manuscripta Mathematica, 67
The Man Who Knew Infinity: A Life of the Genius Ramanujan (Kanigel), 169
The Man Who Loved Only Numbers: The Story of Paul Erdös and the Search for Mathematical Truth (Hoffman), 168
Manzhirov, Alexander, 132
Maor, Eli, 185
Maple: A Comprehensive Introduction (Nicolaides and Walkington), 226
The Maple Handbook: Maple V Release 4 (Redfern), 134
Maple V by Example (Abell and Braselton), 224
Marichev, O. I., 129, 133
Mark Kac: Probability, Number Theory, and Statistical Physics: Selected Papers (Kac), 243
Marsden, Jerrold E., 220
Martello, Silvano, 22
Martin, Clyde F., 199
Martin, George E., 213
Martingale Methods in Financial Modeling (Musiala and Rutkowski), 220

Masani, P. R., 170
Mastering Mathematica: Programming Methods and Applications (Gray), 225
MAST: Minimum Abbreviations of Serial Titles, Mathematics (Tompkins), 43
Matematicheskaia Entsiklopediia (Vinogradov), 100, 103, 104
Matematicheskie Terminy: Spravochnik (Aleksandrova), 79
Matematicheskie Zametki, 67
Matematicheskii Entsiklopedicheskii Slovar' (Prokhorov), 103
Matematicheskii Sbornik, 67
Matematiki Mekhaniki: Biograficheskii Spravochnik (Bogoliubov), 154
Materials for the History of Statistics (University of York Department of Mathematics), 163
MATH, 2
Math2.org, 110
Math Archives, 29
Math Archives: History of Mathematics, 159
Math Dictionary With Solutions (Kornegay), 90
The Mathemagician and Pied Puzzler: A Collection in Tribute to Martin Gardner (Berlekamp and Rogers), 209
Mathematica: A Practical Approach (Blachman), 224
The Mathematica Book (Wolfram), 139
The Mathematica Book (Wolfram), 139
Mathematica in Action (Wagon), 227
Mathematica in Education and Research, 67
"Mathematical Articles and Bottled Water" (Burdzy), 13
Mathematical Association of America, 283
Mathematical Atlas, 29
Mathematical Bioeconomics: The Optimal Management of Renewable Resources (Clark), 216
Mathematical Book Review Index, 1800–1940 (Grinstein), 39

The Mathematical Career of Pierre de Fermat (1601–1665) (Mahoney), 170
Mathematical Circus: More Puzzles, Games, Paradoxes, and Other Mathematical Entertainments from Scientific American (Gardner), 210
Mathematical Cranks (Dudley), 198
Mathematical Encounters of the Second Kind (David), 167
Mathematical Expeditions: Chronicles by the Explorers (Laubenbacher and Pengelley), 184
The Mathematical Experience (Davis and Hersh), 196
Mathematical Foundations of Elasticity (Marsden and Hughes), 220
Mathematical Function Handbook (Baker), 114
Mathematical Gems III (Honsberger), 202
Mathematical Handbook for Scientists and Engineers: Definitions, Theorems, and Formulas for Reference and Review (Korn and Korn), 127
Mathematical Handbook of Formulas and Tables (Liu and Spiegel), 129
Mathematical History of Division in Extreme and Mean Ratio (Herz-Fischler), 181
A Mathematical History of the Golden Number (Herz-Fischler), 181
Mathematical Impressions (Fomenko), 201
Mathematical Inequalities & Applications, 67
Mathematical Intelligencer, 48, 68
Mathematical Journals: An Annotated Guide (Liang), 76
"Mathematical Journals: Past, Present and Future–A Personal View" (Babbitt), 13
A Mathematical Journey (Gudder), 201
"Mathematical Libraries in Europe" (Barrat, Sureau, and Zweig), 287
Mathematical Logic Quarterly. *See* MLQ. Mathematical Logic Quarterly

The Mathematical Magpie (Fadiman), 200
Mathematical Methods for Physics and Engineering (Riley, Hobson, and Bence), 221
Mathematical Methods in the Applied Sciences, 68
Mathematical Methods in the Physical Sciences (Boas), 215
Mathematical Methods of Classical Mechanics (Arnold), 214
Mathematical Modelling and Numerical Analysis. See M2AN. Mathematical Modelling and Numerical Analysis
Mathematical Models & Methods in Applied Sciences, 68
Mathematical Mountaintops: The Five Most Famous Problems of All Time (Casti), 195
Mathematical Museum and Exhibitions, 185
A Mathematical Mystery Tour: Discovering the Truth and Beauty of the Cosmos (Dewdney), 197
Mathematical Notes, 68
Mathematical Olympiad Challenges (Andreescu and Galca), 209
Mathematical Papers (Clifford), 235
Mathematical Papers of George Green (Green), 239
The Mathematical Papers of Isaac Newton (Newton), 249
The Mathematical Papers of Sir William Rowan Hamilton (Hamilton), 240
Mathematical Physics, Analysis and Geometry, 68
Mathematical Physics Electronic Journal, 68
Mathematical Physiology (Keener and Sneyd), 219
The Mathematical Practitioners of Hanoverian England, 1714–1840 (Taylor), 162
The Mathematical Practitioners of Tudor and Stuart England (Taylor), 162

Mathematical Proceedings of the Cambridge Philosophical Society, 68
Mathematical Programming, 68
Mathematical Quotations Server (Furman University), 122
Mathematical Recreations and Essays (Ball and Coxeter), 209
Mathematical Reflections In a Room With Many Mirrors (Hilton, Holton, and Pedersen), 201
Mathematical Research Letters, 68
Mathematical Research Today and Tomorrow: Viewpoints of Seven Fields Medalists (Casacuberta and Castellet), 194
Mathematical Reviews (AMS), 2, 35, 44, 68
Mathematical Reviews and Current Mathematical Publications, 43
Mathematical Reviews Database (AMS), 46
Mathematical Sciences Professional Directory, 148
Mathematical Sciences Research Institute (MSRI), 296
Mathematical Sciences Research Institute Publication, 277
Mathematical Snapshots (Steinhaus), 208
Mathematical Social Sciences, 68
Mathematical Surveys and Monographs, 277
Mathematical Thought from Ancient to Modern Times (Kline), 183
The Mathematical Tourist: New and Updated Snapshots of Modern Mathematics (Peterson), 206
The Mathematical Traveler: Exploring the Grand History of Numbers (Clawson), 176
The Mathematical Universe: An Alphabetical Journey Through the Great Proofs, Problems, and Personalities (Dunham), 198
The Mathematical Work of John Wallis (Scott), 172
The Mathematical Works (Barrow), 231
Mathematical Works of J. H. C. Whitehead (Whitehead), 261

Mathematical World, 277
Mathematical Writing (Knuth, Larrabee, and Roberts), 142
Mathematica Scandinavica, 67
A Mathematician Grappling with His Century (Schwartz), 172
"Mathematicians and the Mathematics Library: A Librarian's Perspective" (Rutter), 291
The Mathematician's Art of Work (Littlewood), 193
"Mathematicians Love Books" (Kaufmann-Buehler, Peters, and Peters), 290
A Mathematician's Miscellany (Littlewood), 193
Mathematicians of the Seventeenth and Eighteenth Centuries, 163, 174
Mathematics, a Human Endeavor: A Book for Those Who Think They Don't Like the Subject (Jacobs), 202
"Mathematics: A Century Ago–A Century from Now" (Ewing), 14
Mathematics: A Concise History and Philosophy (Anglin), 173
Mathematics and Humor (Paulos), 205
Mathematics and Its Applications, 277
Mathematics and Its History (Stillwell), 188
Mathematics and Logic (Kac and Ulam), 182
Mathematics and Mathematicians: Mathematics in Sweden before 1950 (Gårding), 167
Mathematics and Sports (Sadovskii and Sadovskii), 222
Mathematics and the Physical World (Kline), 203
Mathematics and the Unexpected (Ekeland), 199
A Mathematics Citation Index (Schatz), 49
Mathematics Dictionary: English-Arabic (with an Arabic Index): Covering the Terms (and Definitions) of Traditional and Modern Mathematics, Mechanics and Computers (Jordanian Committee for Arabisation), 89

Mathematics Dictionary (James), 88
Mathematics Education in Secondary Schools and Two-Year Colleges: A Sourcebook (Campbell and Grinstein), 22
Mathematics Education Library, 277
"Mathematics Education Resources on the Internet" (DeCarlo), 288
Mathematics Encyclopedia (Shapiro), 103
Mathematics for the Imagination (Higgins), 201
Mathematics from Leningrad to Austin: George G. Lorentz' Selected Works in Real, Functional and Numerical Analysis (Lorentz), 247
Mathematics Genealogy Project, 159
Mathematics Handbook for Science and Engineering (Råde and Westergren), 133
Mathematics Illustrated Dictionary: Facts, Figures, and People (Bendick), 80
Mathematics in Civilization (Resnikoff and Wells), 187
Mathematics in Medicine and the Life Sciences (Hoppensteadt and Peskin), 218
Mathematics in Science and Engineering, 277
Mathematics into the Twenty-First Century (Browder), 194
Mathematics into Type; Copy Editing and Proofreading of Mathematics for Editorial Assistants and Authors (Swanson), 143
Mathematics in Western Culture (Kline), 203
Mathematics, Its Power and Utility (Smith), 207
"Mathematics Journals Should Be Electronic and Free" (Krantz), 15
Mathematics Magazine, 48, 68
Mathematics of Computation, 68
Mathematics of Control, Signals, and Systems, 68
Mathematics of Derivative Securities (Dempster and Pliska), 216

The Mathematics of Financial Derivatives: A Student Introduction (Wilmott, Howison, and Dewynne), 223
Mathematics of Operations Research, 69
Mathematics of Projectiles in Sport (Mestre), 220
The Mathematics of Sonya Kovalevskaya (Cooke), 166
Mathematics on the Web: Mathematical Books, 267
"Mathematics on the Web with MathML" (Froumentin), 289
Mathematics: People, Problems, Results (Campbell and Higgins), 194
Mathematics: Queen and Servant of Science (Bell), 193
"Mathematics Research Libraries: A 1990 Snapshot" (Anderson and Rovnyak), 287
"Mathematics Research Libraries at the End of the Twentieth Century" (Anderson, Dilcher, and Rovnyak), 287
"Mathematics Resources on the Internet" (Roberts), 290
"Mathematics Sites Compared: Zentralblatt MATH Database and MathSciNet" (Fowler), 289
The Mathematics Survey Draft proposal (Pitman), 16
Mathematics Teacher, 69
Mathematics: The Loss of Certainty (Kline), 183
Mathematics: The New Golden Age (Devlin), 197
Mathematics: The Science of Patterns: The Search for Order in Life, Mind and the Universe (Devlin), 197
Mathematics Through History: A Resource Guide (Fauvel), 20, 156
Mathematics Unbound: The Evolution of an International Mathematics Research Community (Parshall and Rice), 186
Mathematics Web Sites Around the World, 148
Mathematics: Who's Who (Dass), 155

Mathematics Without Borders: A History of the International Mathematical Union (Lehto), 184
Mathematics WWW Virtual Library, 30
Mathematika, 69
Mathematische Abhandlungen (Hasse), 241
Mathematische Annalen, 43, 69
Mathematische Nachrichten, 69
Mathematischer Fachwortschatz: Englisch-Deutsch, Deutsch-Englisch (Pfeil), 95
Mathematisches Begriffswörterbuch (Meschkowski), 93
Mathematische Schriften (Leibniz), 245
Mathematisches Fachwörterbuch: Englisch-Deutsche, Deutsche-Englisch (Lewisch and Posamentier), 91
Mathematisches Vokabular (Klaften), 89
Mathematisches Wörterbuch: Alphabetische Zusammenstellung sämmtlicher in die mathematischen Wissenschaften gehörender Gegenstande in erklärenden und beweisenden synthetisch und analitisch bearbeiteten Abhandlungen (Hoffmann), 87
Mathematisches Wörterbuch: mit Einbeziehung der theoretischen Physik (Naas and Schmid), 93
Mathematische Werke (Eisenstein), 236
Mathematische Werke (Wielandt), 261
Mathematische Zeitschrift, 43, 69
MathFile, 2
Math Forum@Drexel, 29
The Math Forum Internet Mathematics Library, 29
Math Forum Internet Mathematics Library, History/Biography, 159
Math Forum Internet Mathematics Library [Dictionaries], 92
Math Forum Internet News, 294
MathGuide (SUB Göttingen), 30
Math Horizons, 67, 208
Math in LATeX (Grätzer), 225
MathJobs.Org, 148

Math Journal Price Survey based on AMS 2001 data (Rehmann), 292
Math-Net: Persona Mathematica, 148
Math on the Web (AMS), 29
Math on the Web: A Status Report, September 2003: Focus: Interactive Math (Miner and Topping), 15
Math Refresher for Scientists and Engineers (Fanchi), 121
MathResource: Interactive Math Dictionary, 92
MathSci, 2
MathSci Disc, 2–3
MathSciNet (AMS), 4, 8, 10, 35, 43–46, 51, 69, 160
"MathSciNet: Mathematical Reviews on the Web: A Review" (Dominy and Bhatt), 288
MathSciNet–Mathematical Reviews on the Web: Guiding You through the Literature of Mathematics (AMS), 46, 129
MathSci on Dialog, 43
MathSci on SilverPlatter, 43
MathSci User Guide, 129
MathSearch [Richardson], 47
MathSoft Constants (Finch), 122
MathWorld. See Eric Weisstein's World of Mathematics (MathWorld) (Weisstein)
The MATLAB 5 Handbook (Redfern and Campbell), 135
Matters Mathematical (Herstein and Kaplansky), 201
Matthews, J. Rosser, 185
Maurer, Stephen B., 210
Maxwell, James Clerk, 248
May, Donald Curtis, Jr., 117
May, Kenneth O., 25, 148, 160
Maz'ya, Vladimir, 170
McArthur, Charles W., 185
McCleary, John, 130, 187
McDowell, C. H., 92
M. C. Escher, Art and Science (Coxeter, et al.), 195
McGraw-Hill Dictionary of Mathematics (Parker), 94
McGraw-Hill Dictionary of Physics and Mathematics (Lapedes), 91

McGraw-Hill Dictionary of Scientific and Technical Terms, 94
McMahon, Timothy E., 290
McNeil, D. B., 88
McZeal, Cassandra M., 196
Medvedev, Fyodor A., 185
Mehrsprachenwörterbuch Mathematischer Begriffe (Meschkowski), 93
Melvyl—The Catalog of the University of California Libraries, 31
Memoirs of the American Mathematical Society, 69, 277
Memorabilia Mathematica: The Philomath's Quotation Book (Moritz), 131
Men of Mathematics (Bell), 166
"Mergers, Acquisitions, and Access: STM Publishing Today" (Robertson), 290
The Merging of Disciplines: New Directions in Pure, Applied, and Computational Mathematics (Ewing, Gross, and Martin), 199
Mermin, N. David, 204
Merzbach, Uta C., 178
Meschkowski, Herbert, 93
Messengers of Mathematics: European Mathematical Journals (1800–1946) (Ausejo and Hormigón), 76
Mestre, Neville de, 220
The METAFONTbook (Knuth), 225
METAFONT: The Program (Knuth), 225
Methods of Mathematical Finance (Karatzas and Shreve), 219
Metrika, 69
Michigan Mathematical Journal, 69
Micula, Gheorghe, 130
Micula, Sandra, 130
Mikisha, A. M., 93
The Millennium Problems: The Seven Greatest Unsolved Mathematical Puzzles of Our Time (Devlin), 197
Miller, Arthur I., 204
Millington, T. Alaric, 93
Millington, William, 93
Milne-Thomson, L. M., 93
Minderovic, Zoran, 163

Mindlin, Raymond D., 248
Miner, Robert, 15
Minkowski, Hermann, 249
Miscellanea Mathematica (Hilton, Hirzebruch, and Remmert), 202
Mitrinovic, D. S., 130
Mittelbach, Frank, 123, 143
MLQ. Mathematical Logic Quarterly, 69
Möbius and His Band: Mathematics and Astronomy in Nineteenth-Century Germany (Fauvel, Flood, and Wilson), 179
Modern Algebra and the Rise of Mathematical Structures (Corry), 176
Modern Mathematics in the Light of the Fields Medals (Monastyrsky), 185
Monastyrsky, Michael, 185
Monatshefte für Mathematik, 69
Monatshefte für Mathematik und Physik, 42
"Monitoring Serials Use in a Science and Technology Library: Results of a Ten Year Study" (Hill, Hill, and Hayes), 289
Monk, J. Donald, 130
Monographs and Textbooks in Pure and Applied Mathematics, 277
Moon, P., 130
Moré, Jorge J., 131
More Mathematical Challenges (Gardiner), 210
More Mathematical People: Contemporary Conversations (Albers, Alexanderson, and Reid), 164
Morishima, Taro, 249
Moritz, Robert Edouard, 131
Morrison, David, 15
Morrison, Philip, 205
Morrison, Phyllis, 205
Morrow, Charlene, 160
Morse, Marston, 249
Mortenson, Michael E., 131
Moser, William O. J., 209
Mosteller, Frederick, 213
Moving Forward (Ewing), 13
MPRESS/MathNet.preprints, the Mathematics Preprint Search System, 47

MR. *See* **Mathematical Reviews**
Muir, Jean, 170
Müller, Felix, 21
Müller, Gert H., 25
Müller, M., 124
Multi-Repository Mathematics Collection, 267
Multiscale Modeling & Simulation, 69
Murray, Margaret A. M., 170
Musiala, Marek, 220
Myers, Dowell, 221

Naas, Josef, 93
Naber, Gregory L., 221
Nagoya Mathematical Journal, 69
Nasar, Sylvia, 170
The National Faculty Directory, 148
National Institute of Standards and Technology, 131
National Research Council. Committee for the Study of Research-Doctorate Programs in the United States, 149
Natural Structure (Williams), 139
Nature, 48
The Nature and Power of Mathematics (Davis), 196
The Nature of Mathematics (Smith), 207
Navia, Luis E., 26, 160
Navier-Stokes Equations and Nonlinear Functional Analysis (Temam), 223
Neave, H. R., 110
Nelson, David, 94
Nelson, R. D., 83
Neugebauer, O., 186
The Neumann Compendium (Von Neumann), 261
Never at Rest: A Biography of Isaac Newton (Westfall), 173
Nevison, Christopher, 109
The New Ambidextrous Universe: Symmetry and Asymmetry from Mirror Reflections to Superstrings (Gardner), 217
New Cambridge Statistical Tables (Lindley and Scott), 110
New Directions in Applied Mathematics (Hilton and Young), 218
New ICMI Studies Series, 277

NewJour, 294
New Journals in Mathematics, 76
New Mathematical Library, 277
Newsletter on Serials Pricing Issues, 294
Newton, Isaac, 205, 249
New York Journal of Mathematics, 4, 69
Neyman, J., 250
Nicolaides, Roy, 226
Nihon Sugakkai Henshu, 102
1999 Joint Directory of Members, 146
Nipp, Gordon L., 110
NoDEA Nonlinear Differential Equations and Applications. *See* Nonlinear Differential Equations and Applications: NoDEA
Noether, Emmy, 250
Nonconvex Optimization and Its Applications, 277
NonElementary Problems in an Elementary Exposition (Iaglom and Iaglom), 202
Nonlinear Analysis. Theory, Methods & Applications, 70
Nonlinear Differential Equations and Applications: NoDEA, 70
Nonlinearity, 70
Nonlinear Mathematics and Its Applications (Aston), 214
Norbert Wiener, 1894–1964 (Masani), 170
North-Holland Mathematical Library, 277
North-Holland Mathematics Studies, 277
Notable Mathematicians: From Ancient Times to the Present (Young and Minderovic), 163
Notable Women in Mathematics: A Biographical Dictionary (Morrow and Pearl), 160
Notations in Elementary Mathematics (Cajori), 176
Notations Mainly in Higher Mathematics (Cajori), 176
Notices of the American Mathematical Society, 70
Notices of the American Mathematical Society, 294

Novak, Josef, 219
NSDL Scout Report for Math, Engineering, & Technology. Internet Scout Project, 294
NSF-CBMS Regional Conference Series in Probability and Statistics, 277
Number, the Languge of Science (Dantzig), 195
The Number Devil: A Mathematical Adventure (Enzensberger), 199
Numbers and Geometry (Stillwell), 208
NUMDAM (NUMérisation de Documents Anciens Mathématiques, 9, 267
Numerical Algorithms, 70
Numerical Functional Analysis and Optimization, 70
Numerical Linear Algebra with Applications, 70
Numerische Mathematik, 70

Obreanu, P. E., 87
OCLC Worldcat, 31
O'Connor, John J., 159
Odeh, Robert E., 110, 111
Odlyzko, Andrew, 5, 15
Oeuvres, Collected Papers (Serre), 256
Oeuvres: Collected Papers (Borel), 233
Oeuvres de Laguerre, Publiées Sous les Auspices de l'Académie des Sciences (Laguerre), 244
Of Men and Numbers: The Story of the Great Mathematicians (Muir), 170
Ogilvie, Marilyn, 161
O'Heigeartaigh, M., 26
OhioLINK Central Catalog, 31
Ohio State University Mathematical Research Institute Publications, 277
Oka, Kiyoshi, 250
Okerson, Ann, 16
Oldham, Keith B., 136
Olver, F. W. J., 250
Omega–Bibliography of Mathematical Logic (Müller and Lenski), 25
101 Careers in Mathematics (Sterrett), 208

On Growth and Form (Thompson), 222
Online! A Reference Guide to Using Internet Resources (Harnack and Kleppinger), 141
Online! A Reference Guide to Using Internet Resources (Harnack and Kleppinger), 141
Online Books Page (University of Pennsylvania), 267
"Online Resources for Mathematics in the Scientific Virtual Reference Desk" (De Robbio), 288
Open Access Scholarly Publishing: Opportunities and Obstacles (Cornell University Faculty Forum), 13
"Open Access to the Scientific Journal Literature" (Suber), 17
Open Archives, 36
Opera Omnia. Series Prima. Opera Mathematica (Euler), 237
Operations Analysis in the U. S. Army Eighth Air Force in World War II (McArthur), 185
Operator Theory: Advances and Applications, 278
Optimization Methods and Software, 70
Optimization Software Guide (Moré and Wright), 131
Order, 70
Order Statistics and Their Use in Testing and Estimation (Harter), 109
The Origins of the Infinitesimal Calculus (Baron), 174
Orlov, V. B., 93, 94
O'Rourke, Joseph, 123
Osaka Journal of Mathematics, 70
Osen, Lynn M., 171
Ostaszewski, Adam, 221
Ostrowski, Alexander, 250
Outliers in Statistical Data (Barnett and Lewis), 115
Out of the Mouths of Mathematicians: A Quotation Book for Philomaths (Schmalz), 136
Owen, D. B., 110, 132

Oxford Figures: 800 Years of the Mathematical Sciences (Fauvel, Flood, and Wilson), 179
Oxford Journals, 267
Oxford Lecture Series in Mathematics and its Applications, 278
Oxford Statistical Science Series, 278

Pacific Journal of Mathematics, 70
Paenson, Isaac, 94
Pais, Abraham, 171
Palais, Richard, 15
PAM Bulletin, 295
PAM Electronic Discussion List [PAMnet], 295
A Panorama of Pure Mathematics: As Seen by N. Bourbaki (Dieudonné), 198
Pao-Lu Hsü Collected Papers (Hsü), 242
Papageorgiou, Nikolas, 126
Pardalos, Panos M., 98, 121, 125
Parke, Nathan Grier, 21
Parker, Phillip E., 120
Parker, Sybil P., 94
Parkinson, Claire L., 160
Parshall, Karen Hunger, 186
The Parsimonious Universe: Shape and Form in the Natural World (Hildebrandt and Tromba), 201
Parts per Million Values for Estimating Quality Levels (Odeh), 111
Patel, Jagdish K., 132
Patil, Ganapati Parashuram, 26
The Pattern Book: Fractals, Art, and Nature (Pickover), 206
Paul Dirac: The Man and His Work (Pais, et al.), 171
Paul Erdös: The Art of Counting. Selected Writings (Elgot), 236
Paulos, John Allen, 205
Pausch, Lois M., 19
Peano: Life and Works of Giuseppe Peano (Kennedy), 169
Pearl, Teri, 160
Pearson, Egon Sharpe, 111
Pearson, E. S., 250, 251
Pedersen, Jean, 201

"The Peer-Review Process" (Rowland), 291
Peeva, K., 83, 94
Peirce, Charles S., 251
Pemberton, John E., 21
Pengelley, David, 184
The Penguin Desk Encyclopedia of Science and Mathematics (Bunch and Tesar), 98
The Penguin Dictionary of Curious and Interesting Geometry (Wells), 97
The Penguin Dictionary of Curious and Interesting Numbers (Wells), 97
The Penguin Dictionary of Mathematics (Daintith and Nelson), 83
The Penguin Dictionary of Mathematics (Nelson), 94
Penrose Tiles to Trapdoor Ciphers . . . and the Return of Dr. Matrix (Gardner), 211
Percy Alexander MacMahon: Collected Papers (MacMahon), 247
Perspectives on the History of Mathematical Logic (Drucker), 178
Peskin, Charles S., 218
Peters, Alice, 290
Peters, Jean, 111
Peters, Klaus, 290
Peterson, Ivars, 206
Peterson's Graduate Programs in the Physical Sciences, Mathematics, Agricultural Sciences, the Environment & Natural Resources, 149
Peterson's Math Review for the GRE, GMAT, and MCAT, 132
Pfeil, Trante, 95
PHB Practical Handbook of Curve Design and Generation (Von Seggern), 139
PhDs.org Science, Math, and Engineering Career Resources, 149
Phillips, Esther R., 186
Pi: A Source Book (Berggren, Borwein, and Borwein), 174
Pickover, Clifford A., 206
Pierre-Simon Laplace, 1749–1827: A Life in Exact Science (Gillispie), 168

Pi Mu Epsilon Journal, 70
Pinfield, Stephen, 290
Pioneers of Representation Theory: Frobenius, Burnside, Schur, & Brauer (Curtis), 177
Pitman, Jim, 16
PlanetMath.Org, 102
Pless, Vera, 221
Plis, Alexander I., 136
Pliska, S. R., 216
Plouffe, Simon, 103
Pocketbook of Integrals and Mathematical Formulas (Tallarida), 137
The Pocket Statistician: A Practical Guide to Quality Improvement (Coleman, et al.), 119
Poggendorff, J. C., 161
Poincaré and the Three Body Problem (Barrow-Green), 165
Poland, Jean, 10
Polianin, Andrei D., 132
Pollard, J. H., 132
Polya, George, 251
Polyominoes: A Guide to Puzzles and Problems in Tiling (Martin), 213
Polyominoes: Puzzles, Patterns, Problems, and Packings (Golomb), 211
Population Biology: Concepts and Models (Hastings), 218
Porkess, Roger, 95
Porter, Roy, 161
Porter, Theodore M., 186
Posamentier, Alfred S., 91
Positivity, 70
"Postcommercial Scholarly Publication" (Quinn), 16
Potential Analysis, 70
Powell, Russell H., 26
Powers of Ten (Morrison and Morrison), 205
Practical Guide to Splines (De Boor), 120
Practical Handbook of Genetic Algorithms (Chambers), 117
Practical Handbook of Spreadsheet Curves and Geometric Constructions (Arganbright), 113

The Practical Statistician: Simplified Handbook of Statistics (Linton and Gallo), 129
Pre-Meiji Works in the Library of Congress (Honda), 24
Prentice-Hall Encyclopedia of Mathematics (West), 105
"The Price Spiral of Mathematics Journals and What to Do About It" (Rehmann), 16
"Pricing of Scientific Publications: A Commercial Publisher's Point of View" (Beschler), 13
PRIME (Platonic Realms Interactive Mathematics Encyclopedia), 103
Primer of Mathematical Writing: Being a Disquisition on Having Your Ideas Recorded, Typeset, Published, Read & Appreciated (Krantz), 142
A Primer of Population Biology (Wilson and Bossert), 224
Princeton Mathematical Series, 278
Princeton Mathematics Community in the 1930's: An Oral History Project, 186
The Principia: Mathematical Principles of Natural Philosophy (Newton), 205
Principles and Practice of Mathematics (COMAP, Inc.), 195
Prizes in Mathematics (Voelker), 150
Probability and Mathematical Statistics, 278
Probability in the Engineering and Informational Sciences, 70
Probability Theory and Related Fields, 70
Problems for Mathematicians, Young and Old (Halmos), 212
Proceedings of Symposia in Applied Mathematics, 278
Proceedings of Symposia in Pure Mathematics, 278
Proceedings of the American Mathematical Society, 71
Proceedings of the Edinburgh Mathematical Society. Series II, 71

Proceedings of the International Congress of Mathematicians, August 18–17, 1998, Berlin (Fischer and Rehmann), 200
Proceedings of the Japan Academy. Series A, Mathematical Sciences, 71
Proceedings of the Royal Society of Edinburgh. Section A. Mathematics, 71
Proceedings of the Steklov Institute of Mathematics, 278
"A Professor, his Periodicals, their Publication and Acquisition" (Rubenstein), 16
Progress in Mathematics, 278
Progress in Nonlinear Differential Equations and Their Applications, 278
Progress in Probability, 278
Project Euclid, 268
Project Mathematics!, 296
Prokhorov, Iu. V., 103
Proquest, 38
Prudnikov, A. P., 133
Publicationes Mathematicae, 71
Publications Mathématiques (Institut des Hautes Études Scientifiques, 71
Publications of the Research Institute for Mathematical Sciences, 71
Public Discussions at The Math Forum, 295
"Publishing Mathematics on the Web" (Cole), 288
"Publishing on the Internet" (Casselman), 13
PubMed (National Library of Medicine), 48
Pullman, Bernard, 221
Pythagoras: An Annotated Bibliography (Navia), 26, 160

Quantification and the Quest for Medical Certainty (Matthews), 185
Quantities and Units of Measurement: A Dictionary and Handbook (Drazil), 84

Quantum Groups and Their Primitive Ideals (Joseph), 218
Quarterly Journal of Mathematics, 71
Quarterly of Applied Mathematics, 71
Quaternary Quadratic Forms: Computer Generated Tables (Nipp), 110
The Queen of Mathematics: A Historically Motivated Guide to Number Theory (Goldman), 180
Queen's Papers in Pure & Applied Mathematics, 278
Quinn, Frank, 5, 16

Rabe-Hesketh, Sophia, 133
Rabinowitz, Stanley, 48
Råde, Lennert, 133
Rademacher, Hans, 251
R. A. Fisher: The Life of a Scientist (Box), 166
Rahtz, Sebastian, 123
Rainich, Gabrielle, 95
Ralley, Thomas G., 121
Ramanujan, Srinivasa, 252
Ramanujan Journal, 71
Ramanujan: Letters and Commentary (Ramanujan), 252
Ramanujan's Notebooks (Ramanjuan), 252
Random Structures & Algorithms, 71
Rao, C. R., 133, 252
"The Rapid Evolution of Scholarly Communication" (Odlyzko), 15
Rara Arithmetica: A Catalogue of Arithmetics Written Before the Year MDCI. . . . (Smith), 27, 162
Ratiu, Tudor S., 220
Reading the Numbers: A Survival Guide to the Measurements, Numbers, and Sizes Encountered in Everyday Life (Blocksma), 116
Recognizing Excellence in the Mathematical Sciences: An International Compilation of Awards, Prizes, & Recipients (Jaguszewski), 147
Redfern, Darren, 134, 135
Reed, Campbell B., 101, 102, 132

Referativnyi zhurnal. Matematika, 48
Referativnyi zhurnal. 13, Matematika, 48
Reflections on Kurt Gödel (Wang), 172
"Reforming Scholarly Publishing in the Sciences: A Librarian Perspective" (Branin and Case), 13
Rehmann, Ulf, 16, 200, 292
Reid, Constance, 164, 171, 206
Reingold, Edward M., 120
Reissner, Eric, 253
Relativity Theory: Concepts and Basic Principles (Harpaz), 218
"Remarks on Math Journals and Libraries" (Levy), 15
Remmert, Reinhold, 202
Rennie, Andrew, 214
"Report of the Treasurer (2002)" (AMS), 14
Reports on Mathematical Physics, 71
Representation Theory, 71
Research-Doctorate Programs in the United States: Continuity and Change (National Research Council), 149
Research Library, 48
Resnikoff, H. L., 187
Resources in Education (U.S. Department of Education), 39
Resources in Mathematics (Physics-Astronomy-Mathematics Division of SLA), 30
Resultate (Jacobs), 203
Reviews in Complex Analysis (AMS), 47
Reviews in Functional Analysis, 1980–86 (AMS), 47
Reviews in Global Analysis, 1980–86 (AMS), 47
Reviews in Graph Theory, 1940–78 (AMS), 47
Reviews in K-Theory, 1940–84 (AMS), 47
Reviews in Mathematical Physics, 71
Reviews in Number Theory, 1940–72 (AMS), 47
Reviews in Number Theory, 1973–83 (AMS), 47

Reviews in Number Theory, 1984–96 (AMS), 47
Reviews in Numerical Analysis, 1980–86 (AMS), 47
Reviews in Operator Theory, 1980–86 (AMS), 47
Reviews in Partial Differential Equations, 1980–86 (AMS), 47
Reviews in Ring Theory, 1980–84 (AMS), 47
Reviews in Ring Theory (AMS), 47
Reviews of Papers in Algebraic and Differential Topology, Topological Groups, and Homological Algebra, . . . 1940–67 (AMS), 47
Reviews on Finite Groups, . . . [1940–1970] (AMS), 47
Reviews on Infinite Groups, . . . [1940–1970] (AMS), 47
"Review Times in Statistical Journals: Tilting at Windmills?" (Carroll), 13
Revista Matemática Iberoamericana, 72
Ribenboim, Paulo, 253
Rice, Adrian C., 186
Richert, Norman, 291
Rider, Robin E., 26, 161
Riemann, Bernhard, 253
Riesz, Marcel, 254
Riley, K. F., 221
Rinnooy Kan, A. H. G., 26
The Rise of Statistical Thinking, 1820–1900 (Porter), 186
Ritter, Gerhard X., 135
Robbins, Herbert, 254
Roberts, Beth A., 290
Roberts, Joe, 207
Roberts, Paul M., 142
Robertson, Edmund F., 159
Robertson, Kathleen, 290
Robinson, Abraham, 254
Rocky Mountain Journal of Mathematics, 72
Roebuck, Laura, 148
Rogers, Tom, 209
Rohlf, F. James, 111
"A Role for Libraries in Electronic Publication" (Quinn), 16

Role of Mathematics in Science (Schiffer and Bowden), 207
Romanian-English Dictionary and Grammar for the Mathematical Sciences (Gould and Obreanu), 87
Rosen, Kenneth H., 135
Rosenberger, Gerhard, 200
Rosenfeld, B. A., 164
Ross, Ian C., 50
Rota, Gian-Carlo, 103, 203
Rovnyak, James L., 287
Rowe, David E., 186, 187
Rowland, Fytton, 291
Rowlett, Russ, 95
Royal Society Mathematical Tables (Royal Society of London), 111
Royal Society of London, 49, 111
Royal Statistical Society, 283
Rubenstein, Dan, 16
Rucker, Rudy, 207
Rudin, Walter, 171
Ruelle, David, 207
Ruiz-Cobo, Maria Reyes, 215
Russian Academy of Sciences. Doklady. Mathematics. *See* **Doklady. Mathematics**
Russian-English Dictionary of Mathematics (Efimov), 84
Russian-English Dictionary of the Mathematical Sciences (Lohwater), 87
Russian-English, English-Russian Dictionary on Probability, Statistics, and Combinatorics (Borovkov), 81
Russian-English/English-Russian Glossary of Statistical Terms (Kotz), 90
Russian-English Mathematical Dictionary: Words and Phrases in Pure and Applied Mathematics (Milne-Thomson), 93
Russian-English Mathematical Vocabulary (Burlak), 82
Russian-English Vocabulary with Grammatical Sketch: To Be Used in Reading Mathematical Papers (Rainich), 95

Russian for the Mathematician (Gould), 123
Russian Journal of Mathematical Physics, 72
Russian Journal of Numerical Analysis and Mathematical Modelling, 72
Russian Mathematical Surveys, 72
Russko-Angliiskii Matematicheskii Slovar'-Minimum (Glushko), 87
Russko-Angliiskii Matematicheskii Slovar'. Russian-English Mathematical Dictionary (Kramer), 91
Russko-Anglo-Nemetsko-Frantsuzskii Matematicheskii Slovar' (Orlov, Skorokhod, and Sosinskii), 94
Rust, John, 113
Rutkowski, Marek, 220
Rutter, Sara, 291
Ryzhik, I. M., 108–9

Sachdev, P. L., 135
Sachs, Gerald E., 254
Sachs, Lothar, 21
Sack, J. R., 135
Sadovskii, A. L., 222
Sadovskii, L. E., 222
Sahai, Hardeo, 95
Salminen, Paavo, 116
Salomon, D., 226
Salzer, Herbert E., 111
Samarin, Alexander, 123
Samuel, Pierre, 254
Sándor, J., 130
Sankhya, 72
Saunders, P. T., 222
Sbornik. Mathematics, 72
Scandinavian Journal of Statistics. Theory and Applications, 72
"A Scenario for Publishing Mathematics in the Future" (Kirby), 14
Scenes from the History of Real Functions (Medvedev), 185
Schaaf, William L., 26
Schabas, Margaret, 172
Schaffner, Ann C., 16
Schatz, Joseph A., 49
Schiffer, M. M., 207

Schläfli, Ludwig, 254
Schlissel, Arthur, 187
Schlote, Karl Heinz, 157
Schmalz, Rosemary, 136
Schmid, Hermann Ludwig, 93
Schoenberg, I. J., 255
"Scholarly Associations and the Economic Viability of Open Access Publishing" (Willinsky), 291
"Scholarly Journals and Grand Solutions" (Crawford), 13
"Scholarly Mathematical Communication at a Crossroads" (Kuperberg), 15
Scholarly Societies Project, 284
Schrödinger, E., 255
Schroeder, Manfred, 207
Schwartz, Jacob T., 203
Schwartz, Laurent, 172
Schwartzman, Steven, 96
Schwarz, Hermann Amandus, 255
Schwinger, Julian, 255
Science, 48
Science Citation Index, 41
ScienceDirect, 268
Scientific English: A Guide for Scientists and Other Professionals (Day), 141
The Scientific Letters and Papers of James Clerk Maxwell (Maxwell), 248
"Scientific Publishing: A Research Mathematician's Viewpoint" (Birman), 13
SciSearch, 40
Sci-Tech Library Newsletter, 295
The Scope and History of Commutative and Noncommutative Harmonic Analysis (Mackey), 184
Scott, J. F., 172
Scott, W. F., 110
The Search for E. T. Bell, Also Known as John Taine (Reid), 171
Search Notices of the AMS, 162
Seeds, Robert S., 291
Seidel, J. J., 255
Selberg, Atle, 256
Selecta (Beno), 235
Selecta (Friedrichs), 238

Selecta (Halmos), 240
Selecta: Selected Works of Benoit M. Mandelbrot (Mandelbrot), 248
Selecta (Spencer), 257
Selected Logic Papers (Sachs), 254
Selected Papers (1937–1976) of Julian Schwinger (Schwinger), 255
Selected Papers (Bishop), 233
Selected Papers (Chern), 234
Selected Papers in Statistics and Probability (Wald), 261
Selected Papers (Lefschetz), 245
Selected Papers. Oeuvres Scientifiques (Leray), 246
Selected Papers of Abraham Robinson (Robinson), 254
Selected Papers of C. R. Rao (Rao), 252
Selected Papers of Demetrios C. Magiros: Applied Mathematics, Nonlinear Mechanics, and Dynamical Systems Analysis (Magiros), 247
The Selected Papers of E. S. Pearson (Pearson), 251
Selected Papers of F. W. J. Olver (Olver), 250
Selected Papers of Kentaro Yano (Yano), 262
Selected Papers of S. Chandrasekhar (Chandrasekhar), 234
Selected Papers of W. T. Tutte (Tutte), 259
Selected Papers (Robbins), 254
Selected Papers: Saunders Mac Lane (Mac Lane), 247
Selected Papers (Wolfowitz), 262
Selected Publications of Eugene L. Lawler (Lawler), 245
Selected Tables in Mathematical Statistics, 112
Selected Works in Applied Mechanics and Mathematics (Reissner), 253
Selected Works of A. N. Kolmogorov (Kolmogorov), 244
The Selected Works of J. Frank Adams (Adams), 229
The Selected Works of V. S. Varadarajan (Varadarajan), 260

Selected Works (Vinogradov), 260
A Selection of Early Statistical Papers of J. Neyman (Neyman), 250
Selkirk, K. E., 96
Semendiaev, K. A., 116, 117
Semigroup Forum, 72
Sen, P. K., 122
Seneta, E., 168
Serben, Saul, 111
Serials and Journals–covered by Zentralblatt MATH, 77
Series in Approximations and Decompositions, 278
Seroul, Raymond, 226
Serre, Jean Pierre, 256
"Setting Up an Institutional E-Print Archive" (Pinfield, Gardner, and MacColl), 290
Set-Valued Analysis, 72
Shafarevich, Igor R., 256
Shapiro, Max S., 103
Shaposhnikova, Tatyana, 170
Shaw, William T., 227
She Hsueh Li Hsueh Pao. English Edition. See Acta Mathematica Scientia. Series B. English Edition
Sheskin, David J., 136
Shikin, Eugene V., 136
Shklarsky, D. O., 213
Shone, Ronald, 222
Shonkwiler, Ronald M., 224
A Short Account of the History of Mathematics (Ball), 174
Short Dictionary of Mathematics (McDowell), 92
Shreve, Steven E., 219
Shu Hsueh Hsueh Pao. English Series. See Acta Mathematica Sinica. English Series
SIAM Journal on Applied Dynamics, 73
SIAM Journal on Applied Mathematics, 72
SIAM Journal on Computing, 73
SIAM Journal on Control and Optimization, 73
SIAM Journal on Discrete Mathematics, 73

SIAM Journal on Mathematical Analysis, 73
SIAM Journal on Matrix Analysis and Applications, 73
SIAM Journal on Numerical Analysis, 73
SIAM Journal on Optimization, 73
SIAM Journal on Scientific Computing, 73
SIAM Journals Online, 268
SIAM News, 73
SIAM Review, 73
SIAM Studies in Applied Mathematics, 278
Siberian Mathematical Journal, 73
Sibirskii Matematicheskii Zhurnal. *See* Siberian Mathematical Journal
"Silicon Dreams and Silicon Bricks: The Continuing Evolution of Libraries" (Odlyzko), 15
Silva, Jorge-Nuno, 210
Simon Stevin. *See* Bulletin of the Belgian Mathematical Society, Simon Stevin
Singer, I. M., 203
Sirovich, Lawrence, 222
Sjöstedt, C. E., 96
Skalskaia, I. P., 220
Skorokhod, N. S., 94
Skula, Ladislav, 23
SLA, Physics-Astronomy-Mathematics Division, 30
Slavutskii, Ilja Sh., 23
Sloane, Neil J. A., 103, 136
Sloane's On-Line Encyclopedia of Integer Sequences (Sloane), 103
Slovar' Matematicheskikh Terminov Na Angliiskom, Russkom, Armianskom, Nemetskom, Frantsuzkom Iazykakh (Tonian), 96
Slovic, Paul, 203
"The Slow Revolution of the Free Electronic Journal" (Jackson), 14
Smale, Stephen, 256
Smarandache, Florentin, 257
Smirnova, G. S., 174
Smith, David Eugene, 27, 162, 187
Smith, Henry John Stephen, 257
Smith, Karl J., 207
Smithies, Frank, 172
Sneddon, I. N., 104
Sneyd, James, 219
Societies and Associations, 284
Society for Industrial and Applied Mathematics (SIAM), 284
Sofroniou, Nick, 143
Sokal, Robert R., 111
Solving Problems in Scientific Computing Using Maple and MATLAB (Gander and Hrebícek), 224
"So Many Problems, So Little Time: Maps and Mathematics" (Figa), 289
Some Eminent Indian Mathematicians of the Twentieth Century (Kapur), 158
Sommerville, D. M. Y., 27
Sonnenschein, Hugo, 125
Sosinskii, A. B., 94
Sound Propagation in Stratified Fluids (Wilcox), 223
Sources and Studies in the History of Mathematics and Physical Sciences, 278
Sources in the History of Mathematics and the Physical Sciences, 278
Sources of Hyperbolic Geometry (Stillwell), 188
Space Kinematics and Lie Groups (Karger and Novak), 219
Spacetime and Singularities: An Introduction (Naber), 221
Spanier, Jerome, 136
SPARC Open Access Newsletter, 295
Sparknotes: Math Study Guides, 137
Special Functions of Mathematics for Engineers (Andrews), 113
The Special Theory of Relativity: A Mathematical Exposition (Das), 216
Spencer, D. E., 130
Spencer, Donald C., 257
Spencer, Donald D., 162
Spiegel, Murray R., 129
Spivak, M. D., 137

Spravochnik po Matematicheskikh Tablits, 110
SpringerLINK, Mathematics Online Library, 268
Springer Series in Computational Mathematics, 279
Spurrier, John D., 137
Squaring the Circle: the War Between Hobbes and Wallis (Jesseph), 182
S. S. Chern: A Great Geometer of the Twentieth Century (Yau), 173
Standard Probability and Statistics Tables and Formulae (Zwillinger and Kokoska), 112
Stanislaw Ulam: Sets, Numbers, and Universes: Selected Works (Ulam), 260
Starting Our Careers: A Collection of Essays and Advice on Professional Development from the Young Mathematicians' Network (Bennett and Crannell), 193
"State of AMS 2004" (Ewing), 288
Statistical Dictionary of Terms and Symbols (Kurtz and Edgerton), 91
Statistical Papers, 73
Statistical Science, 73
Statistical Services Directory, 150
Statistical Society of Canada, 284
Statistical Tables (Rohlf and Sokal), 111
Statistical Tables and Formulae (Kokoska and Nevison), 109
Statistical Tables for Biological, Agricultural and Medical Research (Fisher and Yates), 108
Statistical Theory and Method Abstracts (International Statistical Institute), 49, 74
Statistical Vocabulary, 88
Statistica Neerlandica, 73
Statistica Sinica, 73
Statistician. *See* **Journal of the Royal Statistical Society. Series D. The Statistician**
Statisticians of the Centuries (Heyde and Seneta), 168
Statistics, 74
Statistics & Probability Letters, 74
Statistics and Computing, 74
Statistics Glossary (StatSoft), 96
Statistics on the Table: The History of Statistical Concepts and Methods (Stigler), 188
Statistics Tables: For Mathematicians, Engineers, Economists and the Behavioral and Management Sciences (Neave), 110
Statistics: Textbooks and Monographs, 279
Statistics, Theory and Practice: Selected Papers by Sir Maurice Kendall (1907–1983) (Kendall), 243
Statisztikai Szótar; 1700 Statisztikao Kifejezes het Nyelven. 3. Kiad (Központi Statisztikai Hivatal), 90
StatLib (Carnegie Mellon University, Department of Statistics), 30
StatLib–Web Links, 149
Stats, 74
StatSoft, 96
Steen, Lynn Arthur, 23, 27
Steenrod, Norman E., 143
Stegun, Irene A., 112, 114, 131
Stein, Sherman, 172
Steinberger, Mark, 16
Steiner, Jacob, 257
Steinhaus, H., 208
Sternberg, S., 222
Sternberg, Shlomo, 217
Sterrett, Andrew, 208
Stewart, Ian, 208, 222
Stigler, Stephen M., 187, 188
Stigum, Brent P., 223
Stillwell, John, 188, 208
Stochastic Analysis and Applications, 74
Stochastic Processes and their Applications, 74
Stöcker, Horst, 124
The Story of Mathematics (Mankiewicz), 184
St. Petersburg Mathematical Journal, 72
Strang, Gilbert, 223
A Strategy for Open Access to Society Publications (Pitman), 16
Strøm, Arne, 137
Stroock, Daniel W., 203

Struik, Dirk J., 188
Student Mathematical Library, 279
The Student's Introduction to Mathematica: A Handbook for Precalculus, Calculus, and Linear Algebra (Torrence and Torrence), 227
Studia Mathematica, 74
Studia Scientiarum Mathematicarum Hungarica, 74
Studies in Applied Mathematics, 74
Studies in Logic and the Foundations of Mathematics, 279
Studies in the History of Mathematics (Phillips), 186
Studies in the History of Statistics and Probability (Kendall and Plackett), 188
Studies in the History of Statistics and Probability (Pearson and Kendall), 188
Su, Buchin, 257
Sube, Ralf, 84
Suber, Peter, 17
SUB Göttingen, 30, 43
Su Buchin: Selected mathematical papers/Su Buchin (Buchin), 257
Sugaku Ei-Wa Wa-Ei Jitten. Mathematics: English-Japanese and Japanese-English Dictionary (Komatsu), 90
Sugeno, Michio, 223
Sugihara, George, 125
Sureau, G., 287
Suzuki, Satoshi, 257
Swanson, Ellen, 143
Swetz, Frank J., 188
Sydsæter, Knut, 137
Sylvester, James Joseph, 258
Symmetry (Weyl), 208
Symplectic Techniques in Physics (Guillemin and Sternberg), 217
Syropoulos, Apostolos, 143
Szegö, Gabor, 258
Székely, Gábor J., 213

Table of Integrals, Series, and Products (Gradshteyn and Ryzhik), 108–9
Tables for Converting Polynomials and Power Series into Chebyshev Series (Salzer and Levine), 111
Tables for Lagrangian Interpolation Using Chebyshev Points (Salzer, Levine, and Serben), 111
Tables for Statisticians and Biometricians, 111
Tables of Integral Transforms (Erdelyi), 108
Tables of the SU(MN) Contains SU(M) X SU(N) Coefficients of Fractional Parentage (Chen), 108
Taiwanese Journal of Mathematics, 74
Tallarida, Ronald J., 137
Tanur, Judith M., 102
Tarski, Alfred, 258
Taschenbuch der Mathematik (Bronshtein and Semendiaev), 117
Taschenbuch der Mathematik, Ergänzende Kapitel (Bronshtein and Semendiaev), 117
Taylor, Eva Germaine Rimington, 162
Taylor, Todd W., 143
Teaching Children Mathematics, 74
Technometrics, 74
Temam, Roger, 223
TePaske-King, Bert, 291
Terano, Toshiro, 223
Terquem, M., 27, 162
Tesar, Jenny, 98
TeXbook (Knuth), 226
TeX: The Program (Knuth), 226
Texts in Applied Mathematics, 279
Teoreticheskaia i Matematicheskaia Fizika. *See* **Theoretical and Mathematical Physics**
Teoriia Veroiatnostei i ee Primeneniia. *See* **Theory of Probability and its Applications**
Theoretical and Mathematical Physics, 74
Theory of Computing Systems, 75
The Theory of Interest (Kellison), 219
Theory of Probability and Its Applications, 75
Theory of Probability and Mathematical Statistics, 75

"This Science Isn't Just for Mathematicians Anymore: Mathematics Resources on the Internet" (McMahon), 290
Thisse, Jacques-François, 213
Thomas, Sarah, 10
Thombs, Lori A., 137
Thompson, D'Arcy, 222
Thompson, Thomas M., 189
Thompson, William J., 138
Thomson ISI, 40
Thomson/Peterson's Graduate Program Search, 149
Thoughts about Publishing Mathematics on the Web (Cole), 288
Through a Reporter's Eyes: The Life of Stefan Banach (Kaluza), 169
Tierney, Luke, 227
Tietjen, Gary L., 96
Tigg, Jason, 227
Time-Frequency Representations (Tolimieri and An), 223
Timman, R., 127
Todhunter, I. A., 189
Tohoku Mathematical Journal. Second Series, 75
Tolimieri, Richard, 223
Tolkovyi Matematicheskii Slovar' (Mikisha), 93
Tomber, Marvin, 28
Tomber's Bibliography and Index in Non-associative Algebras (Tomber), 28
Tompkins, Mary L., 43
Tonian, A. O., 96
Tool Kit for the Expert Web Searcher, 52
Topical Dictionary of Statistics (Tietjen), 96
Topics in Cohomology of Groups (Lang), 245
Topology, 75
Topology and its Applications, 75
Topping, Paul, 15
Torelli, Ruggiero, 258
Torrence, Bruce F., 227
Torrence, Eve A., 227
Toward a Formal Science of Economics: The Axiomatic Method in Economics and Econometrics (Stigum), 223
"Toward a Mathematical Markup Language" (Youngen), 17
Towards Excellence: Leading a Doctoral Mathematics Department in the 21st Century (Ewing), 199, 287
"Towards Free Access to Scientific Literature" (Apt), 13
Transactions of the AMS, 44
Transactions of the American Mathematical Society, 75
Transformation Groups, 75
Translations of Mathematical Monographs, 279
A Treatise on Isoperimetrical Problems and the Calculus of Variations (Woodhouse), 189
Trends and Perspectives in Applied Mathematics (Sirovich), 222
Trigg, George L., 102
The Trisectors (Dudley), 198
Tromba, Anthony, 201
Trumbo, Bruce E., 49
Truncated and Censored Samples: Theory and Applications (Cohen), 118
Tsao, C. K., 28
Tsolomitis, Antonis, 143
Tukey, John W., 50, 94, 259
Tuma, Jan H., 138
Turán, Paul, 259
Turpion Limited, 268
Tutte, W. T., 259
Tversky, Amos, 203
20,000 Problems Under the Sea, 48
Twistors in Mathematics and Physics (Bailey and Baston), 214
200% of Nothing: An Eye-Opening Tour Through the Twists and Turns of Math Abuse and Innumeracy (Dewdney), 197
2000 National Doctoral Program Survey, 145
Two-Year College Mathematics Library Recommendations (Steen), 27

Tzelekis, C. P., 97

Ufliand, Y. S., 220
Ulam, Stanislaw, 182, 260
Ulam Quarterly, 4
UMAP Journal, 75
UMI, 38
Understanding Search Engines: Mathematical Modeling and Text Retrieval (Berry and Browne), 215
Unexpected Hanging and Other Mathematical Diversions (Gardner), 211
The Universal History of Numbers: From Prehistory to the Invention of the Computer (Ifrah), 181
The Universe in a Handkerchief: Lewis Carroll's Mathematical Recreations, Games, Puzzles, and Word Plays (Gardner), 211
University Lecture Series, 279
University of Michigan Historical Mathematics Collection, 9, 43, 265, 268
University of Wisconsin–Madison Libraries, 292
University of York Department of Mathematics, 163
Unrolling Time: Christiaan Huygens and the Mathematization of Nature (Yoder), 173
Upton, Graham J. G., 97
Urrutia, J., 135
U.S.A. Mathematical Olympiads, 1972–1986 (Klamkin), 212
U.S. Department of Education, 39
A User's Guide to Algebraic Topology (Dodson and Parker), 120
A User's Guide to Operator Algebras (Fillmore), 121
A User's Guide to Principal Components (Jackson), 126
User's Guide to Spectral Sequences (McCleary), 130
"Using Online Catalogs to Evaluate Science Collections for a Group of Institutions" (Ebersole), 288

Using the Mathematical Literature (Fowler), 20
U.S. National Bureau of Standards, 112
Uspekhi Matematicheskikh Nauk. *See* Russian Mathematical Surveys
The USSR Olympiad Problem Book: Selected Problems and Theorems in Elementary Mathematics (Shklarsky, Chentzov, and Yaglom), 213
Utilitas Mathematica, 75

Van der Geer, Gerard, 17
Van Loan, Chalres, 119
Varadarajan, V. S., 260
Varian, Hal R., 14
Vaughan, Jerry E., 127
Verstraelen, L. C. A., 120
Vieweg Mathematik Lexikon (Kerner, et al.), 89
Vinogradov, I. M., 104
Vinogradov, Ivan Matveevic, 260
The Visual Mind: Art and Mathematics (Emmer), 199
Vita Mathematica, 279
VNR Concise Encyclopedia of Mathematics (Gellert), 99
Vocabularie Mathematic in Interlingue. Con Traduction in Angles (English), Frances (Français) a German (Deutsch) (Sjöstedt), 96
Voelker, Margie L., 150
Von Neumann, John, 260, 261
Von Seggern, David H., 138, 139
Vorlesungen über die Entwicklung der Mathematik im 19.Jahrhundert (Klein), 183
Vorlesungen über Zahlentheorie (Lejeune Dirichlet), 184
Vydaiushchiesia Matematiki: Biograficheskii Slovar'-Spravochnik (Borodin and Bugai), 154

Wadsworth, Harrison M., Jr., 139
Wagon, Stan, 227
Wald, Abraham, 261

Walker, Janice R., 143
Walkington, Noel, 226
Walsh, Norman, 227
Walsh, Ronald A., 138
Wang, Hao, 172
Wanner, G., 180
Wavelets: A Mathematical Tool for Signal Processing (Chui), 216
The Way I Remember It (Rudin), 171
Web Pages That Perform Statistical Calculations! (StatPages.net), 139
Webster's New World Dictionary of Mathematics (Karush), 89
"WEBWATCH: Innumeracy" (Kessinger), 290
"We *Can* Make a Change" (Van der Geer), 17
Wegner, Bernd, 17, 291
Weil, André, 173
Weisstein, Eric W., 104, 156
Wellcome Library for the History and Understanding of Medicine, 158
Wells, David, 97
Wells, D. G., 97
Wells, R. O., Jr., 187
West, Beverly Henderson, 105
Westergren, Bertil, 133
Westfall, Richard S., 163, 173
Weyl, Hermann, 208
What's Happening in the Mathematical Sciences, 75
"Where Does the Money Go?" (Barr), 13
White, Alvin M., 208
Whitehead, J. H. C., 261
Whitney, Hassler, 261
"Whose Article Is It Anyway?," 16
Wielandt, Helmut, 261
Wiener, Norbert, 262
Wilcox, Calvin H., 223
Wiley Interscience, 269
Wilhelm Magnus: Collected Papers (Magnus), 248
Wilkins, David R., 163
Williams, Frank J., 86
Williams, Kenneth S., 212
Williams, Pamela J., 196
Williams, Robert, 139

Willinsky, John, 291
Wills, J. M., 124
Wilmott, Paul, 223
Wilson, Edward O., 224
Wilson, Joseph N., 135
Wilson, Robin, 179
Winning Ways for Your Mathematical Plays (Berlekamp, Conway, and Guy), 193
Winning Women into Mathematics (Kenschaft and Keith), 203
Witomski, P., 217
Witte, Edith, 92
The Wohascum County Problem Book (Gilbert, Krusemeyer, and Larsen), 211
Wold, Herman, 28
Wolfowitz, Jacob, 262
Wolfram, Stephen, 139, 140
Wolfram Research's Mathematical Functions, 140
Women and Mathematics, Science and Engineering: A Partially Annotated Bibliography with Emphasis on Mathematics and with References on Related Topics (Høyrup), 24
Women Becoming Mathematicians: Creating a Professional Identity in Post-World War II America (Murray), 170
Women in Mathematics (Osen), 171
Women of Mathematics: A Bio-bibliographic Sourcebook (Grinstein and Campbell), 157
Woodhouse, Robert, 189
Woodrow, Robert E., 211
The Words of Mathematics: An Etymological Dictionary of Mathematical Terms Used in English (Schwartzman), 96
Worked Problems in Applied Mathematics (Lebedev, Skalskaia, and Ufliand), 220
World Biographical Index, 163
World Directory of Historians of Mathematics (May and Roebuck), 148

World Directory of Mathematicians, 150
The World of Learning, 150
A World Ruled by Number: William Stanley Jevons and the Rise of Mathematical Economics (Schabas), 172
World Scientific, 269
World Scientific Series in 20th Century Mathematics, 279
World Wide Web Virtual Library: Statistics, 151
Wörterbuch der Mathematik (Eisenreich and Sube), 84
Wright, Stephen J., 131
Writing Mathematics Well: A Manual for Authors (Gillman), 141
Writings of Charles S. Peirce (Peirce), 251
Wussing, Hans, 189
WWW Virtual Library History of Science, Technology & Medicine, 155

XploRe—Learning Guide (Härdle, Klinke, and Müller), 124

Yaglom, I. M., 213
Yamabe, Hidehiko, 262
Yano, Kentaro, 262
Yates, Frank, 108
Yau, S. T., 173
Yeargers, Edward K., 224
"A Year Without Print at Princeton, and What We Plan Next" (Goodman), 289
Yoder, Joella G., 173
Young, Elizabeth, 289
Young, Gail S., 218
Young, Robyn V., 163
Youngen, Ralph, 17
Yu, Song, 289

Zadeh, L. A., 262
Zariski, Oscar, 263
Zaslavsky, Claudia, 209
Zayed, Ahmed I., 140
Zdravkovska, Smilka, 189
Zeitschrift für Analysis und ihre Anwendungen, 75
Zentralblatt für Mathematik und Ihre Grenzgebiete, 2, 35, 50, 75
Zentralblatt Math, 50–51
Zentralblatt MATH, 4, 8, 10, 35, 50–51, 75, 164
Zhang Shu-yu, 28
Zhong, Jia Qing, 263
Zweig, L., 287
Zwillinger, Daniel, 109, 112, 140

About the Authors

MARTHA A. TUCKER received her B.A. in Russian Studies from Hollins College in Roanoke, Virginia, and her M.L.S. from the University of Washington in 1978. She has been head librarian of the Mathematics Research Library at the University of Washington since 1983. A member of the Physics, Astronomy, and Mathematics Division of Special Libraries Association since 1983, she has worked as Bulletin Editor and as Treasurer. Martha is also a member of the American Mathematical Society and served on the AMS Library Committee for three years.

NANCY D. ANDERSON received her B.A. in Geology from Smith College and her M.S. (Library Science) from Columbia University in 1966. She was Mathematics Librarian at the University of Illinois at Urbana-Champaign from 1972 to 2000; she now holds the title of Emeritus Professor there. Her many professional library activities include long and high-level involvement with the Physics, Astronomy, and Mathematics Division of Special Libraries Association (SLA PAM), the Science-Technology Division of Special Libraries Association (SLA Sci-Tech), and with the International Federation of Library Associations and Institutions (IFLA). She also served as co-chair of the American Mathematical Society's Library Committee for eight years. Nancy was honored with the PAM Division Award in 1994 and the PAM Achievement Award in 1999. Her many publications include articles and two books on topics relating to mathematics librarianship.